VALORIZING THE BARBARIANS

*Ashley and Peter Larkin Series in Greek and Roman Culture*

VALORIZING
THE BARBARIANS

*Enemy Speeches*

*in Roman*

*Historiography*

ERIC ADLER

UNIVERSITY OF TEXAS PRESS

*Austin*

Requests for permission to reproduce material from
this work should be sent to:
    Permissions
    University of Texas Press
    P.O. Box 7819
    Austin, TX 78713–7819
    www.utexas.edu/utpress/about/bpermission.html

♾ The paper used in this book meets the minimum requirements
of ANSI/NISO Z39.48-1992 (R1997) (Permanence of Paper).

LIBRARY OF CONGRESS CATALOGING-IN-PUBLICATION DATA
Adler, Eric, 1973–
    Valorizing the Barbarians : enemy speeches in Roman historiography /
by Eric D. Adler. — 1st ed.
        p.      cm. — (Ashley and Peter Larkin series in Greek and Roman
culture)
    Includes bibliographical references and index.
    ISBN 978-0-292-74403-5
    1. Rome—History—Empire, 30 B.C.-284 A.D.—Historiography.
2. Imperialism—Historiography.    3. Enemies—Rome—Provinces—
Historiography.    4. Roman provinces—Historiography.    5. Speeches,
addresses, etc., Latin—History and criticism.    6. Mithridates VI
Eupator, King of Pontus, ca. 132–63 B.C.    7. Hannibal, 247–182 B.C.
8. Boadicea, Queen, d. 62.    9. Rome—Foreign public opinion.
10. Rome—Intellectual life.    I. Title.
DG271.A35   2011   937'.03072—dc22

                                                    2011003847

ISBN: 978-0-292-72991-9 (E-book)


First Paperback Printing, 2012

*For my parents*

# CONTENTS

# ACKNOWLEDGMENTS

This book began its life as a doctoral dissertation in classical studies at Duke University. Accordingly, I would like to thank my dissertation committee: Mary T. Boatwright, Kent Rigsby, Diskin Clay, Grant Parker, and George Houston. I am particularly indebted to Mary Boatwright, who served as my advisor at Duke and has aided me immeasurably, both during and after my graduate career.

Various colleagues at Connecticut College have selflessly offered me guidance: Dirk Held, Richard Moorton, David Greven, Lindsey Harlan, Geoffrey Atherton, and Andrew Pessin. Richard Moorton deserves special mention, since he greatly improved my clunky translations. As a faculty member at Connecticut College, I was fortunate to receive summer research stipends from Judith Opatrny.

Thanks are also due to Gregory Nagy, who allowed me access to the Center for Hellenic Studies during the summer of 2008. Temple Wright and the staff at the Center were helpful as well. During that summer I used the house of my sister, Amy Adler, and my brother-in-law, Mike Donahue, as home base for my research, and I would like to acknowledge their kindness to me.

An earlier iteration of small portions of chapters 1 and 2 originally appeared in *Classical Journal* ("Who's Anti-Roman? Sallust and Pompeius Trogus on Mithridates," *CJ* 101 [2006]: 383–407). I would like to thank S. Douglas Olson for permitting me to reprint an altered and expanded version of that article. The same thanks are due to Matthew S. Santirocco, since small portions of chapters 5 and 6 originally appeared in different form in *Classical World* ("Boudica's Speeches in Tacitus and Dio," *CW* 101 [2008]: 173–195).

Various scholars offered me good advice during the long process of expanding and altering my dissertation into a monograph: Alexander Beecroft, Scott McGill, Christopher Nappa, and Jeffrey Stackert. I fear I have forgotten to name others; if so, I apologize.

I owe a debt of gratitude also to the staff at the University of Texas Press, especially Jim Burr, Leslie Tingle, Kerri Cox Sullivan, and Nancy Bryan. The same holds true for Victoria Pagán and the anonymous referees for UT Press, whose comments and suggestions greatly improved this book.

Additionally, I would like to acknowledge friends and loved ones who offered me support: Leah Ammon, Will Baker, James Barondess, Matthew Diamond, Calvert Jones, Lili Jones, Rachel Kaplan, Daniel Mathews, Jeremy Pienik, Anna Stroman Rittgers, and Akira Yatsuhashi.

Most of all, however, I would like to thank my parents, Joel and Nancy Adler. I could never have written this monograph—or even persevered through a career in classics—without their love and support. Accordingly, I dedicate this book to them.

# AUTHOR'S NOTE

All translations are my own. Abbreviations of Latin authors' names and works stem from P. G. W. Glare, ed., *Oxford Latin Dictionary* (Oxford, 1996); abbreviations of Greek authors' names and works stem from H. G. Liddell and R. Scott, *A Greek-English Lexicon*, 9th edition (Oxford, 1996). Journal abbreviations conform to those found in *L'Année philologique*; other abbreviations conform to those found in S. Hornblower and A. Spawforth, eds., *The Oxford Classical Dictionary*, 3rd edition (Oxford, 2003).

VALORIZING THE BARBARIANS

# INTRODUCTION

*The white man, strangely enough, tries to describe himself in the same oversimplified and malicious terms once used by the colonizer to describe the colonized.*

PASCAL BRUCKNER, *THE TEARS OF THE WHITE MAN:*
*COMPASSION AS CONTEMPT*

## SETTING THE SCENE:
## ROMANS AND THE COLONIAL "OTHER"

It is no secret that scholarly views of Roman imperialism and colonialism have altered considerably in the past few decades. In a recent article appearing in the journal *Helios*, Stephen H. Rutledge refers to Tacitus' *Agricola* as "an abettor in the colonial process."[1] According to Rutledge, this work—despite its famous Calgacus speech (30–32) decrying the injustices of Roman imperialism—serves as a colonialist document aimed at perpetuating "the further expansion and spread of the *Romanitas* Agricola imposes on Britain."[2] Amounting to a more forceful articulation of current positions, Rutledge's article seems to be in sympathy with the dominant view of Roman expansion and colonialism among contemporary classical scholars. In short, Rome the reflective, self-conscious power is out; Rome the self-assured maligner of other cultures is in.

Accordingly, much recent discussion of Roman imperialism has centered on the ways in which ancient Roman historians consciously or unconsciously denigrate non-Romans.[3] In some cases, contemporary historians have perceived ancient authors' seemingly trenchant criticisms of Rome as subtly undermining the anti-imperialist positions they superficially appear to support.[4] By this means, some of the most glaring examples of anti-Roman sentiment—such as Calgacus' speech in the *Agricola*—have been cast as pro-Roman in effect. In a similar vein, contemporary scholars have downplayed Roman elite anxiety about their empire's expansion. Benjamin Isaac, for example, discussing numerous ancient literary sources on Roman imperialism, argues that "all speak exclusively in terms of utility, of cost and benefit, in addition to the desire for glory. Nowhere is it argued that one should refrain from foreign conquest for moral reasons or from considerations of justice or humanity."[5]

More expansively, even the subtlest recent scholarly works that pertain to Roman perceptions of foreigners focus the large majority of their attention on Roman self-assurance and denigration of others.[6] To some extent this is entirely appropriate; Roman writers offer much evidence of Roman self-aggrandizement. Yet this does not tell the whole story. This book aims in part to challenge such conclusions by testing the degree to which ancient historians of Rome were capable of valorizing foreigners and presenting criticisms of their own society.

Clearly, contemporary positions on the general nature of Roman expansion have influenced perceptions of Roman attitudes toward their colonial subjects. During the late nineteenth century, as well as the early and mid-twentieth century, many scholars believed that Rome's foreign policy was essentially "defensive" in nature.[7] That is to say, the Romans, who were traditionally hesitant to annex territory, did not intend to become masters of a huge empire; rather, they stumbled into a series of wars that compelled them to take control of a large number of provinces and a vast dominion. Since the 1970s, numerous Roman historians have questioned this thesis.[8] In part as a result of more negative views of modern Western imperialism, scholars have criticized the notion of "defensive imperialism" as an elaborate exoneration of Roman conduct. This has especially been the case among British historians of Rome who came of age during their own country's post-imperial period.[9] And given current political vicissitudes, discussions of American imperialism are likely to have a great influence on such conclusions in the years to come.[10]

Nor are these the only intellectual influences on contemporary positions regarding Roman perceptions of conquered peoples. Some recent work on the topic appears influenced by the spirit, if not the specifics, of postcolonial theory.[11] Much as Edward Said argued that Orientalists offered a demeaning portrait of Easterners in order to justify their exploitation and domination at the hands of the West,[12] a number of contemporary scholars of Roman history have detected a penchant on the part of ancient authors to characterize non-Romans in a derogatory fashion.

All this amounts to an understandable rejection of earlier views of Roman imperialism and the perception of colonial subjects in antiquity. Although contemporary critics may be too quick to suggest that political judgments regarding the modern West lie behind the erstwhile attraction to "defensive imperialism,"[13] it is undoubtedly true that some scholars proved too sanguine about Roman motivations for their nation's expansion. The American classical scholar Tenney Frank (1876–1939), for example, discussing the Romans' character, argued, "A sense of fair play and respect for legal orderliness permeates the whole early history of this people."[14] Unsurprisingly, perhaps, Frank judged that the Romans had earnest regard for fetial law well into the Republican period.[15]

Moreover, earlier scholars occasionally appear to stress a sense of kinship between the ancient Romans and modern Westerners. For instance, Francis Haverfield (1860–1919),[16] in the inaugural address to the Society for the Promotion of Roman Studies, highlights the similar roles of the Roman and British empires. Regarding the former, he argues: "We know that by desperate efforts it stayed for centuries the inrush of innumerable barbarian tribes and that the pause insured to European civilisation not only a survival but a triumph over invading peoples."[17] Similarly, Haverfield avers, "our own civilisation is firmly planted in three continents and there is little to fear from yellow or other peril."[18] Overall, Haverfield, a founding father of the professional study of Romano-British archaeology, believed that both Rome and Britain were essential preservers of Western civilization.[19] Contemporary scholars have good reason to distance themselves from these perspectives on Roman expansionism and colonial rule—especially in light of the intellectual currents of the last few decades, which are far more critical of Western imperialism.

There remains a danger, however, that current studies on these topics will overreact to the earlier scholarship, and thus leave later generations with assessments lacking sufficient nuance. In many ways this predicament calls to mind some critics' views of the work of Said, who has been (directly or indirectly) a major influence on contemporary perspectives on Roman imperialism and colonialism.[20] According to Sadik Jalal al-'Azm, for instance, Said's argument that Westerners have consistently and similarly maligned the East from Greek antiquity to the present amounts to "Orientalism in Reverse."[21] That is to say, al-'Azm believes that Said painted with too broad a brush, thus essentializing the West by making Orientalism appear to be an ineluctable component of the "European mind." Furthermore, Said occasionally offered statements seemingly designed more for polemical effect than argumentative rigor. For instance, in his landmark work *Orientalism* he claimed, "It is therefore correct that every European, in what he could say about the Orient, was consequently a racist, an imperialist, and almost totally ethnocentric."[22]

It is perhaps in the context of such remarks—which demonstrate the influence of Third Worldism on the flowering of postcolonial theory[23]—that we should understand the more spirited reactions to early scholarship on Roman imperialism and colonialism. Additionally, contemporary historians of Roman expansionism may choose to mirror the openly political tone of much postcolonial criticism, and thus produce more deliberately ideological work. This would prove unfortunate, given the subtle discussions of Roman imperialism that have appeared in recent years.[24] Either way, some scholars might suppose that Said's pioneering oeuvre suggests that earlier classicists felt sympathetic to Rome as an imperial power. Hence Richard Hingley, a major voice in the contemporary debate on the nature of Roman rule, argues, "The agenda for twentieth-century Roman studies was set within the context of a wildly, uncritically pro-imperial Britain."[25]

## THE PURPOSE OF THIS BOOK

This book will not contend that earlier views on the nature of Roman expansionism and colonialism were correct. It will not maintain, for example, that "defensive imperialism" is the proper intellectual framework through which to view Rome's rise to power in the Mediterranean world. After all, the notion that the Romans unwittingly came to control a vast empire rightly strikes modern scholars as far-fetched. Nor will it gainsay the import of contemporary perspectives on these topics—perspectives that often serve as useful correctives to previous positions. But it will test aspects of these new approaches—specifically in their de-emphasis of Roman societal self-criticism. It will argue that recent views of Roman imperialism and colonialism can overlook ways in which ancient historians of Rome demonstrated deep-seated criticisms of Roman society. Although it would be foolish to assert that these ancient historians were either stalwart anti-imperialists or postcolonial theorists avant la lettre, this book will contend that it is incorrect to assume that they were incapable of presenting serious reflections on the failings of Roman imperialism and Roman rule. More expansively, it will investigate a variety of topics important to discussions of imperial expansion that are highlighted in numerous speeches in Roman historiography: recourse to fetial law; administrative corruption; greed and plunder; gender and sexuality; the "Noble Savage"; ethnic stereotyping; and senatorial *libertas*.

In order to do so, the book offers exegeses of speeches (and one letter)—crafted by a variety of Greco-Roman historians (Polybius, Sallust, Livy, Pompeius Trogus/Justin, Tacitus, and Cassius Dio)—that are put in the mouths of Rome's enemies. These rhetorical creations often contain the most polemically anti-Roman sentiments to be found in ancient literature. They can potentially serve as a window, therefore, into ancient authors' criticisms of Roman imperialism and, more broadly, Roman society. Through a close examination of various orations of enemies in Roman historiography, then, the book will attempt to determine how much resistance can be built in to the imperial project—how critical of Rome's empire a variety of Roman historians prove to be.

Such a study of what might be termed "Roman self-criticism" will also allow us to touch upon a number of ancillary issues regarding Greco-Roman historiography: the historicity of speeches; the uses of orations in historical works; the import of emulation in speech composition; the potential reasons for authors' inclusion of orations in their writing. In addition, the book will attempt to discern which ancient historians of Rome proved more critical of Roman imperialism and colonialism and which proved less so. If we can identify—however tentatively—those ancient writers most outspoken in their second thoughts about Rome's empire, we may be able to answer more general questions pertaining to the intellectual history of the Greco-Roman elite. Why, for instance, do some historians seem more condemning of Roman society than do others? Did Roman self-criticism peak at any particular point in time, and, if so, what might explain that peak? Are Greek authors more disapproving of Rome's conquests than writers of Latin descent? If not, why not? What do enemy speeches tell us about ancient regard, or disregard, for waging "just wars"? How do Roman historians use ethnicity and sexuality to characterize the nature of Roman rule?

In order to offer answers to these and kindred queries, this book will proceed as follows. Part I (chapters 1 and 2) chiefly focuses on two compositions attributed to the same Pontic king—Sallust's so-called *Epistula Mithridatis* ("Letter of Mithridates") and Pompeius Trogus' lengthy Mithridatic speech. Part II (chapters 3 and 4) examines two key Polybian orations of Hannibal, along with Livy's versions of these addresses. Part III (chapters 5 and 6) concentrates on Tacitus' Boudica oration (found in the *Annales*) and Cassius Dio's lengthier version of this speech. In chapter 7 we shall turn to some general conclusions regarding ancient historians' criticisms of Roman imperialism and colonialism. Although the chapters will focus mostly on close readings of select enemy orations, they will also provide discussions of a larger number of speeches that appear elsewhere in the historians' work and the way these orations fit into the context of their thought. In this way we should be able to make broader conclusions regarding the writers' capacity for criticism of Rome.

Over the course of my preparing this book, a few interlocutors interested in the project were surprised to learn that the study does not provide a full-scale examination of some of the most famous examples of speeches by Rome's enemies—principally, Calgacus' aforementioned speech in the

*Agricola*, which has yielded one of the most memorable phrases in the history of classical literature: *ubi solitudinem faciunt pacem appellant* ("They [the Romans] make desolation and label it peace"; *Ag.* 30.5).[26] I was not trying to avoid this or any other of the manifold speeches condemning Rome. Rather, given the difficulty inherent in determining the degree of criticism present in any particular oration, it seemed more useful to focus the investigation chiefly on pairs of compositions—two speeches of Boudica as found in the work of two different historians, for example. This allows us, at the very least, to offer conclusions based on a *comparative* approach to these orations.

Recourse to such a comparative method naturally restricts our study to specific ancient historians whose major enemy orations appear in other surviving sources. For this reason we shall not discuss a number of ancient authors who crafted similar addresses—e.g., Caesar and Josephus. Even so, the book's chronological scope ranges from the earliest extant texts of the Roman historiographical tradition to the mid-Imperial period. It does not extend its purview into late antiquity; the dearth of major overlapping enemy orations from works of this period and the rise of Christianity render such an extension problematic. The book's chapters have been arranged according to its comparative approach (e.g., chapters 1 and 2 deal chiefly with Mithridates) and have been placed in the chronological order of the authors when possible.[27] Hence, for example, an examination of Sallust appears before a chapter on Livy. Since the study will touch upon a variety of speeches and, more expansively, historians' commentary on Roman expansionism and colonialism, it is hoped that the book musters sufficient evidence to shed light on issues pertaining to the intellectual world of the Greco-Roman elite from the late Republic to the mid-Empire.

## ANCIENT BATTLE SPEECHES — REAL OR INVENTED?

Before we can turn to our examination of enemy orations in Roman historiography, however, we need to discuss a few topics that have direct bearing on the subject at hand. Of paramount importance is the thorny issue of the historicity of speeches in Greco-Roman historiography. Although we shall have reason briefly to return to this topic in the context of the individual orations discussed in the chapters to come, it will prove useful to present some general discussion now, since this has direct relevance on what one can deduce from the speeches of Rome's rivals in ancient historiography. After all, the degree to which such orations serve as accurate reflections of actually delivered speeches influences the nature of the conclusions that we can draw. If, say, Pompeius Trogus' Mithridates oration is somehow found to conform to the sentiments actually pronounced by the king of Pontus himself to his troops, we shall be left with much less confidence about the link between this speech and Trogus' inclination to criticize Rome.[28]

It is unlikely, however, that anyone will conclusively solve the matter of the historicity of speeches in Greco-Roman historiography. For well over a century much debate, controversy, and disagreement have swirled around this topic.[29] Even so, we should have little reason to conclude that the kinds of orations discussed in this book offer either *ipsissima verba* renditions of actually delivered speeches or even semi-accurate accounts of historical orations.[30] With the exception of Sallust's *Epistula Mithridatis* and the pre-Zama colloquy in Polybius and Livy, all the speeches we shall examine in detail are exhortations addressed to troops before battle. These are perhaps the most likely category of orations to have been invented by ancient historians.[31] They contain certain stock elements and themes in common, which suggests that dramatic and rhetorical considerations weighed heavily on their inclusion. One could, furthermore, question the historicity of such speeches on the basis of logistics: without amplification systems, generals may not have spoken to all their assembled troops at one gathering.[32] After all, the soldiery's inability to hear these orations would naturally reduce their effectiveness. Furthermore, it is clear that the audiences for such speeches—if not all speeches—were unrealistically portrayed in ancient historiography: one seldom learns of noises from the crowd, applause, jeers, and other forms of response.[33]

It is key to recognize, moreover, that the speakers of these orations are all foreigners, and that, as a result, the historians would not have had nearly as good a chance of acquiring adequate information as to these speeches' contents as they would in regard to harangues delivered to Roman troops. Mithridates, Boudica, and Hannibal addressed their soldiers (as we might imagine) in their own first languages—that is, not in Latin.[34] In order to be able to decide in favor of the historicity of these orations, we must presume that Tacitus and Cassius Dio, for example, either took the trouble to translate Boudica's remarks or worked from a source that offered such a translation. Perhaps it is more probable, given the existence of pro-Carthaginian and pro-Mithridatic historical traditions, that Polybius, Livy, Sallust, and Pompeius Trogus had access to genuine information to serve as the basis of their Hannibalic and Mithridatic compositions. As we shall see anon,[35] however, this is highly unlikely.

To this we can add another consideration. The pre-battle speeches of Hannibal and Mithridates, given these leaders' use of mercenary troops, would have been addressed to soldiers who spoke different languages. Under such circumstances, one cannot help but doubt the likelihood of a general or king declaiming to troops en masse without taking this reality into account. Yet in the context of these speeches as they appear in the histories, we are never told about interpreters or other necessary arrangements. This amounts to one more reason to doubt that the texts under examination stem even remotely from actually delivered orations. In addition, as we shall see in the chapters to follow, a number of details specific to the relevant individual speeches speak against their historicity.[36]

A historian's choice to render a speaker's words in either direct discourse (*oratio recta*) or indirect discourse (*oratio obliqua*), furthermore, is no guarantee of a speech's veracity. In the pages to come, we shall take note of Roman historians' use of both direct and indirect discourse. Modern readers have often assumed that *oratio recta* amounts to a more veridical means of reporting speeches. As Andrew Laird has persuasively demonstrated, however, a historian's recourse to *oratio recta* and *oratio obliqua* tells us virtually nothing about the historicity of an oration; rather, it is a clue only to matters of style.[37] As a result, we need not put more stock in the veracity of addresses presented in direct discourse. Overall, it seems safe—although not perfectly safe—to suppose that at least the majority of the elements in these compositions were not the product of a recording of the remarks or writings of the personages to whom they were attributed.

Even so, it would be shortsighted to assume that the opinions in these speeches necessarily reflect their authors' judgments on the topics of Roman imperialism and colonialism. Since juxtaposed orations played an important part in Greco-Roman historiography, one may reasonably infer that matters of tradition loomed large in their inclusion. A given historian could add pre-battle harangues to highlight the generals' characters, strategies, and motivations, or simply to demonstrate the significance of a particular clash—among other possibilities.[38] In addition, such speeches serve as a break from the main narrative in which they are found and add an element of dramatic tension. These important caveats notwithstanding, we shall attempt to find strong evidence that numerous ancient historians were capable of presenting ambivalent discussions of Roman imperialism and of portraying foreigners in a semi-sympathetic light. This should help us highlight, furthermore, Roman historians' discussions of administrative corruption, martial aggressiveness, and a variety of other topics germane to imperial expansion.

## ROMAN READER, MODERN READER

We have not yet exhausted the topics we need to consider before turning to our examination. For instance, we must discuss the matter of the ancient readership for Roman histories. After all, to a great extent this book focuses on evaluating deliberative orations ancient historians put in the mouths of Rome's enemies.[39] This begs the following question: How are we to know if Roman readers would have shared our assessments of these speeches?

This query highlights a number of unfortunate gaps in our knowledge about Roman historiography and rhetoric—gaps that have an admitted impact on this study. To begin with, there is the issue of the audience for ancient histories. We know little about the readership of Roman historiography, other than the fact that we can fairly safely presume it was small.[40] If such works were regularly delivered in public performances, their audiences could have been more sizeable, but we do not possess sufficient evidence to determine whether this was the case.[41] Scholars, moreover, disagree about literacy rates in the ancient world,[42] and this necessitates conclusions regarding the basic makeup of history's ancient readership that are replete with guesswork and surmise.

In regard to the appeal of specific historians, we stand on slightly firmer ground. Largely on the basis of testimony from the historians themselves, for example, John Marincola has argued that Tacitus and Cassius Dio aimed their works at a senatorial audience.[43] Yet this does not mean that their readerships were made up exclusively—or even largely—of Roman senators. As Marincola notes, Polybius' clear regard for an audience of statesmen did not preclude mention of his work's appeal to the lay reader.[44] Though an author might explicitly invoke a certain readership, furthermore, we need not conclude that this accounted for the bulk of his audience.[45] Nor is difficult prose necessarily an indicator of a work's popularity, or lack thereof.[46] Overall, although ancient readers of Roman histories were presumably elites, we cannot speak conclusively about them or their tastes.

We possess, in addition, few clues about Roman readers' perceptions of the strength of individual examples of deliberative speeches. And this is the case despite the great attention the Romans paid to oratory and the elaborate rules about speech composition found in ancient rhetorical handbooks. For example, ancient guides to rhetoric disagree on the ultimate goal of deliberative oratory. According to both Aristotle (*Rh.* 1.3.5 [1358b]) and the author of the *Rhetorica ad Herennium* (3.3), expediency should be the deliberative orator's essential focus.[47] Quintilian, however, explicitly criticizes this approach, agreeing with Cicero that deliberative oratory primarily concerns what is honorable.[48] More importantly, these authors' assessments of individual examples of deliberative oratory are highly subjective. Despite their obvious regard for the proper format of speeches, they leave us with very little notion of what arguments are considered more persuasive. This is unsurprising, since ancient authors appear to use very different rhetorical guidelines to craft deliberative orations.[49]

Unfortunately, ancient literary critics do not serve as better guides. Most often their praise of historians' speeches is either unrelated to their persuasiveness or too unspecific to be of much use. For instance, in regard to Livy's rhetorical prowess, Quintilian merely informs us that his orations are supremely eloquent (*Inst.* 10.1.101), without offering any details.[50] It hardly needs to be stressed that such evaluations offer us little assistance.

In addition, ancient rhetorical handbooks and literary critics mention a number of other important aspects of deliberative oratory, any of which could easily dilute a historian's concern for crafting persuasive speeches. Quintilian tells us, for example, that the deliberative orator must give thought to the sort of audience a speech has, since this could have an effect on the kind of arguments likely to win over listeners (*Inst.* 3.8.37–38). For instance, those who lack honor will show more regard for praise, appeals to popularity, and advantage (3.8.39). For historians, moreover, the matter of the audience for orations is more complex: their speeches must consider both the dramatic audience (say, Mithridates' troops) and the actual audience of readers. An argument aimed at the presumed tastes of the former might not suit those of the latter, and vice versa.

Ancient commentary on historians' speeches, moreover, demonstrates a keen regard for verisimilitude—the crafting of orations that seem authentic. As such, Plutarch excoriates Herodotus for including speeches that clearly offer the historian's own opinions (*De Herod. malig.* 15) or prove unrealistically prophetic (38).[51] In Dionysius of Halicarnassus' discussion of Thucydides, furthermore, the criterion of verisimilitude looms large.[52] Key to this concern is the matching of an address's words to the character of its speaker.[53] Quintilian even suggests that impersonating the character of the speaker—an essential task for a writer (*Inst.* 3.8.51)—is the most difficult necessity attached to the creation of a deliberative oration (*Inst.* 3.8.49). Lucian in large part directs his sparse instructions on speechifying to the criterion of verisimilitude:

ἢν δέ ποτε λόγους ἐροῦντά τινα δεήσῃ εἰσάγειν, μάλιστα μὲν ἐοικότα τῷ προσώπῳ καὶ τῷ πράγματι οἰκεῖα λεγέσθω, ἔπειτα ὡς σαφέστατα καὶ ταῦτα. πλὴν ἐφεῖταί σοι τότε καὶ ῥητορεῦσαι καὶ ἐπιδεῖξαι τὴν τῶν λόγων δεινότητα. (*Hist. conscr.* 58)[54]

If ever it may be necessary to introduce someone to make a speech, let him first and foremost say things that fit his character and are suitable to the circumstances, then let his remarks be as clear as possible. On these occasions, however, you can both be an orator and display the awesome power of your words.

This passage also clues us in to another likely concern for Greco-Roman historians composing speeches: the stylishness of their rhetorical creations. Despite Polybius' admonitions that one should record the actual words of one's speakers,[55] it seems clear that many—if not all—ancient historians used their orations to some extent as opportunities to demonstrate their rhetorical prowess. To this we can add other factors. The outcome of historical events could affect the degree to which an ancient historian would craft a persuasive address. When composing counterpoised pre-battle exhortations, for instance, the historian might aim to put a superior oration in the mouth of the general whose troops ultimately prevail. In addition, as we shall see in the chapters to come, one could compose an oration partly in homage to an earlier historian.

Even a brilliant oration need not be considered the work of an author particularly attuned to writing a speech aimed at persuading his readership. In the context of discussing classical Greece, Øivind Andersen notes that the ancients often demonstrate suspicion of those who spoke too well, too convincingly.[56] Accordingly, as Andersen stresses, it proved useful for orators to mention their own supposed rhetorical shortcomings in comparison with the verbal facility of their opponents.[57] A very compelling speech, then, could have been intended as an example of linguistic legerdemain, not of arguments the historian deemed persuasive.

This calls to mind another essential point. Ancient readers—much like modern readers—would naturally have reacted to these speeches differently. Although, as noted above, we can say little about the specific audience for Roman historiography, we can presume that some readers lacked a full education in the rules of ancient rhetoric. Even those who had rhetorical training would not necessarily come to similar conclusions regarding specific orations. After all, despite the penchant for categorization in ancient rhetorical handbooks, discriminations about the persuasiveness of particular speeches often seem subjective and appear to offer little guidance to the reader. We should remember, furthermore, that the ancients were capable of arriving at some views on orations that likely strike the modern reader as peculiar. Photius (*Bibl.* 71), for example, informs us that he prefers Cassius Dio's speeches to those of Thucydides.[58]

All in all, then, how are we to know if particular arguments—to say nothing of particular speeches—had resonance with Roman readers? How are we to recognize what the ancients would have regarded as powerful criticism of Roman imperialism and colonialism? Although there is ultimately—and admittedly—a good deal of subjectivity involved in this enterprise, we are left with a few possible clues. There are in fact numerous ways of detecting the potential import of particular arguments in the speeches. None of them amounts to a foolproof guide to the strength of a given historian's orations, but together they can help us make the necessary discriminations in the chapters that follow.

First—and unsurprisingly—the overall repetition of specific points in a historian's speeches may suggest that their author put particular stock in them. If we find, for example, discussion of *libertas* ("freedom") appearing repeatedly in Tacitus' orations, we might have reason to conclude that this topic was of specific interest to him. This seems even more the case if points presented in speeches conform to sentiments that also appear in the historian's narratives. As we shall see, one can sometimes detect an overlap between arguments put in the mouths of Rome's foreign enemies and opinions expressed by the historian himself. To this we can add other considerations. If a historian presents an oration that is clearly an homage to a speech in the work of a predecessor, this could signal the power of that earlier address in the eyes of a Roman audience. Although one need not presume that the later historian found the earlier speech persuasive, at the very least he deemed it sufficiently compelling to warrant recasting in his own work. An ancient historian could also offer other hints to suggest that a given oration contains salient arguments. If he depicted the audience listening to the address as approving of its contents, for example, this could indicate to us the historian's own assessment of its power.[59]

We might also glean information about a historian's *modus scribendi* if his speech fails to comply with Quintilian's advice on winning over an address's audience (*Inst.* 3.8.37–39).[60] Throughout his discussions of the Carthaginians, for example, Livy highlights perfidy as a quintessential Punic trait.[61] Under such circumstances, if Livy were to follow Quintilian's judgments on concern for an oration's listeners, he would naturally craft Hannibalic pre-battle harangues that eschewed the topics of honor and righteousness. After all, Quintilian informs us:

> (38) Et honesta quidem honestis suadere facillimum est; si vero apud turpes recta optinere conabimur, ne videamur exprobrare diversam vitae sectam cavendum, (39) et animus deliberantis non ipsa honesti natura, quam ille non respicit, permovendus, sed laude, vulgi opinione, et, si parum proficiet haec vanitas, secutura ex his utilitate, aliquanto vero magis obiciendo aliquos, si diversa fecerint, metus. (*Inst.* 3.8.38–39)

(38) Indeed, it is extremely easy to give honorable advice to honorable men; but in fact if we are going to make an attempt to make foul men do what is right, we must beware lest we seem to reproach a way of life merely because it is different from our own. (39) For the mind of such an audience cannot be influenced by the very nature of honor, which it does not respect, but by flattery and by regard for the opinion of the crowd, and, if these specious trifles prove insufficiently effective, by the advantage that will accompany the recommended course of action, or even better, indeed, by arousing some fears of the results if they decide differently.

Accordingly, Livy's harping on moral considerations in his versions of Hannibal's exhortations to his troops might signal a greater concern for crafting powerful orations than for adherence to the dictates of verisimilitude.

We can, moreover, turn to our ancient rhetorical treatises for another potential sign of the persuasiveness of orations found in the Roman historiographical tradition. Both Cicero (*De orat.* 2.313) and the author of the *Rhetorica ad Herennium* (3.18), when discussing the proper arrangement of arguments in speeches, instruct orators to place their strongest points at the start and conclusion of an address.[62] If historians offer cogent and relevant arguments at these integral places in their speeches, this might lead us further to conclude that the authors have endeavored to present the reader with compelling orations.

Don Fowler's work on "deviant focalization" also points to ways in which these enemy addresses may seem powerful.[63] To be sure, as Fowler himself might have reminded us, such speeches amount to the imagined grievances of Rome's rivals; in Roman historiography, of course, Rome's enemies lack the ability to speak for themselves.[64] This may seem particularly important in the case of the orations under consideration in this book, which, as we shall see, often employ elements common to Roman rhetorical abuse and expand on themes dear to Roman elites and on their likely anxieties. Yet the mere incorporation of speeches from Rome's rivals is itself significant—whether or not their authors agreed with the viewpoints found therein. Their inclusion, after all, allows readers to determine their efficacy for themselves. As Fowler put it, "Merely to allow these viewpoints to exist is an ideological act."[65] And, in the chapters to follow, we shall see that Roman historians were often capable of putting arguments in the mouths of Rome's adversaries that, at the very least, may appear convincing to readers.

Overall, given the numerous other concerns a historian might have had in crafting the speeches of Rome's foreign enemies, the very existence of arguments in them that strike modern readers as trenchant and persuasive speaks to the power of these rhetorical creations. Further, our examination of these speeches will allow us to come to conclusions about Roman regard for fetial law, colonial administrative malfeasance, and other topics of import to Roman imperialism. We need not, of course, make a determination of the degree to which given addresses prove convincing, but merely root out potentially powerful arguments found therein. Our criteria for judging these orations are obviously imperfect, but they are not hopeless.

Let us turn then to our first author.

The Roman politician–turned-historian Sallust hailed from Sabine country; Jerome informs us that he was born in the town of Amiternum.[1] Pompeius Trogus, the author of a forty-four-book world history and a natural scientist during the age of Augustus, was from Gallia Narbonensis.[2] Unlike the Italian Sallust, Trogus was only a third- or fourth-generation Roman citizen.[3] It is chiefly for this reason, it seems, that numerous scholars inspecting the speech of Mithridates found in Justin's abridgment of Trogus' world history (38.4–7) consider his composition "anti-Roman,"[4] whereas those examining Sallust's *Epistula Mithridatis* (*Hist.* 4.69M; *EM*) never claim that this letter's vehemence proves its composer's hatred of Rome.[5]

Modern historians have expatiated on Sallust's criticisms of then-contemporary Roman politics. After all, the decay of Roman society after the Third Punic War is among the most prominent themes in Sallust's monographs.[6] Even so, scholars tend to conclude that Sallust's discussions of Roman failings can be chalked up to what Arthur Lovejoy and George Boas termed "chronological primitivism"—uncritical lauding of the past at the expense of the present.[7] Sallust, that is to say, believed that the destruction of Carthage in 146 B.C. marked the end of Roman virtue and the beginning of Roman moral degeneration (see *Cat.* 10). To numerous modern historians, then, Sallust's criticism of Rome in the *EM* does not betray any hatred of Rome; rather, it conforms to Sallust's framework of Roman decline.

Those who perceive a distinctly negative attitude toward Rome in Pompeius Trogus' speech of Mithridates, however, generally do not conclude that this resulted from an intellectual framework we might also label "chronological primitivism." Instead, modern historians often conclude that Trogus was genuinely "anti-Roman."[8] This is odd, since Trogus' description of early Rome, at least as it survives in Justin's abridgment, is generally positive.[9] Trogus may have presented a view of Roman history similar to that of Sallust, but contemporary historians have not perceived it as such.

Modern scholarly discussion of Sallust's *EM* and Trogus' speech of Mithridates, then, presents us with an assortment of views that appear to fit current positions on Roman imperialism. For while many classicists argue that Trogus' speech of Mithridates is genuinely "anti-Roman," the same argument is never made about Sallust's *EM*. A discussion of the compositions at hand appears to be of secondary consideration to the details of their authors' biographies. Too often the assumption is made that Trogus, the Gaul, can be anti-Roman; Sallust, the Italian, however, cannot.

Accordingly, the argument the first two chapters of this book advance—that Sallust's *EM* is in fact more condemning of Roman actions than is Trogus' speech of Mithridates—will do much to prove that Roman historians did not always cast foreigners as inferior, nor did they incessantly denigrate non-Romans. As we shall see in chapter 1, in the *EM* the "Roman" Sallust was capable of criticizing Rome and even valorizing barbarians' complaints against it. Chapter 2 will demonstrate that the "foreigner" Trogus, in his corresponding speech of Mithridates, pulled most of his punches. It is thus incorrect to assume that Roman historians inevitably discussed barbarians with the implicit motive of justifying Roman conquest. On the contrary: at times Roman historians present deep-seated criticisms of their own society. As we shall detect in the chapters to follow, such criticism, by no means confined to the periphery of Rome's territory, is detectable in an array of ancient historians' works.

## Chapter 1

# "A DEEP-SEATED LUST FOR EMPIRE AND RICHES": SALLUST'S *Epistula Mithridatis*

## A GENUINE LETTER FROM A PONTIC KING?

The *EM* purports to be a letter from Mithridates VI Eupator, the king of Pontus, addressed to Phraates III Theos, the twelfth Parthian king of the Arsacid line.[1] It requests Parthian aid against Lucullus and his troops, most likely shortly after the Battle of Tigranocerta in 69 B.C.[2] The *EM* presents a series of arguments in favor of the Parthians joining an alliance with Mithridates and Tigranes, the king of Armenia. Some of these arguments are based on selected examples from the history of Roman foreign policy in the East—more specifically, from Roman treatment of Eastern kings. In reality, any diplomatic correspondence between Mithridates, Tigranes, and Phraates proved ineffective, since Phraates ultimately decided to remain neutral in the conflict, even though he had apparently made some sort of deal with both sides.[3] The *EM* comes to us among a collection of Sallustian speeches and letters (Vatican Lat. 3864) probably originally produced in the first or second centuries A.D.[4] This means that the context of the *EM* is wholly lost to us.

Before we can conclude that the *Letter of Mithridates* offers us an opportunity to glean sentiments concerning Roman imperialism that are Sallust's invention, we must determine that this composition is largely of his own making. A few scholars have asserted that the *EM* owes its origin to a document culled from the archives of Mithridates, which Sallust somehow acquired and translated or adapted into Latin.[5] Some claim that Pompey discovered this epistle in a secret archive after the Third Mithridatic War, and then presumably brought it to Rome.[6] Others have supposed that the *EM* is an expression of authentic Pontic propaganda, and thus based on arguments that are not Sallust's own.[7]

There are a number of reasons to doubt these assertions, and it seems more reasonable to assume that the letter is a free invention—a composition of Sallust with, at best, minimal concern for any historical missive or genuine pro-Pontic propaganda.[8] First, Fronto mentions the *EM* as one of the letters in Greco-Roman historiography that is not entirely the work of an actual historical subject.⁹ In addition, all our supposed sources for pro-Pontic propaganda amount to very little. We possess one inscription of a Mithridatic letter (Welles no. 74)¹⁰ and a few purported mentions in our Greek and Roman literary sources of a pro-Mithridatic tradition.¹¹ None of these examples, however, has much in common with the text of the *EM*; in fact, the inscription's discussion of the Romans is far more reminiscent of Sallust's *oratio obliqua* speech of Jugurtha to King Bocchus (*Jug.* 81.1).¹² In short, Sallust would not have needed to examine any Mithridatic propaganda or explicitly pro-Pontic sources in order to compose his diatribe against Rome—even though it is possible that he consulted pro-Pontic works during his research for the *Historiae*.¹³ We can be reasonably certain, then, that the *EM* is the creation of Sallust and is the product of a Roman historian's attempt to reconstruct the likely arguments of an anti-Roman Eastern king.

### THE TEXT

### *The* Exordium *(EM 1–4)*

On to the letter itself. The *EM* opens with a greeting and a highly rhetorical *exordium* that offers the principles by which the appeal to Phraates ought to be judged:

> (1) Rex Mithridates regi Arsaci salutem. Omnes, qui secundis rebus suis ad belli societatem orantur, considerare debent, liceatne tum pacem agere, dein, quod quaesitur, satisne pium tutum gloriosum an indecorum sit. (2) Tibi si perpetua pace frui licet, nisi hostes opportuni et scelestissumi, egregia fama, si Romanos oppresseris, futura est, neque petere audeam societatem et frustra mala mea cum bonis tuis misceri sperem. (*EM* 1–2)¹⁴

> (1) King Mithridates to King Arsaces, Greetings. Everyone who is entreated to enter a war alliance when his circumstances are good must consider whether it is right to keep the peace, and then whether what is sought from him is sufficiently reverent, safe, honorable, or disgraceful. (2) If it is right for you to enjoy enduring peace, if there were not a susceptible and vicious enemy, and there would not be extraordinary fame if you should overcome the Romans, I would not dare to seek your alliance and hope in vain to entangle your good situation with my bad one.

Elias Bickerman's valuable article on the *EM* demonstrates that this *exordium* follows Greco-Roman rhetorical commonplaces, and establishes the questions to be posed in a standard manner, with its focus on *possibile, iustum, tutum,* and *laudibile*.¹⁵ From its very first sentence, we have reason to believe that Sallust, when composing this epistle, was attuned to earlier speeches in the Greco-Roman historiographical tradition: section 1, which discusses the concerns any nation should weigh before entering into a military alliance, bears similarities to the opening of the Corcyreans' speech to the Athenians in Thucydides: [16]

δίκαιον, ὦ Ἀθηναῖοι, τοὺς μήτε εὐεργεσίας μεγάλης μήτε ξυμμαχίας προυφειλομένης ἥκοντας παρὰ τοὺς πέλας ἐπικουρίας, ὥσπερ καὶ ἡμεῖς νῦν, δεησομένους ἀναδιδάξαι πρῶτον, μάλιστα μὲν ὡς καὶ ξύμφορα δέονται, εἰ δὲ μή, ὅτι γε οὐκ ἐπιζήμια, ἔπειτα δὲ ὡς καὶ τὴν χάριν βέβαιον ἕξουσιν· εἰ δὲ τούτων μηδὲν σαφὲς καταστήσουσι, μὴ ὀργίζεσθαι ἢν ἀτυχῶσιν. (1.32.1)[17]

It is just, Athenians, that those coming to their neighbors for assistance without either having offered a great service or a preexisting alliance, as we do now, show clearly if it is possible first how it will be expedient, and, if not, how at least it will not be hurtful, and then that they will have stead-fast gratitude; and if they cannot clearly establish either of these things, they should not be upset if they fail.

If Sallust was in fact attempting to echo this oration, he has done so subtly: *EM* 1 tweaks the argument found in the Thucydidean model. Mithridates, unlike the Corcyreans, weighs the potential for an alliance against the prospect of remaining at peace. This is key to the *EM*: as we shall see, Sallust's Mithridates makes the inevitability of a war between Rome and Parthia a major part of his argument.

In sections 3 and 4, Sallust continues with the preamble to the main arguments offered in the *EM*. Section 3 highlights Phraates' anger with Tigranes. Mithridates argues that the Parthians now may ask for the terms they desire from the king of Armenia; ostensibly, this means that Phraates is free to demand Parthian land from Tigranes that Armenia had previously seized.[18] In section 4, Sallust's Mithridates writes of his potential use to Phraates in a military alliance: he can serve as a source of knowledge, since he has much experience fighting the Romans.

*Roman Perfidy in the East, 200–74 B.C. (*EM *5–9)*

Having completed the letter's lengthy prologue, Sallust has Mithridates begin the composition's overarching anti-Roman thesis. This commences with a broad indictment of Roman imperialism:

Namque Romanis cum nationibus populis regibus cunctis una et ea vetus causa bellandi est: cupido profunda imperi et divitiarum. (*EM* 5)

> For the Romans, there is a single age-old cause for instigating war on all
> nations, people, and kings: a deep-seated lust for empire and riches.

This sentiment amounts to a direct attack on Roman foreign policy. Roman
fetial law specified that wars were justifiable only if it could be demonstrated
that they were fought on the basis of proper cause.[19] It is unsurprising that
Mithridates' description of Roman martial motives has remained the most
memorable quotation from the entire *EM*: it is a powerful phrase, reminiscent of Calgacus' famous quip in the *Agricola: ubi solitudinem faciunt pacem
appellant* ("when the Romans make desolation, they name it peace"; 30.5).

The main argument of the *EM* starts strong, that is to say: it begins with
a general indictment of Roman foreign policy. Sallust has Mithridates offer a
distinctly moral argument, not a tactical one;[20] the author aims to undercut
Roman moral superiority. Mithridates presents his case in this way ostensibly
to persuade Phraates that his kingdom will never be at peace with Rome. As
such, the letter seems to be directed more at a Roman audience than at its
supposed recipient, the king of Parthia. It focuses on hypocrisy at the expense
of tactical matters that would have been pressing to a potential martial ally.

Mithridates' general indictment of Roman foreign affairs then gives way
to a number of specific examples of Roman misconduct in Rome's experiences
with the East—the very part of the world both Mithridates and Phraates
inhabit. To some modern historians, these *exempla* are filled with exaggera-
tions and distortions.[21] And to a certain extent, as we shall see, this is true.
Yet when examining these examples, we must recognize a few essential facts.
First, we do not possess any of the numerous historical sources that were sympathetic to Mithridates.[22] Accordingly, we can test Mithridates' sentiments
only against Roman sources—or Greek sources broadly sympathetic to the
Roman cause. With the pro-Pontic tradition of historiography lost to us except in name, it is often difficult to pronounce upon the distortions that can
be gleaned from an inspection of the surviving Greco-Roman sources.

Second, the historical examples that Mithridates introduces in his letter to Phraates were mostly beyond the scope of Sallust's *Historiae*, since the
large majority of these incidents occurred earlier than the starting date of
this work's narrative. In order for the ancient reader to recognize the exag-
gerations in Mithridates' letter, then, he would have to possess an encyclopedic knowledge of Roman foreign policy in the East. It is hard to believe
that many ancient Romans could have immediately discovered the distortions
Sallust's Mithridates offers—distortions that modern scholars were able to
detect only after extended careful research.[23] And third, most of the arguments that Mithridates presents have at the very least a kernel of truth. They
cannot, that is to say, be dismissed as utter fabrications.

For example, in sections 5 and 6 of the *EM*, Sallust's Mithridates turns to the topic of the Roman treatment of Philip V of Macedon.[24] Sallust has Mithridates charge that:

> Qua primo cum rege Macedonum Philippo bellum sumpsere, (6) dum a Carthaginiensibus premebantur, amicitiam simulantes. (*EM* 5-6)

> They [the Romans] first took up war with Philip, the king of the Macedonians, (6) while pretending friendship with him as long as they were hard pressed by the Carthaginians.

To be sure, the argument that Sallust has Mithridates present is simplified and distorted.[25] Philip had in fact intensified Rome's difficulties through his alliance with Hannibal, and the Romans felt justified in their actions against him, since they were obliged to give aid to allies whom Philip had wronged.[26] Accordingly, Mithridates' claim that the Romans had proved disloyal to an ally seems far-fetched. Yet the Romans eventually decided to attack Philip *both* because he had become an ally of a mortal enemy of Rome *and* because there was a danger that he would come to dominate Greece.[27] The Roman annalistic tradition, that is to say, forged a pretext for the Second Macedonian War.[28] This does not imply that Sallust necessarily concurred with this view of the origin of the Second Macedonian War. Philip, after all, supplied his own pretexts.[29] Still, Mithridates' complaints of Roman maltreatment of Philip underline an essential point about Roman dealings with him: the Romans did *not* fight Philip merely for defensive reasons. In many respects, despite the rationalizations of the Roman annalistic tradition, they had been the aggressors.

Accordingly, Sallust's first example of Roman perfidy is a powerful one.[30] In addition, we should note that Sallust's *Historiae* did not discuss the Second Macedonian War, at least in the course of the main narrative. Thus ancient readers would not have happened upon any corrective to Mithridates' claims about Roman treatment of Philip in the *Historiae*. One would require an impressive background in Roman foreign policy to detect the conflations, simplifications, and distortions in Mithridates' argument. Some of Sallust's ancient readers undoubtedly possessed this background, but others surely did not.

Sallust's Mithridates next excoriates Rome for its purported maltreatment of Antiochus III (*EM* 6). The letter charges the Romans with diverting Antiochus from aiding Philip and then plundering his land. By presenting the situation in this manner, Sallust's Mithridates quickly passes over an important point: Livy attests that Antiochus made a pact with Philip.[31] The Romans deemed Antiochus' aid to Philip tantamount to aggression. Even so, it is reasonable to consider Mithridates' assessment of these events a likely view on the part of the enemy; Antiochus would naturally have denied that he betrayed Rome. This does not mean that the *EM* here reflects genuine Seleucid propaganda; rather, Sallust could have concluded what the arguments from Rome's opposition were likely to have been. Although distorted, the point Sallust has Mithridates introduce highlights Roman military action against a king who could not reasonably be considered a dire threat to Roman security. And it presents an example of the Romans alienating monarchs from one another in order to conquer each one individually. Accordingly, it serves as a dramatic example of the letter's main thesis: Phraates should join Mithridates because the Romans aim to demolish him anyway. Again, the *Historiae* would not have discussed Rome's conflict with Antiochus in its narrative, so the ancient reader would have required a strong background in Roman history to recognize the unfairness of Mithridates' characterization.

The letter moves on to discuss Roman perfidy in regard to yet another Hellenistic monarch, Perseus.[32] Rome, Mithridates argues, promised Perseus protection, but then killed him by depriving him of sleep (*EM* 7). As Leo Raditsa notes, the *EM* here conflates two distinct historical occurrences: Perseus' escape to Samothrace and his *in fidem* relationship with Rome.[33] And, to be sure, Mithridates exaggerates the case against Rome in this instance. Still, this view of Roman treachery, albeit greatly oversimplified, is not ridiculous.[34] Though the *EM* presents the more unpleasant version of Perseus' death, Sallust has not concocted it: Plutarch (*Aem.* 37) informs us that it was held by a minority of authorities. Additionally, Diodorus highlights the fact that the Romans did have some qualms about their actions in regard to *in fidem* relations (30.7.1; 31.9.4–5).[35] Once again, the *Historiae* did not cover the historical events mentioned here, so the lay reader would have to be very aware of Roman history to criticize this oversimplified—though not absurd—view. All the same, Sallust's letter demonstrates a degeneration in the strength of the historical illustrations presented. Whereas the *EM*'s account of Philip's treatment is a powerful deflation of Roman concern for waging justifiable wars, the discussions of Antiochus and Perseus, though not baseless, are increasingly tendentious.

This degeneration continues in section 8, where the subject turns to Eumenes, the king of Pergamum. Sallust's Mithridates claims:

> Eumen<en>, quoius amicitiam gloriose ostentant, initio prodidere Antiocho pacis mercedem; post, habitum custodiae agri captivi, sumptibus et contumeliis ex rege miserrumum servorum effecere, simulatoque inopio testatemento filium eius Aristonicum, quia patrium regnum petiverat, hostium more per triumphum duxere; Asia ibsis obsessa est. (*EM* 8)

They betrayed Eumenes, whose friendship they boastfully exhibited, first to Antiochus as a price of peace; afterward they transformed him, as guardian of a captured territory, from a king to the most wretched of slaves through charges and insults, and they led his son Aristonicus in a triumph in the manner of enemies, after a dishonest will was counterfeited, because he aimed at his ancestral realm; Asia was besieged by them.

The specifics of the *EM*'s argument here contradict our tradition, which does not mention betrayal to Antiochus.[36] This, however, is no different in the case of the claims found in sections 5–7 of the letter, with which the bulk of our received tradition disagrees. Yet this argument is distinctly weaker: Mithridates leaves out essential information regarding Roman dealings with Aristonicus, and refers to a forged will that our sources never mention. His assertion that Eumenes only nominally controlled his territory, moreover, is merely polemical. Although Raditsa notes a sentiment in Livy 44.24.1–7 akin to the *EM*'s criticisms,[37] we must conclude that Mithridates' contentions here are weaker than those regarding Philip, Antiochus, and Perseus.

The growing weakness of the examples Mithridates proffers intensifies in section 9, which concerns Nicomedes IV Philopator of Bithynia. Here Mithridates avers that Rome, having taken away all of Asia, then seized Nicomedes' territory, even though the late king had a legitimate heir to the throne. According to Hans Stier, this claim is an outrageous fib.[38] Our tradition asserts that Nicomedes had disowned his children and thus left Bithynia to Rome in his will.[39] Mithridates' concern for Nicomedes' kingdom seems particularly duplicitous, given the king of Pontus' own history of scheming against Bithynia. It is also likely that Sallust discussed Nicomedes' will in the narrative of the *Historiae*, since its contents pertain to the time period it covered. The ancient reader, then, would likely have a sign of Mithridates' distortion in Sallust's very text. Overall, section 9 does not contain a strong argument.

## More Roman Faithlessness, 88–69 B.C. (EM 10–15)

When Mithridates takes up his own dealings with the Romans, however, his arguments become more compelling. For in this part of the letter Sallust has Mithridates assert:

> Nam quid ego me appellem? Quem diiunctum undique regnis et tetrarchiis ab imperio eorum, quia fama erat divitem neque serviturum esse, per Nicomedem bello lacessiverunt, sceleris eorum haud ignarum et ea, quae adcidere, testatum antea Cretensis, solos omnium liberos ea tempestate, et regem Ptolemaeum. (*EM* 10)

Truly, why should I mention myself? They provoked me, separated on all sides by kingdoms and tetrarchies from their empire, into war through Nicomedes, because of the rumor that I was rich and would not be a slave; I was not ignorant of their crimes, and I previously appealed to the Cretans—the only free people at that time—and to King Ptolemy about the things that had happened.

According to Sallust's Mithridates, then, Rome provoked the First Mithridatic War by forcing Nicomedes to raid his territory. Although Mithridates has conveniently omitted key details of the story, his case is essentially strong, and is close to that of Appian (*Mith.* 11). David Magie, discussing the outbreak of the First Mithridatic War, asserts that M'. Aquilius and C. Cassius made a tactical blunder when they compelled Nicomedes to raid Pontus: this would allow Mithridates to contend that he was fighting against Roman aggression.[40] Sallust, then, has Mithridates seize upon this strong argument, instead of compelling him to legitimize his less upstanding conduct.[41] He has offered a damaging argument against Roman claims to righteousness in its foreign policy.

In the short section 11, Mithridates presents his reaction to this perceived Roman pugnacity. He took vengeance, he claims, driving Nicomedes from his kingdom, and loosened Asia from Rome's clutches. Sallust, furthermore, has Mithridates assert that *Graeciae dempsi grave servitium* ("I took Greece away from harsh servitude"). Once again Mithridates is guilty of the sin of omission: he disregards his more dubious conduct in order to depict himself as the wronged party. His claim for revenge, however, still seems plausible, given the machinations of Aquilius and Cassius. One could perceive the notion that Mithridates "freed" Greece as a subtle insult to Mithridates: monarchs of his ilk had no knowledge of, or use for, freedom—save their own. Yet perhaps his claim to have granted "freedom" highlights the horrors of Roman conduct in Greece: if Mithridates can claim to have liberated the Greeks, Rome's provincial administration in the East must have been very bad indeed.[42] We should note, moreover, that this regard for the liberation of Greece is clearly aimed at the *EM*'s Roman audience, not at Phraates. Would a Parthian king care if Mithridates had "freed" anyone? Of course not: he had no concern for Greek autonomy. Thus Mithridates' contention amounts to a moral appeal to Sallust's readership.

Not every portion of the *EM* appears designed to cause doubts about Rome's provincial conduct, however. In section 12, for instance, the king of Pontus blames his failures in the First Mithridatic War on his erstwhile underling Archelaus. Mithridates even implies that Archelaus' defection after the Peace of Dardanus (85 B.C.) proves that he intentionally lost battles for the Pontic side. This dubious argument conveniently allows Mithridates to shift blame from himself. The main narrative of the *Historiae* did not cover the First Mithridatic War, and thus the ancient reader would not necessarily find a corrective to Mithridates' claim about the cause of the Pontic loss. Even so, this does not seem like an assertion that would require wide learning to doubt; it appears as if Mithridates is concocting a suspect excuse. Such an argument, furthermore, might not induce much self-reflection on the part of a Roman readership. By the time Sallust began composing the *Historiae*, Mithridates had already lost his battles with Rome; he was dead. It would not much matter, then, if Sulla had outwitted Mithridates, or if Archelaus were fully responsible for the king of Pontus' failure. Even if the latter were true, this does not impugn Rome's conduct or motives.[43]

Yet the *EM* returns to morally charged arguments in section 13:

> Equidem quom mihi ob ipsorum interna mala dilata proelia magis quam pacem datam intellegerem, abnuente Tigrane, qui mea dicta sero probat, te remoto procul, omnibus aliis obnoxiis, rursus tamen bellum coepi, Marcumque Cottam, Romanum ducem, apud Calchedona terra fudi, mari exui classe pulcherruma. (*EM* 13)

> Indeed, since I understood that their [the Romans'] internal strife postponed war rather than offered peace, although Tigranes (who now appreciates my advise too late) declined to join me, and you were far away, and everyone else spineless, nevertheless I began war anew. On land I vanquished Marcus Cotta, the Roman commander at Calchedon, and at sea I deprived him of a most superb fleet.

Rome, Mithridates claims, can be at peace abroad only when it is preoccupied by civil disturbances. Sallust's Mithridates mentions Tigranes' original refusal to ally with Pontus—a mistake the king of Armenia now recognizes. The king of Pontus then boasts that he renewed the war with Rome (the Third Mithridatic War) and routed M. Aurelius Cotta. By admitting his part in starting the conflict, Sallust's Mithridates places heavy emphasis on the bad faith with which Sulla negotiated the Peace of Dardanus. We possess evidence from our ancient literary sources in support of this assertion. Appian (*Mith.* 69) essentially offers the same view of Sullan treachery, and informs us that L. Licinius Murena argued this as his justification for his aggressions in the Second Mithridatic War.[44] By contending that the Romans would cease their quest for territory only when internal conflicts compelled them, Sallust's Mithridates reintroduces the main theme of the letter: Roman lust for riches and dominion is insatiable (5). This amounts to a repetition of the central argument of the *EM*, and, however oversimplified and distorted, issues a challenge to Roman pretensions of engaging in "just wars."

Still, having presented this critique of Roman imperial excesses, Sallust's Mithridates returns to shifting the blame for Pontic military failures away from himself. In section 14 Mithridates holds shortages of provisions and shipwrecks responsible for his poor showing in the ongoing Third Mithridatic War; he ignores the generalship of Lucullus. Even Plutarch, who is hostile to Lucullus' conduct soon before his replacement in 66 B.C.,[45] notes the Roman general's impressive string of victories in this conflict. It is highly unlikely, then, that Sallust's *Historiae* did not directly contradict the claims that Mithridates offers in this section. Given the presumptive proximity of the discussion of these events in the narrative of the *Historiae*, the ancient reader would likely recall the ways in which the *EM*'s account contradicts Sallust's explanation in the main narrative.

Nor is this the end of Mithridates' self-exonerations for failures in the Third Mithridatic War. In the first portion of section 15, Mithridates blames a shortage of rations for his lack of success. Having done so, however, the king of Pontus then claims *secutique Romani non me, sed morem suom omnia regna subvortundi, quia multitudinem artis locis pugna prohibuere, inprudeniam Tigranis pro victoria ostentant* ("and the Romans followed me—or, rather, followed their custom of subverting all monarchies—and paraded the bad judgment of Tigranes as a victory, since they kept a great number of troops from a battle by hemming them in"). Though Eastern criticism of Rome may have possessed an element of concern for Rome's supposed hatred of monarchies,[46] we need not conclude that Sallust incorporated Eastern propaganda in the *EM*.[47] Romans, after all, were proud of their hatred of kings, since they had established the Republic upon the expulsion of the tyrannical Tarquinius Superbus.[48] The mention of Roman disdain for kings might actually inspire pride in a Roman reader. Section 15 of the *EM* contains exactly the sort of criticism that a Roman might concoct: it highlights Roman political sophistication and portrays the East as backward, under the guise of supposedly bashing Rome. Even so, Sallust here sticks to the main point of the letter—the Romans will never stop their conquests.

Mithridates' exoneration of his own conduct at the expense of Tigranes, however, appears weak: the *Historiae*'s narrative must have demonstrated this claim to be unfounded. Phraates, moreover, in order to join this alliance, would have to trust both Mithridates and Tigranes. It was necessary that he deem both kings competent. Thus the sentiments in section 15 of the letter appear tactically foolish.

## Roman Rapacity Knows No Bounds (EM 16–23)

Having completed a discussion of Rome's foreign policy malefactions in the East, Sallust's Mithridates returns to his main theme.

> Nunc quaeso considera, nobis oppressis utrum firmiorem te ad resistundum an finem belli fururum putes? Scio equidem tibi magnas opes virorum, armorum et auri esse; et ea re a nobis ad societatem. Ab illis ad praedam peteris. Ceterum consilium est, Tigranis regno integro meis militibus <belli prudentibus> procul ab domo [parvo labore] per nostra corpora bellum conficere, quo[m] neque vincere neque vinci sine tuo periculo possumus. (*EM* 16)

> Now I ask you to consider whether, when we have been overwhelmed, you will be more able to resist the Romans or if there will be an end of war. Indeed, I know that you have great abundances of men, of weapons, and of gold; and for this reason we have sought you as an ally, they as a spoil. Yet the plan is to finish the war far from home at the expense of our bodies while Tigranes' kingdom is intact, with my soldiers skilled in war—a war in which we are not able to conquer or be conquered without it being a danger to you.

Rome, he asserts, will never cease its conquering, and thus Phraates should align himself with Pontus and Armenia now, when it is strategically advantageous. In the strictest sense, this forecast did not prove true; neither Lucullus nor Pompey attacked Parthia, and it is unlikely that Lucullus ever envisioned such a strategy.[49] But Mithridates' prediction is only false in a technical sense. Rome continued to menace Parthia after the conclusion of the Third Mithridatic War, and Sallust could have been pondering these ill-fated campaigns when composing the *EM*.[50]

In section 17, Mithridates continues to harp on this topic. Rome's expansion in the East, he claims, began only when it could not move farther West. In addition to a few polemical denunciations of Rome, this portion of the letter contains a direct refutation of Roman pretenses to engaging in "just wars." Neither human nor divine will, he opines, stops the Romans from ruining their friends and allies. Sallust intensifies this sort of rhetoric in sections 18–23. Even so, section 18 offers an obviously Roman conceit: few people, asserts Mithridates, actually desire freedom. Naturally, this sentiment makes little sense in the context of arguments advanced by a king. Neither Phraates nor Mithridates would be concerned about their subjects' desire—or lack of desire—for political liberty. They were monarchs and presumably had no use for non-autocratic means of governance. Perhaps the argument about Rome's incessant pugnacity made a certain amount of sense to Sallust, who, unlike the Pontic king, had knowledge of unprovoked Roman aggression against the Parthians after the conclusion of the Third Mithridatic War.[51] Either way, the *EM* concludes with a restatement of the advice offered at the start of the letter: Phraates should fight now, or Parthia will face inevitable ruin.

## ECHOES OF THE *EM*

Before turning to our conclusions regarding Sallust's *Letter of Mithridates*, we ought to note that some sentiments found therein echo criticisms from other parts of Sallust's oeuvre—in both set speeches and the narratives proper. C. Memmius' oration to the Roman people after the return of L. Calpurnius Bestia in the *Bellum Iugurthinum* (31), for example, focuses its attention on the *nobiles'* rapacity, which supposedly left Roman commoners *de facto* slaves (31.11).[52] Sallust has Memmius assert:

> At qui sunt ii, qui rem publicam occupavere? Homines sceleratissumi cruentis manibus, immani avaritia, nocentissumi et idem superbissumi, quibus fides decus pietas, postremo honesta atque inhonesta omnia quaestui sunt. (*Jug.* 31.12)[53]

> But who are those men who have taken possession of the state? The most impious men, with bloodstained hands, of enormous greed, utterly pernicious but also utterly arrogant, who have sought faith, glory, piety, in sum all honorable and dishonorable attainments, out of a desire for gain.

Although Memmius does not explicitly harp on the impact these men had on Roman foreign affairs, his outrage at the *nobiles'* malefactions echoes the *EM*'s criticisms of Roman greediness (cf. 5, 16). In his preamble to the speech, moreover, Sallust champions Memmius as an eloquent detractor of the *nobilitas*.[54] Sallust could easily have expanded his criticisms of second- and first-century B.C. *nobiles* found in his monographs into a more general excoriation of Roman rapacity and its relation to the Roman state's foreign policy. Since such men, according to Sallust, were essentially in control of the Republic, their avarice could be deemed responsible for Rome's foreign entanglements.

Sallust has Marius invoke similar themes in a speech before an assembly of the people (*Jug.* 85), which in part aimed at irritating the *nobilitas* (84.5).[55] For example, Sallust's Marius claims:

> (45) Primum omnium de Numidia bonum habete animum, Quirites. Nam quae ad hoc tempus Iugurtham tutata sunt, omnia removistis: avaritium,

inperitiam atque superbiam. Deinde exercitus ibi est locorum sciens, sed mehercule magis strenuos quam felix. (46) Nam magna pars eius avaritia aut temeritate ducum adtrita est. (*Jug.* 85.45–46)

(45) First of all, citizens, have good faith regarding Numidia. For you have withdrawn all the things that, up to this time, have protected Jugurtha: avarice, incompetence, and arrogance. Besides, there is an army there knowledgeable about the place, but—by Hercules—more vigorous than lucky. (46) For a large part of it has been destroyed on account of the greed or rashness of its leaders.

Here Sallust connects Rome's early difficulties in the Jugurthine War with the avarice of its commanders. The parallel with the *EM* is not perfect: in this instance, Sallust does not contend that Rome had no business involving itself in Numidian affairs. Rather, the ruling class' susceptibility to bribery originally allowed Jugurtha to escape Rome's retribution. Sallust, unlike Mithridates in the *EM*, criticizes Roman inaction. Hence Sallust presents the reader with a speech (14) and letter (24.2–10) of Adherbal urging Roman intervention, both of which he portrays sympathetically.[56] All the same, Sallust appears attuned to the impact the *nobiles'* greed could have on Roman foreign affairs, and it seems a simple step to apply this criticism to the Romans tout court, as he does in the *EM*.

For this reason, Jugurtha's *oratio obliqua* remarks to King Bocchus of Mauretania regarding the evils of Rome (81.1) read much like a truncated version of the *Letter of Mithridates*:

Igitur in locum ambobus placitum exercitus conveniunt. Ibi fide data et accepta Iugurtha Bocchi animum oratione adcendit: Romanos iniustos, profunda avaritia, communis omnium hostis esse; eandem illos causam belli cum Boccho habere, quam secum et cum aliis gentibus, lubidinem imperitandi, quis omnia regna advorsa sint; tum sese, paulo ante Carthaginiensis, item regem Persen, post uti quisque opulentissumus videatur, ita Romanis hostem fore. (*Jug.* 81.1)

Thereupon the armies gathered in a location that was agreeable to them both. There, after pledging themselves to mutual loyalty, Jugurtha provoked Bocchus' wrath with a speech: the Romans, he said, were unjust on account of their boundless greed and were the common enemies of mankind. They had the same rationale for war with Bocchus as with himself and with other nations—namely, a lust for rule and a hatred for all kingships. He was the Romans' enemy at that time; a little before it was the Carthaginians and King Perseus; afterward it would be anyone who seemed the most powerful.

Although the dramatic date of the oration has compelled Sallust to offer the Carthaginians as one of his examples of Roman rapacity,[57] Jugurtha's speech has much in common with the *EM*.[58] In both compositions Sallust has used chronologically and geographically pertinent instances of purported Roman malefactions to strengthen a similar point: Rome, an inexorably imperialistic state, aims to divide and conquer. We need not assume that Sallust has great sympathy with Jugurtha's complaints. Sallust's lauding of pre-146 B.C. Rome (cf. *Cat.* 9–10) leads us to believe that he would hardly have viewed the Punic Wars as examples of aggressive imperialism on the part of the Romans.[59] Even so, the *EM*'s repetition of themes found in Jugurtha's oration might speak to Sallust's desire to question Rome's foreign policy decisions through attacks on its claims to justifiable warfare and purported inattention to material rewards.

It should come as no surprise, then, to discover that Sallust's speech of Cato the Younger to the Roman Senate (*Cat.* 52.2–36) contains an explicit link between Roman moral failings and the Republic's unjust colonial administration:[60]

> (19) Nolite existumare maiores nostros armis rem publicam ex parva magnam fecisse. (20) Si ita esset, multo pulcherrumam eam nos haberemus: quippe sociorum atque civium, praeterea armorum atque equorum maior copia nobis quam illis est. (21) Sed alia fuere, quae illos magnos fecere, quae nobis nulla sunt: domi industria, foris iustum imperium, animus in consulendo liber, neque delicto neque lubidini obnoxious. (22) Pro his nos habemus luxuriam atque avaritiam, publice egestatem, privatim opulentiam. Laudamus divitias, sequimur inertiam. (*Cat.* 52.19–22)

> (19) Don't reckon that our ancestors fashioned a great state from an insignificant one by force of arms. (20) If that were so, we ought to have a far fairer state, since we have a greater abundance of allies and citizens than they—not to mention weapons and horses. (21) But there were other things that made those men great: industriousness at home; just rule abroad; an independent spirit in matters of council, free of crime and concupiscence. (22) Instead of these qualities, we have luxury and avarice, public impoverishment and private opulence. We praise riches and pursue laziness.

To Sallust's Cato, contemporary Roman indolence and avarice are responsible for, inter alia, the Republic's unjust colonial rule.[61] This need not imply that Sallust's *Historiae*, despite its author's high regard for Cato (*Cat.* 53.6–54), proved critical of Rome's entry into the Third Mithridatic War. All the same, as our ancient literary sources describe in detail, Mithridates' conflicts with Rome—and the king's popularity with many Roman subjects in the East— were at the very least exacerbated by Rome's promotion of fiscal misery in the provinces.[62] If Sallust desired to magnify the theme of Roman greed and its impact on Roman foreign policy, he would have found a description of the Mithridatic Wars fully amenable to his designs.

These concerns are not confined to Sallustian speeches, but also appear in his works' main narratives. In the *Bellum Catilinae*, for instance, Sallust ex-patiates on the ruinous morals of contemporary Romans. He avers:

> (3) Sed lubido stupri ganeae ceterique cultus non minor incesserat: viri mu-liebria pati, mulieres pudicitiam in propatulo habere; vescendi causa terra marique omnia exquirere; dormire prius quam somni cupido esset; non famem aut sitim, neque frigus neque lassitudinem opperiri, sed ea omnia luxu antecapere. (4) Haec iuventutem, ubi familiares opes defecerant, ad facinora incendebant: (5) animus inbutus malis artibus haud facile lubidini-bus carebat; eo profusius omnibus modis quaestui atque sumptui deditus erat. (*Cat.* 13.3–5)[63]

> (3) But the passion for lust, dissipation, and other immoralities did not wane: men submitted to sex like women; women publicly offered their chastity; for the sake of engorging themselves people ransacked land and sea; they slept before they required rest; they did not wait for hunger, thirst, cold, or weariness, but allowed their self-indulgence to anticipate their physical needs. (4) These vices incited the youth to crimes when their familial resources were exhausted. (5) Their minds, infected by evil pur-suits, could scarcely lack wantonness. Thus they abandoned themselves all the more extravagantly to all kinds of greed and waste.

In this instance, Sallust has not specifically targeted Roman moral collapse as responsible for dubious foreign policy adventures. Yet the import of using avarice to describe contemporary Roman society is clear enough.[64] It is not surprising that such a mindset led Sallust to criticize Roman expansionism as an example of Rome's unbridled acquisitiveness. And the repetition of this theme in both Jugurtha's speech to Bocchus[65] and the *EM*[66] potentially demonstrates that this line of argument piqued his interest. With the context of the *EM* lost to us, we cannot speak definitively about Sallust's prospective affinity with some of its arguments. Still, it would be odd if Sallust, given his great concern for contemporary Roman greed and corruption, did not in part use the epistle to reiterate criticisms found elsewhere in his monographs.

## CONCLUSIONS

Having examined the *EM* at length, in addition to similar sentiments found in Sallust's oeuvre, we can now turn to some conclusions regarding the force of the criticism of Rome detectable in the *Letter of Mithridates*, as well as what forms this criticism takes. Overall, the *EM* presents a hodgepodge of arguments of varying strength.[67] In accordance with proper Roman rhetorical practice, it tends to proffer the stronger arguments first.[68] The overarching theme of Roman perfidy is polemically presented but persuasive. The same is true to a lesser extent of Mithridates' take on Roman maltreatment of Philip V. And the argument regarding Rome's commencement of hostilities with Mithridates via Nicomedes may be the most powerful point in the *EM*. The letter focuses mostly on moral concerns; it contains several forceful denunciations of Roman greed, treachery, and lust for empire. At the same time, it must be admitted that some arguments in the letter are weak and do not appear to be designed to elicit self-reflection on the part of the Roman reader. Mithridates' excuses for Pontic military losses seem particularly feeble. More generally, his complaints about Roman hostility to monarchies may have been more likely to encourage Roman pride than self-doubt.

Even so, the *EM* offers a consistent denunciation of Roman foreign policy in the East—with occasional lapses into less substantial complaints. This does not imply that Sallust himself entirely agreed with this criticism any more than he agreed with Catiline's criticism of Rome in the *Bellum Catilinae*. The possibility exists that the *EM* at least partly aims at criticizing Rome's foreign policy vis-à-vis Parthia.[69] In a sense, Mithridates' predictions of Roman desire for a larger empire proved true: Rome continued to menace Parthia after Mithridates' death. After all, 53 B.C. marked the ignominious defeat and death of Crassus in his unprovoked attack on Parthia. Only assassination in 44 B.C. deterred Julius Caesar's intended campaign against the Parthians. By 41 B.C., Q. Labienus had defected to Parthia and was inciting them to invade the Roman East. And M. Antonius suffered great losses at the hands of the Parthians in 36 B.C. Sallust appears to have composed the *EM* shortly after this,[70] and thus this missive could signal—among other things—his criticism of Roman interventionism in Parthia.[71]

All the same, we do not possess the requisite evidence to conclude whether Sallust's aim in the *EM* was to criticize Rome's current dealings with Parthia, or, as Richard Geckle suggests, to lambaste the corruption of the Republic while highlighting the hypocrisy of Mithridates himself.[72] Perhaps there is a bit of both. Even so, it is clear that the *EM* presents cogent criticism of

Roman foreign policy: Sallust has chosen pertinent historical examples, proffered arguable (though distorted) readings of these examples, and consistently harped on the general moral failings of Rome's conduct in the East.

We need not assume, however, that the *EM* offers a glowing portrait of Mithridates. To some extent, the epistle, despite its claim that its author liberated Greece (11), emphasizes the king's opposition to the political freedom of his subordinates (18). In fact, in Sallust's work both Jugurtha (81.1) and Mithridates mention a Roman detestation of monarchies that is not highlighted in the author's Roman addresses critical of the vicissitudes of the late Republic. This sentiment helps to pigeonhole Sallust's Mithridates as an Eastern monarch whose way of life was unvaryingly hostile to the Romans' supposedly superior political culture. As hinted at above, it may signal a sense of Roman contentment with its purported hostility to autocracy. It may also signal one means by which Sallust differentiates the complaints of foreigners from those of Rome's internal critics. Sallust's Romans concern themselves with the injustices of Rome's colonial administration; foreign enemies concentrate on its hostility to monarchies. If there is an ethnic stereotype at play here (and, given our limited evidence, it is perhaps unwarranted to say so), it appears as if Sallust contributes to the notion that Asians and Africans are congenitally ill-disposed to political freedom.[73]

Otherwise, though, the *EM* presents arguments that often seem compatible with Roman complaints appearing in Sallust's oeuvre about omnipresent greed and corruption. In fact, Sallust's Mithridates demonstrates a keen regard for "just war" rationales, in keeping with Roman concern for fetial law. The missive's request for an alliance with Phraates is based chiefly on its intrinsic defensiveness: Rome will inevitably attempt to destroy Parthia, and thus it is both appropriate and just for the Parthians to join Mithridates' cause. Sallust's Mithridates minimizes both tactical concerns and other sorts of anti-Roman criticisms he might have mustered in order to focus his ire on incessant Roman aggression.

In essence, the *EM* makes it appear as if Pontus acts as the just combatant. The epistle flips Roman pretensions to engage in defensive warfare on their head. To be sure, the historical Mithridates' philhellenism renders the *EM*'s focus on Roman bellicosity less surprising, given the Greeks' contribution to "just war" theory.[74] It would obviously be wrongheaded to assume that anxiety about martial aggression was somehow the Romans' exclusive preserve. But, as we have seen, Sallust's Jugurtha, a North African king, shares the *EM*'s focus in truncated form. This perhaps clues us into the import Sallust places on Roman pugnacity in his speeches of foreign enemies.

Nor is this the only tendency we can glean from the predilections detectable in Sallust's orations. As we have seen, the *EM* is akin to other Sallustian addresses critical of the late Republic in presenting greed as the primary motivating factor in Roman foreign policy. Sallust's Jugurtha and Mithridates, however, do not trouble themselves to provide specific examples of this charge. Rather, they both assume the role of rapacity as the cause of Rome's foreign entanglements and focus the brunt of their attention on the specifics of the Romans' failure to live up to their self-professed standards of waging justifiable wars. Although we ultimately cannot know for sure, this suggests at least some nervousness on Sallust's part with Rome's rapid expansion.

Perhaps the repetition of themes in various Sallustian orations also highlights aspects of their author's unease. It is interesting that so much kinship exists between Sallust's own excoriations of the late Republic, the views of foreign enemies found in the historian's work, and those of Sallust's internal critics of Roman conduct. But Sallust's speakers do not present identical arguments. The most salient distinction must be the following: Sallust's Roman critics recognize—as does the author himself—Rome's deviation from its former righteousness; his foreign enemies, on the other hand, do not perceive any differences between the Rome of its halcyon days and the debased version of the second and first centuries B.C. Thus neither Sallust's Jugurtha nor his Mithridates speaks of the Republic's numerous failings in terms of a degeneration from erstwhile glory, as do Sallust's Roman critics.

Though Sallust may have partly attributed to foreign enemies sentiments that correspond to his own views, these leaders' lack of historical perspective serves to differentiate them from Rome's native critics, with whom Sallust appears to share a stronger bond. More than anything else, this marks the distinction between Sallust's criticisms of then-contemporary Rome and the assessments of his foreigners. The belief in Rome's descent from idyllic perfection becomes quintessentially Roman. It is not that Sallust's barbarians lack a sense of history. After all, in the *EM* Sallust's Mithridates demonstrates intricate knowledge of the annals of Roman foreign policy. Rather, Sallust's barbarian enemies lack the perspective of the historian's "chronological primitivism" and, in Sallust's view, mistakenly castigate the Romans for congenital depravity, though their wrath would be more properly focused on late Republican Rome. In essence, they are unfair to Rome's illustrious *maiores* ("ancestors"), though not to the Romans of Sallust's own day.

Overall, as we have seen, the *EM* amounts to an extended attack on Roman claims to engaging in warfare solely on the basis of proper cause. It picks up themes regarding contemporary Roman rapacity and self-indulgence that appear elsewhere in Sallust's work; this hints at the possibility that Mithridates' complaints piqued his interest.[75] We cannot say that Sallust agreed with the *EM*'s arguments, either in part or in whole. Still, as we shall see in the next chapter, in comparison with another rhetorical composition attributed to Mithridates found in the annals of Roman historiography, this is very strong criticism indeed.

## THE MYSTERIOUS JUSTIN

Although it is difficult to imagine many modern scholars shedding tears over the loss of Pompeius Trogus' forty-four-book world history, the *Historiae Philippicae*, we would obviously be able to say much more about Trogus' view of the Roman world if this work survived from antiquity. With this history in our hands, we would be far better acquainted with the mindset of a man of Gallic origins who lived during the age of Augustus. The survival of Trogus' world history could also cast light on early Imperial views of Roman expansionism. After all, in some sense, Trogus' *Historiae Philippicae* was a history of imperialism. The start of the work likely discussed how, in the early days, there were no imperialists (Justin 1.1.3)—and thus the history commenced with the Assyrian king Ninus, who was the first to desire to increase his realm (1.1.4). To Trogus, it appears, without imperialism there is no history.

As it is, however, Trogus' work comes to us only in greatly abridged form from the pen of M. Iunian[i]us Iustinus, better known as Justin.[1] Although Justin's work has been titled an "epitome," this term is not accurate. Justin himself, in the preface of his work, claims that he has made a *florum corpusculum* ("little body of flowers")—a *florilegium*, not an "epitome" (*Praef.* 4).[2] Justin claims, furthermore, to have selected the pleasurable bits from Trogus' history, as well as those parts that would provide moral instruction to his readership. The *Prologi* of the *Historiae Philippicae*, which were composed by an unknown hand and are akin to the *Periochae* of Livy, demonstrate that Justin did, in fact, delete much material from Trogus' original. Although there is no general consensus on how truncated Justin's text is,[3] one can presume that Justin was highly selective. As a result, we know far less about the context surrounding Trogus' speech of Mithridates (38.4–7)—the focus of this chapter's discussion—than we would like. Naturally, this renders it more difficult for us to determine the degree to which this oration demonstrates Trogus' inclination to criticize the vicissitudes of the Roman Empire.

There exists, in fact, a lack of scholarly consensus concerning almost every aspect of the *Historiae Philippicae*. Justin informs us that the speech of Mithridates, found in Trogus'/Justin's thirty-eighth book, was sufficiently important to merit word-for-word inclusion (38.3.11). The speech, by far the longest in Justin's abridgment, is in *oratio obliqua*; Justin tells us that Trogus was critical of Sallust and Livy for offering numerous speeches in *oratio recta*.[4] The oration was supposedly delivered by Mithridates to his troops sometime around the beginning of the First Mithridatic War.[5] As we shall see, this harangue presents many arguments similar to those found in Sallust's *EM*, though it harps more on the lowly origins of the Romans and discusses different historical examples of bad conduct on the Romans' part.

Unfortunately, the gaps in our knowledge about the original *Historiae Philippicae* make it more difficult to pass judgment on the nature of this speech. In fact, we have inadequate information regarding both Trogus and Justin. There is, for instance, no scholarly consensus regarding the dates of the latter's life. Proposals concerning his *floruit* range from the early second century to the late fourth century A.D.[6] It appears as if Justin was not from the city of Rome (*Praef.* 4); save this fact, however, we do not know from what area of the Empire he hailed.[7] Other problems present themselves. There is little agreement regarding the amount of input Justin offered in—and liberties he took with—his abridgment of Trogus' history.[8] It seems more likely, however, that Justin's contribution was minimal: with the exception of excising and occasional errors, he was essentially a copyist. The abridgment has a slapdash feel to it; its chronology is muddled in numerous places. Justin appears most interested in the rhetorical aspects of historiography (cf. *Praef.* 1). Accordingly, he may have altered a few phrases, or added flourishes of his own. It is unlikely that a man of his oratorical preoccupations modified the tenor of the historical narrative—except by way of heavy excising.

## A GENUINE SPEECH?

No consensus exists regarding the historicity of Trogus' speech of Mithridates.[9] A few scholars consider the speech to be at least partly based on pro-Pontic sources.[10] Others posit that Trogus invented it.[11] The latter contention is the most probable. In addition to the general arguments against the historicity of pre-battle exhortations discussed in the introduction, we can discern a few specific problems arising from the conclusion that this particular oration is not a free invention. As we shall see, at points a clear kinship exists between the *EM* and Trogus' speech of Mithridates.[12] This should lead us to conclude that Trogus has the *EM* in mind more than any pro-Pontic sources.

Additionally, as we shall have opportunity to elaborate on below, one detects obvious parallels between Trogus' speech of Mithridates and two other sizeable *oratio obliqua* orations found in Justin's abridgment: the speech of the Aetolians (28.2.1–13) and that of Demetrius, king of Illyria (29.2.2–6). All three Trogan compositions offer a range of historical examples of supposedly perfidious Roman conduct. The Aetolians' speech and the Mithridatic oration both discuss the Gallic sack of Rome and Roman incompetence in the face of the Gauls.[13] Both the speech of Demetrius and Mithridates' oration, moreover, harp on the purported Roman hatred of kingship.[14] The kinds of historical *exempla* offered in all three speeches correspond more often than do those in Mithridates' speech and the *EM*. It is unlikely that all three speakers—Mithridates, the Aetolians, and Demetrius—presented strikingly similar arguments. It is also improbable that Aetolian and Illyrian propaganda (if they existed) were similar to Pontic propaganda. As a result, it seems safe to conclude that Trogus' speech of Mithridates is essentially the product of its author.

## WAS THE *Historiae Philippicae* "ANTI-ROMAN"?

Before turning to the oration itself, we must discuss the general attitude Pompeius Trogus' world history demonstrates toward Rome—at least as it survives in Justin's abridgment. Unfortunately, modern scholars do not agree on this matter either. According to some, Trogus' history is not "anti-Roman."[15] A larger number of scholars, however, detect a distinct anti-Roman bias in Trogus' history.[16] In fact, for a brief time, some classicists found Trogus' abridgment sufficiently hostile to Rome that they supported Alfred von Gutschmid's so-called Timagenian thesis,[17] which argued that Trogus' work was nothing more than a Latin adaptation of a Greek history composed by the anti-Roman Timagenes of Alexandria (*FGrH* 88).[18] There is a reason for this disagreement: one can find all sorts of disparate opinions in the "epitome." In fact, the text contains so many seemingly contrary views that it calls to mind Kurt Tucholsky's quip about Nietzsche: "Tell me what you need and I will supply you with a Nietzsche citation."[19]

Consider the following. One can find examples of Trogus'/Justin's displeasure with imperial expansion, regardless of the state that undertakes it. Justin's rosy portrayal of the primitive Scythians offers one of the most prominent instances of this sentiment: in Justin's description of these people, the text laments that other races are not as unselfish with others' property (2.2.9–11).[20] Even so, Justin elsewhere labels world empire a *gloria* ("glorious enterprise"; 9.8.21).[21] Overall, one can glean that imperialism remains an important theme in Trogus' work, and that he proves more critical of it than many other ancient historians. Still, it appears difficult to ascertain his precise thoughts on the subject.

Parts of Justin's text display obvious nods to primitivism.[22] Justin, for instance, praises the virtues of early Romans (18.2.7–10; 31.8.8–9) and blames the Roman conquest of Asia for the metastasizing of vices to Italy (36.4.12).[23] He also depicts the first inhabitants of Italy as living without slavery or private property (43.1.3). And Justin seems interested in glorifying aspects of less advanced societies, as one can learn from his description of the Spanish:

> (1) Corpora hominum ad inediam laboremque, animi ad mortem parati. Dura omnibus et adstricta parsimonia. (2) Bellum quam otium malunt; si extraneus deest, domi hostem quaerunt. (3) Saepe tormentis pro silentio rerum creditarum inmortui; adeo illis fortior taciturnitatis cura quam vitae. (44.2.1–3)[24]

> (1) The bodies of these people [the Spanish] can survive hunger and hardship; their souls are ready for death. All of them live in harsh and stringent frugality. (2) They prefer war to peace; if a foreign enemy is lacking, they seek out one at home. (3) When tortured, they have often died to maintain their silence about secrets entrusted to them; to such a degree do they possess a stronger will to keep quiet rather than to live.

Despite this lauding of their bravery, Justin elsewhere praises Augustus for granting the Spanish a more civilized way of life (44.5.8). Trogus' potential anti-imperialism may have influenced his penchant for primitivism. It remains difficult to decipher, however, the degree to which either of these attributes contributes to supposed anti-Romanism.

Alas, Trogus'/Justin's views of Rome are particularly inscrutable. To be sure, Justin praises early Rome (e.g., 18.2.7–10; 31.8.8–9) and perceives that it is the world's capital (43.1.1). In other portions of his abridgment, Justin lauds Augustus' Romanization of Spain (44.5.8) and, in an *oratio obliqua* speech of Hannibal to King Antiochus III (31.5.2–9), compliments the Romans for their courage (31.5.5). All the same, numerous portions of Justin's text (apart from the speeches of Mithridates, the Aetolians, and Demetrius, which we shall discuss below) seem critical of Rome and its foreign policy. Justin claims, for instance, that Roman ambassadors to Antiochus III intended to spy on the king under the guise of an official delegation (31.4.4). He also asserts that Rome, frightened of Greece, sought any pretext to go to war with her (31.4.3). Elsewhere Justin highlights Roman covetousness in regard to Jewish property

(36.3.9), criticizes the Roman acquisition of Asia (36.4.8–9), and contends that the Romans, insatiable after their domination of Italy, yearned to rule the kingdoms of the East (39.5.3). There is also the matter of Justin's claim that Rome owed its success to *fortuna* ("fortune"), not *virtus* ("valor"; 30.4.16). This may amount to a slighting of Rome's imperial accomplishments, since elsewhere Justin claims (7.14) that, for the Macedonians, *virtus*, not *fortuna*, was the key.[25] In addition, some might question Trogus' desire to compose a "world history" with a heavy emphasis on the Macedonian Empire. He wrote, after all, the *Philippic Histories*, not the *Augustan Histories*.

Despite these complications, it appears certain that Justin's abridgment contains some sentiments critical of Rome—particularly in comparison with its treatment of the Macedonians. Still, Trogus'/Justin's attitudes toward Rome are complex. Their discussions of Rome—like those of other nations—seem too various for the tag "anti-Roman." We should be wary, in appraising Trogus' work, of coming to overly stark conclusions—that, for example, the historian was either critical of Rome wholesale, or not. Naturally, like anyone else, Trogus could be critical of aspects of Roman practices and martial aims and still remain supportive of other elements of Roman society.

Perhaps an examination of Trogus' speech of Mithridates—the most detailed example of its author's purported anti-Romanism—can shed light on the likely outlook of the *Historiae Philippicae*. Before we even lay eyes on this oration, however, we should note that Justin makes claims in his abridgment that undercut many of the king of Pontus' assertions.[26] Justin informs us, for instance, that Mithridates, from the very start of his reign, desired a large empire (37.3.1). Moreover, he stresses that Mithridates had battle with Rome on his mind well before the commencement of the First Mithridatic War (37.3.4; 38.3.5; 38.3.7). Readers of Trogus' world history thus had reason to suspect Mithridates' assertions to his soldiers.

## THE ORATION

### *The* Exordium *(38.4.1–3)*

Let us turn, then, to the oration itself. The *exordium* of Trogus' speech of Mithridates reads much like the opening of Sallust's *EM*:[27]

> (1) Optandum sibi fuisse ait, ut de eo liceret consulere, bellumne sit cum Romanis an pax habenda; (2) quin vero sit resistendum inpugnantibus, ne eos quidem dubitare, qui spe victoriae careant; quippe adversus latronem, si nequeant pro salute, pro ultione tamen sua omnes ferrum stringere.

(3) Ceterum quia non id agitur, an liceat quiescere non tantum animo hostiliter, sed etiam proelio congressis, consulendum, qua ratione ac spe coepta
bella sustineant. (38.4.1–3)

(1) He [Mithridates] said that it would have been desirable for him to
consider whether it might be permissible to be at peace or in war with the
Romans; (2) yet not even those who lack the hope of victory doubt that
attackers must be resisted—since everyone draws his sword against a robber, if not for his own safety, at least for revenge. (3) Otherwise, since it is
not a question of whether it is permissible to keep quiet, since they have
come not only with hostile intentions but also fighting as they go, it must
now be considered by what rationale and hope they may sustain the war
that has been begun.

Both compositions commence with elaborate disquisitions on the necessity
of going to war or remaining at peace. In Trogus' version, Mithridates informs his troops that Pontus cannot possibly maintain peace with Rome, even
though it would be desirable to have such an opportunity. Rather, the war
has already begun, and Pontus must contemplate how best to defend itself.
Although Trogus has set up the start of this oration differently from the *EM*'s
appeal to Phraates, it is clear that both compositions present similar introduc-
tions. It seems likely—if not certain—that Trogus modeled this *exordium* on
the beginning of Sallust's letter, which itself may hearken back to the introduction of Thucydides' speech of the Corcyreans (1.32.1). Semi-philosophical
ruminations on the necessity of warfare in a particular historical circumstance
seem to fit the recipient of the *EM* more than the soldiers whom Mithridates
ostensibly would have addressed. It is difficult to fathom soldiers requiring
such careful insight into Pontic foreign affairs.

Interestingly, however, Trogus, again like Sallust in the *EM*, has Mithridates start with a moral point, albeit of a less elevated sort: in 38.4.2, Trogus'
Mithridates likens the Romans to a *latro* ("robber"). The speech thus first
introduces a distinctly moral argument about Rome's foreign entanglements
and immediately positions the Romans as the aggressors.

*Rome, the Paper Tiger (38.4.4–16)*

Trogus' Mithridates next presents a series of historical examples that attempt
to prove that Rome is by no means invincible. This list commences with
Mithridates' brief mention of Pontic military victories against M'. Aquilius in
Bithynia and Mallius Maltinus in Cappadocia, which solidifies 88 B.C. as the
dramatic date for the oration.[28] Next is proffered the example of King Pyrrhus

of Epirus, who, Mithridates claims, routed Rome on three different occasions (4.5). First, we should note that Trogus does not have Mithridates focus on an argument related to the Roman East, or one that was chronologically close to the oration's dramatic date. Trogus himself, moreover, had covered the history of the Roman war with Tarentum, and thus the astute reader may have recognized that Mithridates is fibbing: Justin 18.1 and 23.3.11 make clear that Rome lost to Pyrrhus only twice. Also, we should note that this is not a strong line of argument if Trogus' aim was to encourage Roman introspection regarding their nation's imperialism. The Roman reader, after all, already recognized that Mithridates was dead and that Sulla, Lucullus, and Pompey were more than capable of handling his onslaught. Accordingly, the mention of Pyrrhus is weaker than Sallust's panoply of historical *exempla* in the *EM*.

The same is true of Mithridates' next example, Hannibal's near defeat of Rome in the Second Punic War (4.6). Again, Trogus has not chosen to home in on Roman foreign affairs in the East. Having briefly related Carthaginian success against Rome, Trogus' Mithridates eschews a chronological arrangement in order to mention the Gallic sack of Rome ca. 390 B.C. (4.7–10). Trogus relates:

> (7) Audire populos transalpinae Galliae Italiam ingressos maximis eam pluribusque urbibus possidere et latius aliquanto solum finium, quam in Asia, quae dicatur inbellis, idem Galli occupavissent. (8) Nec victam solum dici sibi Romam a Gallis, sed etiam captam, ita ut unius illis montis tantum cacumen relinqueretur; nec bello hostem, sed pretio remotum. (38.4.7–8)

> (7) He [Mithridates] heard that the people of Transalpine Gaul had invaded Italy and possessed most of the greatest of its cities, and that the same Gauls had seized a somewhat broader territory than that in Asia, a place that is called unwarlike. (8) And it was said to him that Rome had not only been conquered by the Gauls, but even captured, so that only the top of a single hill was left for them; and that the enemy was removed by a bribe, not by war.

Pompeius Trogus spends a comparatively lengthy time discussing Gaul, and this may stem from his own Gallic background. It seems as if Trogus, when crafting a speech of Mithridates to deliver to his troops, was intent on engaging in regional cheerleading.[29] The historical example of the Gauls, moreover, would hardly rouse Mithridates' troops into a bellicose frenzy: Trogus' Mithridates argues that his Pontic forces should not fear the Romans because the Gauls had sacked Rome *a full three hundred years earlier*. Unlike the points found in Sallust's *EM*, this is a bookish argument—one obviously fashioned by a Roman historian, not a Pontic king. It would be odd if Mithridates offered a potted discussion of remote portions of Roman history to encourage his troops. This sort of argument continues in 4.11–12, in which Trogus has Mithridates claim that Rome never entirely subdued Italy and refers obliquely to the Roman disaster at the Caudine Forks. Again, this seems far removed from the concerns of Pontic troops. The Roman defeat at the hands of the Samnites in 321 B.C. is another example of Trogus' fondness for bookish references to Rome's martial past.

Even when touching upon more recent historical events, Trogus' Mithridates offers comparatively weak arguments. After mentioning the Social War and civil strife in Rome (4.13–14), he attempts to prove that the Romans are bogged down in a sufficient number of conflicts to render his undertaking successful. To this end, he claims that the invasion of the Cimbri speaks to the Romans' inability to maintain control in Italy (4.15). This rationale seems strange: the Romans had pacified the Cimbri by 101 B.C., more than a decade before the war with Mithridates began.[30] Like the other historical examples Trogus offered,[31] that of the Cimbri was featured elsewhere in his world history (32.3.11; 38.3.6). It appears, then, that Trogus selected examples for this speech from the research he did for the rest of his work, without much concern for the potency of the examples he chose.

### War Is Already upon Us (38.5)

After offering an argument similar to one found in the *EM*—that Pontus must decide *when* to take up arms, not *if* to take up arms[32]—Trogus' Mithridates shifts to a different theme: Rome, he claims, has already begun a war against his kingdom through its previous actions (5.3–10). When he was a child, the king of Pontus asserts, the Romans took away Greater Phrygia, which was a reward they had granted to his father (5.3). This appears to be a comparatively potent point. Appian (*Mith.* 56–57) presents evidence to suggest that this was in fact the case. According to Appian (57), Sulla informed Mithridates that the Romans seized Phrygia because they had previously awarded it to Pontus as the result of a bribe. According to Appian's Sulla, then, Pontus received this territory illegally. Even so, by mentioning the recent history of Phrygia, Trogus has brought up an example of Roman maladministration, since a Roman politician was complicit in this sordid deal.

Nor is this the end of Mithridates' complaints about Roman conduct. He claims that Rome's commanding him to leave Paphlagonia was another form of war, given that it was a portion of his father's inheritance (5.4). In this instance, we have direct testimony from Justin's abridgment to suggest that Trogus had little sympathy for this argument. As Ernst Schneider has pointed out, elsewhere Justin himself labels this very point *superbus* ("arrogant"; 37.4.5).[33] We should conclude, therefore, that Trogus did not bring up this matter in his speech of Mithridates in order to cast aspersions on Roman conduct in the lead-up to the First Mithridatic War. The same seems to hold true for the king of Pontus' next argument, which relates that Pontic acquiescence to Roman demands has failed to mollify his antagonists. Trogus informs us that:

> (5) Cum inter hanc decretorum amaritudinem parendo non tamen eos mitigaret, quin acerbius in dies gerant, non obtinuisse. (6) Quod enim a se non praebitum illis obsequium? Non Phrygiam Paphlagoniamque dimissas? Non Cappadocia filium eductum, quam iure gentium victor occupaverat? (38.5.5–6)

> (5) He [Mithridates] did not soften them [the Romans] amidst this bitterness of decrees by being obedient, and he did not stop them from becoming even harsher day by day. (6) For what act of submission did he not offer them? Had he not let go of Phrygia and Paphlagonia? Was his son not removed from Cappadocia, which he had taken by the right of nations?

Mithridates claims that he departed from Phrygia and Paphlagonia, and removed his son from Cappadocia. According to our tradition, however, these assertions are only partly true and gravely distort Mithridates' role in the scheming of both sides prior to the First Mithridatic War.[34] The king of Pontus, after all, had in fact dismissed his son from Cappadocia, but then had placed him back on the throne (App. *Mith.* 15). The readers of Trogus' world history presumably would have happened upon a detailed account of these pre-war dealings soon before turning to the speech of Mithridates. Such a claim, then, would not likely fool even the credulous among them.

Perhaps the next argument is more compelling. Rome, Mithridates says, owes its territory to military victories, but keeps Pontus from its own conquests (5.7). Although such a point highlights the supposed hypocrisy of Rome, it appears somewhat inconsistent, in light of the earlier portion of this speech. At the start of the oration, Mithridates expatiated on the military weakness of the Romans (4.4–16); now, he appears to view Rome as a powerful conqueror. Still, the king of Pontus has here emphasized supposed Roman duplicity.

Yet Trogus seems incapable of, or, more likely, uninterested in, presenting compelling arguments about the evils of Roman foreign policy. Thus Trogus' Mithridates next presents another seemingly weak point about purported Roman misbehavior (5.8). More specifically, Mithridates asserts that he killed Socrates Chrestus, his puppet king of Bithynia, to satisfy the Romans. Even so, he says, Rome claims Mithridates personally responsible for the actions of both Gordius (who had killed Ariarathes VI of Cappadocia) and King Tigranes of Armenia. This is, in fact, the only mention of Socrates Chrestus' murder in surviving ancient sources, and this may cast doubt on Mithridates' statement. Elsewhere in Justin's text, however, Mithridates is made responsible for the actions of Gordius (38.1.1). In addition, Justin informs us that the king of Pontus desired Tigranes' alliance (38.3.2). Trogus, that is to say, made his readers aware that Mithridates was the mastermind behind these Anatolian machinations. Unless the ancient reader of Trogus' text had skipped the relevant portions of book 38, he would have seen through Mithridates' fabrications.

The king of Pontus' discussion of affairs in Cappadocia is equally tendentious:

> Libertatem etiam in contumeliam sui a senatu ultro delatam Cappadociae, quam reliquis gentibus abstulerunt; dein populo Cappadocum pro libertate oblata Gordium regem orante ideo tantum, quoniam amicus suus esset, non obtinuisse. (38.5.9)

> Besides, freedom was granted to Cappadocia by the Senate as an insult to him [Mithridates]—freedom that they had taken away from all other races; then, with the people of Cappadocia begging for Gordius to be the king instead of the freedom that was granted, they did not obtain this, because he was his friend.

According to Mithridates, Rome granted Cappadocia its independence to spite him. In reality, however, it appears as if Rome did so in order to seem neutral in the conflicts of Asia Minor.[35] Mithridates further claims that the Cappadocians clamored for Gordius to be their ruler; as he was an underling of the Pontic king, however, Rome would not allow it. We possess no other source that mentions the Cappadocians' supposed eagerness to retain Gordius as their king. Trogus likely added this argument about the Roman liberation of Cappadocia because it demonstrated Mithridates' hostility to republican governance. To Trogus' Mithridates, unaware of the benefits of "freedom," the people of Cappadocia must pine for a king. Accordingly, such a statement may not be anti-Roman in tenor, but anti-Eastern instead.

Given the kinds of criticisms Trogus' Mithridates has mustered so far, it should come as no surprise that it is not until 5.10 that the king of Pontus offers a forceful complaint against Rome:

Nicomeden praecepto illorum bellum sibi intulisse; quia ultum ierit se, ab ipsis ventum obviam in eo; et nunc eam secum bellandi illis causam fore, quod non inpune se Nicimedi lacerandum, saltatricis filio, praebuerit. (38.5.10)

Nicomedes waged war against him [Mithridates] at the behest of the Romans; and because he had come to take revenge, they were coming after him; and now their reason for going to war with him would be that he had not surrendered himself without resistance to be torn to pieces by Nicomedes, the son of a dancing girl.

The Romans, he asserts, bid Nicomedes to ravage his territory. As we have discussed in the context of Sallust's *EM*,[36] this is both true and Mithridates' greatest pretext to conclude that he engaged in a "just war." Still, Mithridates does not linger on this topic, but refers to it in one sentence, and then moves on to dilute his claim with a haughty—and irrelevant—attack on Nicomedes' pedigree. Unlike Sallust, who attempted to grant prominent placement to Mithridates' most telling criticisms, Trogus prepared a smorgasbord of arguments, seemingly unconcerned about highlighting particularly withering points.

## Rome, the Enemy of Kings (38.6)

Thus Trogus, having offered Mithridates a comparatively strong complaint, immediately commences with a new line of attack. Romans, Mithridates exclaims, detest kings—not for their malefactions, but on account of their majesty (6.1). This appears to be a tip of the cap to Sallust, since Roman hatred of kings fits the context of the *EM* better than it does Trogus' speech of Mithridates. After all, this point would be a far greater concern to Phraates—himself a king—than to Mithridates' soldiers. Moreover, Trogus' first illustration of Rome's purported anti-monarchism (6.2) is feeble: Mithridates mentions Roman mistreatment of his grandfather, Pharnaces I. He does not proffer any specifics, or any reasoning at all. On the contrary: he merely drops his name and moves on to another point.

Trogus' Mithridates next presents another example: supposed Roman maltreatment of Eumenes, the king of Pergamum (6.3–4).[37] The Romans, he avers, made great use of Eumenes' services in their battles against Antiochus the Great, the Asian Gauls, and Perseus (6.2). Schneider correctly pointed out that here Mithridates proves rather selective in his interpretation of Roman dealings with Eumenes; Appian (*Syr.* 22), for instance, informs us that the Romans did not rely on Eumenes' fleet as fully as Mithridates asserts.[38] In addition, Trogus dealt with this history in his own work, and thus the reader of his entire world history would have reason to be skeptical of Mithridates' claims. Still, we need not infer that ancient readers would have possessed either encyclopedic knowledge of Roman history or a perfect memory for the details in Trogus' work. It remains possible that Mithridates' discussion of Eumenes—though simplified and distorted according to our pro-Roman sources and Trogus' own history—could have some resonance with a Roman audience.

The same holds true for Mithridates' half-truths regarding Aristonicus and Masinissa of Numidia:

> (4) et ipsum pro hoste habitum eique interdictum Italia, et quod cum ipso deforme sibi putaverant, cum filio eius Aristonico bellum gessisse. Nullius apud eos maiora quam Masinissae, regis Numidarum, haberi merita; (5) huic inputari victum Hannibalem, huic captum Syphacem, huic Karthaginem deletam, hunc inter duos illos Africanos tertium servatorem urbis referri: (6) tamen cum huius nepote bellum modo in Africa gestum adeo inexpiabile, ut ne victum quidem patris memoriae donarent, quin carcerem ac triumphi spectaculum experiretur. (38.6.4–6)

> (4) [A]nd they [the Romans] considered him [Eumenes] an enemy and barred him from Italy, and because they had thought it unbecoming to wage a war with him, waged it with his son Aristonicus. No one had favor with the Romans more than Masinissa, king of Numidia; (5) they ascribe the conquering of Hannibal, the capture of Syphaces, and the destruction of Carthage to him; they consider him, along with the two famous Africani, a third savior of the city: (6) even so, the war they waged with his grandson was so merciless that they did not even grant a concession to the memory of his father when he was conquered, so that he wouldn't have to endure imprisonment and the spectacle of a triumph.

Naturally, the king of Pontus' praise of Masinissa (6.5) comes across as overstated: according to Mithridates, he is responsible for Hannibal's defeat, the capture of Syphax, and the ultimate destruction of Carthage. Mithridates compounds this excessive laudation with a dubious claim regarding Rome's dealings with Numidia. Trogus' Mithridates asserts that the Roman victory over Jugurtha amounted to an example of bad faith in regard to Masinissa (6.6). Naturally, this misses the obvious fact that Masinissa's legitimate son Adherbal sought Roman aid against Jugurtha (*Jug.* 14; 24.2–10). Once again, this subject appears elsewhere in Justin's text (33.1.2), and thus ancient readers would have had reasons to be skeptical of Mithridates' assertions.

After presenting these examples of Rome's supposed perfidious conduct vis-à-vis various monarchs, Trogus' Mithridates expands on the Roman hatred of kings tout court. He asserts:

(7) Hanc illos omnibus regibus legem odiorum dixisse, scilicet quia ipsi tales reges habuerint, quorum etiam nominibus erubescant, aut pastores Aboriginum, aut aruspices Sabinorum, aut exules Corinthiorum, aut servos vernasque Tuscorum, aut, quod honoratissimum nomen fuit inter haec, Superbos; atque ut ipse ferunt conditores suos lupae uberibus altos, (8) sic omnem illum populum luporum animos inexplebiles sanguinis, atque imperii divitiarumque avidos ac ieiunos habere. (38.6.7-8)

(7) They [the Romans] affirmed this law of the hatred for every king, of course, because they had such kings that they even blush at their names: either Aboriginal shepherds, or Sabine soothsayers, or Corinthian exiles, or Etruscan slaves, or—that name that was most honored among them—the Superbi; and they themselves say that their founders were nourished by the teats of a wolf, (8) and thus their whole population has the spirit of wolves, insatiably bloodthirsty and sordidly greedy for power and riches.

The end of this passage calls to mind Sallust's *EM*, which excoriates the Romans for their lust for empire (5).[39] Yet Trogus' Mithridates has diluted a potentially forceful argument by combining it with snootiness. This harsh commentary appears neither genuinely Mithridatic nor designed to incite Roman self-doubt. Rather, Trogus has watered down Sallust's powerful criticism with another bookish discussion, this time of Rome's early origins.[40] We can also tell from Justin's praise of early Italy that Mithridates' insults were not supported by the speech's author.[41] Trogus appears more interested in highlighting the arrogance of Mithridates and his own learning than in eliciting Roman self-reflection.

## The Great Mithridates (38.7)

Having denigrated the remote Roman past, Trogus' Mithridates then contrasts its lowliness with his own impressive pedigree (7.1-2). He claims descent not only from Alexander the Great, but also from King Darius (7.1). And he asserts that all those under his rule have experienced the leadership only of those of their race—a claim that is proven wrong elsewhere in Justin's text (13.4.16).[42] Continuing with his braggadocio, Mithridates next discusses his successes against the Scythians (7.3-5), a people who seem to have interested Trogus himself, given the lengthy praise of them found in Justin's text

(2.2.9–15). Trogus has Mithridates introduce the Scythians, it seems, in order to contrast them with the inhabitants of Asia (7.6–8). Asia, he says, is incomparably mild, fertile, and full of riches (7.6). The campaigns in Asia, he asserts, should be a cakewalk—a festival rather than a struggle. Naturally, this commentary contains an unrealistically Western view of the First Mithridatic War. The East, according to Trogus' Eastern king, is wealthy and decadent. We can easily discount the idea that a king of Pontus would offer such a view to his troops. This sort of argument, moreover, does not question Roman foreign policy in the East.

The same is true of the conclusion of Trogus' speech of Mithridates. In this section of the harangue, Trogus' Mithridates encourages his troops by listing his military successes and giving witness of his fairness and generosity. He boasts:

> (9) Sequantur se modo fortiter et colligant, quid se duce posit efficere tantus exercitus, quem sine cuiusquam militum auxilio suamet unius opera viderint Cappadociam caeso rege cepisse, qui solus mortalium Pontum omnem Scythiamque pacaverit, quam nemo ante transire tuto atque adire potuit. (10) Nam iustitiae atque liberalitatis suae ne ipsos milites quin experiantur testes refugere et illa indicia habere, quod solus regum non paterna solum, verum etiam externa regna hereditatibus propter munificentiam adquisita possideat, Colchos, Paphlagoniam, Bosphorum. (38.7.9–10)

> (9) Only let them follow him [Mithridates] bravely and consider what so great an army could do with him as a leader—whom they had seen seize Cappadocia without the aid of any soldiers by the work of him alone, with its king slaughtered, who alone of all mortals had subdued all of Pontus and Scythia, which no one had ever been able to cross and enter safely. (10) As for his fairness and generosity, he did not object to his soldiers being called as witnesses to give evidence that he not only possessed his paternal authority, but also external land that he had obtained through inheritance on account of his munificence, namely Colchis, Paphlagonia, and the Bosporus.

Although this amounts to a reasonable exhortation to his soldiers, it contains a fib about Mithridates' patrimony that astute readers of Trogus' history would have recalled. The ancient reader of Trogus' history, already alert to the machinations of Mithridates highlighted in books 37 and 38, would see through this palaver: Paphlagonia had hardly been Mithridates' willing subject. In addition, the conclusion of the speech serves as an opportunity for Mithridates to indulge in self-congratulation. It does not, unlike Sallust's *EM*, focus on Roman perfidy.

## DIFFERENT ORATIONS, SIMILAR COMPLAINTS

Before we turn to some conclusions about Pompeius Trogus' speech of Mithridates, we should note that a few shorter Trogan orations found in Justin's abridgment present commentary similar to that offered in his Mithridatic harangue. For instance, we can examine Trogus' *oratio obliqua* speech of the Aetolians in response to a Roman delegation demanding the withdrawal of garrisons from Acarnania ca. 240–230 B.C.: [43]

(1) Sed Aetoli legationem Romanorum superbe audivere, Poenos illis et Gallos, a quibus tot bellis occidione caesi sint, exprobrantes (2) dicentesque prius illis portas adversus Karthaginienses aperiendas, quas clauserit metus Punici belli, quam in Graeciam arma transferenda. (3) Meminisse deinde iubent, qui quibus minentur. (4) Adversus Gallos urbem eos suam tueri non potuisse captamque non ferro defendisse, sed auro redimisse; (5) quam gentem se aliquanto maiore manu Graeciam ingressam non solum nullis externis viribus, sed ne domesticis quidem totis adiutos universam delesse, sedemque sepulcris eorum praebuisse, quam illi urbibus imperioque suo proposuerant; (6) contra Italiam trepidis ex recenti urbis suae incendio Romanis universam ferme a Gallis occupatam. (7) Prius igitur Gallos Italia pellendos quam minentur Aetolis, priusque sua defendenda quam aliena appetenda. (8) Quos autem homines Romanos esse? nempe pastores, qui latrocinio iustis dominis ademptum solum teneant, (9) qui uxores cum propter originis dehonestamenta non invenirent, vi publica rapuerint, (10) qui denique urbem ipsam parracido condiderint murorumque fundamenta fraterno sanguine adsperserint. (11) Aetolos autem principes Graeciae semper fuisse et sicut dignitate, ita et virtute ceteris praestitisse; (12) solos denique esse, qui Macedonas imperio terrarum semper florentes contempserint, qui Philippum regem non timuerint, qui Alexandri Magni post Persas Indosque devictos, cum omnes nomen eius horrerent, edicta spreverint. (13) Monere igitur se Romanos, contenti sint fortuna praesenti nec provocent arma, quibus et Gallos caesos et Macedonas contemptos videant. (28.2.1–13)

(1) But the Aetolians arrogantly listened to the Roman embassy, reproaching them in regard to the Carthaginians and the Gauls, by whom the Romans had been cut down in many wars, (2) and saying that before invading Greece they ought to open up their gates, which they closed on account of their dread of a Punic War, to take on the Carthaginians. (3) Then they ordered them to recall who was threatening whom. (4) They said that the Romans were not able to protect their own city against the Gauls and,

when it was captured, could not defend it by iron but had to buy it back with gold; (5) when the Roman people attacked Greece with a slightly larger force, the Greeks destroyed them not only without the aid of foreign troops but not even with all their own, and that they had furnished the proposed seat of their empire with their tombs; (6) on the other hand, Italy had been almost entirely seized by the Gauls, since the Romans were alarmed on account of the recent burning of their city. (7) Therefore, they said that they should eject the Gauls from Italy before they menace the Aetolians and ought to defend their own lands before striving for others'. (8) Moreover, they wondered, what sort of men were the Romans? As everyone knew, shepherds who possess land stolen from its rightful owner through robbery, (9) who, as a result of their base stock, could not find wives and were compelled to kidnap them through the use of violence in broad daylight, (10) who, in sum, founded their city on parricide and sprinkled the foundations of its walls with the blood of brothers. (11) The Aetolians, however, had always been the leaders of Greece and just as they had surpassed the others in eminence, so they had in regard to courage as well. (12) Indeed, they were the only ones who had always despised the Macedonians when they were flourishing with a world empire, who did not fear King Philip, who spurned the edicts of Alexander the Great after the Persians and the Indians had been subdued, when everyone else shuddered at his name. (13) Therefore, they said that they recommended that the Romans be content with what they had and not stir up arms with which they saw the Gauls slaughtered and the Macedonians defied.

This passage, like Trogus' speech of Mithridates, contains a reference to the Gallic sack of Rome (28.2.4; 38.4.7).[44] It offers, that is to say, a bit of cheerleading for Trogus' ancestors, rather than an indictment of Roman conduct. In fact, the oration's continued focus on Gaul leads one to believe that a discussion of erstwhile Gallic military endeavors was of greater import to Trogus than withering criticisms of Roman foreign policy.

The appeal to Gallic martial prowess, moreover, relates to another tendency detectable in Justin's speech of the Aetolians and Trogus' Mithridatic oration. In the course of their comments (28.2.8–10), the Aetolians discuss congenital Roman shortcomings by referring to legends that surround the early history of the Roman kingship. This is another example of Trogus' penchant for presenting his reader with bookish arguments based on remote events—something we have also detected in the speech of Mithridates (cf. 38.4.5–9, 38.6.7–8). Just as it seems far-fetched to assume that Mithridates' insults aimed at the upbringing of Romulus and Remus would inspire much introspection on the part of Roman readers, it is hard to imagine that the Aetolians' disparaging of Rome's legendary pedigree would cause Romans to reflect upon the sins of their nation's martial past. Rather than hunt for more potent examples of Roman malefactions, Trogus appears to have been content to offer weaker allusions to remote Roman mythology. Romulus' fratricide, after all, does not tell us much about the character of Rome's foreign affairs, and amounts to little more than name-calling. Certainly one can find stronger indictments of Roman imperialism in the annals of ancient historiography.[45] We should also note that Justin has presented the Aetolians' remarks in a manner that bears similarities to Trogus' Mithridatic oration. In both cases, the Romans' pedigree is excoriated and then contrasted with the presumed majesty of the speakers' lineage (28.2.8–12; 38.6.7–7.2).[46]

Similarities also abound between Trogus' Mithridatic speech and Justin's *oratio obliqua* oration of Demetrius of Pharus, which attempts to incite anti-Roman animus in Philip V of Macedon after the Second Illyrian War (29.2.2–6).[47] The young Philip, Justin informs us, aimed to fight the Aetolians (29.1.11), but Demetrius' counsel compelled the king to wage war against Rome instead—a task made more manageable by the recent Roman loss to Hannibal at Trasumenus in 217 B.C. (29.2.7).[48] Justin introduces the speech thus:

> (1) Quae agitantem illum Demetrius, rex Illyriorum, nuper a Paulo, Romano consule, victus supplicibus precibus adgreditur, (2) iniuriam Romanorum querens, qui non contenti Italiae terminis, imperium spe inproba totius orbis amplexi, bellum cum omnibus regibus gerant. (3) Sic illos Siciliae, sic Sardiniae Hispaniaeque, sic denique totius Africae imperium adfectantes bellum cum Poenis et Hannibale suscepisse; (4) sibi quoque non aliam ob causam, quam quod Italiae finitimus videbatur, bellum inlatum, quasi nefas esset aliquem regem iuxta imperii eorum terminos esse. (5) Sed et ipsi cavendum exemplum esse, cuius quanto promptius nobiliusque sit regnum, tanto sit Romanos acriores hostes habiturus. (6) Super haec cedere se illi regno, quod Romani occupaverint, profitetur, gratius habiturus, si in possessione imperii sui socium potius quam hostes videret. (29.2.1–6)

> (1) With Philip deliberating on these matters, Demetrius, the king of Illyria, having recently been conquered by Paullus, the Roman consul, came to him with humble entreaties, (2) complaining about the abuses of the Romans, who, not satisfied with the boundaries of Italy, and having embraced the idea of controlling the whole world with an outrageous hope, were waging war with all kings. (3) Thus, pursuing rule over the populations of Sicily, Sardinia, Spain, and finally all Africa, he said, they had taken up a

war with the Carthaginians and Hannibal. (4) Also, he said, Hannibal had been attacked merely because he seemed to be neighboring Italy—as if it were criminal for any king to be near the borders of their empire. (5) And Philip must beware of his example, since his kingdom was closer at hand and better known, he would have the Romans as fiercer enemies. (6) In addition to these things, Demetrius said that he was handing over his kingdom, which the Romans had seized, to Philip; he professed that he would be happier if he saw an ally in control of his realm rather than an enemy.

In some sense, Demetrius' speech seems more powerful than its Mithridatic and Aetolian corollaries, since it focuses more closely on relevant historical *exempla*—in this case Roman actions vis-à-vis Carthage. Still, its distortions are, if anything, even more obvious: given Hannibal's famous trek across the Alps, it appears difficult to argue that the Romans commenced hostilities in the Second Punic War.[49] The fame of this episode renders it unlikely that Roman readers would take Demetrius' commentary at face value. All the same, Roman detestation of monarchs amounts to the overarching theme of the speech; this same sentiment, as we have already noted, informs Trogus' Mithridatic oration as well (38.6.1, 7). This demonstrates that Trogus likely had little regard for crafting speeches that stayed true to the sentiments actual enemies of Rome delivered.

The correspondences between these three Trogan creations seem more numerous than those of the Mithridatic oration and Sallust's *EM*. In addition, Demetrius' speech elucidates a theme potentially inclined to encourage Roman pride, not doubt: Republican Rome was hostile to tyranny.[50]

CONCLUSIONS

From the preceding examination we can determine that Pompeius Trogus' speech of Mithridates appears far less successful at offering powerful criticism of Roman conduct than did Sallust's *EM*, although we can find a few examples of it in the oration. Overall, Trogus harps on Roman lowliness—a charge unlikely to lead to introspection on the part of the Romans. And Trogus makes Mithridates appear like a braggart. His historical examples seem bookish, and are almost all undercut by the text of Justin's abridgment. Although Trogus' Mithridates offers a few forceful examples of Roman misconduct, Trogus, unlike Sallust, sees no need to place these examples in powerful places in the oration; rather, the speech both begins and ends with weak points.

Even though Trogus appears interested in presenting a few passages critical of Roman foreign policy in the East, other matters seem to concern him as well. He probably composed his speech of Mithridates with Sallust's letter in mind: the oration contains a number of tips of the cap to Sallust. At the same time, Trogus seems to have gone out of his way to mention historical examples that Sallust did not discuss. He did so even though these *exempla* dramatically undercut the force of his speech of Mithridates. Trogus likely included this oration partly as a tribute to Sallust's rhetorical powers in the *EM* and partly to demonstrate the knowledge he had acquired in researching his world history. Still, the overlap we detected in this speech and those of the Aetolians and Demetrius of Pharus suggests that Trogus wanted to convey anti-Roman arguments to his readership.

Nor is this the only thing we can learn from the enemy orations appearing in Justin's "epitome." As was the case with Sallust's *EM*, Justin's speeches offer us the opportunity to examine a Roman author's attitude toward Easterners. Overall, they leave us with similar impressions: one detects stereotypes of the East in Trogus'/Justin's addresses that echo themes in Sallust's work. In the aforementioned orations of Mithridates and Demetrius, part of Trogus' animus seems to stem from the East's perceived effeminacy and softness, and part of it derives from the intrinsic connection between autocracy and the East. The latter association, which we have also uncovered in the *EM*, is more striking in the Trogan context, since Trogus, unlike Sallust, lived under a de facto monarch. The lack of anti-Augustus sentiment found in Justin's "epitome" suggests that Trogus did not attempt to use this line of argument to criticize the vicissitudes of the early Roman Empire. Rather, we may insinuate that when biases against foreigners appeared in the Roman historiographical tradition, matters of convention loomed large. Thus Trogus felt free to highlight the lack of political freedom in the East without appearing to deprecate the Roman present.

The casting of Asia as pliant and weak in Trogus' Mithridatic oration (38.7.6–8) is made particularly striking by the fact that the historian puts these sentiments in the mouth of an Eastern king. After all, Trogus' Mithridates portrays Asia, due to its fecundity and wealth, as a veritable Valhalla for prospective invaders. Either Trogus assumed that foreigners harbored the same stereotypes about other groups as did members of the Roman elite, or in this instance he failed to demonstrate regard for verisimilitude, and thus offered the prejudices of a semi-Roman Mithridates. If this granting of "Roman" sentiments about the East to Mithridates was a lapse on Trogus' part, it is not the only mistake appearing in his foreign addresses: elsewhere his Demetrius incorrectly labels Hannibalic Carthage a monarchy (29.2–3). Yet the latter contention could also serve to intensify anti-Eastern animus in the work, since Trogus/Justin could have intentionally associated the Carthaginians, as Phoenician colonists, with Eastern autocracy.

In a similar vein, Trogus also has his Mithridates discuss Western barbarian groups in a manner that reflects Greco-Roman stereotypes. Thus the king of Pontus characterizes the Cimbri as *inmensa milia ferorum atque inmitium populorum* ("immense thousands of savage, harsh people"; 38.4.15).[51] In Trogus'/Justin's enemy addresses, even the portrayal of the Gauls fits aspects of Greco-Roman perceptions of Westerners, although, as we have seen, Trogus' Gallic background appears to have compelled him to stress the Gauls' martial prowess. As a result, Trogus'/Justin's Mithridates and Aetolians both laud Gallic ferocity at length.

And while Trogus'/Justin's foreign orations demonstrate their own regard for military valor, they also focus much attention on Roman pretensions to engage in defensive warfare. For instance, Trogus' Mithridates portrays Rome as unappeasable and therefore irrational. This helps characterize Rome as unconcerned either with righteous conduct in its foreign entanglements or with the mere maintenance of order. As Trogus' king of Pontus views matters, the Romans constantly aim to defeat monarchs and conquer territory. His speech dilutes its criticism of Roman aggressiveness, however, by elsewhere portraying imperialism in a positive light—e.g., the Gallic sack of Rome (38.4.8) and the forthcoming Pontic invasion of Asia (38.7.6–8).

More broadly, in the speeches we have surveyed Trogus' foreigners view Roman aggression and lust for empire as axiomatic. Thus they do not seem compelled to elaborate on the specifics of Roman motives with the detail of Sallust's Mithridates. Still, for both Trogus and Sallust, ruminations on the Romans' failures to live up to the details of fetial law—however vague—remain the key way to criticize Rome's foreign policy and colonial rule. As we have detected, Sallust's *exempla* of Rome falling afoul of engagement in justified warfare often seem more convincing than the more generalized denunciations Trogus'/Justin's foreigners muster. Even so, the focus on Roman pugnacity is essentially the same.

In keeping with Sallust's orations critical of Roman imperialism, Trogus'/Justin's foreign addresses present greed as a key force in Roman foreign policy. As was the case with Sallust's speeches, however, Trogus'/Justin's do not elaborate on specific examples of Roman acquisitiveness. In the eyes of Trogus' anti-Roman speakers, it appears, Rome's failure to engage in morally justifiable warfare should lead one to surmise that the Romans must have expanded due to an insatiable desire for riches. Thus Trogus' foreign enemies do not countenance other possible motives for Roman imperialism—tactical incentives, for example, or the obsession with martial valor on the part of the

Roman elite. As a result, greed actually plays a minor role in Trogus'/Justin's anti-Roman orations, as does Roman administrative corruption.

All in all, though, the preceding chapters have shown that it is the historian who hails from a town close to Rome—Sallust—who seems more concerned with presenting criticism of Roman conduct than does the man from Gallia Narbonensis. Criticism of Rome, that is to say, did not appeal only to those on the periphery of the Roman world; rather, as we shall continue to see in the chapters to come, it is detectable in a broad range of historians.

It remains difficult to discern how much this self-critical cast of mind, if you will, affected Roman readers of history. It is instructive to recall that Justin, who produced our version of Pompeius Trogus' world history, considered the speech of Mithridates so important that—alone of all the orations in his abridgment—he offered it word-for-word (38.3.11). Similarly, the preservation of Sallust's *EM* in a collection of orations likely intended for educational purposes demonstrates that many Romans may have been comfortable studying rhetoric from a letter filled with anti-Roman arguments.[52] In order for the *EM* to serve as a rhetorical example, moreover, it was wrenched from its historical context, and would likely seem stronger on its own than in the text of Sallust's *Historiae*. Accordingly, the prominence given to both Trogus' speech of Mithridates and Sallust's letter of Mithridates after their original composition suggests that ancient readers welcomed—if they did not openly seek out—criticism of Rome.

This appears particularly noteworthy in the case of Justin himself. In fact, perhaps more telling than the existence of speeches critical of Rome in Pompeius Trogus' *Historiae Philippicae* is the prominence Justin afforded them in his abridgment. In a work containing few extended orations, Justin's "epitome" emphasizes the anti-Roman speeches of the Aetolians, Demetrius of Pharus, Hannibal (31.5.2–9), and Mithridates. Unfortunately, our hazy knowledge of his life and intellectual predilections leaves us in the dark about Justin's rationale for offering conspicuous placement to anti-Roman orations from Trogus' world history. All the same, it appears to speak to a level of comfort with the sorts of criticisms of Rome Trogus featured in his original work.

All this suggests that some Roman elites were interested in discussions of their society's collective failings. Far from inevitably undermining anti-Roman arguments, Roman historians appear capable of powerful criticism of Roman conduct. More specifically, Sallust does in the *EM* what he does elsewhere in his monographs:[53] he uses a foreigner to assail Roman political, diplomatic, and military conduct. Pompeius Trogus was also capable of presenting cogent anti-Roman arguments. Although this by no means implies that either Sallust or Pompeius Trogus was a diehard anti-imperialist, it does intimate that they could see both the blessings and the curses of Roman expansionism.

Is such a perspective confined to Sallust and Trogus? Does it relate to enemies of Rome who lived in an earlier period than the first century B.C.—the age previous generations of classical scholars have deemed home to uncharacteristic Roman pugnacity and duplicity?[54] In the next chapter, we shall determine, inter alia, an answer to these questions by spotlighting another figure who waged war against Rome.

Of all the ancient historians of Rome, Livy, by virtue of being heir to the Roman annalistic tradition, is among the most likely to be accused by modern scholars of introducing patriotic and even jingoistic sentiments that distort his work.[1] As a result, many scholars focus on his orations—which were the most heralded feature of Livy's history during antiquity[2]—as at least in part celebrations of Roman superiority.[3] In contrast, though there is no firm consensus on the subject, modern classical scholars tend to stress Polybius' stance vis-à-vis Rome as more ambiguous.[4] In short, the "Roman" Livy seems pro-Roman; the Greek Polybius comes across as evenhanded.

Yet, as we shall see in the next two chapters, an examination of two key speeches found in the works of both historians (and the addresses with which they are counterpoised) demonstrates that Livy is in fact equally, if not more, capable of sympathizing with Rome's greatest enemy. The orations, those of Hannibal and P. Scipio before the Battle of Ticinus (Polybius 3.63–64; Livy 21.40–44) and those of Hannibal and the man who would come to be known as Scipio Africanus before the Battle of Zama (Polybius 15.6.4–8; Livy 30.30.3–31.1–9), are important parts of the respective works in which they are found. This is especially true in regard to Livy, since his pre-Ticinus and pre-Zama speeches act as bookends for his Third Decade.[5] Far from offering pro-Roman bromides, these orations present a variety of arguments that can reasonably be construed as critical of Roman imperialism. To be sure, the speeches do not contain only anti-Roman commentary. Rather, Livy—much like Polybius—criticizes both the Carthaginians and Hannibal himself. But, as we shall see, an exegesis of these Livian speeches, side by side with a discussion of their Polybian counterparts, reveals that Livy was fully capable of presenting cogent critiques of Roman society.[6] Polybius too, as is less surprising, uses his orations at times to question and find fault with Roman conduct.

In chapter 3 we shall chiefly examine Polybius' version of these speeches; in chapter 4 we shall turn to the Livian corollaries.

# "HE CONSIDERED IT TO BE IN NO WAY WORTHY TO CONTEMPLATE THE HOPE OF LIVING DEFEATED": POLYBIUS' SPEECHES OF HANNIBAL

## ON THE HISTORICITY OF POLYBIUS' PRE-TICINUS AND PRE-ZAMA ORATIONS

Before we examine Polybius' speeches prior to the battles of Ticinus and Zama, we must quickly discuss the matter of these addresses' potential historicity. After all, if one can demonstrate that Polybius was recording the actual sentiments of Hannibal in these orations, they would tell us very little about Polybian views on Roman foreign policy and colonialism. This will require a quick foray into the world of *Quellenforschung*, though we need not proffer any definitive claims about Polybius' sources for these speeches.

In general, it has long been presumed that Polybius used many literary sources when composing his history.[1] This seems related to the comparatively high opinion modern scholars have of Polybius as a historian. In addition to postulating his employment of earlier written histories, one might conclude that Polybius engaged in original research (which would have stemmed from his proximity to the so-called Scipionic circle) for events extending back to the beginning of his work. Still, little effort has been expended on determining the possible sources for Polybius' pre-Ticinus and pre-Zama orations,[2] and we have little reason to believe that we can do so. As a result, we must conclude that Polybius, for his pre-Ticinus orations and pre-Zama conference, used (an) unknown source(s) and, further, that we cannot tell the degree to which these speeches were Polybius' own creation, as opposed to the product of ideas put forward in his source(s). As we shall see, however, we can be certain that Polybius put these addresses into his own style,[3] and that they appear to reflect concerns typical of this historian.

Additionally, there are numerous reasons to doubt the historicity of these Polybian orations—many, if not all, of which apply also to their Livian corollaries. It is possible that the pre-oration violence among the Carthaginians' Gallic captives (which is featured in both Polybius' and Livy's accounts of the lead-up to the Battle of Ticinus)[4] was invented in order to make the Carthaginians—and especially Hannibal—appear more savage and barbaric.[5] More importantly, P. Scipio's address to his troops prior to the Battle of Ticinus is surely ahistorical, since Scipio did not envision fighting Punic forces at this time.[6] Consequently, it is likely that at some point in the historiographical tradition someone created a Scipionic speech to complement Hannibal's pre-Ticinus harangue—if, that is, the Hannibalic oration itself is in any way genuine.

In regard to Polybius' version of the pre-Zama colloquy, we have reason to suspect its accuracy, although on the whole there are fewer compelling reasons to doubt the historicity of the two orations. The notion that this conversation stems from a passage found in Ennius, as some have asserted,[7] and is thus a wholesale invention, does not seem sound.[8] Still, one might find dubious Polybius' (15.6.3) and Livy's (30.30.1) claim that translators were required for the meeting. Hannibal, we know, spoke both Greek[9] and Latin.[10] This purported inconsistency need not trouble us, however: Hannibal may have found it either easier or more politic to speak in his native tongue. Further, since the pro-Punic historians Silenus and Sosylus, who had traveled in Hannibal's entourage, served as sources for later historians, it remains conceivable that Polybius had access to comparatively well-informed writers for information on this conference.

As we shall see, however, the pre-Zama conferences presented in the works of Polybius and Livy differ to such an extent that one can justifiably conclude that ancient historians allowed themselves great liberties in their speechifying. This seems a less controversial opinion in regard to Livy, since his orations are so often deemed essentially ahistorical.[11] But in this chapter we shall happen upon evidence that casts doubt on the historicity of Polybius' speeches as well.[12] In fact, the faith in Polybius' concern for crafting historically accurate orations appears to be based on two—shaky—elements: first, Polybius' polemical criticism of the rhetorical excesses found in other historians' speeches (notably those of Timaeus); and, second, the relative lack of stylistic polish and rhetorical τόποι detectable in Polybius' orations. In regard to the former concern, reasons certainly exist to doubt that Polybius' polemical historiographical commentary necessarily translated into a keen concern for offering *ipsissima verba* oratorical contributions. Also, we need not conclude that Polybius' criticisms of rhetoric's ancient employment necessarily amounted to *historical* criticism, but rather to *literary* criticism.[13] Polybius did not reject the use of rhetoric per se, only its shoddy use. Though this may be overstated, we still have reason to be wary of Polybius' polemical commentary, especially since Timaeus' work does not survive from antiquity.

The latter contention—namely that Polybius' lack of stylistic concerns in his speeches makes it more likely that his orations capture the gist of what was actually spoken—is not without merit. Unlike Livy, as we shall see, Polybius does not appear obsessed with crafting rhetorically sound orations replete with mellifluous phrases. On the contrary: his *oratio recta* addresses (which often commence in *oratio obliqua* and then transition into direct discourse)[14] frequently seem bland and stylistically similar to the narratives in which they appear. Under such circumstances, it is reasonable to conclude that Polybius had less regard for the literary trappings of his speeches, and more regard for their reflection of reality.

Even so, there are reasons to be skeptical of this assumption. First, although more subtly employed, there remains a discernible influence of ancient rhetoric on Polybius' orations. Far from ineluctably presenting dry, factual arguments, Polybius crafted speeches that owe much to Demosthenes' orations and, to a lesser extent, Thucydides'.[15] Polybius' speeches, like Demosthenes', tend to focus on a single argument (rather than a multiplicity of τόποι) and often lack *prooemia* and perorations.[16] What at first appears a desiccated summary of actually delivered addresses is in fact nothing of the sort. Although Polybius presented his orations in such a manner as to make them appear more historically grounded, we have little reason to conclude that they offer anything more than arguments deemed appropriate for their respective situations.

## POLYBIUS ON ROMAN IMPERIALISM
## AND THE CARTHAGINIANS

It is necessary to discuss Polybius' general attitude toward Roman imperialism, specifically as it applies to Hannibal and the Carthaginians. This should help us determine more about the context in which the speeches appear, which will in turn allow us more easily to come to conclusions regarding the import of the sentiments found therein. Unfortunately, however, it remains difficult to discern Polybius' stance on these topics.[17] Perhaps, like Paul Jal, we must conclude that Polybius never explicitly answers his own questions regarding his attitude toward Roman imperialism, even though this was a key goal of his work.[18]

We can identify Polybius' views on Hannibal and the Carthaginians with greater precision, however.[19] Overall, there is reason to consider Polybius partially sympathetic to the Carthaginian leader in the Second Punic War. In some places in his work, in fact, Polybius appears to possess distinctly positive impressions of Hannibal. He praises Hannibal's courage and shrewdness (2.36.3); considers him brave (3.116.4); blames fortune for Hannibal's failure as a general (instead of Hannibal himself) (9.1–6); exonerates Hannibal from charges of excessive cruelty (9.23.20, 24, 26); and lauds his skills as a general (11.19; 15.15.6–16).

In addition, we can detect Polybius' sympathy for the Carthaginian people. Polybius believes, for instance, that one could argue that Carthage was not responsible for the commencement of the Second Punic War (3.30.4), and recognizes that the Carthaginians, at the Battle of Zama, were fighting for the preservation and control of Africa, whereas the Romans were aiming at a world empire (15.9.2).[20] Polybius also appears capable of criticizing Roman actions. Both in his speeches (3.28.2–4; 5.90) and in his narrative (5.104.1; 9.37) Polybius calls the Romans barbarians. At one point in his work, he also lambasted the Roman Senate (31.25.2–8).

Still, we must admit that at times Polybius also proves highly critical of Hannibal and the Carthaginians. He makes clear, for example, that the Carthaginians desired the establishment of a big empire in Spain (2.13); he claims that from the start of his campaigns in Spain, Hannibal intended to wage a war against Rome (2.36.3); he avers that Hamilcar's unreasonable wrath was a cause of the Second Punic War (3.9.6); he argues that Carthaginian success in Spain was another cause of the war (3.10.6); he expatiates on how unjust Hannibal was to wage a war under his own pretexts (3.15.8–13); he explicitly criticizes Hannibal for his unsound justification of war to the people of Carthage (3.15.9); he labels Hannibal irrational at a crucial point in the war's germination (3.15.10); he calls Hannibal's dressing up in wigs and costumes to avoid assassination attempts Φοινικικῷ στρατήγματι ("Punic artifice"; 3.78.1–5); he asserts in passing that Hannibal is the cause of the war (9.23.1); he labels Hannibal greedy (9.25.1). In addition, as we shall see below, Polybius offers a Hannibalic speech before the Battle of Cannae that comes across as nakedly imperialistic; this address presents the goal of Hannibal's campaign as the control of Italy and the winning of spoils (3.111.2–10).[21] Polybius thus demonstrates a mixed attitude toward Hannibal and, more expansively, toward the Carthaginian people. As we shall see in the next chapter, this amounts to a far more positive assessment than Livy musters. Accordingly, one might expect Polybius' pre-Ticinus and pre-Zama addresses to prove more equivocal than Livy's versions.

## POLYBIUS' PRE-TICINUS SPEECHES (3.63–64)

With all this in mind, we can commence with an examination of Polybius' orations of P. Scipio and Hannibal to their respective troops before the Battle of Ticinus of 218 B.C. (3.63–64).[22] This conflict marked the first confrontation between the Romans and Carthaginians in the Second Punic War, and amounted to a setback for the Roman side.

Polybius introduces this speech pair by noting that both Scipio and Hannibal saw fit to offer an oration to their own troops that was suitable for the occasion (3.62.1). Polybius then presents the lead-up to Hannibal's address. Before speaking, Polybius informs us, Hannibal roused his troops by compelling a single pair of Gallic captives, whom the Carthaginians had taken prisoner over the course of their trek across the Alps, to fight to the death for prizes. When Hannibal sought two Gauls to serve as his volunteers, all the captives desired to be chosen. Polybius also tells us that the assembled Gauls and Carthaginians praised both the victor and the vanquished of this single combat, the latter of whom was sufficiently fortunate to die instead of remaining a captive (3.62.2–11).

Much has been made of this event in Polybius, which also exists in different forms in the work of Livy and Dio.[23] Some might say that the mere addition of this story—whether true or fabricated—makes the Carthaginians (and Hannibal in particular) appear barbaric. Indeed, there is a gruesome quality to this spectacle, though we ought not view it on the basis of modern standards of conduct. Even so, we can point to a reason to suppose that Polybius did not include a description of this single combat to highlight the cruelty of the Carthaginian general. Clearly, Hannibal, through the use of the Gallic combatants, exhorts his soldiers by demonstrating that his army finds itself in the same situation as the prisoners themselves. The story's power can only serve as motivation for the Punic forces, then, if the comparison holds true: Hannibal, that is to say, is implying that the Carthaginians are Rome's captives. Accordingly, much as was the situation for the Gallic prisoners, the Carthaginians have the choice of fighting or remaining enslaved. However overwrought this argument may appear, it still amounts to a moral sentiment. Through this bloody demonstration, Hannibal proves to his troops (and, perhaps, to ancient readers) that theirs is a fight for both glory and freedom.

The preamble to Polybius' Hannibalic pre-Ticinus oration, then, offers a distinctly moral appeal to the reader. And Polybius informs us that this theatrical ploy was effective: Hannibal electrified his troops as desired (3.63.1).

### Spoils or Enslavement (3.63.1–6)

Having thus invigorated his soldiers, Polybius' Hannibal begins his oration, which starts in *oratio obliqua*. The speech commences with a direct reference to the combat that has just taken place before the army:

(1) Ἀννίβας δὲ διὰ τῶν προειρημένων τὴν προκειμένην διάθεσιν ἐνεργασάμενος ταῖς τῶν δυνάμεων ψυχαῖς, (2) μετὰ ταῦτα προελθὼν αὐτὸς τούτου χάριν ἔφη παρεισάγειν τοὺς αἰχμαλώτους, ἵν᾽ ἐπὶ τῶν ἀλλοτρίων συμπτωμάτων ἐναργῶς θεασάμενοι τὸ συμβαῖνον, βέλτιον ὑπὲρ τῶν σφίσι παρόντων βουλεύωνται πραγμάτων. (3) εἰς παραπλήσιον γὰρ αὐτοὺς ἀγῶνα καὶ καιρὸν τὴν τύχην συγκεκλεικέναι καὶ παραπλήσια τοῖς νῦν ἆθλα προτεθεικέναι. (3.63.1–3)[24]

(1) Hannibal, having produced the present disposition in the minds of his forces through this means, (2) came forward after these things and said he set up the prisoners before them so that, having seen manifestly in the fortunes of others what might befall them, they might take better counsel regarding the present matters. (3) He says that Fortune has enclosed them in a similar and opportune contest, and has now put forward similar prizes.

The soldiers, having witnessed what could befall them, should take better stock of the situation they face, he says (3.63.2). Fortune (τὴν τύχην), he claims, has placed the Carthaginian soldiers in the same circumstances as those of the Gallic captives (3.63.3). There are already signs that Hannibal's points have appealed to Polybius' interests: the oration begins with a discussion of τύχη ("fortune"), a subject of great import to Polybius.[25]

Hannibal continues in this vein:

δεῖν γὰρ ἢ νικᾶν ἢ θνήσκειν ἢ τοῖς ἐχθροῖς ὑποχειρίους γενέσθαι ζῶντας. εἶναι δ᾽ ἐκ μὲν τοῦ νικᾶν ἆθλον οὐχ ἵππους καὶ σάγους, ἀλλὰ τὸ πάντων ἀνθρώπων γενέσθαι μακαριωτάτους, κρατήσαντας τῆς Ῥωμαίων εὐδαιμονίας. (3.63.4)

For it is necessary either to conquer, die, or become living subjects of the enemy. For the prize for winning the contest is not horses and cloaks, but to become the most blessed of all people, having power over Roman prosperity.

In this portion of the speech Polybius has introduced an all-or-nothing argument, according to which the troops are compelled to fight. Importantly, his introductory salvo to his soldiers does not assert that Rome has maltreated the Carthaginians, or acted in a manner that requires revenge. Rather, his appeal focuses on the importance of maintaining a martial ethos. Perhaps one might argue that Hannibal's overwrought rhetoric implies the impossibility of dealing with the Romans through diplomatic channels. According to Polybius' Hannibal, after all, the Carthaginians' choice is stark: complete victory or enslavement. Yet this seems tangential to the matter at hand as Hannibal presents it—the winning of Rome's wealth tout court.

Polybius' Hannibal next discusses what he deems the prize of death:

a quick end to an honorable struggle for a most beautiful hope (ὑπὲρ τῆς καλλίστης ἐλπίδος) without enduring suffering (3.63.5). Hannibal does not, however, specify what he considers "the most beautiful hope." According to him, it appears, mere fighting in battle deserves such accolades. This sentiment may serve to rally his troops more effectively, but it hardly convinces us of the justice of Hannibal's cause. Even so, Polybius' Hannibal continues on with a similar theme. Those who flee or are captured, he argues, will meet every calamity (3.63.6). Again, Polybius' focus on the import of martial valor, as well as its inherent glory, seems an apposite theme for a commander who seeks to win victory in battle. And it magnifies the notion that the Punic forces must win or perish.

## Pragmatic Advice for the Soldiery (3.63.7–13)

Having presented this stark assessment of the impending conflict, Polybius' Hannibal then offers more pragmatic arguments:

(7) οὐδένα γὰρ οὕτως ἀλόγιστον οὐδὲ νωθρὸν αὐτῶν ὑπάρχειν ὃς μνημονεύων μὲν τοῦ μήκους τῆς ὁδοῦ τῆς διηνυσμένης ἐκ τῶν πατρίδων, μνημονεύων δὲ τοῦ πλήθους τῶν μεταξὺ πολεμίων, εἰδὼς δὲ τὰ μεγέθη τῶν ποταμῶν ὧν διεπέρασεν ἐλπίσαι ποτ᾽ ἂν ὅτι φεύγων εἰς τὴν οἰκείαν ἀφίξεται. (8) διόπερ ᾤετο δεῖν αὐτούς, ἀποκεκομμένης καθόλου τῆς τοιαύτης ἐλπίδος, τὴν αὐτὴν διάληψιν ποιεῖσθαι περὶ τῶν καθ᾽ αὑτοὺς πραγμάτων ἥνπερ ἀρτίως ἐποιοῦντο περὶ τῶν ἀλλοτρίων συμπτωμάτων. (9) καθάπερ γὰρ ἐπ᾽ ἐκείνων τὸν μὲν νικήσαντα καὶ τεθνεῶτα πάντες ἐμακάριζον, τοὺς δὲ ζῶντας ἠλέουν, οὕτως ᾤετο δεῖν καὶ περὶ τῶν καθ᾽ αὑτοὺς διαλαμβάνειν καὶ πάντας ἰέναι πρὸς τοὺς ἀγῶνας μάλιστα μὲν νικήσοντας, ἂν δὲ μὴ τοῦτ᾽ ᾖ δυνατόν, ἀποθανουμένους. (10) τὴν δὲ τοῦ ζῆν ἡττημένους ἐλπίδα κατὰ μηδένα τρόπον ἠξίου λαμβάνειν ἐν νῷ. (3.63.7–10)

(7) For no one among you is so irrational or slow that, remembering the length of the journey he has accomplished from his fatherland, and recalling the number of enemies in between and knowing the size of the rivers he crossed, he thought that he could arrive home by fleeing. (8) Therefore Hannibal thought, since all such hope had been knocked out of them, that it was necessary to take the same distinction concerning their own situation that they readily made regarding the others' chances. (9) For as everyone considered both the victorious and the dead blessed and pitied the living, thus he thought it necessary to believe this about themselves, and all go to the battles to conquer, and if this was not possible, to die. (10) He considered it to be in no way worthy to contemplate the hope of living defeated.

None of us, Hannibal claims, is sufficiently foolish to believe that we can flee home (3.63.7). Although this point should seem excruciatingly obvious to the men who ventured across the Alps, it grants a sense of urgency to Hannibal's kill-or-be-killed argument. Accordingly, Polybius' Hannibal next exhorts his army to forget any hopes of safety, and instead view the situation much as the Gallic combatants addressed their own circumstances (3.63.8–9). In a similar vein, he implores his soldiers not to ponder life after defeat (3.63.10).

If you follow my advice, Polybius' Hannibal continues, you will prevail, because no one who has chosen not to flee has ever failed to put his enemies to flight (3.63.11–12). Obviously, this historical claim is absurd. One wonders whether it would even rally troops to battle, let alone convince readers of its truth. Even so, Hannibal continues with this theme in the conclusion of his oration. The Romans, he says, have the opposite hope, since they are confident in the safety of flight. As a result, Carthaginian courage would win the day (3.63.13). Polybius then informs us that the Gallic combat and Hannibal's oration were well received by the troops, who became more enthusiastic about the prospects of battle and more confident in victory (3.63.14).

Overall, Polybius' Hannibalic address before the Battle of Ticinus possesses a rather monochromatic feel: it focuses almost exclusively on the matter of courage. In addition, Hannibal never explains why the Romans were banking on flight. To be sure, given the proximity of their homes, the Romans would be more capable of fleeing. Yet this does not guarantee that the Romans would retreat, as Hannibal concludes in his oration. The Carthaginian general's discussion of purported Roman pusillanimity, moreover, might be unlikely to disconcert Polybius' Roman (or Greek) readers. After all, everyone knew who was the ultimate victor in the Second Punic War.

The speech's most compelling element, perhaps, remains Hannibal's focus on the stark choice between slavery and the ultimate subjugation of Rome. According to this view, one cannot deal with Rome through negotiation and compromise. Even so, Polybius' Hannibal merely assumes that this is true, without offering any specific complaints about Roman conduct or the reasons the Romans were incapable of such actions. In short, Polybius never fleshes out an argument, never augments Hannibal's contentions with examples of Roman misconduct. In addition, Polybius appears to treat Hannibal as deeply deceptive: only the most careless or selective reader would not know of Hannibal's passion to destroy Rome (cf. 3.10.7–11). Yet Polybius concocts a comparatively passionless and quasi-logical rationale for the war—however shoddy or misleading its foundation. All this leads us to conclude that Polybius does not appear particularly interested in allowing Hannibal to speak convincingly.

We need not be too strong in our conclusions, however. Polybius—like Demosthenes—tended to concentrate on one argument in his orations, rather than present the reader with a series of τόποι.[26] Thus Polybius' focus on the do-or-die nature of the conflict—rather than the reasons for fighting in the first place—may not be the result of an attempt to downplay the Carthaginians' justifications for war. It could, on the contrary, stem from Polybius' historiographical method—the sorts of points he aimed to offer in speeches. Still, for an oratorical stylist known for eschewing rhetorical commonplaces,[27] Polybius has presented a fair number of bromides in this short speech.[28] Perhaps this suggests that he did not aim to convince his readership of the Carthaginian cause's justice.

## Scipio's Retort (3.64.2–8, 10)

With this in mind, we can now examine Polybius' counterpoised speech of P. Scipio prior to the battle. Around the same day, Polybius tells us, Scipio advanced with his troops to the Ticinus River, ordered a bridge built, and summoned his army for an oration (3.64.1). Before presenting the details of Scipio's address, Polybius informs us that most of what Scipio discussed with the soldiers pertained to Rome's great status and the achievements of its ancestors. Polybius mentions that he will offer the arguments Scipio presented that related to the situation at hand (3.64.2). Interestingly, Polybius here acknowledges that he has cut out portions of the speech as it was supposedly delivered. He has decided, moreover, to skip the more generic arguments about Rome's might and glorious past. Perhaps this was done to spare the readers from the oration's duller moments. Yet it could also serve as a means by which Polybius tells his readership that Scipio included such patriotic sentiments, without subjecting it to potentially arrogant remarks about Rome's former glories.[29] This could signal, that is to say, Polybius' desire to shield the Roman general from charges of pomposity.

Scipio's oration commences (in *oratio obliqua*) with the claim that the Romans should have unqualified hope in victory, even though they have not recently fought the Carthaginian army (3.64.3).[30] In fact, Polybius' Scipio continues, the Roman soldiers should perceive that Carthage's attempt to face Rome in war is outrageous, since it has previously lost battles, paid tribute, and served almost as a slave to Rome for many years (3.64.4). As we can see, unlike Polybius' Hannibalic address, Scipio's oration centers on the First Punic War, bolstering Roman pride by recalling erstwhile Roman success against the Republic's current adversaries. According to Ragnar Ullmann, such an argument seems more typical of Polybius' speeches than do the points Hannibal presents in his pre-Ticinus oration—points essentially unmoored from any chronological context.[31] Interestingly, though, Polybius has not chosen to eschew the lauding of the Roman past in the speech, as he previously maintained (cf. 3.64.2). Additionally, Scipio's point, though certainly serving to underline Roman military superiority, appears unabashedly imperialistic. He boasts about the near-slavery status of the Carthaginian adversary—potentially a far more condemning charge concerning Roman foreign policy than anything Hannibal musters in his pre-Ticinus oration. Some ancient readers, of course, may have delighted in the notion of Punic subservience. But Roman historians' pretensions to engaging in justifiable warfare—combined with the ruminations on the injustice of Roman colonial conduct found in the works of, say, Sallust and Tacitus—suggest that such a bold claim could have caused others to bristle.

Polybius next has Scipio switch into *oratio recta*. Our adversaries, Scipio claims, cannot even look us in the eyes:

> ὅταν δέ, χωρὶς τῶν προειρημένων, καὶ τῶν νῦν παρόντων ἀνδρῶν ἔχωμεν ἐπὶ ποσὸν πεῖραν ὅτι μόνον οὐ τολμῶσι κατὰ πρόσωπον ἰδεῖν ἡμᾶς, τίνα χρὴ διάληψιν ποιεῖσθαι περὶ τοῦ μέλλοντος τοὺς ὀρθῶς λογιζομένους; (3.64.5)

And when, apart from what has been said beforehand, we can determine essentially by our own experiences that the men who are present now do not dare to look us in the face, what distinction should we make about the future, if we compute it correctly?

Here again Scipio discusses the matter of courage, rather than focusing on the justice or injustice of Roman actions. Switching back to *oratio obliqua*, Scipio continues with this line of argument. The Carthaginians, he says, did not even fare well in a cavalry battle against the Romans near the Rhone River (3.64.6). Polybius' Scipio avers that this loss forced Hannibal to flee across the Alps out of sheer terror (3.64.7). Naturally, it is difficult to fathom that Polybius himself—or many of his ancient readers, for that matter—believed a word of this argument. In fact, it seems just as ridiculous as Hannibal's prior claim that no army disregarding the option of flight has ever failed to rout his enemy (3.63.12). In the context of Scipio's address, it appears as if Polybius was interested in making the Roman general's reasoning seem weak. Although the Romans had obviously outmatched the Carthaginians in many previous conflicts, we have little reason to suspect that ancient readers would be unaware of Hannibal's initial successes in the Second Punic War. Scipio's sentiments, then, read like ignorant bluster. One might suppose that Scipio's discussion of Carthaginian fear—however distorted and overwrought—amounts to a direct refutation of Hannibal's praise for Punic derring-do. This could have inspired Scipio's troops, but is unlikely to have made much of an impression on Polybius' ancient readers, especially since Scipio's dismissal of Punic valor proved so wrongheaded.

Scipio next presents more details regarding the supposed catastrophe of Hannibal's crossing of the Alps:

(8) παρεῖναι δὲ καὶ νῦν ἔφη τὸν Ἀννίβαν, κατεφθαρκότα μὲν τὸ πλεῖστον μέρος τῆς δυνάμεως, τὸ δὲ περιλειπόμενον ἀδύνατον καὶ δύσχρηστον ἔχοντα διὰ τὴν κακουχίαν, ὁμοίως δὲ καὶ τῶν ἵππων τοὺς μὲν πλείστους ἀπολωλεκότα, τοὺς δὲ λοιποὺς ἠχρειωκότα διὰ τὸ μῆκος καὶ τὴν δυσχέρειαν τῆς ὁδοῦ. (9) δι᾽ ὧν ἐπιδεικνύειν ἐπειρᾶτο διότι μόνον ἐπιφανῆναι δεῖ τοῖς πολεμίοις. (3.64.8–9)

(8) He [Scipio] said that Hannibal was now present, having lost the greatest part of his forces, the remnants of which were weak and nearly useless because of hardship; he had similarly lost most of his horses, and the remaining ones he had rendered useless on account of the length and difficulty of the journey. (9) Through these remarks he tried to show that it was merely necessary to be seen by the enemy.

The Carthaginian army present at the Ticinus River is greatly depleted due to its difficult trek (3.64.8). Having presented this contention, Polybius then breaks away from the speech for a moment, informing us that Scipio employed such arguments to convince his troops to engage with the enemy (3.64.9). Though one could make too much of this point, this sentiment, which interrupts the oration's flow, calls into question the validity of Scipio's entire harangue, which attempts to lull its listeners into a false sense of military confidence. By harping on purported Punic pusillanimity, Polybius' Scipio actually casts his own soldiers as hesitant. They, after all, seemingly require Scipio's expatiation on Carthaginian cowardice to tamp down their fear.

Polybius then returns to the speech itself. Scipio, Polybius tells us, encouraged his men to rest assured in his presence: he would not have abandoned his Spanish campaign if he did not think that fighting Hannibal in Italy amounted to requisite public service for his country (3.64.10). At this point in the oration, Polybius finally has Scipio present a line of reasoning that does not hinge on an exhortation to courage. Rather, Scipio here makes clear that he fights on behalf of the state, not for any personal gain or hope for treasure. This seems different from Hannibal's address, which never offers an appeal to his soldiers that focuses on the overall plight of Carthage and the state's current needs. Perhaps this serves to make Scipio appear comparatively selfless, though we ought not stress this point too much, given Polybius' brief mention of it and its placement in a comparatively weak portion of the oration.[32]

At the speech's conclusion, Polybius tells us that Scipio's authority as a speaker and the truth of his words (τὴν τῶν λεγομένων ἀλήθειαν) incited his troops to battle (3.64.11). It would be odd for Polybius to use the word ἀλήθεια ("truth") if in fact he deemed Scipio's arguments wrongheaded. Yet it seems hard to believe that Polybius considered the Punic crossing of the Alps to be motivated by fear. Some might view Polybius' Hannibalic address as more convincing than its Scipionic counterpart precisely because the former focuses on his own troop's strengths, whereas the latter discusses the enemy's supposed weaknesses.[33] But this need not be so. Before launching into Scipio's speech, Polybius informs the reader that Scipio had expounded on Rome's former glories. Accordingly, the address contained some pro-Roman sentiments, however cursorily mentioned. The notion that Scipio's speech is inferior because of its concern for Punic futility should also strike us as an ex post facto rationalization. Scipio's side, after all, loses the Battle of Ticinus, and it seems easy to conclude that the orations foreshadow this outcome. In reality, it appears possible, given the orations themselves, to believe that Scipio's speech remains more powerful, more convincing.

In reality, then, neither address comes across as either particularly strong or particularly feeble. Polybius appears to have favored neither general in his pair of opening addresses, and, curiously enough, has not fashioned orations that highlight the import of Scipio's and Hannibal's first encounter. Both speeches seem chiefly concerned with pragmatic matters and exhortations to courage. Perhaps Polybius chose this line of argument in order to make the counterpoised harangues appear more appropriate to the situation at hand. Regardless, we must confess that Polybius' speeches before the Battle of Ticinus turn neither general into a hero or a villain.

## THE VICISSITUDES OF FORTUNE
## IN THE PRE-ZAMA ORATIONS

Having examined Polybius' pre-Ticinus speeches in detail, we can now move on to his orations from the conference between Hannibal and Scipio Africanus, which took place shortly before the Battle of Zama (202 B.C.). In addition to Polybius' and Livy's versions of this event, both Appian (*Lib.* 39) and Cornelius Nepos (*Hann.* 6.2) present iterations of this meeting. Before offering his version of the pre-Zama meeting, Polybius informs us that Hannibal and Scipio—the former attempting to avoid the upcoming battle—met alone, with the exception of one interpreter apiece.

*Hannibal's Address (15.6.4–7.9)*

Hannibal, the general proposing the end of hostilities, naturally spoke first. He begins:

(4) δεξιωσάμενος δὲ πρῶτος Ἀννίβας ἤρξατο λέγειν ὡς ἐβούλετο μὲν ἂν μήτε Ῥωμαίους ἐπιθυμῆσαι μηδέποτε μηδενὸς τῶν ἐκτὸς Ἰταλίας μήτε Καρχηδονίους τῶν ἐκτὸς [τῆς] Λιβύης· (5) ἀμφοτέροις γὰρ εἶναι ταύτας καὶ καλλίστας δυναστείας καὶ συλλήβδην ὡς ἂν εἰ περιωρισμένας ὑπὸ τῆς φύσεως. (6) "ἐπεὶ δὲ πρῶτον μὲν ὑπὲρ τῶν κατὰ Σικελίαν ἀμφισβητήσαντες ἐξεπολεμώσαμεν ἀλλήλους, μετὰ δὲ ταῦτα πάλιν ὑπὲρ τῶν κατ' Ἰβηρίαν, τὸ δὲ τέλος ὑπὸ τῆς τύχης οὔπω νουθετούμενοι μέχρι τούτου προβεβήκαμεν ὥστε καὶ περὶ τοῦ τῆς πατρίδος ἐδάφους τοὺς μὲν κεκινδυνευκέναι, τοὺς δ' ἀκμὴν ἔτι καὶ νῦν κινδυνεύειν, (7) λοιπόν ἐστιν, εἴ πως δυνάμεθα δι' αὐτῶν παραιτησάμενοι τοὺς θεοὺς διαλύσασθαι τὴν ἐνεστῶσαν φιλοτιμίαν. (8) ἐγὼ μὲν οὖν ἕτοιμός εἰμι τῷ πεῖραν εἰληφέναι δι' αὐτῶν τῶν πραγμάτων ὡς <εὐ>μετάθετός ἐστιν ἡ τύχη καὶ παρὰ μικρὸν εἰς ἑκάτερα ποιεῖ μεγάλας ῥοπάς, καθάπερ εἰ νηπίοις παισὶ χρωμένη." (15.6.4–8)[34]

(4) Hannibal, having greeted Scipio, first began to speak, saying that he wished that neither the Romans had ever desired anything outside of Italy nor the Carthaginians outside of Libya; (5) for these were perfect empires for both, and empires that are held together as if nature had marked their boundaries. (6) "But since first we have gone to war over Sicily and afterwards over Spain, finally, ignoring the lessons of Fortune, we have gone so far that your fatherland was formerly in danger and ours is still even now, (7) what we are left with is the matter of through what means we are able to prevail upon the gods to put an end to our present rivalry. (8) And so I am ready, having learned through actual experiences how capricious Fortune is, and how by the slightest move either way she tips the scales the most, as if she were playing with silly children."

Polybius relates Hannibal's opening salvo in indirect discourse: would that Rome had been content with ruling Italy and Carthage with Africa (15.6.4). According to Polybius' Hannibal, Italy and Africa were natural boundaries for these respective empires (15.6.5). The speech thus commences with a criticism of imperialism. It also serves to equate the interests of both these empires. Rome and Carthage, Polybius' Hannibal believes, are guilty of the same brand of imperial ambition. In an attempt to win over Scipio (and, perhaps, Polybius' readership) to his side, Hannibal portrays both Carthage and

Rome as engaged in pernicious expansionism. Perhaps this demonstrates that Polybius' Hannibal deemed all powerful states guilty of overweening ambition. Yet his argument singles out Rome and Carthage alone, eschewing Thucydidean speculation about the nature of empires.

As Hannibal switches from the vicissitudes of the current situation to a more philosophical argument, Polybius switches from *oratio obliqua* to *oratio recta*. Having gone to war over Sicily and Spain, and refusing to heed the warnings of fortune (τῆς τύχης), he says, Carthaginians and Romans have progressed in their designs to such an extent that their fatherlands have been in danger (15.6.6). This leads to a discussion of fortune's fickleness, which Polybius' Hannibal claims to have learned through experience (15.6.8). Hannibal, the commander in the weaker position, attempts to persuade Scipio to enter into a peace agreement through an elaboration on his own experiences, because they serve as a potential warning for the young Roman. Since the Carthaginian general here addresses the whims of fortune—a topic that figured into Polybius' own historiographical method[35]—we may assume that Polybius finds this an interesting topic, even though it remains difficult to assess the degree to which the author agrees with the sentiments his Hannibal here relays.

Polybius' Hannibal continues with this line of reasoning. He fears that Scipio, given his youth and inexperience with calamity, may not be convinced of his argument (15.7.1).[36] As a result, he inveighs the Roman commander to ponder Hannibal's own career as an example (15.7.2–5). Polybius' Hannibal contrasts his erstwhile success in the Second Punic War with the lowliness of his current position (15.7.3–4). As a result, Hannibal cautions humility (15.7.5), noting that failure in the upcoming battle will destroy Scipio's current glory, though victory will add little to his country's fame (15.7.6). Although one may suppose that Hannibal's general argument amounts to a comparatively sound rationale for a general in a weak position to proffer, this last sentiment seems absurd. Surely Scipio recognized—as did Hannibal—that he would gain great renown for defeating Rome's most gifted and feared adversary.

This general argument about fortune's uncertainty complete, Polybius' Hannibal next switches to the purpose of the colloquy itself (15.7.7). He proposes that Sicily, Sardinia, and Spain, among other territories, become part of Rome's undisputed domain (15.7.8). Hannibal sums up his offer succinctly. These terms, he says, would allow Carthage to feel secure and would be most honorable to Scipio and the Romans (15.7.9). This appeal to Scipio seems typical of Polybian speechifying: it is short and to the point. The peace terms

Hannibal suggests, however, are less than just, as Polybius' readers may note. Carthage had already essentially offered the terms Hannibal proposes,[37] and Polybius' Hannibal here fails to mention the payment of any indemnity to Rome. The oration's conclusion, in fact, makes it appear as if Hannibal attempted to dupe his younger counterpart, who presumably may not have realized that the more experienced general was proposing an ungenerous peace agreement. All the same, however, the oration commences with a mildly anti-imperialistic sentiment—one aimed at both perceived Punic and Roman imperial overstretch. This may have been a contention with which Polybius had some sympathy.

## Scipio Africanus Responds (15.8)

Now to Polybius' Scipionic retort. It begins forcefully (in *oratio obliqua*) and immediately touches on Hannibal's arguments:

(1) Ἀννίβας μὲν οὖν ταῦτ' εἶπεν. ὁ δὲ Πόπλιος ὑπολαβὼν οὔτε τοῦ περὶ Σικελίας ἔφη πολέμου Ῥωμαίους οὔτε τοῦ περὶ τῆς Ἰβηρίας αἰτίους γεγονέναι, Καρχηδονίους δὲ προφανῶς· (2) ὑπὲρ ὧν κάλλιστα γινώσκειν αὐτὸν τὸν Ἀννίβαν. μάρτυρας δὲ καὶ τοὺς θεοὺς γεγονέναι τούτων, περιθέντας τὸ κράτος οὐ τοῖς ἄρχουσι χειρῶν ἀδίκων, ἀλλὰ τοῖς ἀμυνομένοις. (15.8.1–2)

(1) And so Hannibal said these things. Scipio, retorting, said that the Romans were responsible neither for the war around Sicily nor for that around Spain, but clearly the Carthaginians were; (2) Hannibal knew this especially well. He said that the gods were witnesses of these matters, conferring the victory not upon those beginning the war unjustly, but upon those warding off attackers.

Polybius' Scipio claims that the war over Sicily was Carthage's fault (15.8.1). According to him, the gods recognized this, which is why the Romans had proved victorious in the First Punic War (15.8.2). In a clear juxtaposition, Scipio here puts his faith in the gods, as opposed to Hannibal's faith in fortune (or, perhaps more accurately, in the inevitability of misfortune).[38]

And although it amounts to a powerful retort, Scipio obviously simplifies matters in his barebones account of the First Punic War.[39] Hannibal would certainly not agree with this assessment, which Scipio offers perhaps as a means for him to demonstrate that he will not be cowed by the older man's gravitas. The statement could come across to readers as an example of intellectual hectoring: Scipio replies with a polemical opening statement because he is the man in the stronger position. Alternatively, however, readers could view this opening salvo as laudable, especially given Hannibal's blatantly in-equitable peace terms. Rome's champion, it asserts, will not be fooled.

Polybius' Scipio next moves on to discuss the issue of fortune. No one, he claims, knows about fortune's fickleness more than he, and he takes stock of this as much as possible (15.8.3). Although this amounts to a direct retort to Hannibal's ruminations on fortune, Scipio does not expand on this theme. In-stead, Scipio immediately turns (in *oratio recta*) to the conditions of the peace themselves. He stresses that Hannibal would have had reason to be satisfied with these terms had he proposed them before departing Italy: [40]

> ἀλλ᾽ εἰ μὲν πρὸ τοῦ τοὺς Ῥωμαίους διαβαίνειν εἰς Λιβύην αὐτὸς ἐξ Ἰταλίας ἐκχωρήσας προύτεινας τὰς διαλύσεις ταύτας, οὐκ ἂν οἴομαί σε διαψευσθῆναι τῆς ἐλπίδος. (15.8.4)

> "But," he [Scipio] said, "if you, having departed from Italy and crossed into Libya, proposed this cessation of hostilities, I do not think that you would have been mistaken in your hope."

This amounts to a compelling retort. Polybius' Scipio highlights Hannibal's weak position and the bad faith with which he presents his supposedly just terms.

At this point, Scipio touches on the current situation regarding Rome and Carthage, a topic he introduces with a rhetorical question (15.8.6). Rome had already made a treaty with the losing Carthaginians that offered what Han-nibal proposed in addition to the handing over of prisoners, the surrender of warships, the payment of 5,000 talents, and the offer of hostages (15.8.7).[41] Although these were the agreed terms, Scipio says, the Carthaginians have treacherously violated this peace (15.8.8–9). Now Polybius' Scipio returns to presenting rhetorical questions. Loath to reward Hannibal's treachery, the Roman commander asserts that nothing can be gained from this colloquy (15.8.14). It is time to fight.

Other than the quick dismissal of fortune's import and Scipio's simplis-tic blaming of the Carthaginians wholesale for the outbreaks of the First and Second Punic Wars, the reply seems forceful—and uncharacteristically florid for Polybius, with its numerous rhetorical questions. The oration has both moral and practical dimensions. It also responds directly to Hannibal's ap-peal, which is partially moral in content as well. And while Polybius may have harbored some sympathy for Hannibal's arguments, he has certainly allowed Scipio a withering retort.

## PAULLUS AND HANNIBAL PRE-CANNAE

Before offering some conclusions about the speeches before the battles of Ticinus and Zama, we must quickly examine a few other relevant orations in Polybius' work. Chief among these must be the counterpoised exhortations of L. Aemilius Paullus (3.108–109) and Hannibal (3.111), which were delivered to their respective forces before the Battle of Cannae (216 B.C.).

Although the Romans had obviously not fared well against Hannibal up until this time, Paullus' address seems so downcast and full of equivocations that it must cause one immediately to doubt its historicity.[42] It is as if the Roman general, doomed to failure and an early demise, recognizes the impending disaster and musters a handful of uninspired rationales in order (rather feebly) to contest the ineluctability of a Roman defeat. Hannibal, Polybius' Paullus argues, has gotten the better of Roman forces under advantageous circumstances; now that these circumstances have altered, however, one ought to expect a Roman victory (3.108.4–109.3).

Among numerous contentions of this sort, Polybius' Paullus proffers a more interesting point for our purposes:

(6) τοῖς μέν γε μισθοῦ παρά τισι στρατευομένοις ἢ τοῖς κατὰ συμμαχίαν ὑπὲρ τῶν πέλας μέλλουσι κινδυνεύειν, οἷς κατ' αὐτὸν τὸν ἀγῶνα καιρός ἐστι δεινότατος, τὰ δ' ἐκ τῶν ἀποβαινόντων βραχεῖαν ἔχει διαφοράν, ἀναγκαῖος ὁ τῆς παρακλήσεως γίνεται τρόπος· (7) οἷς δέ, καθάπερ ὑμῖν νῦν, οὐχ ὑπὲρ ἑτέρων, ἀλλ' ὑπὲρ σφῶν αὐτῶν καὶ πατρίδος καὶ γυναικῶν καὶ τέκνων ὁ κίνδυνος συνέστηκεν, καὶ πολλαπλασίαν τὰ μετὰ ταῦτα συμβαίνοντα τὴν διαφορὰν ἔχει τῶν ἐνεστώτων ἀεὶ κινδύνων, ὑπομνήσεως μόνον, παρακλήσεως δ' οὐ προσδεῖ. (8) τίς γὰρ οὐκ ἂν βούλοιτο μάλιστα μὲν νικᾶν ἀγωνιζόμενος, εἰ δὲ μὴ τοῦτ' εἴη δυνατόν, τεθνάναι πρόσθεν μαχόμενος ἢ ζῶν ἐπιδεῖν τὴν τῶν προειρημένων ὕβριν καὶ καταφθοράν; (3.109.6–8)

(6) Indeed, for mercenary soldiers or those intending to face danger on behalf of their neighbors due to an alliance, the most dreadful time occurs during the battle itself, and the results have little impact on them, and in such a circumstance there is need of a speech. (7) But for those like you right now, who are not about to risk your lives for others, but for yourselves, your fatherland, your wives, and your children, and for whom the outcome is many times more important than the present dangers, there is need of a reminder alone, not an exhortation. (8) For who, fighting under these circumstances, would not wish to be victorious, and if this is not possible, to die fighting, rather than to live and look upon the outrage and destruction of what I just said we have at stake?

This sentiment manages to address, inter alia, the great significance of the battle ahead. It also portrays the Romans, unlike, presumably, their Punic foes, fighting for their state's continued existence. Though this turned out to be an overwrought prognostication—for the Romans, of course, ultimately regrouped after the disaster at Cannae—it amounts to an argument similar to those offered by Rome's enemies in different circumstances.[43] In this case, Rome was battling for its livelihood; Carthage aimed to conquer and to reap the material benefits of victory. Paullus' speech thus conjures up a portrait of an imperiled Rome that is typically more fitting for Rome's enemies than for the Romans themselves. Though its rhetoric may appear overblown in places, the address may have induced a sense of sympathy for Rome in some ancient readers.

Hannibal's retort, as recorded by Polybius, only serves to underscore Rome's precarious position pre-Cannae. It may also portray the Carthaginian general, as well as the Carthaginians themselves, in unflatteringly imperialistic terms. Among Hannibal's claims in his speech (3.111.8–10), which, Polybius tells us, won the general assent of his troops (3.111.11), is the following:

(8) διὰ μὲν οὖν τῶν πρὸ τοῦ κινδύνων κεκρατήκατε τῆς χώρας καὶ τῶν ἐκ ταύτης ἀγαθῶν κατὰ τὰς ἡμετέρας ἐπαγγελίας, ἀψευστούντων ἡμῶν ἐν πᾶσι τοῖς πρὸς ὑμᾶς εἰρημένοις· ὁ δὲ νῦν ἀγὼν ἐνέστηκεν περὶ τῶν πόλεων καὶ τῶν ἐν αὐταῖς ἀγαθῶν. (9) οὗ κρατήσαντες κύριοι μὲν ἔσεσθε παραχρῆμα πάσης Ἰταλίας, ἀπαλλαγέντες δὲ τῶν νῦν πόνων, γενόμενοι συμπάσης ἐγκρατεῖς τῆς Ῥωμαίων εὐδαιμονίας, ἡγεμόνες ἅμα καὶ δεσπόται πάντων γενήσεσθε διὰ ταύτης τῆς μάχης. (10) διόπερ οὐκέτι λόγων, ἀλλ' ἔργων ἐστὶν ἡ χρεία· θεῶν γὰρ βουλομένων ὅσον οὔπω βεβαιώσειν ὑμῖν πέπεισμαι τὰς ἐπαγγελίας. (3.111.8–10)

(8) And so through your earlier enterprises you have gotten possession of the land and its wealth, as I promised, speaking nothing but the truth to you. The battle ahead will be for the cities and their wealth. (9) Having proved victorious, straightaway you will be the masters of all Italy, freed from the present hardships, in possession of all Rome's wealth, and you will be sovereigns and masters of all on account of this battle. (10) Wherefore there is want of deeds, not words; for, with the gods willing, I am convinced that I shall quickly make good my promises to you.

Polybius' Hannibal makes clear that he and his troops hope to plunder Roman Italy, acting as the lords and masters of their new territory. This is a far cry from his previous insistences, in sentiments that ought to be chalked up to Polybius' creation,[44] that the Carthaginians aimed to liberate the Italians from Roman rule (cf. Plb. 3.77). Clearly this should signal Polybius' distrust in Hannibal's rhetoric, which thereby renders the Carthaginian general's plea at Zama less compelling.

But would ancient readers—unable to augment their understanding of Polybius' work with the aid of modern scholarship, and possessing far more cumbersome copies of his text—recall Hannibal's duplicity in book 3 when they happened upon the pre-Zama colloquy in book 15? It does not seem too bold to suggest that some may have forgotten. (Others, of course, may have only read portions of Polybius' history, and thus would not have happened upon all of Hannibal's pre-battle addresses in any case.) Further, Polybius, in his discussion of the Second Punic War's conclusion, may have hinted at the notion that Hannibal, having learned about the vicissitudes of fortune, was now earnestly repenting for his prior sins. There are, to be sure, reasons to doubt this conclusion—Hannibal's prior duplicity, for example, as well as his inveterate hatred of Rome (3.10.7-11). Yet the change in tone from Polybius' Hannibalic speeches before Cannae and Zama still presents a dramatic portrait of fortune's reverses. Since the Romans were themselves in dire straits during the early years of the Second Punic War, Hannibal's pre-Zama discussion of impending Punic catastrophe could compel readers to ponder conquest's necessary hardships.

## CONCLUSIONS

We are left, then, with some general conclusions about Polybius' Hannibalic addresses and their Roman corollaries. Overall, it appears as if Polybius favored monochromatic orations that often seem notably bereft of moral and ethical content. This could stem from the historian's approach to speechifying. The harangues before the Battle of Ticinus, for example, focus much attention on pragmatic matters and exhortations to courage. Interestingly, Polybius' addresses have a tendency to view the Second Punic War—and, perhaps, military conflict in general—as a struggle leading either to utter collapse or to complete victory. There is little sense of compromise, little notion of the possibility of peaceful acquiescence. Perhaps this relates to Polybius' Thucydidean take on the nature of states, or maybe to his knowledge of Carthage's ultimate fate in the Third Punic War.

It is possible that Polybius chose to give the most forceful oration to the general who would prove victorious in the upcoming conflict. To add some (admittedly slight) evidence for this conclusion, we can note that Polybius allowed the winning leader of the battles of Ticinus, Cannae, and Zama to speak last.[45] Of these addresses, Scipio Africanus' prior to the Battle of Zama may come across as the most powerful. Yet even it—though amounting to a strong answer to Hannibal's contentions that could have earned the esteem of Roman readers—contains its share of simplifications and distortions.

Perhaps the Polybian pre-battle addresses that we have examined are most notable for what they lack. Hannibal's speeches neither highlight Roman greed and desire for plunder nor harp on the baneful aspects of Roman foreign policy. In fact, in his pre-Ticinus harangue, Polybius' Hannibal seems to make Rome's conduct indistinguishable from that of any other strong state. Accordingly, the Carthaginian general hopes that his troops will either strip Rome of all its possessions or meet their death (3.63.5–6). A Punic victory, in the eyes of Polybius' Hannibal, would merely replace a pugnacious and prosperous Rome with a similarly bellicose and thriving Carthage. This is in marked contrast to the addresses of Sallust and Pompeius Trogus/Justin we have discussed in previous chapters. As we have seen, both Sallust and Trogus focused the brunt of their attention on Roman martial aggression and failure to live up to the dictates of justifiable warfare. Polybius, however, does not appear to have been interested in using his pre-battle addresses to ruminate on such themes.

We cannot be certain why Polybius chose to focus his enemy orations as he did. It remains possible, however, that verisimilitude was of cardinal import to him. After all, as we noticed in chapter 2, Pompeius Trogus, in order to concentrate his Mithridates speech on Rome's foreign policy malefactions, had the king of Pontus deliver unrealistically bookish arguments based on remote episodes in Roman history. In all likelihood, Trogus chose to do this as an homage to Sallust, whose *Letter of Mithridates* seems a more agreeable repository for criticisms of Roman foreign affairs. Polybius' pre-Ticinus orations, however, to a great extent are tied up in exhortations to courage. Although such remarks rob readers of the sorts of arguments likely to lead to introspection about Roman expansionism, they fit their contexts quite well. After all, in an address to soldiers before combat, calls to take courage make more sense than intricate arguments about Roman pugnacity.

Polybius' lack of specifics about Roman foreign policy in his speeches also allows them to come across as more philosophical than other orations in the Roman historiographical tradition. One notes more airy contemplation of both the glories of conquest and the calamities of defeat. To some extent, this serves to make Polybius' pre-battle addresses seem comparatively interchangeable. None of Polybius' generals offers strong evidence to counter the contention that it is in the nature of powerful states to expand. To be sure, in Polybius' version of the pre-Zama meeting, Scipio Africanus assumes that Rome's erstwhile successes against the Carthaginians resulted from the justness of its foreign policy (15.8.1-2). But Polybius' Scipio does not expatiate on this topic, preferring to harp on Hannibal's personal perfidy. Similarly, Polybius' Hannibal implies that greed motivates Rome's inexorable expansion (cf. 3.63.4-5), yet, unlike Sallust's and Trogus' Mithridates, he does not construct his addresses around this theme.

This relates to Polybius' general depiction of Hannibal. In the orations we have surveyed, Polybius adds little that highlights the Carthaginian general as the "Other." With the potential exception of the inequitable peace terms he proposes, for instance, Hannibal in his pre-Zama address does not seem markedly "Punic" in his argumentation. In fact, he proffers points that would seem reasonable from a Roman speaker, if directed against the Carthaginians. One gets the impression that Polybius did not show much interest in using his Hannibalic speeches to present an unflattering portrait of a Punic leader or to engage in ethnic stereotypes. Again, this contrasts with the approaches of Sallust and Trogus, both of whom paint Mithridates as an Eastern tyrant par excellence.

Polybius' disinclination to distinguish Roman from non-Roman addresses may be intensified by Aemilius Paullus' speech, which, as we noted above, conjures up the image of an endangered Rome on the brink of extinction—an image usually more appropriate for Rome's adversaries than for Rome itself. From our preceding examination, one gets the sense that Polybius did not believe generals from disparate backgrounds presented different sorts of orations, but rather harbored similar thoughts about the requirements of pre-battle exhortations. In the Hannibalic addresses we have surveyed, these requirements did not include ruminations on Roman administrative corruption. Further, Polybius' speeches of Hannibal offer no explicit focus on Roman greed, far fewer "just war" themes than can be found in other ancient authors' orations, and little in the way of ethnic stereotypes.

Overall, it seems very difficult to determine the comparative strength of the Roman and Carthaginian speeches in Polybius' discussion of the Second Punic War. On its own, this may be instructive. The fact that we cannot discount the possibility of sympathy for Carthage's plight (however limited) in his work suggests that Polybius was capable of producing a semi-sympathetic portrayal of Rome's quintessential enemy.

As we shall see in our next chapter, Polybius was not alone in his ability to muster some sympathy for Rome's Punic foe.

## LIVY, THE ROMAN ANNALISTIC TRADITION, AND POLYBIUS

Livy, like his fellow Roman annalists, supposedly maintains a consistently pro-Roman outlook in his history, at least in the portions that survive from antiquity.[1] After all, the annalists, beginning ca. 200 B.C. with the work of Q. Fabius Pictor, aimed to champion Rome's arrival on the Mediterranean scene and shine a spotlight on its grand history, hoping to prove that Rome well deserved its lofty position in the ancient world.[2] It was supposedly embarrassing to the Romans, so powerful after their victory in the Second Punic War, that they did not possess any written histories cataloging their state's dramatic rise. The annalists, we are told, hoped to supply the world—at first, particularly the Greek intellectual world—with a compelling narrative of these events. Hence the annalists, who understandably knew little about Rome's remote history, purportedly created and elaborated on versions of the Roman past that would emphasize the Romans' grandeur and courage.

Although there has been some recent speculation about Livy's purported hyper-patriotism,[3] there are good reasons to suggest that this portrait of the Roman annalistic tradition is largely correct. Even so, as we shall see in this chapter, Livy seems capable of using his speeches to glorify Hannibal, Rome's dire enemy, who actually appears to have been an unexpected recipient of Livy's sympathy. In fact, Livy's orations of P. Scipio and Hannibal before the Battle of Ticinus (21.40–44) and those of Hannibal and the man who would come to be known as Scipio Africanus before the Battle of Zama (30.30.3–31.1–9) offer surprisingly sympathetic portraits of Rome's quintessential antagonist and, through him, of the Carthaginian people. Although Livy, much like Polybius, in part criticized Hannibal and the Carthaginians in these orations, a careful exegesis of them reveals that Livy was fully capable of broaching the subject of criticism of Rome.

We need not trouble ourselves too much here with the matter of these speeches' historicity. In the previous chapter we addressed the reasons allowing us to conclude that Polybius' pre-Ticinus and pre-Zama orations were likely to be the product of their author's invention.[4] Virtually all these arguments hold true for Livy's versions as well.[5] In addition, we should note that modern scholars almost without exception deem Livy's orations essentially ahistorical.[6] Even so, we must still concern ourselves with a related matter: Livy's potential sources for these harangues. To be sure, while we ought not to get tangled up in overlong discussions of Livian *Quellenforschung*, we still should take up the possibility of Livy's use of Polybius as a source for his pre-Ticinus and pre-Zama orations. If we could demonstrate that Livy merely copied Polybius, we would be left with less faith in his concern for the shortcomings of Roman imperialism.[7]

Unfortunately, even in the case of Livy's use of Polybius, there are numerous reasons to conclude that definitive answers remain elusive. The matter of Livy's source material—and particularly his potential use of Polybius throughout his Third Decade—has for much time been the subject of considerable debate.[8] In regard to what we might now deem "original research" done by Livy, we can safely conclude that he did none: scholarly consensus (not to mention time considerations on Livy's part) strongly suggests that Livy did not consult the *Annales maximi*, senatorial records, or other "primary sources."[9] Still, even in regard to Livy's use of Polybius, we find ourselves on shaky ground. In his landmark work on the subject, Heinrich Nissen argued that Livy directly consulted Polybius only as far back as the material for Livy's twenty-fourth book.[10] According to Nissen, then, Livy did not employ Polybius for his pre-Ticinus harangues, since they appear in book 21.

Though numerous modern critics have agreed with Nissen's view,[11] others find it dubious.[12] In regard to the speeches before the Battle of Ticinus, there have been only a few guesses about the probability that Polybius was a direct source for Livy.[13] One detects, however, a bit more of a consensus regarding Livy's potential use of Polybius for his rendition of the conference between Hannibal and Scipio at Zama. According to Nissen's influential view, it is possible that the material found in Livy's thirtieth book stems directly from Polybius.[14] As a result, manifold critics have deemed Polybius a likely source for at least portions of this book.[15] Moreover, numerous classical scholars have related these conclusions to the pre-Zama colloquy itself, which they perceive (in part, at least) as an example of Livy's direct use of Polybius.[16]

The possibility still remains, however, that the correspondence between the two historians' pre-Ticinus harangues and the pre-Zama conferences is the result of an indirect link between Polybius and Livy, not a direct one. In fact, numerous potential sources for Livy's Third Decade have been proposed: Coelius Antipater, Valerius Antias, Claudius Quadrigarius, Fabius Pictor, and others.[17] The writer most often deemed a major and direct influence on Livy's Third Decade is Coelius Antipater, whose monograph on the Second Punic War appears to have been both detailed and, conveniently enough for Livy's purposes, composed in Latin.[18] One of the fragments from Coelius' work, moreover, appears to stem from his version of Hannibal's speech before the Battle of Ticinus.[19]

Although it remains likely that Livy consulted Coelius Antipater for his Third Decade, we know too little about his work (as well as about the histories of Fabius Pictor, Claudius Quadrigarius, Valerius Antias, and others) to detect whether he was in fact a major, direct source for this portion of Livy's history. As we shall see, moreover, we cannot precisely determine the degree to which the sentiments presented in Livy's pre-Ticinus and pre-Zama speeches are the products of his intellect or those of his sources. In regard to Livy's putative direct use of Polybius for these orations, we are on firmer ground. But, even in this case, we cannot ultimately distinguish whether Livy used Polybius directly, or has offered similar sentiments as the result of employing a common source.

## LIVY ON HANNIBAL AND THE CARTHAGINIANS

Having dealt with the historicity of the pre-Ticinus and pre-Zama addresses as well as Livy's sources, we may now turn to another important topic—Livy's views on Roman imperialism, most especially as they pertain to Hannibal and the Carthaginians. As was the case with the other authors we have discussed, we must get a sense of the overall context in which these speeches appear in order to determine the import of the sentiments found therein.

In comparison with Polybius, Livy's views on these topics, while eschewing the facile label of propaganda, appear far more pro-Roman and anti-Carthaginian. At a few points during the course of his narrative, for instance, Livy explicitly justifies Roman imperialism (5.27; 22.13)—something Polybius was loath to do, even though he considered it the essential raison d'être of his work. Livy is also unequivocal about the unjust side in the Second Punic War—the Carthaginian side.[20] Additionally, Livy offers numerous derogatory remarks about the Carthaginian people.[21] He implies that they, by their very nature, are untrustworthy (21.4.9). He deems a lack of regard for the established rules of postwar conduct a typically Punic trait (22.6.12). He also asserts that during the Second Punic War the Carthaginians perfidiously acquiesced to a peace with Rome merely to buy time for Hannibal's regrouping (30.16.10–11).

But surely Livy aims the brunt of his criticism of Carthaginian actions at Hannibal himself. Livy's famous elaboration on Hannibal's character (21.4.2–9) bears a striking resemblance to Sallust's description of Catiline (*Cat.* 5.1–5): both men had almost preternatural abilities, but, along with such innate strengths, they possessed horrendous vices. Livy also asserts that Hannibal desired and engineered a war with Rome from the start (21.5.2)—and even manipulated the Carthaginian Senate into following his machinations (21.9.4). He also mentions Hannibal's cruelty on numerous occasions (e.g., 21.4.9; 21.14.3; 26.38.3). Moreover, Livy questions Hannibal's bravery by reporting a rumor that the Carthaginian general contemplated fleeing to Gaul during setbacks that occurred in the war (22.43.3–4). In addition, he characterizes Hannibal as treacherous (25.1.1; 25.22.14; 27.26.1–2). He even castigates Hannibal for being utterly unreligious (21.4.9; 24.12.4), a label belied by a prayer Hannibal offers in order to avert a bad omen (30.25.12).[22]

Livy's assessment of Hannibal appears very negative indeed. Yet we must admit that Livy also occasionally presents a decidedly pro-Punic view. For instance, Livy notes (however noncommittally) that the Carthaginians resented the Romans' maltreatment of them after the First Punic War (21.1.3). Even though Livy offers no hint that he agrees with this sentiment, it at least amounts to an acknowledgment of Punic grievances. Livy also has the eldest member of a Spanish tribe, the Volcani, excoriate the Romans (21.20.8)—although this man's view is dramatically qualified by the fact that Hannibal had been bribing the Gauls to side with the Carthaginians. In addition, Livy mentions that the Romans planned a trick on the Carthaginians (27.28.3), the kind of stunt Livy usually regards as typically Punic in its duplicity. He gives his readers the distinct impression, however, that, whereas the Romans occasionally resort to treachery in order to obtain their military goals, perfidy was not an integral part of the Roman character per se, as was the case with the Carthaginians. As a result, when the Romans ambush Hannibal (27.41.6), Livy claims that they are merely employing Hannibal's own means.

Even so, Livy does not portray these tactics as beneath the dignity of the Romans. In discussing the end of the Second Punic War, Livy also includes a sentiment that potentially indicts Scipio Africanus. After the conference at Zama, Scipio, Livy asserts, was free to say what he felt would be advantageous to his troops about their adversary, since his meeting with Hannibal had been private (30.32.8). In this instance, at least, Livy portrays Scipio as something less than a beacon of veracity. And, in regard to the Battle of Zama itself, Livy reports that Hannibal did not escape until he had attempted every expediency (30.35.4)—a clear heralding of the Carthaginian general's resourcefulness and courage.

Despite these desultory pro-Punic and pro-Hannibalic comments appearing throughout the course of Livy's narrative, however, one is left with the distinct impression that Livy's description of the Carthaginians and their leader in the Second Punic War is, on the whole, more negative than Polybius' assessment. Naturally, neither historian inhabits the extreme end of the spectrum: neither Polybius nor Livy presents pro-Roman propaganda; both authors, moreover, do not offer an extended attack on Roman imperialism and kindred injustices related to Roman misrule. All the same, it seems clear that Polybius' narrative remains more nuanced than Livy's. And this is precisely what one might have expected from a Greek captive who was not as closely tied to the Roman annalistic tradition as was his Augustan fellow historian.[23]

## THE ADDRESSES BEFORE THE BATTLE OF TICINUS

What, then, about the counterpoised speeches of Roman and Carthaginian generals in Livy's Third Decade? We might expect, given Polybius' and Livy's aforementioned tendencies, that the orations before the battles of Ticinus and Zama, which appear in the works of both historians, would offer similar results: Polybius' accounts would appear more nuanced, and Livy's would strike us as more nationalistically pro-Roman. This is not, however, the case.

Livy chose (if in fact no earlier source he used had not chosen beforehand) to invert the order of the orations—Scipio speaks first (21.40–41), and then Hannibal afterward (21.43.2–44).[24] Before either general delivers his harangue, however, Livy establishes the mise-en-scène. The armies drew close to each other, Livy informs us, and each commander—although not well acquainted with one another—had a keen admiration for his opponent (21.39.7). Both generals, Livy continues, were renowned among their enemies (21.39.8–9). Scipio was first to cross the Po River, leading his troops to the Ticinus, and, from there, offered *talem orationem* ("such an oration"; 21.39.10).[25]

### Scipio: "You Have the Leftover Vestiges of an Enemy, Not an Enemy"

In Livy's work, Scipio delivers the entire speech in *oratio recta*. Livy's Scipio commences by informing his troops that he would have no need to address them if they had comprised the army he possessed in Gaul (21.40.1).

(1) Si eum exercitum, milites, educerem in aciem, quem in Gallia mecum habui, supersedissem loqui apud vos; (2) quid enim adhortari referret aut eos equites, qui equitatum hostium ad Rhodanum flumen egregie vicissent, aut eas legiones, cum quibus fugientem hunc ipsum hostem secutus confessionem cedentis ac detractantis certamen pro victoria habui? (21.40.1-2)[26]

(1) If, soldiers, I were leading into battle formation the army that I had with me in Gaul, I would have refrained from addressing you; (2) for what advantage would there be to exhort those horsemen who had brilliantly conquered the cavalry of the enemy at the Rhone River, or those legions with whom I followed after the routed enemy, whose withdrawal and flight from battle I considered a confession of our victory?

Here Livy seems to attempt to generate a reason for Scipio, who did not expect a major confrontation at Ticinus, to address his troops.[27] Why, he asks his soldiers, would I need to speak to the men who in Gaul had pursued a fleeing enemy (21.40.2)? This argument echoes one offered by Polybius' Hannibal (3.63.7), although, naturally, it does not proffer the same language.[28]

With the former army under the control of his brother (21.40.3), Scipio informs us that he had decided to address his new troops (21.40.4). Thus far, Scipio, in the portion of the speech Otto Kohl and Ragnar Ullmann deem the *prooemium*,[29] focuses on the reasons for delivering the oration itself, and obliquely boosts the confidence of the Roman troops under his command. My previous soldiers, Scipio asserts, fared well against the Carthaginians. This obviously implies that Scipio's new army can reasonably expect similar results. Additionally, Scipio flaunts his own acumen as a general, as well as his family's pedigree.

Having related his rationale for uttering this oration, Livy's Scipio next offers a different course of argument.[30] Scipio tells his assembled troops that he does not aim to keep them uninformed about the Romans' enemy—an enemy that had ignominiously lost the First Punic War and suffered various indignities as a result (21.40.5).[31] This amounts to an obvious attempt to boost the Roman army's confidence. In the course of this boasting, Livy's Scipio delights in the tribute Carthage has paid Rome and the snatching of Sicily and Sardinia. In this regard, one may reasonably take him to be an unapologetic imperialist—according to this argument, at least, might makes right, and the Romans should be proud of the fact that they have compelled an enemy to pay tribute. And, as far as Livy's Scipio is concerned, the Romans ought to cheer the fact that this tribute has poured into Rome as a result of their opponent's weakness, not because of the justness of the Roman cause in the First Punic War.

Scipio continues with this theme:

(6) Erit igitur in hoc certamine is vobis illisque animus, qui victoribus et victis esse solet. Nec nunc illi, quia audent, sed quia necesse est, pugnaturi sunt; (7) nisi creditis, qui exercitu incolumi pugnam detractavere, eos duabus paene partibus peditum equitumque in transitu Alpium amissis, cum plures perierint quam supersint, plus spei nactos esse. (8) 'At enim pauci quidem sunt, sed vigentes animis corporibusque, quorum robora ac vires vix sustinere vis ulla possit.' (9) Effigies immo, umbrae hominum, fame frigore inluvie squalore enecti, contusi ac debilitati inter saxa rupesque; ad hoc praeusti artus, nive rigentes nervi, membra torrida gelu, quassata fractaque arma, claudi ac debiles equi: (10) cum hoc equite, cum hoc pedite pugnaturi estis; reliquias extremas hostis, non hostem habetis; ac nihil magis vereor quam ne cui, vos cum pugnaveritis, Alpes vicisse Hannibalem videantur. (21.40.6–10)

(6) In this struggle, therefore, you and they will have the spirit that is usual for the victors and the defeated. And those men will not fight you because they are daring, but because they must, (7) unless you believe that those who declined battle when their army was whole became more hopeful when they lost two thirds of their infantry and cavalry in crossing the Alps. (8) [Someone may claim,] "Truly they are few, but strong in mind and body, whose vigor and strength hardly any force could withstand." (9) No indeed: they are imitations, specters of men, plagued by hunger, cold, filth, and squalor, battered and crippled among rocks and cliffs; in addition to this, their limbs are frostbitten, their muscles stiffened by the snow, their bodies sluggish with ice, their battle gear flimsy and broken, their horses limping and frail. (10) You will have to do battle with this cavalry, with this infantry; you have the leftover vestiges of an enemy, not an enemy. And I fear nothing more than that it may seem as if the Alps conquered Hannibal, even though you fought him.

The Romans ought to enter battle with the mindset of victory, he claims, whereas the enemy should fear defeat. In fact, the Carthaginians, he says, are now forced to fight (21.40.6). Here Livy's Scipio attempts to take one of the most compelling arguments in favor of the Carthaginian side (according to Hannibal)—the necessity of war under the logistical circumstances—and turn it into a boon for the Romans.[32] In the next sections of the oration Scipio explains his contention about Carthaginian strategic weakness, mentioning Hannibal's devastating trek across the Alps (21.40.7–9)[33] and the greatly depleted army the Romans are facing as a result (21.40.10).[34] Up to this point,

Livy's Scipionic speech seems similar to Polybius' version—both have thus far focused chiefly on perceived Carthaginian weaknesses.

Livy's Scipio now offers a new line of attack, however. It is right, he asserts, that the gods should decide a war with a treaty-breaking general and populace, and that the Romans, harmed along with the gods, should complete it (21.40.11).[35] For the first time in the address, Scipio has uttered a distinctly moral argument. Though it is tangled up in a prognostication that ultimately proves incorrect, it directly assails the Carthaginians for acting unjustly, and thus defends (implicitly, at least) Roman actions against their foe. But Livy's Scipio quickly retreats from this assault on Carthaginian machinations. He claims that he is unconcerned that someone may think he offers strong sentiments without believing them (21.41.1).[36] This amounts to a feeble addition to the Roman general's previous argument: here Scipio abandons his moral concerns, focuses again on military confidence, and implicitly offers his troops reason to doubt—despite remarks to the contrary—that he has faith in his own words. Regardless of its comparative impotence, Livy's Scipio continues with this theme. The Roman general claims that he could have remained in Spain, battling a less difficult adversary than Hannibal (21.41.2). This sentiment, in addition to seeming uninspiring, appears anachronistic: would Scipio already know—before Ticinus, before Cannae, before Trasumenus—that Hannibal would prove the master general that he did, one far superior to Hasdrubal, as Livy's Scipio implies?

Scipio next continues with his feeble point, brashly attempting to demonstrate to his troops his personal eagerness to fight Hannibal (21.41.3-5).[37] To be sure, this manages to highlight, however simplistically, the courage and competence of Scipio himself, who rushed out to engage the Carthaginian general. But, if Scipio were so certain of his inevitable victory, would he need to dilate on his own lack of fear? Even among arguments that focus on bravery (which, as we have seen, in some ways could fail to seem compelling to readers), these sentences appear particularly feckless.

At this point in the oration, Livy's Scipio alters his course, now turning to the enemy's purported feebleness:

> (6) Experiri iuvat, utrum alios repente Carthaginienses per viginti annos terra ediderit, an idem sint, qui ad Aegatis pugnaverunt insulas et quos ab Eryce duodevicenis denariis aestimatos emisistis, (7) et utrum Hannibal hic sit aemulus itinerum Herculis, ut ipse fert, an vectigalis stipendiariusque et servus populi Romani a patre relictus. (21.41.6–7)

> (6) It would please me to test whether the earth suddenly produced another kind of Carthaginian in the last twenty years, or if they are the same men

who fought at the Aegatian islands and whom you released from Eryx for a ransom of eighteen denarii a head, (7) and whether this Hannibal is a rival of the wandering Hercules, as he himself says, or has been left behind by his father as a tributary, taxpayer, and slave of the Roman people.

Scipio archly contemplates whether the earth, in the last twenty years, has fashioned a new species of Carthaginian (21.41.6). This sentiment recalls the speech's *prooemium*, which also highlighted Carthaginian incompetence in the First Punic War. Continuing in this wry vein, Scipio wonders whether Hannibal's quest is akin to Hercules' (as the Punic general himself believes), or if Hamilcar left him to be the Romans' taxpayer and slave (*vectigalis stipendiariusque et servus populi Romani*; 21.41.7).[38] The latter sentiment seems wholeheartedly and unapologetically imperialistic. If the Romans prove victorious, Hannibal—and, by extension, the Carthaginians—will become the Romans' slaves. Such a comment is very far from the Romans' supposed concerns for waging "just wars."[39]

Livy's Scipio again turns to a very different argument. He claims that Hannibal, if he truly understood his crimes vis-à-vis Saguntum, would be concerned for his country (21.41.8).[40] However overwrought this analysis may be, it clearly manages to blame the Carthaginian side for the siege of Saguntum and the germination of the Second Punic War itself. It is interesting that this sentiment, which appears to be in tune with the notion of "defensive" warfare, follows the brazen statement of the preceding sentence (21.41.7). It remains unclear, however, whether Livy deliberately attempted such a juxtaposition for the reader, or simply presented as many arguments as he could muster, regardless of their effect on the speech's overall coherence.

Scipio now describes his rationale for this assessment. Hannibal's father withdrew from Mount Eryx under orders from a Roman consul; Hamilcar also said that he would depart from Sicily and pay tribute to Rome (21.41.9).[41] Again, Livy's Scipio offers his soldiers (and, more importantly, Livy's readership) explicit justification for Roman actions against Hannibal. Yet Livy again presents a striking incongruity: Scipio next claims that his soldiers should fight with rage, as if their slaves had taken up arms against them (*velut si servos videatis vestros arma repente contra vos ferentes*; 21.41.10).[42] This sentiment is nakedly imperialistic. Livy's Scipio here equates a defeated people with slaves. The highlighting of the Romans' defensive actions against the Carthaginians again gives way to a might-makes-right line of reasoning.

But the argument shifts once more:

(11) Licuit ad Erycem clausos ultimo supplicio humanorum, fame, interficere; licuit victricem classem in Africam traicere atque intra paucos dies

sine ullo certamine Carthaginem delere; (12) veniam dedimus precantibus, emisimus ex obsidione, pacem cum victis fecimus, tutelae deinde nostrae duximus, cum Africo bello urgerentur. (21.41.11-12)

(11) We had them trapped at Mount Eryx and could have starved them to death—the most extreme punishment of human beings. We could have transferred our victorious fleet to Africa, and within a few days destroyed Carthage without any struggle; (12) yet we pardoned them when they begged us to do so, we discharged them from a siege, we made peace with the conquered, and, when they were burdened with the African war, we at last considered them as under our guardianship.

Livy's Scipio claims that the Romans could have utterly annihilated the Carthaginians after the First Punic War if they had so desired (21.41.11). In this instance, Scipio casts the Roman people as magnanimous, since they refrained from obliterating the Carthaginians wholesale. Such an opinion (which does not offer one much confidence in the Romans' righteousness) is undercut by the former talk of Punic slavery. Still Livy's Scipio continues, averring that the Romans presented Carthage with what it sought—peace and protection (21.41.12). This amounts to a simplification, to be sure, but it does offer a defense of Roman conduct.

And for this, Scipio archly queries, we deserve a "young firebrand" (*furiosum iuvenem*) fighting against us (21.41.13)! This does not make sense in light of what appears in 21.41.2, in which Scipio himself implies that Hannibal—now seen as an impetuous tyro—is a far greater menace than Hasdrubal. Again, Livy's oration lacks consistency. Such incongruities in the portrayal of the Carthaginian general suggest that Livy was more intent on ruminating on Rome and its expansion than on presenting a realistic portrait of an enemy. As perhaps is typical of Roman historians expounding on foreigners, Livy here betrays an intense inward focus, as if Hannibal were merely a foil for Roman unease with their state's expansionism.[43]

Having provided this mocking reference to Hannibal, Livy's Scipio next avers that Rome's very survival hangs in the balance (24.41.13-15).[44] This, of course, turned out to be false, since Rome managed to see many other days, despite its defeat in the Battle of Ticinus, as ancient readers would well know. Here, however, Livy's Scipio raises the stakes for his troops, albeit through a dubious argument. Yet these statements appear to nullify the former views Scipio proffered concerning the Punic army's supposed weaknesses. If the adversary's troops were truly so impotent, there would be little need for such histrionics. Once again, Livy's Scipionic address presents arguments that fly in the face of one appearing before it. Livy's Scipio, however, continues with this theme. We do not protect ourselves alone, he argues, but also our wives and children (21.41.16).[45] Portentously, Scipio claims that Rome's fortune rests upon his troops' might and bravery (21.41.7). Again, Livy's Scipio appears to add grandeur to his oration, even though it ends up confusing his logic.

One is left with the sense that Livy has deliberately added as many arguments to the harangue as he could muster, in order to vary the rhetorical sentiments found therein.[46] Unlike Polybius, who attempted to stick with a few key themes, Livy offers a portmanteau oration, one that amounts to a congeries of stronger and weaker arguments.[47] Thus, whereas Livy's Scipio presents sentiments with a distinctly moral dimension that justify Roman conduct, he also presents some unambiguously pugnacious rhetoric that seems anathema to the spirit of Roman "just war" ruminations and fetial law.[48] Readers are perhaps left with a mixed view of the oration, in comparison with Polybius' version. It is at times more pro-Roman, at times less so.[49] At this point in the narrative, furthermore, Livy does not relay the soldiers' reaction.

### Hannibal's Rejoinder: "This Most Cruel and Arrogant Nation"

We can now move on to Livy's speech of Hannibal before the Battle of Ticinus. Prior to this address, Hannibal (so Livy informs us) decided to encourage his troops by means of an object lesson (21.42.1). He arranged the Carthaginian forces in a circle and placed some captive Gauls in the center. He then asked if any of these prisoners would engage in individual life-or-death combats knowing that, if they won, they would receive a horse, weapons, and their freedom. Livy tells us that all the captives desired to take part (21.42.2). Those chosen for the single combats celebrated and received the others' congratulations (21.42.3). In regard to the fights themselves, all the onlookers expressed equal praise, Livy claims, for those who died as for those who won and survived (21.42.4). After numerous pairs of Gallic captives fought, Hannibal ended the demonstration, having roused his troops as he desired (21.43.1).

Livy clearly expanded the deadly contests between the captives from what appears in Polybius' narrative (although it is unclear, of course, whether Polybius was his direct source for this episode).[50] Some modern scholars perceive that the discussion of these pre-battle single combats aimed to make Hannibal appear cruel and inhuman.[51] If this were true, Livy's greater emphasis on this story would reflect heightened animosity toward the Carthaginians. But perhaps it remains more likely that Livy (or his source) found this scene of single combat dramatic, and thus augmented it in order to offer his narrative a more theatrical appeal. Either way, we should note that Livy's elaboration on the single combat makes clear that the Gallic captives fought for two things: booty and freedom. This detail is less explicit in Polybius' version, and it has some bearing on the addresses themselves.

On to Hannibal's speech. Livy has Hannibal commence (in *oratio recta*) by referring to the single combats that immediately preceded the address:

> (2) Si, quem animum in alienae sortis exemplo paulo ante habuistis, eundem mox in aestimanda fortuna vestra habueritis, vicimus, milites; neque enim spectaculum modo illud, sed quaedam veluti imago vestrae condicionis erat. (3) Ac nescio an maiora vincula maioresque necessitates vobis quam captivis vestris fortuna circumdederit; (4) dextra laevaque duo maria claudunt nullam ne ad effugium quidem navem habentis, circa Padus amnis maior [Padus] ac violentior Rhodano, ab tergo Alpes urgent, vix integris vobis ac vigentibus transitae. (21.43.2–4)

> (2) If, soldiers, you presently will have the same spirit in contemplating your fortune that you had a bit before in others fighting for theirs, then we have won; for that was not merely a spectacle but a clear representation of your own condition. (3) And I do not know whether fortune has locked you up in greater chains and greater constraints than your captives. (4) On the right and left two seas enclose you, and you do not even have a ship for flight; the Po River is around you—a greater and more turbulent river than the Rhone; at your back the Alps press upon you, which you barely crossed when you were unwounded and strong.

According to Livy's Hannibal, these combats should inspire the Carthaginian troops, since they find themselves in the same plight as the Gallic captives (21.43.2).[52] Like Polybius' Hannibal, Livy's links his soldiers' situation to that of the Gallic combatants, albeit more explicitly. It seems a bit far-fetched for an army that has just crossed the Alps to meet its foe to label itself captive. Even so, Hannibal continues with this theme, remarking that fortune has given his troops strong bonds (21.43.3)[53] and that the current geographical constraints have left them surrounded (21.43.4). It appears as if Hannibal's argument regarding purported Carthaginian captivity essentially relays a tactical point, not a moral one: due to the logistical vicissitudes, the Carthaginians find themselves at Rome's mercy. Thus Livy does not have Hannibal offer ethical sentiments about slavery—which he could have done to some effect, given Scipio's comments about the Carthaginians in his preceding oration.

Livy's Hannibal now introduces another line of reasoning, declaring that his soldiers must prevail here or die (21.43.5).[54] Fortune (*eadem fortuna*) has established matters, Hannibal says, in such a way that if the Carthaginians were to prove victorious, they would not ask more from the gods. Again, we should note that Livy's Hannibal attempts to win over his troops with talk of treasure, not moral considerations. Still, he offers strong (if tactical) language—the conquer-or-die theme seems more powerful and direct than Scipio's earlier remarks concerning the necessity of victory. Hannibal continues. Their reward would be sufficiently great if only they could re-obtain Sicily and Sardinia, both of which were purloined from their ancestors (21.43.6).[55] Here, at least, Livy's Hannibal has presented an argument grounded in foreign policy, one that implies the injustice of Roman actions in the First Punic War and its aftermath (i.e., the capture of Sicily and Sardinia). Perhaps this line of reasoning, given its lack of specificity, would be unlikely to incite some of Livy's readers to criticize Roman foreign affairs. Still, it amounts to a more direct indictment of Roman conduct than anything Polybius' Hannibalic address musters.

But it is immediately undercut—at least to some extent. Livy's Hannibal now urges his troops to ready themselves and to win a great victory with the gods' help (21.43.7). Obviously, the reference to divine aid implies Punic justness in pursuing the conflict. Even so, the Carthaginian general focuses here too on the treasure to be obtained, not the righteousness of the endeavor. As a result, he argues that the army, having risked life and limb in the Alps, deserves a good reward (21.43.8-9). In a bold sentiment that will reappear in the pre-Zama colloquy, Livy's Hannibal avers that fortune (*fortuna*) has made this victory the final goal of his army's hardships (21.43.10).

Having stressed the booty that his troops will receive, Livy' Hannibal next highlights the impending victory's ease, opining that the Romans merely possess a renowned name, and nothing more (21.43.11-12).[56] Not only, of course, does Hannibal underestimate the actual hardships involved in the war to come, but he also presents a sentiment more likely to make some Roman readers angry rather than self-reflective. After all, he inveighs against—incorrectly, as it turns out—the Roman people's valor and military acumen. This, however, does not stop Livy's Hannibal from continuing with this theme. Scipio's army, he asserts, replete with neophytes, was routed by the Gauls (21.43.13-14). In order to hammer home the Romans' purported weaknesses, Livy's Hannibal engages in a bit of braggadocio, which highlights his military roots and erstwhile successes. Further, he contrasts his martial prowess with P. Scipio's, which is found wanting (21.43.15). Naturally, this is greatly at variance with Scipio's own presentation of the events leading up to the Battle of Ticinus (cf. 21.40.2-10). Livy, moreover, has Hannibal offer an argument that could irk the Roman reader. Hannibal's descriptions of his earlier achievements come across as overwrought: Hannibal, to be sure, skillfully led his troops across the Alps, but he did not "conquer" these regions in any real sense, as the speech maintains (21.43.15).[57] Hannibal's version of Scipio's activity seems equally tendentious; it is as foolish as Livy's Scipio asserting that Hannibal ventured across the Alps to avoid an encounter with him.

Still, Livy's Hannibal adds to his denigration of the Roman commander. He archly suggests that Scipio, if shown the opposing armies without standards, would not know which was the Roman side (21.43.16). All this bluster demonstrates that Livy aims to highlight Hannibal's overconfidence. This allows Hannibal to transition into delivering more praise for his Carthaginian forces, which he lauds as tested, decorated, and noble (21.43.17–44.1).[58] In addition, Livy's Hannibal asserts that he views Carthaginians and their faithful allies prepared to fight on behalf of the native land "as the result of a most righteous indignation" (*ob iram iustissimam*; 21.44.2). Again the Carthaginian general presents a morally charged argument. Though hasty and unspecific, it still amounts to the sort of sentiment missing from Polybius' more workmanlike pre-Ticinus Hannibalic oration. Yet Hannibal's next sentence undercuts his previous contention. Now he claims that the Carthaginian army, more courageous than its foe, is on the offensive (21.44.3). To be certain, Hannibal could here refer to the logistics of the upcoming battle, rather than imply that Rome overall acts defensively. Even so, the sentiment could allow ancient readers to conclude that Rome was not an aggressor.

But Livy's Hannibal then turns to the most morally charged portion of the address—a mode of argument more likely to incite reflection on Rome's foreign affairs, and missing from Polybius' version of this Hannibalic speech:

> (4) Accendit praeterea et stimulat animos dolor iniuria indignitas. Ad supplicium depoposcerunt me ducem primum, deinde vos omnes, qui Saguntum oppugnassetis; deditos ultimis cruciatibus adfecturi fuerunt. (5) Crudelissima ac superbissima gens sua omnia suique arbitrii facit. Cum quibus bellum, <cum> quibus pacem habeamus, se modum inponere aequum censet. Circumscribit includitque nos terminis montium fluminumque, quos non excedamus, neque eos quos statuit terminos observat. (21.44.4–5)

> (4) In addition, outrage, wrongs, and insults inflame and goad our spirits. First they demanded I, your leader, be punished, then of all of you who attacked Saguntum; they were going to set upon those who surrendered with the most brutal tortures. (5) This most cruel and arrogant nation considers all things its own and for its own pleasure. This nation thinks it fair that only they should decide with whom we should have war, with whom

we should have peace. This nation circumscribes and confines us by the boundaries of mountains and rivers from which we may not depart; yet it does not observe those boundaries that they established.

The Carthaginian general argues that the Punic side should be angry as a result of the wrongs and insults to which the Romans have subjected it. The Romans sought for Carthage to give up, and would surely compel it to undergo unspeakable tortures after it did so (21.44.4).[59]

According to Ursula Händl-Sagawe, Livy here follows pro-Roman propaganda, and thus has Hannibal present bald-faced lies.[60] To be sure, Livy's Hannibal offers a distorted picture of Roman intentions—one that is at variance with Livy's own account. Even so, he does not present an argument that seems entirely far-fetched. After all, Scipio, in his pre-Ticinus address, glories in the quasi-enslaved position of the Carthaginians vis-à-vis the Romans (cf. 21.41.10). Is it impossible to imagine that the Romans would be intent on punishing the Carthaginians soundly for their actions? However simplified, this line of reasoning allows Hannibal to seem as if he acted justifiably. Hannibal then adds to this argument. The Romans, he contests, are the "most cruel and arrogant nation" (*crudelissima ac superbissima gens*; 21.44.5). Acting on their whims alone, they think it is up to them to decide with whom the Carthaginians may fight. And, according to Livy's Hannibal, the Romans are inveterate hypocrites: although they attempt to limit the Carthaginians to certain boundaries, they blithely transgress their own. Here we reach the peak of Hannibal's anti-Roman fervor. In fact, this portion of the speech reads a bit like Sallust's *EM*.[61] It presents a general yet dramatic portrait of Roman misconduct and double standards. To be sure, the statements are overblown and lack nuance. Even so, Livy's Hannibal here presents withering criticism of Rome's strong-man tactics.

The oration's next sentence relates a series of Roman rhetorical commands—"Do not involve yourself with Saguntum," etc.—and answers them, lending an even more dramatic character to the ethically charged sentiments found in this portion of the oration (21.44.6). Then Livy's Hannibal transitions to a few rhetorical questions that highlight Rome's machinations. Having purloined Carthage's ancient provinces of Sicily and Sardinia, and having entered Spain, he argues, the Romans have already headed to Africa.[62] Again, Hannibal focuses on Roman rapacity. The argument remains distorted and simplistic, but could have more resonance for Livy's ancient readership in light of events occurring after the Second Punic War—for example, the annihilation of Carthage in the Third Punic War and Lucullus' and Pompey's expansionism in the East. Livy's Hannibal here views the war as, at its heart, a defensive enterprise for the Carthaginians. This seems paradoxical, given that Hannibal previously admitted that Carthage was on the attack (cf. 21.44.3). The contradiction, in fact, causes the speech to appear unbalanced, as if Livy added every sort of argument he could conjure up.

From here, Livy's Hannibal returns to a theme he articulated earlier in the address: the Carthaginians are compelled to seek victory or death, banishing any hope in flight (21.44.8). This amounts to a skillful weaving of two ideas presented elsewhere in the speech—the Carthaginians, up against a wall thanks to Roman rapacity, must fight to the death. And Hannibal claims that victory is already in his army's grasp, since the gods offer no greater tool for conquest than contempt for death (21.44.9).[63] This amounts to a strikingly bold conclusion, one that—suspiciously, perhaps—makes it appear as if Hannibal already knows what will occur in the upcoming battle.

After the oration, Livy states that both sides were perked up by their respective commanders' addresses (21.45.1).

Overall, one detects fewer correspondences between Polybius' and Livy's Hannibalic speeches pre-Ticinus than in their respective orations of P. Scipio.[64] To be certain, in both Livian versions of these harangues, there is a greater concern for the inclusion of various rhetorical τόποι. Yet it remains important to distinguish the sorts of arguments Livy was capable of adding to his orations, which seem missing from their Polybian counterparts: moral arguments. Indeed, strategically placed at the conclusion of Livy's pre-Ticinius Hannibalic *tractatio* is a strident moral appeal. This could strike readers as particularly forceful, since Livy's Scipionic address did not expound on themes of this sort.

Livy, then, supposedly a jingoistic Roman patriot, presents moral appeals in his Hannibalic oration, whereas the purportedly evenhanded Polybius includes no such category. This does not imply, of course, that Livy ultimately sympathized with Hannibal and the Carthaginians' plight. In fact, we can see that Livy's Hannibalic address before the Battle of Ticinus amounts to a hodgepodge of stronger and weaker sentiments. Still, the inclusion of genuine ethical concerns means that, for whatever combination of reasons, Livy aimed to introduce moral appeals from Rome's dire enemy, even though he need not have done so.

## THE ORATIONS BEFORE THE BATTLE OF ZAMA

The same holds true, as we shall see, for Livy's two speeches prior to the Battle of Zama (202 B.C.). Before discussing Hannibal's and Scipio Africanus' conference, Livy specifies that the Roman general was located in the city of

Naraggara, and his Punic counterpart was close by (30.29.9). The commanders met between these two locales, each bringing with him one interpreter (30.29.10–30.1). For a moment, Livy histrionically informs us, the generals were silent in mutual admiration.

### Hannibal: "What I Was at Trasumenus, at Cannae, You Are Today"

Hannibal spoke first (30.30.2). Livy relays Hannibal's sentiments in *oratio recta*. He begins as follows:

> (3) Si hoc ita fato datum erat, ut qui primus bellum intuli populo Romano quique totiens prope in manibus victoriam habui, is ultro ad pacem petendam venirem, laetor te mihi sorte potissimum datum a quo peterem. (4) Tibi quoque inter multa egregia non in ultimis laudum hoc fuerit, Hannibalem, cui de tot Romanis ducibus victoriam di dedissent, tibi cessisse, teque huic bello vestris prius quam nostris cladibus insigni finem imposuisse. (5) Hoc quoque ludibrium casus ediderit fortuna, ut cum patre tuo consule ceperim arma, cum eodem primum Romano imperatore signa contulerim, ad filium eius inermis ad pacem petendam veniam. (30.30.3–5)[65]

> (3) If it is fated that I, who have first waged war on the Roman people and who have so often had victory nearly in my hands, come to seek peace, I am glad that chance has given me you, a man of the first order, as the person from whom I sue for peace. (4) This will also be one of your most outstanding accomplishments, and by no means the least praised, that Hannibal, to whom the gods have given victory over so many Roman leaders, yielded to you, and that you have made an end to this war, a war that was remarkable for your disasters and then our own. (5) Fortune also made a laughingstock of our expectations, so that, although I took up arms when your father was consul, and though I first went to battle with him as the Roman general, unarmed I come to his son in order to seek peace.

Livy's Hannibal commences by claiming that, despite his erstwhile victories, he is content to ask for peace (30.30.3).[66] It is important to note that Hannibal, in the introduction to his oration, immediately mentions fate—an important part of Polybius' version of this speech.[67] It appears as if Livy's Hannibal admits that he himself began this war, though it is unclear whether this means that Livy painted Hannibal as responsible for the hostilities tout court. Hannibal continues: My appeal to you, Scipio, will bring you honor (30.30.4). Here Livy's Hannibal comes across as more self-impressed than one detects him to be in Polybius' account. This, Hannibal says, could be fortune's joke—having first fought against your father, I now appeal to you for peace (30.30.5). This amounts to an explicit reference to the addresses delivered prior to the Battle of Ticinus, perhaps serving to highlight the fact that these four speeches act as bookends for Livy's Third Decade.

Next Livy's Hannibal delves into the heart of the appeal:

> (6) Optimum quidem fuerat eam patribus nostris mentem datam ab dis esse, ut et vos Italiae et nos Africae imperio contenti essemus. (7) Neque enim ne vobis quidem Sicilia ac Sardinia satis digna pretia sunt pro tot classibus, tot exercitibus, tot tam egregiis amissis ducibus; sed praeterita magis reprehendi possunt quam corrigi. (8) Ita aliena appetivimus ut de nostris dimicaremus, nec in Italia solum nobis bellum, vobis in Africa esset; sed et vos in portis vestris prope ac moenibus signa armaque hostium vidistis, et nos ab Carthagine fremitum castrorum Romanorum exaudimus. (9) Quod igitur nos maxime abominaremur, vos ante omnia optaretis, in meliore vestra fortuna de pace agitur. Agimus ii quorum et maxime interest pacem esse, et qui quodcumque egerimus ratum civitates nostrae habiturae sunt; animo tantum nobis opus est non abhorrente a quietis consiliis. (30.30.6–9)

> (6) Indeed it would have been best if the gods had put into our fathers' minds that you should be content to rule over Italy and we to rule over Africa; (7) for not even for you have Sicily and Sardinia been a worthy exchange for the loss of so many fleets, so many armies, and so many excellent leaders. But it is easier to blame the past than correct it. (8) Thus we sought after others' possessions and ended up contending over our own, and for us it was not only a war in Italy, and for you not only one in Africa, but you have seen the standards and weapons of the enemy near by your gates and walls, and we hear from Carthage the rumblings of the Roman camp. (9) Thus we discuss peace when Fortune smiles on you—something we should most detest, and you desire above all else. We, for whom peace is of the greatest interest, are seeking it out, and whatever terms we have made, our states will approve. All we need is a state of mind that does not abhor calm deliberations.

Interestingly, Livy's Hannibal asserts that it would have been optimal if the generals' ancestors had been content to control Africa and Italy respectively (30.30.6).[68] Sicily and Sardinia, he claims, have not been worth the loss of so many ships, troops, and commanders. Yet it remains easier to fault the past than to alter it, Hannibal suggests (30.30.7). With the exception of this last *sententia*, this essentially rehashes the points Polybius' Hannibalic speech presents in 15.6.4.[69] Livy's version is perhaps more characteristically garrulous, but the sentiments seem basically the same. This also proves true for the next few sentences of Livy's Hannibalic oration, in which Hannibal outlines the zenith of Carthaginian success in the Second Punic War as well as their current desperate plight, which necessitates peace terms amenable to Roman interests (30.30.8–9).[70]

Livy's Hannibal now delves into his personal experiences in the Second Punic War. Informing his younger colleague that age has taught him to follow reason, not chance (30.30.10), Hannibal claims that he is concerned about Scipio's youth and history of unremitting success, since they could lead him to harbor a cavalier attitude toward the vicissitudes of fortune (30.30.11). Again, this seems akin to Polybius' version of this speech,[71] though Livy appears to place even more emphasis on fortune's import. Not content to offer only what is found in the Polybian account, Livy presumably augments it: his Hannibal informs Scipio that he finds himself in the same position as Hannibal once did in the early portion of the war (30.30.12).[72] The supplementary commentary is noteworthy. Livy's Hannibal views the Carthaginians as, in essence, the same as the Romans. Both need to be wary of fortune, which treats all alike. More to the point, Hannibal sees Scipio as a younger version of himself. The Punic commander dismisses the supposed differences of character between the Carthaginians and the Romans.

Hannibal turns to complimenting his adversary. Scipio, he says, obtained honor by avenging his father's and uncle's deaths, and regained the lost Spanish provinces by defeating Punic armies (30.30.13). In this instance Livy's Hannibal is more specific than Polybius' regarding the Carthaginians' imperialistic designs. He may even make Rome appear to be acting defensively in the Second Punic War. Hannibal also commends Scipio for his boldness in traveling to Africa, which compelled the Carthaginian general to retreat from Italy (30.30.14). Hannibal praises both Scipio and his own abilities in this sentence, since he compliments himself, it seems, for controlling Italy for sixteen years.

The Punic commander next offers a *sententia* claiming that the heart can desire a victory instead of peace, as he well knows (30.30.15). But, he continues, if the gods grant humans reason, they can ponder future happenstances (30.30.16).[73] Livy's Hannibal returns to suggesting his own experiences as an example. Although he formerly came close to sacking Rome, he now must rescue his own city from the terrors he almost inflicted upon the Republic (30.30.17). Again, this distraught rhetoric seems to add weight to his sentiments. It also potentially serves to portray Hannibal as a sympathetic character—a man who has learned from his prior machinations, thanks to the uncertainties and reversals that plague all empires. To this is added yet more appeals to fortune (30.30.18–20), which, Hannibal emphatically stresses, must not be trusted. Additionally, Livy's Hannibal mentions peace, which, unlike war, he avers, will bestow great honor on Scipio (30.30.18–22).[74] In order to solidify this point, Hannibal presents an example not found in Polybius' oration—that of M. Atilius Regulus, a commander during the First Punic War who was captured after offering unacceptable peace terms (30.30.23). Since Livy proffers this *exemplum* elsewhere in his oeuvre (28.42.1; 28.43.17), it seems unlikely that this detail came from Livy's sources for the current episode. Rather, he appears to have suggested it himself.

At this point in the address Livy's Hannibal comes to the terms of peace, which he himself introduces:[75]

> (24) Est quidem eius qui dat, non qui petit, condiciones dicere pacis; sed forsitan non indigni simus qui nobismet ipsi multam inrogemus. (25) Non recusamus quin omnia propter quae ad bellum itum est vestra sint, Sicilia Sardinia Hispania, quidquid insularum toto inter Africam Italiamque continetur mari. (26) Carthaginienses, inclusi Africae litoribus vos—quando ita dis placuit—externa etiam terra marique videamus regentes imperio. (27) Haud negaverim propter non nimis sincere petitam aut exspectatam nuper pacem suspectam esse vobis Punicam fidem; multum per quos petita sit ad fidem tuendae pacis pertinet, Scipio. (28) Vestri quoque, ut audio, patres nonnihil etiam ob hoc, quia parum dignitatis in legatione erat, negaverunt pacem. (29) Hannibal peto pacem, qui neque peterem nisi utilem crederem, et propter eandem utilitatem tuebor eam propter quam petii; (30) et quemadmodum, quia a me bellum coeptum est, ne quem eius paeniteret quoad ipsi invidere di praestiti, ita adnitar ne quem pacis per me partae paeniteat. (30.30.24–30)

> (24) It is, in fact, he who gives peace, not the one seeking it, who sets the conditions; but perhaps we might not be unworthy of inflicting a penalty on ourselves. (25) We accept the term that all the possessions for which we went to war are to be yours: Sicily, Sardinia, Spain, and all the islands between Africa and Italy that are bound by the sea. (26) Let us Carthaginians, restricted to the shores of Africa, behold you ruling even lands and seas, since it so pleased the gods. (27) I would not deny that, due to the fact that we recently sought or anticipated peace without real sincerity, Punic trustworthiness is suspect in your view. Much of the credibility of the peace depends on the quality of those through whom it has been sought, Scipio. (28) Your senators too, as I hear, denied the peace in part because there was a lack of men of stature in the embassy. (29) I, Hannibal, seek peace, I who

would not seek it unless I believed it beneficial, and I shall maintain it on account of the same benefit that led me to seek it. (30) And in the same way, since I began the war, I saw to it that that no one faulted my conduct of the war (until the gods themselves grew hostile), so I shall take pains that no one will regret the peace gained through me.

The Carthaginian general first asserts that his people are content to rule Africa, leaving the rest to the Romans (30.30.25-26). Interestingly, Hannibal does not speak of any indemnity, even though Scipio specifically called for one (30.16.10-12). This perhaps suggests that Livy aimed to highlight the unrealistic terms Hannibal offered, and possibly hints at the notion that the Carthaginian commander acted in bad faith. Nevertheless, from here Livy's Hannibal turns to appeals missing from Polybius' version of the speech.[76] Admitting that the Romans are reasonably hesitant to accept a peace, in part given previous Punic perfidy (30.30.27-28), Hannibal stresses that he himself asks for an agreement, which the Carthaginians will then uphold (30.30.29). Hannibal is clearly touting his own name and fame as a means to sway Scipio to accept his (less than completely generous) terms. On a similar note, this leads Livy's Hannibal to finish the oration by stating that he started this war, ensuring that no one would regret it, until the gods became envious. Now he will prevent anyone from regretting a peace gained through him (30.30.30). This serves to augment Hannibal's gravitas. Yet it also seems to remind Livy's readership—at the tail end of the address—of Hannibal's personal responsibility for the Second Punic War's fruition.

Overall, we should note that this pre-Zama oration is far closer to the Polybian version than is either of Livy's pre-Ticinus harangues. This need not prove that Polybius was Livy's direct source, though it certainly makes this contention more feasible. Livy's Hannibal speech is also highly rhetorical, even by his standards. It is chockablock with *sententiae* and various oratorical figures.[77] Additionally, Livy has expanded the argument found in Polybius' text. He has discussed Hannibal's and Scipio's deeds in the Second Punic War at greater length, repeated the concerns about fortune numerous times, and offered a striking conclusion that refers to the gods' anger at Hannibal, to which we shall turn anon.

## Scipio Africanus' Retort: "Prepare for War, Since You Have Not Been Able to Endure Peace"

After offering Hannibal's sentiments, Livy grants Scipio Africanus a response. Before presenting this oration in *oratio recta*, Livy tells us that Scipio *in hanc fere sententiam respondit* ("offered essentially this judgment"; 30.31.1). Again we happen upon an example of Livy specifically refraining from giving his readers the impression that he reproduces the actual words that were spoken.

Scipio begins by telling the Punic leader that Carthage did not desire peace before his arrival in Africa, and that his terms are less than equitable:[78]

> (1) Adversus haec imperator Romanus in hanc fere sententiam respondit: "Non me fallebat, Hannibal, adventus tui spe Carthaginienses et praesentem indutiarum fidem et spem pacis turbasse; (2) neque tu id sane dissimulas, qui de condicionibus superioris pacis omnia subtrahas praeter ea quae iam pridem in nostra potestate sunt. (3) Ceterum ut tibi curae est sentire cives tuos quanto per te onere leventur, sic mihi laborandum est ne, quae tum pepigerunt, hodie subtracta ex condicionibus pacis praemia perfidiae habeant. (4a) Indigni quibus eadem pateat condicio, etiam ut prosit vobis fraus petitis. (4b) Neque patres nostri priores de Sicilia, neque nos de Hispania fecimus bellum; et tunc Mamertinorum sociorum periculum et nunc Sagunti excidium nobis pia ac iusta induerunt arma." (30.31.1-4)

> (1) In answer to these words, the Roman commander offered essentially this judgment: "I was not deceived, Hannibal, that the Carthaginians, in hope of your arrival, confounded both the present pledge of the armistice and the hope of peace; (2) and of course you do not conceal it, when you withdraw all the elements of the former terms for peace except those that have been in our power for some time. (3) Still, as it is a concern to you by how much you free your citizens from a burden, thus I must make sure that they are not rewarded for their treachery through remission of peace terms to which they had previously agreed. (4a) Unworthy of the terms that lie open to you, you even hope to profit from your deceit. (4b) Our fathers were not the aggressors in Sicily, and we did not incite the war in Spain; then the danger to our allies the Mamertines and now the destruction of Saguntum clad us in holy and righteous arms."

At the start of the address Livy's Scipio notes the unfairness of Hannibal's offer. And he continues with this idea, claiming that he cannot reward Hannibal's perfidy by relaxing the peace terms (30.31.3).[79] Although unworthy of the prior terms, Scipio claims, Hannibal now desires an even more advantageous agreement (30.31.4a).[80]

Importantly, Livy's Scipio next contends that the Romans did not act as aggressors in Sicily or Spain, but justifiably defended the Mamertines and reacted to the Punic siege of Saguntum (30.31.4b).[81] Although greatly simplified, Scipio's point is nevertheless forceful and clear: the Carthaginians alone are to blame for the First and Second Punic Wars, and the Romans were morally justified in opposing them. This sentiment appears particularly powerful given that, in his preceding address, Hannibal did not deny initiating the second war.

Livy's Scipio proceeds in this vein, stressing that the Romans will win, since the gods side with the just (30.31.5). Scipio here makes clear that he places more stock in the gods than in the vicissitudes of fortune. His is a notably more moral universe than Hannibal's, since he believes that those in the right will eventually triumph. He does not contend that everyone must suffer the blows of capricious fortune. Even so, we must admit that Hannibal, in his counterpoised oration, does not come across as an atheist, cowering at the prospect of an inevitably wretched fate. Rather, he blamed the gods' jealousy for his downfall. As a result, the contrast between Scipio's concern for cosmic justice and Hannibal's regard for fortune may not be so stark.

Yet Livy's Scipio intensifies this contrast by implicitly criticizing Hannibal's notion of fortune:

> (6) Quod ad me attinet, et humanae infirmitatis memini et vim fortunae reputo, et omnia quaecumque agimus subiecta esse mille casibus scio. (7) Ceterum quemadmodum superbe et violenter me faterer facere si, priusquam in Africam traiecissem, te tua voluntate cedentem Italia et imposito in naves exercitu ipsum venientem ad pacem petendam aspernarer, (8) sic nunc, cum prope manu conserta restitantem ac tergiversantem in Africam attraxerim, nulla sum tibi verecundia obstrictus. (9) Proinde si quid ad ea in quae tum pax conventura videbatur, quasi multa navium cum commeatu per indutias expugnatarum legatorumque violatorum, adicitur, est quod referam ad consilium; sin illa quoque gravia videntur, bellum parate, quoniam pacem pati non potuistis. (30.31.6–9)

> (6) As for me, I remember human weakness, and I think about the force of fortune and know that all the things we do are exposed to a thousand chances; (7) still, I would admit that I would be acting in an arrogant and violent way if after you had withdrawn from Italy by your own volition and embarked your army in ships before I came to Africa, I should spurn your overtures of peace; (8) as things stand, since I have dragged you back to Africa resisting almost to the point of blows and equivocating besides, I have been bound by no reverence for you. (9) Thus if anything is added to the terms of a peace treaty that seemed imminent, like compensation for our supply ships seized during the armistice or our mistreated ambassadors, I could bring this to the council, but if those additions also seem too harsh, prepare for war, since you have not been able to stomach peace.

The Roman general claims, perhaps hubristically, that he understands human weakness and the fact that fortune exposes everyone to chance (30.31.6).[82] From here, Scipio criticizes the timing of Hannibal's overture to peace, arguing that it would have deserved more of the Roman commander's attention if Hannibal had offered it in Italy, rather than in his current dire circumstances (30.31.7–8). This could come across as haughty, since Carthage—or any other ancient power—would obviously be highly unlikely to sue for peace when it possessed the upper hand or, perhaps, was not clearly defeated. Scipio's contention, therefore, may appear unreasonable. Unless Hannibal is willing to add compensation to Rome as part of his proposed deal, Livy's Scipio contends, he ought to prepare for war (30.31.9).[83]

The most striking feature of this speech is its length. Livy, normally intent on adding numerous arguments and rhetorical flourishes to his orations, has truncated what appears in the typically more taciturn Polybius.[84] Why did Livy do this? Answers to this question should touch on the degree to which Livy appears sympathetic to Hannibal's plight before the Battle of Zama, and, more generally, to that of the Carthaginians. One might suppose that Livy crafted a long speech for Hannibal before the Zama conflict in order to highlight his maniacal nature: he acts obsequiously, so as to fool Scipio into agreeing to an unfair peace.[85] Yet one could also posit that Livy gave Hannibal a longer oration in order to demonstrate the greatness of Scipio and Rome, since they defeated such a worthy adversary.[86] There is probably some truth to both these arguments.

But this does not fully explain the curtness of Livy's Scipionic reply. Livy tended to compose counterpoised speeches of equal length for stylistic purposes.[87] This makes the brevity of Scipio's oration even more striking. Some might suppose that Scipio presents a brief retort because he need not offer anything more: his speech, that is to say, is powerful—a great contrast to Hannibal's rambling request.[88] Yet Livy himself calls the validity of this argument into question, since he admits (30.32.8) that Scipio could tell his troops whatever he wanted about what Hannibal said, since it was a private conversation. The Roman general, that is to say, may have chosen to fabricate Hannibal's contentions because his actual sentiments were potentially compelling. This could signal that Livy implicitly concedes the power of Hannibal's appeal. Since Livy does not offer any commentary regarding the quality of the two pre-Zama addresses, this is as close as we can get to an acknowledgment that Hannibal's speech was, at the very least, not a disaster in the eyes of its author.

More tellingly, the conclusion that Livy purposely crafted a feeble Hannibalic speech and a withering Scipionic retort overlooks Gottfried Mader's significant article, according to which Hannibal, throughout Livy's Third Decade, can be seen as a tragic figure.[89] As Mader notes, Livy includes two speeches by Hanno, a Carthaginian senator opposed to the Barcid faction (21.3.3–6; 21.10.2–13). In both of these orations, with which Livy appears to agree[90] (and perhaps even concocted, given that they do not appear in Polybius' narrative), Hanno acts as a kind of soothsayer—one who forecasts Hannibal's later doom.[91] To be sure, Mader's notion of a "tragic" Hannibal may be overstated. But his article presents cogent points. It is possible to read Hannibal's pre-Zama speech (especially in light of his prior pre-Ticinus oration) as a turn from ignorance to knowledge.[92] It is also true that the address makes Hannibal appear both pathetic *and* prophetic, given Scipio's later political downfall and Rome's subsequent decay, according to Livy (*Praef.* 11–12). We should also note that Livy, by casting Hanno as critical of the Barcids, portrays the Carthaginians as capable of societal self-criticism. Indeed, Hanno may simply be a foil for Livy's own views. More importantly, Livy does not demonize all the Carthaginians as mindlessly supportive of Hannibal. Rather, he makes Carthage appear very much like Rome—with factions, one pro-war and one anti-war.[93]

We need not, then, view Livy's Hannibalic address prior to the Battle of Zama as merely degrading to the Carthaginian leader. Rather, it could serve as a warning about the limits of imperialism—while still amounting to a commendation of Scipio Africanus' martial performance. Perhaps Livy's lauding of Scipio only serves to make his later political defeat appear more ignominious.[94] Furthermore, Livy could have attempted to intensify the horrors of Rome's purported embrace of vice and immorality by highlighting Scipio's glorious victory. Thus Livy's version of the pre-Zama conference cannot be breezily attributed to its author's supposed pro-Roman or anti-Punic outlook.

## ECHOES OF HANNIBAL?

Hannibal's pre-Ticinus and pre-Zama addresses, of course, are not the only enemy orations Livy includes in his history. Far from it. As a result, it seems reasonable to examine more briefly a few other examples of such speeches, so that we may get a sense of, inter alia, the Hannibalic addresses' typicality.

In his discussion of the aftermath of Rome's debacle at the Caudine Forks (321 B.C.), for instance, Livy grants a few addresses to individual Samnites (9.1.3–11, 3.6–13, 4.4–6, 11.1–13). Among these is the withering oration of C. Pontius[95] (9.11.1–13), the Samnite commander whose army trapped the Romans' forces. This speech, in fact, amounts to the last direct address pertaining to this particular conflict. Pontius' oration, delivered in response to

Spurius Postumius' antics vis-à-vis Rome's hewing to fetial law and its continuation of anti-Samnite activities,[96] contains some seemingly forceful contentions. Among them are the following:

> (6) Nunquamne causa defiet cur victi pacto non stetis? Obsides Porsinnae
> dedistis; furto eos subduxistis. Auro civitatem a Gallis redemistis; inter
> accipiendum aurum caesi sunt. (7) Pacem nobiscum pepigistis ut legiones
> vobis captas restitueremus; eam pacem inritam facitis. Et semper aliquam
> fraudi speciem iuris imponitis. (9.11.6–7)[97]

> (6) Even in defeat, will you never lack a rationale for failing to abide by an
> agreement? You gave hostages to Porsenna; you then secretly took them
> back. With gold, you bought back your state from the Gauls; they were
> murdered while receiving this gold. (7) You agreed upon a peace with us, so
> that we might give back your captured legions to you; now you nullify this
> peace. And you always impose some semblance of legality to your deceit.

As S. P. Oakley correctly asserts, this attack on Roman good faith in its
martial history is not necessarily an overwhelmingly powerful indictment.[98]
Earlier in his work, Livy himself proffered an incongruous version of Rome's
dealings with Lars Porsenna (cf. 2.13.9), and highlighted the Gauls' duplicity
in regard to the ransoming of Rome (cf. 5.48.9–49.7).[99] One might reasonably wonder, furthermore, whether condemnations that pertain to legendary
details from chronologically distant Romano-Etruscan warfare would elicit
much embarrassment from Livy's Roman readership.

All the same, there are reasons to conclude that these arguments are more
compelling than one might immediately suppose. Livy's own versions of the
historical episodes Pontius mentions would likely be remote to many of his
readers, since they appear at least four whole books prior to Pontius' speech.[100]
Can we assume that ancient readers possessed a sufficiently detailed understanding of Rome's conflict with Lars Porsenna ca. 509 B.C. to note that Pontius' reading of it seems tendentious? With the exception of those possessing
a splendid memory for Roman foreign policy in the early Republic, we are
correct to deem it far-fetched. More importantly, Livy's Pontius argues in
a manner consistent with that of Sallust's *EM*: he proffers relevant historical *exempla* of Roman misconduct in an attempt to prove an overarching—
and damning—contention regarding Rome's history of bad faith.[101] Despite
the potential shakiness of Pontius' examples, his assertions may seem potent,
since the Romans certainly made dubious recourse to fetial law in the aftermath of the disaster at the Caudine Forks. Given the dramatic date of Pontius' speech, moreover, Livy was compelled to employ examples from legend-

ary struggles removed from more immediate Roman concerns for martial fair play. And, of course, Livy allows Pontius the final words on the matter. This does not imply that Livy agreed with the assertions he attributes to Pontius, but it suggests that ancient—and modern—readers could come to disparate conclusions about their efficacy.

To some extent, at least, the same appears true regarding a speech Livy puts in the mouth of L. Annius Setinus (8.4.1-11),[102] a Latin praetor involved in diplomacy with the Romans prior to the Great Latin War (340-338 B.C.). In an oration delivered at a Latin assembly, Livy's Annius presents the reader with numerous complaints about Roman conduct vis-à-vis the Latin League. For instance, Annius says:

> (3) Sin autem tandem libertatis desiderium remordet animos, si foedus [est], si societas aequatio iuris est, si consanguineous nos Romanorum esse, quod olim pudebat, nunc gloriari licet, si socialis illis exercitus is est quo adiuncto duplicent vires suas, quem secernere ab se consilia bellis propriis ponendis sumendisque nolint, cur non omnia aequantur? cur non alter ab Latinis consul datur? (4) Ubi pars virium, ibi et imperii pars est. (5) Est quidem nobis hoc per se haud nimis amplum quippe concedentibus Romam caput Latio esse; sed ut amplum videri posset, diuturna patientia fecimus. (8.4.3-5)[103]

> (3) But if at last a longing for freedom eats away at our hearts, if a treaty, if an alliance means an equal distribution of rights, if it is now permitted for us to pride ourselves on being kinsmen of the Romans (though previously it was shameful to us), if to them an allied army is one that, added in the mix, doubles its strength, one that they do not want to separate from themselves in matters of war and peace, why aren't all things made equal? Why isn't one of the consuls furnished by the Latins? (4) Where part of the strength lies, there part of the power should lie, too. (5) Indeed, this is hardly too much for us, since we have allowed Rome to be Latium's capital, but by our long-lasting acquiescence, we have made it possible for this to be viewed as excessive.

Despite this passage's heightened rhetoric, we have reason to doubt Livy's interest in making Annius' speech particularly cutting. After all, Livy informs us that Annius himself soon met an ignominious fate, tumbling down the steps of Jupiter's temple (perhaps to his death), as the result of his spurning of the god (8.6.1-3). Livy also tells us that T. Manlius Torquatus' orations in response to Annius' complaints were well received by the Roman Senate (8.6.1) and people (8.6.7).[104] This could signal that Livy did not hope to offer

Annius compelling criticisms of Rome. In fact, Oakley counts this address as an example of Livian "[s]peeches by foreigners which are critical of Rome, but the contents of which are refuted by the later turn of events."[105]

To be sure, Annius' hopes do not come to fruition; Rome would soon prevail in war and dissolve the Latin League. Yet this need not entirely gainsay the arguments Livy's Annius presents. Annius' complaints appear ahistorically similar to the Italian allies' grievances on the cusp of the Social War.[106] The idea that the Latin League wished for an annual consul of its own, as Annius implores, seems especially far-fetched.[107] Importantly, the link between this speech and Italian concerns up through the first century B.C.—even if unintentional on Livy's part—demonstrates that Annius' aims were not necessarily a dead letter. Rather, they speak to Italian allies' recurring dismay over the Romans' heavy-handed treatment. Furthermore, they resonate with criticisms of Rome ventured in late Republican history—a period Livy himself deemed distinctly inferior to the remote Roman past (*Praef.* 11–12).

It may prove instructive to note that in this episode Livy treats Annius—an Italian from Setia—much like an unenlightened barbarian. Annius, after all, impiously scoffs at the power of Capitoline Jupiter, and straightaway pays the price for his anti-Roman transgression. Livy, moreover, has the consul Torquatus ridicule the idea of accepting peace terms from such a bumpkin (8.5.7). In the course of his first address pertaining to the matter, Torquatus specifically links Annius' requests with unwanted and unbecoming "alien" influence on Roman policy:

> Et conversus ad simulacrum Iovis, 'audi, Iuppiter, haec scelera' inquit; 'audite, Ius Fasque. Peregrinos consules et peregrinum senatum in tuo, Iuppiter, augurato templo captus atque ipse oppressus visurus es?' (8.5.8)

> And, turning to Jupiter's statue he [Torquatus] says: "Listen, Jupiter, to these wicked words; listen, Law and Right. Jupiter, can it be that you will be captured, enslaved, and passively behold foreign consuls and a foreign Senate in your consecrated temple?"

At this early date in Republican history, Livy's hometown of Patavium was not even close to becoming Rome's subject.[108] If we are to believe that Livy considered Torquatus' stance impregnable, we must also recognize that he countenanced the consul's xenophobic castigation of his Italian ancestors. The implicit likening of Livy's forebears to barbarians does not appear to trouble the historian. All in all, the addresses of Annius and Torquatus should allow us to conclude that Livy, though by no means a disparager of Republican valor or awash in nostalgia for the Latin League, is capable of presenting earnest critiques of Roman foreign policy.

The same appears to hold true with regard to a speech Livy assigns to an unnamed Macedonian ambassador at a meeting of the Aetolian League in the spring of 199 B.C. (31.29.1–16), against which he counterposes both an Athenian (31.30) and a Roman retort (31.31).[109] In the course of this address, Livy's Macedonian delegate presents criticisms of specific instances of Roman foreign policy. For example, he claims:

> (6) Messanae ut auxilio essent, primo in Siciliam transcenderunt; iterum, ut Syracusas oppressas ab Carthaginiensibus in libertatem eximerent; (7) et Messanam et Syracusas et totam Siciliam ipsi habent vectigalemque provinciam securibus et fascibus subiecerunt. (8) Scilicet sicut vos Naupacti legibus vestris magistratus a vobis creatos concilium habetis, socium hostemque libere quem velitis lecturi, pacem ac bellum arbitrio habituri vestro, sic Siculorum civitatibus Syracusas aut Messanam aut Lilybaeum indicitur concilium: — praetor Romanus conventus agit; (9) eo imperio evocati conveniunt; excelso in suggestu superba iura reddentem, stipatum lictoribus vident; virgae tergo, secures cervicibus imminent; et quotannis alium atque alium dominum sortiuntur. (31.29.6–9)[110]

> (6) At first they crossed into Sicily to be an aid to Messana; the second time to restore the Syracusans, subjected by the Carthaginians, to liberty. (7) They themselves hold both Messana and Syracuse and all Sicily, and have submitted them—their commission and revenue—to their axes and rods. (8) Of course, just as you have a council at Naupactus that follows your laws, with magistrates chosen by you, to select freely allies and enemies as you see fit, and to be at peace or at war according to your decision, thus a council of Sicilian cities is summoned to Syracuse, or Messana, or Lilybaeum:—a Roman praetor presides over these assemblies; (9) summoned by his authority they gather; they see him bestowing arrogant laws from his lofty platform, surrounded by lictors; rods threaten their backs, axes threaten their necks; and annually they draw lots for one master after another.

This serves as a vivid rebuke to Roman pretensions to engaging in warfare on justifiable grounds. It offers a clear—albeit disingenuous—juxtaposition between Greek freedom and the sham democracies of local communities living under Roman control. Livy's Macedonian ambassador highlights the Roman entry into the First Punic War—likely a sore spot for those defending Roman foreign policy, given the Mamertines' dubiousness.

Even so, it must be admitted that the context in which these remarks appear drastically undercuts their effectiveness. In the course of their *oratio obliqua* response, the Athenians call into question the Macedonian monarch's magnanimity (31.30.1–11), on which his delegate had harped (31.29.13). Additionally, Livy's Roman ambassador then provides a point-by-point refutation of the Macedonians' charges. At this speech's conclusion, Livy informs us that the Aetolian League leaned in favor of the Roman side (31.32.1)—a clear sign that he had fashioned a powerful retort to Philip V's contentions.

All the same, one major point in the Roman delegate's response potentially undercuts his argument. As an example of Rome's comparatively altruistic foreign policy, Livy's Roman ambassador says:

> (15) Sed quid ego Capuam dico, cum Carthagini victae pacem ac libertatem dederimus? (16) Magis illud est periculum, ne nimis facile victis ignoscendo plures ob id ipsum ad experiundam adversus nos fortunam belli incitemus. (31.31.15–16)

> (15) But why am I speaking about Capua, when we have bestowed peace and freedom upon conquered Carthage? (16) There is a greater danger that, by forgiving the vanquished too readily, we may encourage more people to try their fortune in war against us.

This might have amounted to a powerful retort at this assembly in 199 B.C., though its rosy claim about Carthaginian "peace" and "liberty" in the aftermath of the Second Punic War could have rung hollow.[111] To Livy's ancient readership, however, given Rome's ultimate destruction of Carthage in 146 B.C., this contention—a key point in the Roman ambassador's arsenal—must have seemed quite weak. One might even wonder whether it was ironically intended. Overall, then, even in this example, in which a Roman response appears to get the better of Macedonian complaints, we are left with questions about Rome's righteousness in her foreign affairs.

## CONCLUSIONS

Our examination of Livy's pre-Ticinus and pre-Zama addresses—combined with a few other examples of anti-Roman orations in *Ab urbe condita*—demonstrates that Livy was quite interested in offering a range of τόποι in his speeches. This is in marked contrast to Polybius, who tended to favor monochromatic orations. Most assuredly, this must be related to Livy's concern for composing artful harangues that follow ancient rhetorical precepts. In all the speeches we have discussed, one can detect Livian enthusiasm for presenting the reader with various purple passages.

Still, we can note other differences between Livy's and Polybius' Hannibalic addresses—differences more germane for our purposes. Whereas

Polybius' speeches (as we saw in chapter 3) tend to be very light on moral and ethical content, Livy's addition of new τόποι addresses distinctly moral concerns—concerns that often focus on the good or ill of Roman imperialism and colonialism. We have seen that such sentiments are not confined to Livy's Hannibalic orations, but appear in other enemy speeches as well. Thus, it appears as if Livy desired both to demonstrate his rhetorical prowess and to craft harangues that are less singularly focused than those of Polybius. In fact, one can occasionally detect a pell-mell cast to Livy's enemy orations, as if Livy tried to supply his speakers with a full panoply of arguments. This penchant on Livy's part allows the possibility for far more moral criticism of Rome to creep into his speeches in general. And these are not the sorts of arguments one would expect to discover in the work of the supposedly ultra-patriotic Livy. Perhaps Livy's attachment to the lost cause of Pompey—though Augustus supposedly found it unthreatening (Tac. *Ann.* 4.34)—drove him to present such sentiments.

Yet we must admit that our examination of some enemy orations in Livy's work leaves us with complicated and, to some extent, contradictory assessments of Livy's treatment of imperialism and colonialism. In fact, Livy's various addresses present an assortment of views, some of which appear ambiguous. Different orators in Livy's work proffer disparate opinions about the nature of expansionism—and, in the case of Livy's Hannibal, one speaker's take on this subject changes over the course of the Second Punic War. Hence it remains difficult to offer clear-cut conclusions about Livy's portrait of ancient imperialism, since his characters' thoughts are so diverse and (at times) antipathetic.

In a few of the speeches we have discussed, Livy seems to portray conquest as both a great boon to the victor and a calamity for the vanquished. For instance, in his oration before the Battle of Ticinus, Livy's P. Scipio boasts about previous Punic defeats at the hands of the Romans, the tribute Rome exacted from Carthage, and the colonization of Sicily and Sardinia as spoils of war (21.40.5). The Roman general presents this as the natural course of events for the successful conqueror. As we have seen, P. Scipio even equates the Carthaginians with slaves (21.40.10). Further, Livy's P. Scipio displays a patronizing attitude toward Rome's colonial subjects: according to him, the Romans could have utterly destroyed Carthage in the First Punic War, but magnanimously chose to take on the role of its guardian instead (21.41.11–12). As far as Scipio sees it, Roman colonial maltreatment of the Carthaginians may be to some extent excusable, if not appropriate, since Carthage ought to have demonstrated gratitude toward Rome for being spared in the first place. At times Hannibal's pre-Ticinus response appears equally engaged in imperial apologetics. Livy's Hannibal, after all, hoped to turn Carthage into a new Rome, seizing Rome's former territories upon its collapse (21.43.6). This suggests a bellicose approach to foreign affairs, but it is unclear whether Livy aimed to criticize such a stance by putting these views in the mouths of two ultimately unsuccessful generals.

Regardless, these pugnacious sentiments seem compatible with the Polybian notions of Realpolitik we encountered in the previous chapter. In places Livy's counterpoised addresses make it appear as if powerful states clamor for the same prize—empire—and that impotent states complain about injustice merely because they are weaker. This renders greed for riches pandemic and further serves to make all peoples appear similarly motivated. Importantly, such a position questions Roman pretenses to engage in wars for morally appropriate reasons, since it portrays the drive for expansion as the natural result of omnipresent avarice and lust for power.

All the same, in Livy's speeches one can find strikingly different assessments of imperialism and colonialism. In the pre-Zama colloquy, for instance, Livy's Hannibal proves far more critical of expansionism tout court (30.30.6–8). In fact, the Carthaginian general offers a negative appraisal of imperialism, as if he has learned his lesson about the inescapable horrors of unbridled pugnacity for both sides in a conflict. In portions of their speeches, furthermore, Livy's Roman generals also appear concerned with matters of propriety in foreign affairs. P. Scipio, though he takes pride in Roman colonialism, still makes a point of asserting that Rome was the just party in its wars with Carthage (21.41.11–13). In his pre-Zama address, Livy's Scipio Africanus also stresses Rome's purportedly fair-minded dealings with the Carthaginians (30.31.4–5). Despite these protestations on behalf of an ethical approach to foreign policy, one still wonders precisely what Livy's Scipio Africanus means when he claims that it was the Romans *qui et illius belli exitum secundum ius fasque dederunt et huius dant et dabunt* ("who gave a favorable, just, and lawful end to the former war [the First Punic War], and give and will give one to the latter one"; 30.31.5). With such incongruous sentiments strewn throughout Livy's speeches, it seems impossible to tell.

In regard to Livy's view of the Carthaginians in the pre-Ticinus and pre-Zama addresses, we stand on firmer ground. One does not see many examples in these orations of Livy presenting a stereotypical portrayal of a Carthaginian leader.[112] In fact, the complaints Livy's generals present in their speeches seem somewhat interchangeable. The closest approximation of anti-Carthaginian bias in the orations themselves is surely Hannibal's pre-Zama reference to *Punicam fidem* ("Punic trustworthiness"; 30.30.27), a loaded term having negative associations pertaining to supposed Carthaginian treachery.[113] Yet even this phrase, uttered as it is by Livy's Hannibal, does not amount to much. Scipio Africanus' pre-Zama oration homes in on perceived Punic perfidy, but, as we have noted, Pontius' address makes much of Roman faithlessness. In fact, we have seen sufficient evidence of foreigners harping on Roman deception in the enemy orations of Sallust, Trogus, and Livy to suggest that members of the Roman elite worried that treachery was a trait barbarians assigned to them. Additionally, in his speech of Torquatus, Livy may have even proved critical of Roman xenophobia, since the objects of Torquatus' prejudice were Livy's fellow Italians.

Still, we have no reason to suppose that Livy aimed to use his pre-Ticinus and pre-Zama orations to present an idealized portrait of either Hannibal or the Carthaginian people. Rather, one can point to some incongruities in Livy's depiction of Hannibal in these speeches. Livy's P. Scipio views the Carthaginian general as both an able adversary (21.41.2) and a feeble tyro (21.41.8). This bifurcation, typical of Roman discourses on foreigners,[114] demonstrates the possibility that Livy was chiefly focused on Rome's actions and missteps. For this reason, perhaps, Hannibal's harangue to his troops before the Battle of Ticinus, in keeping with Greco-Roman stereotypes of Westerners,[115] portrays the peoples of Spain and Gaul as ferocious (21.43.13–14), despite the fact that many of Hannibal's soldiers must have been mercenaries from the West themselves. All in all, though, Livy's Hannibalic and Scipionic speeches do not seem devoted to offering a demeaning take on the Carthaginian people. This is striking, since, as we have detected, in his narrative Livy expends much energy castigating Hannibal and the Carthaginians for their "Punic" traits.

It is undeniable that Livy paints Hannibal in a less flattering light overall in his account of the Second Punic War than does Polybius. We have also discovered reasons to gainsay the power of other enemy orations appearing in Livy's oeuvre. Polybius, moreover, neither demonizes Hannibal nor valorizes his enemies in the pre-Ticinus and pre-Zama speeches. But this does not suggest that Livy was incapable of sympathy for Hannibal, even though he also proved quite critical of him in places. Nor was Livy unable to fashion at least mildly persuasive addresses to be delivered by other enemies of Rome. It is striking that Livy crafted Hannibalic speeches—before both the Battle of Ticinus and the Battle of Zama—that are in many ways more appealing, and in some ways more powerful than the corresponding orations in Polybius' history. We can see that Livy sometimes allowed his role as a master orator to trump his regard for presenting readers with patriotic sentiments. This exponent of the Roman annalistic tradition, though assuredly no maligner of Rome, was hardly an uncritical jingoist.

Does the same conclusion hold true for other historians of the Imperial period? In the next two chapters we shall turn to an examination of Tacitus' and Cassius Dio's Boudica orations in order to answer this and kindred questions.

Scholars have often viewed the numerous speeches Tacitus put in the mouths of Rome's enemies—for instance, those of Calgacus (*Ag.* 30–32), Civilis (*Hist.* 4.14.2–4, 17.2–6), Arminius (*Ann.* 1.59), Boiocalus (*Ann.* 13.55–56), and Boudica[1] (*Ann.* 14.35)—as a collective example of his merits as a historian.[2] According to Ronald Syme, for example, such orations serve as proof that "[n]o other writer reveals so sharply the double face of Roman rule [as does Tacitus]."[3] Likely of Italian extraction,[4] Tacitus, think critics such as Syme, had the requisite critical faculties to expatiate on his own society's shortcomings.

This perception of Tacitus as capable of censuring Rome also conforms to a conventional picture of his speeches: that they generally clarify a historical situation and/or offer a detailed picture of the character that is speaking.[5] Tacitus did not, that is to say, compose orations merely to demonstrate his rhetorical prowess. Overall, these views seem divorced from an assessment of Tacitus as "anti-Roman" in his outlook. Modern historians tend to believe that Tacitus' inclination to provide Roman enemies with powerful, compelling speeches demonstrates his critical cast of mind—one that is requisite for a "good" historian.

This does not appear to be the consensus in regard to the history of L.(?) Claudius(?) Cassius Dio.[6] On the contrary, Cassius Dio is often seen as essentially uncritical of Rome. This perception is not necessarily the result of Dio's purported allegiance to Rome,[7] but rather arises because he is supposedly a "bad" historian—a fundamentally naïve writer. Accordingly, the conventional view of Dio's speeches, unlike those of Tacitus, is that they are mere rhetorical showpieces, replete with quasi-philosophical platitudes and oratorical boilerplate.[8] In part for this reason, it seems, comparatively little attention has been paid to Dio's view of Roman rule. The degree to which Dio was attuned to the sins of Roman expansionism and colonialism appears to be a subject of less interest.

In the following two chapters, however, we shall question these views by means of a case study: the Boudica orations found in the works of Tacitus (*Ann.* 14.35) and Cassius Dio (62.3-6).[9] Through an examination of these compositions—as well as others written by these two historians—we shall discover that Dio's speeches do not in fact prove less critical of Rome than Tacitus' versions. In regard to their respective Boudica orations, Dio and Tacitus employ different strategies by which to highlight Roman maladministration in Britain. Both historians' accounts of Boudica's rebellion contain a mixture of anti-imperialist and pro-Roman sentiments.

Modern readers on the whole seem more convinced of the power of Tacitus' Boudica oration in large part because they have (incorrectly) associated concise writing with stronger arguments. Our contemporary aesthetic sensibilities perceive Tacitus as having crafted a superior Boudica speech.[10] But this does not imply that his version of the harangue presents a more cogent critique of Roman rule. On the contrary: these two authors offer impressions of Roman colonialism that are both jingoistic and censorious. Their respective speeches also give us clues as to Tacitus' and Dio's perceptions of barbarians, colonial maladministration, Roman bellicosity, and other matters pertaining to imperial expansion.

## TACITUS ON BOUDICA'S REBELLION

In either A.D. 60 or 61, Boudica, the widow of Prasutagus, the recently deceased client king of the Celtic Iceni tribe, led an unsuccessful revolt against Rome.[1] We possess only three narratives of this rebellion, two by the same author.[2] Tacitus presents an extremely terse account of the revolt in *Agricola* 14.3–16.2, and a longer, yet still concise, version in *Annales* 14.29–39. As we shall discuss at length in the next chapter, Cassius Dio provides a discussion of the revolt in 62.1–2, which has come down to us from antiquity only in the form of Xiphilinus' epitome of Dio's history.[3] Unfortunately, Tacitus and Dio do not agree on major details pertaining to the revolt, which renders our understanding of it shaky.[4]

Tacitus first presented a description of Boudica's rebellion in the *Agricola*. Since the revolt merely served as background information regarding the history of Britain prior to Agricola's governorship, he discusses the uprising only very briefly. Although Tacitus does not firmly date the rebellion, he notes that it occurred while Suetonius Paulinus, then governor of Britain, was attacking the island of Mona (modern Anglesey) (14.3). Tacitus does not mention that the principal tribe to rebel from Rome was the Iceni,[5] and does not discuss any specific causes for the revolt.

With their governor elsewhere, Tacitus informs us, the Britons began to discuss the *mala servitutis* ("evils of slavery") and foment discontent (15.1). Right from the start of his description of the uprising, Tacitus mentions a theme typical of his sentiments on the Roman Empire in general: *servitium* ("slavery") versus *libertas* ("freedom").[6] This is a sign, perhaps, that the rebellion is an object of special interest to him. Tacitus then relates, in *oratio obliqua*, the various musings of unnamed disgruntled Britons (15). Nowadays, they assert, we possess two kings—a governor and a procurator (15.2). Both of these men and their henchmen, they continue, are insatiably greedy and lusty. In a powerful and memorable sentence, they claim, *Nihil iam cupiditati, nihil libidini exceptum* ("They take part in every conceivable act of avarice and lust"). Interestingly, this remark appears similar to the contention Sallust advanced in the *EM*: Roman greed knows no bounds.[7]

The anonymous Britons offer further complaints. The Romans in Britain—cowards all—go to great lengths to plunder from them. In fact, these men were prepared to die for anything, save their country (15.3). This criticism, we should note, fits well with Tacitus' longing for the "good old days" of Republican Rome, when statesmen and officials would supposedly sacrifice all in service to the state. It also serves as a counterpoise to the behavior of Agricola, whose upstanding conduct is a reminder of an earlier and better time. One gets the sense, then, that Tacitus presents the Britons' protestations in a manner that fortifies some of his own complaints about contemporary Rome. The unnamed Britons then offer a cursory exhortation to battle, arguing that the Roman soldiers in Britain are few, thanks to Paulinus' endeavors on Mona (15.3). Britons fight for their countries, wives, and parents; the Romans, they aver, fight for *avaritiam et luxuriam* ("greed and luxury"; 15.4). The speech concludes with a paean to the Britons' courage and the assertion that the gods are on their side (15.4–5).

After offering this oration, Tacitus proceeds to discuss the outcome of the revolt. Under the leadership of a woman of royal stock named Boudica, he says, all Britain erupted in a revolt (16.1). Pursuing and capturing various Roman soldiers, these Britons eventually invaded the Roman colony of Camulodunum (modern Colchester), exacting horrible punishments on their victims. As a result, Tacitus explains, Paulinus returned from Mona and restored order after one battle (16.2). This ends Tacitus' discussion of the uprising—a discussion markedly bereft of political and military details. The reader may be left with the impression, however, that Tacitus had an interest in likening the Britons' criticism of Roman colonialism to his own concerns about failings of the Roman Empire.

Tacitus' other description of the revolt (*Ann.* 14.29–39) is a bit more thorough. After introducing the revolt with a reference to the consular year A.D. 61 (*Caesennio Paeto et Petronio Turpiliano consulibus*, "With Caesennius Paetus and Petronius Turpilianus consuls"; 14.29.1), Tacitus mentions that it occurred under the governorship of Suetonius Paulinus, whom he lauds as the military rival of Corbulo (14.29.2).[8] As a result (*igitur*), Tacitus informs us, Paulinus prepared to attack Mona, which was serving as a safe-haven for refugees (14.29.3). He next discusses Paulinus' venture on the island of Mona, focusing particular attention on the Druidic appearance of the natives there (14.30.1).[9] According to Tacitus, Paulinus exhorted his soldiers not to fear such a *muliebre et fanaticum agmen* ("feminine and fanatical herd"; 14.30.2).

As Paulinus was managing affairs on Mona, he was informed of the sudden revolt of his province (14.30.3).

It is curious, to say the least, that Tacitus does not tell us why Paulinus, an ostensibly competent governor and commander, had no inkling of the impending rebellion and was caught entirely off guard.[10] Perhaps this relates to the account's favoritism regarding Paulinus—a favoritism that appears to cause some discrepancies between this narrative and Tacitus' earlier version in the *Agricola*.[11] If this is so, we should not be surprised that Tacitus ignored this matter, preferring to view Paulinus' attention to Mona as befitting the actions of a great commander (14.29.2–3).

Tacitus next discusses affairs among the Iceni—the Celtic tribe chiefly responsible for the uprising. Their late ruler, Prasutagus, a client king of Rome, left his inheritance to his two daughters and the emperor Nero, presumably as a way to protect his descendants (14.31.1).[12] The results of this action were precisely the opposite: upon his death, Roman centurions pillaged his realm; slaves laid waste to his household; his wife Boudica was whipped; and his daughters were raped. In addition to the maltreatment of Prasutagus' family, Tacitus informs us that the *praecipui* ("chief men") among the Iceni had their ancestral estates confiscated. As a result of these actions, Tacitus informs us, Boudica led a revolt against Rome, inciting the Trinovantes and other tribes to join them (14.31.2).[13] As he had in his account of the uprising in the *Agricola*, Tacitus casts the rebellion as the result of the natives' desire for *libertas* ("freedom") as opposed to *servitium* ("slavery").[14] Tacitus does not claim that the seizing of the king's and nobles' property was technically illegal. There is a reason for this: agreements between the government of Rome and client kings only pertained to the ruler himself; once he died, all previous arrangements were null and void.[15] Still, Tacitus' discussion of events appears aimed at eliciting sympathy for the Iceni and, more specifically, for Prasutagus' family.

The rebels' first target was, naturally, Camulodunum, the seat of Roman power in Britain (14.31.3–4). The colonists who inhabited this city, Tacitus tells us, had mistreated the natives, and thus its temple of Claudius was a beacon of contempt for the Britons. After relating a series of omens that presumably forecast the trouble to come (14.32.1), Tacitus informs us that an appeal for protection was made to Decianus Catus, the procurator of Britain, since Paulinus was far off on the island of Mona (14.32.2). Catus seems to have had nowhere near the requisite number of soldiers at his disposal for the task, and thus Camulodunum was destroyed (14.31.2–3). Tacitus demonstrates particular scorn for Catus, who crossed the English Channel to Gaul in order to remain safe from the rebelling Britons. In fact, Tacitus claims that Catus was responsible for the uprising in toto, though he does not offer any details to explain why this might be so (14.32.3).[16] The rebels also defeated the Roman commander Petilius Cerialis, who had led the ninth legion to what he had hoped would amount to the rescue of the colony.

Tacitus next discusses the actions of Paulinus, which he clearly offers as a counterpoise to the cowardly incompetence of Catus (14.33.1). Paulinus marched straight to London, but soon recognized that his troops would be unable to save the city. Undeterred by the inhabitants' protestations, Paulinus abandoned London, which was sacked, along with the *municipium* of Verulamium. At this point, according to Tacitus, Paulinus readied his soldiers and prepared to fight a pitched battle (14.34.1). Whereas Paulinus expertly arranged his men for the combat, the Britons, overconfident, moved about in a desultory fashion, eagerly anticipating the struggle. Tacitus here introduces a theme that resurfaces in his speeches of Boudica and Paulinus—the contrast between the professional orderliness of the Roman troops and the Britons' undisciplined bravado.

The description of the rebels' arrogant jubilation leads Tacitus to introduce Boudica, the ostensible leader of the revolt (14.35.1).[17] Here, before what would amount to the final battle between the Roman forces and the Britons,[18] Tacitus has Boudica deliver her speech (14.35) in *oratio obliqua*, which we shall discuss at length below. Directly thereafter, Tacitus has Paulinus address his own troops (14.36.1-2). He then describes the Roman victory, offering scarcely believable casualty figures (14.37.1-2).[19] Boudica, Tacitus informs us, committed suicide by taking poison, thus ending the revolt (14.37.3).

Overall, it is safe to conclude that Tacitus' account of the rebellion, though demonstrating obvious respect for Paulinus and his abilities as a commander, is at least partially sympathetic to the cause of the rebels. Over the course of the narrative, Tacitus does not enlarge on Roman injustices in Britain. Rather, he mentions the excesses of the Roman government quickly, without offering too many details—save those directly related to Boudica and her daughters. Still, Tacitus employs the highly charged vocabulary of *libertas* and *servitium*—key concerns in his historical writing. Moreover, Tacitus places at least partial responsibility for the revolt on Decianus Catus, the procurator of Britain.

## A GENUINE SPEECH?

Before turning to Tacitus' Boudica speech itself, we should quickly address the possibility that this composition reflects actual sentiments the rebel leader presented to her troops. Just as is the case with the speeches of many other ancient historians, unfortunately, there is no consensus regarding the historicity of Tacitus' orations.[20] As to the Boudica exhortation, however, the matter is more straightforward. As we have noted previously, there are numerous reasons to doubt that Tacitus would have—or could have—presented an accurate reflection of Boudica's address to her troops. In order for Tacitus' Boudica speech to reflect what was actually said, a Roman sufficiently fluent in Celtic would have had to be present during the harangue to inform one of Tacitus' sources about what was uttered. It does not seem cavalier to rule out this possibility.

In this context, we need not preoccupy ourselves with Tacitean *Quellenforschung*. Simply put, we do not possess sufficient evidence regarding the potential literary sources for Tacitus to allow us to label them with any real authority.[21] If Tacitus did use Suetonius Paulinus' memoirs and Paulinus discussed his activities in Britain in this work, we may have reason to suppose that Tacitus' version of this Roman general's retort (which we shall discuss anon) corresponds roughly to reality.[22] But, as we shall see in this and the next chapter, Tacitus and Dio offer such disparate versions of both the Boudica and Paulinus orations that it seems far-fetched to believe that either historian aimed to offer an accurate account of the speeches.[23]

## "THEY DO NOT EVEN LEAVE BODIES, OLD AGE, OR MAIDENHOOD UNSOILED": TACITUS' BOUDICA ORATION

With all this in mind, we can move on to Tacitus' terse Boudica oration. The speech, which is in *oratio obliqua*, commences with Boudica on a chariot with her daughters in front of her assembled troops:

> Boudicca curru filias prae se vehens, ut quamque nationem accesserat, solitum quidem Britannis feminarum ductu bellare testabatur, sed tunc non ut tantis maioribus ortam regnum et opes, verum ut unam e vulgo libertatem amissam, confectum verberibus corpus, contrectatam filiarum pudicitiam ulcisci. Eo provectas Romanorum cupidines, ut non corpora, ne senectam quidem aut virginitatem impollutam relinquant. (*Ann.* 14.35.1)

> Boudica, riding in a chariot with her daughters before her, said as she approached each tribe that it was customary for the Britons to wage war under the leadership of women; but then, she said, she was avenging not her kingdom and her power as a woman born from noble ancestors, but rather her lost freedom, her body worn out by whips, and the defiled chastity of

her daughters as one of the people. The rapaciousness of the Romans had advanced so far, she said, that they do not even leave bodies, old age, or maidenhood unsoiled.

She first argues that it is customary for the Britons to fight under female commanders (14.35.1). There is already reason to doubt the historicity of the oration: the Britons would be well aware of what was customary for their people, and thus the sentiment seems to be aimed at Tacitus' readership, not an imagined audience of Britons.[24] The remark, furthermore, makes little sense in light of a comment that Tacitus has the Caledonian rebel Calgacus offer in the *Agricola* (31.4). Calgacus, in order to stir up his troops, refers to the prior fortunes of the Britons under an unnamed female commander (clearly either Boudica or Cartimandua);[25] the Britons, he claims, even fared well against the Romans when led by a woman. It is likely that Tacitus began his Boudica oration in this manner in order to highlight both Boudica's gender and the foreignness of the Britons, who—unlike the Romans—would engage in battle under female leadership.[26]

The start of Boudica's oration also offers sentiments similar to those found in Calgacus' harangue. Both focus on the gender of the Britons' commanders. Calgacus' speech also mentions the Romans' sexual defilement of Celtic women,[27] just as Tacitus discussed the rape of Boudica's daughters in the lead-up to the Boudica oration (14.31.3) and in the oration itself (14.35.1). In both cases, Tacitus appears interested in concentrating on the oppression of the Britons through the metaphor of sexual misconduct.[28]

Tacitus' Boudica turns to her next argument. She does not, she claims, act in the capacity of a ruler, but of a woman of her people, since her freedom has been lost, her body whipped, and her daughters raped (14.35.1). The speech continues to discuss Roman imperial injustices through the lens of gender, restating the charges of abuse Tacitus presented in the narrative of the rebellion itself. In addition to focusing on the gender of the speaker, the remark also allows Boudica to downplay her noble stature, and potentially makes her argument more compelling to readers. Boudica does not act like a haughty, foreign queen, but like an outraged woman.[29] This highlights something noticed by other scholars examining this oration: Tacitus in some ways turns Boudica into a wronged Roman matron.[30] He does not, that is to say, always transform Boudica into the "Other"; rather, he views her in part as a slightly idealized Roman woman.

Boudica's focus on the sexual mistreatment of her daughters offers another potential link between foreign and Roman women. Elsewhere in the Roman historiographical tradition, rape looms large as an event that validates an uprising. Famously, Sex. Tarquinius' rape of Lucretia hastens the demise of the kingship, serving as a catalyst for the anti-monarchical rebellion led by Brutus and Collatinus.[31] To be sure, the parallel is not perfect—Boudica is not personally the victim of sexual violence, and she certainly does not respond in the same fashion as that attributed to Lucretia. Still, it is interesting to note that this historical connection serves both to "Romanize" Boudica and to present a justification for the rebellion somewhat akin to Rome's impetus for the expulsion of a "foreign" monarchy.

Boudica then turns to a complaint regarding Roman misrule in Britain. The Romans' avarice has become so all-encompassing, she claims, that their very bodies are not free from it (14.35.1). By means of this comment, Boudica fashions her familial suffering at the hands of the Romans into a more general argument concerning the provincial misconduct of an imperial power. The sentiment is somewhat reminiscent of Sallust's powerful line in the *EM* that we encountered in chapter 1:

Namque Romanis cum nationibus populis regibus cunctis una et ea vetus causa bellandi est: cupido profunda imperi et divitiarum. (*EM* 5)

For the Romans there is a single age-old cause for instigating war on all nations, peoples, and kings: a deep-seated lust for empires and riches.

In both cases, greed—not concern for the justice of Roman actions—is presented as the motivating force behind Roman expansionism, and this avarice has lascivious overtones (*cupido profunda*, "a deep-seated lust"). Tacitus allows Boudica to expand what was originally fashioned as a personal grievance (i.e., the suffering of Boudica and her daughters) into a general argument concerning Roman provincial misrule.[32] It is a damning indictment—one that undercuts Roman claims to being the wronged party.

Boudica also refers to the earlier successes of the revolt, claiming that the gods were just in granting revenge on the Romans:

Adesse tamen deos iustae vindictae; cecidisse legionem, quae proelium ausa sit; ceteros castris occultari aut fugam circumspicere. Ne strepitum quidem et clamorem tot milium, nedum impetus et manus perlaturos. Si copias armatorum, si causas belli secum expenderent, vincendum illa acie vel cadendum esse. Id mulieri destinatum: viverent viri et servirent. (14.35.2)

Nevertheless, the gods of just revenge were present: a legion that dared battle had fallen; others hid in the camp or searched intently for an escape. She said that the Romans would not even be able to endure the roar and clamor of so many thousands, much less their fury and violence: if the

Britons considered the abundance of troops and the motives of the war, they would know that their battle line must either conquer or fall. That was the resolve of a woman: the men might live and be slaves.

One of their legions (that of Petilius Cerialis) has perished, she says, and the remaining Romans were hiding in their camp or searching for an escape (14.35.2). In offering this sentiment, Boudica shifts her focus to Roman military weakness and pusillanimity. Tacitus has now distanced Boudica from her previous role as a Roman matron; unlike the legendary Lucretia, Boudica, having suffered a wrong, exhorts her troops to continue with their uprising, which she characterizes as just (*iusta vindicta*). To be sure, it is possible that this criticism of supposed Roman cowardice is not the kind of sentiment that would elicit much sympathy in the hearts of many Romans. After all, later events demonstrate that Boudica's remarks are untrue: the Romans ultimately defeat the rebellion. Such an argument, however, could serve to highlight the tragic character of Boudica; even in the face of superior Roman military might, the Britons' leader rallies her army with optimistic, yet inaccurate, assessments of their foe.

In presenting this point, Tacitus' Boudica refers to the customs associated with the Britons' military endeavors. *Ne strepitum quidem et clamorem tot milium . . . perlaturos* ("They [the Romans] would not even be able to endure the roar and clamor of so many thousands"), Tacitus reports her as saying, offering an explicit mention of the Britons' war cry—the typical cacophonous fanfare that barbarians bring into battle (14.35.2). In this instance, Tacitus demonstrates that he has not fully "Romanized" Boudica: he has not merely reinvented her as a wronged Roman matron, but has cast her as part Roman, part Briton.[33] His is a complex portrayal of an enemy of Rome, which relies neither on an ahistorically Roman Boudica nor an "Otherized" barbarian.

This complexity of presentation can also be gleaned in Boudica's conclusion. The view she has presented, she says, is that of a woman, though men might live on as slaves (14.35.2).[34] By concluding in this manner, Tacitus appears to show little regard for verisimilitude: if females were in fact regular leaders of Celtic military expeditions, as Boudica claimed at the start of her oration (14.35.1), it is improbable that she would offer a conclusion that highlights the peculiarity of her role as a woman leading the rebellion. Yet Boudica's final remark allows Tacitus to return to the subject of the speaker's gender—the subject with which the oration commenced. And Tacitus has clearly offered this sentiment as mellifluously as possible: *viverent viri et servirent* ("the men might live and be slaves"). This conclusion also appears to offer a strikingly downcast view of the final battle on the part of the Iceni: it is as if

Boudica knows that she and her people are doomed to failure, and thus must elect death.

All in all, Tacitus' Boudica oration is a complex and compact excoriation of Roman imperialism. Notably, Tacitus refers to the gender of the speaker on more than one occasion and has Boudica offer a largely anecdotal response to Roman misrule. Although this may simply reflect how Tacitus envisioned a woman arguing, it is also possible that he has Boudica speak in this fashion in order to avoid the occurrence of another Calgacus-like oration.[35] At the time Tacitus wrote the *Annales*, oratorical complaints against Roman expansionism and colonialism were already fairly common occurrences in his work. In the *Agricola*, Tacitus has unnamed Britons discuss their grievances against Rome (15),[36] and has Calgacus offer a strong indictment of Roman misrule in Britain (30–32). In the *Historiae*, as we shall see below, the Batavian prince Civilis delivers two addresses against Roman misrule (4.14.2–4, 17.2–6). Most significantly, Tacitus neither demonizes Boudica nor presents a simplistic characterization of her. His Boudica is a hybrid—part maltreated Roman matron, part determined Celtic leader. This fits Tacitus' penchant for offering ambivalent descriptions of barbarian revolts in his histories, which, as Nancy Shumate has stressed, often focus on their leaders as bifurcated figures.[37] Their hybridity, perhaps, renders these barbarian enemies particularly potent threats to Roman imperial ideology.[38]

Even those elements of the speech that cast Boudica as a barbarian connect with themes Tacitus elsewhere casts as quintessentially Roman. The oration's appeal to the cardinal import of *libertas* ("freedom")[39] relates to Tacitus' discussion of the kinds of criticisms Thrasea Paetus and the senatorial Stoic resistance offered about the government of the Roman Empire.[40] Much like Thrasea, Boudica couches her appeal in the language of freedom versus slavery. At the very least, this suggests that Boudica's cause held a specific appeal for Tacitus.

## SUETONIUS PAULINUS' RETORT

Overall, we have reason to suggest that Tacitus' Boudica oration amounts to an impassioned attack on Roman foreign affairs. We are fortunate, in addition, to have a further opportunity to evaluate its strength—by examining Tacitus' speech of Suetonius Paulinus to his troops before the same battle (14.36.1–2), which was clearly intended as a counterpoise to Boudica's harangue. The power of this retort can speak to Tacitus' designs in crafting these orations. If it appears particularly compelling, it may serve to cancel out—or at least greatly diminish the effect of—Boudica's arguments. If it seems weak, it may reinforce her contentions.

The text begins as follows:

> Quamquam confideret virtuti, tamen exhortationes et preces miscebat, ut spernerent sonores barbarorum et inanes minas: plus illic feminarum quam iuventutis adspici. Imbelles inermes cessuros statim, ubi ferrum virtutemque vincentium totiens fusi agnovissent. (14.36.1)

> Although he [Paulinus] trusted his soldiers' courage, he nevertheless mixed exhortations and entreaties that they should scorn the clamor of the barbarians and their empty threats: in their ranks there were more women than young men to be seen. Unwarlike and unarmed, they would give up immediately when, so often routed, they recognized the iron and courage of the conquerors.

Tacitus implies that Paulinus was usually a taciturn character, but found the battle so important that even he could not remain silent. This already casts Paulinus as laconic and well mannered, in contrast to the noisy, raucous Britons. Fittingly, then, Tacitus has Paulinus first instruct his men to dismiss the barbarians' noise and menace (14.36.1). He next elaborates on this point, offering the reason they should deem their opponents' din meaningless: in the barbarian ranks, he claims (no doubt speciously), women outnumber men. In this way, Tacitus has Paulinus touch upon the gender-related themes that his Boudica presented.

Paulinus further calls the Britons unwarlike and unarmed; they are accustomed to defeat and will easily meet it again. Along with this disparagement of the Britons' valor, Paulinus also praises Roman courage. These are all essentially stock elements of a typical pre-battle exhortation: our side possesses more fortitude; our enemy is poorly equipped. The argument, moreover, sticks fairly close to the tenor of the other oration Tacitus puts in the mouth of Paulinus, which is found in the *Historiae* (2.32). In this instance, too, Paulinus delivers a tactical speech—one noticeably removed from the realm of moral justifications for Roman actions.

After explaining that it will be particularly glorious for such a small number of Roman troops to defeat a colossal horde of Britons, Paulinus then discusses tactical specifics:

> Etiam in multis legionibus paucos, qui proelia profligarent; gloriaeque eorum accessurum, quod modica manus universi exercitus famam adipiscerentur. Conferti tantum et pilis emissis post umbonibus et gladiis stragem

caedamque continuarent, praedae immemores: parta victoria cuncta ipsis
cessura. (14.36.2)

Even in many legions, he said, there are a few people who win battles; that
a small band would win the fame of an entire army would add to their glory.
Only let them cast their javelins from a tight formation and, indifferent
to plunder, carry on with the havoc and slaughter with shield-bosses and
swords: when they had won, everything would be theirs.

Keep your order close, he says. Discharge your javelins; use your swords; and
pile up their dead. Naturally this amounts to generic military information.
Paulinus then instructs his army to eschew plundering. All will be yours when
victory is attained, he avers. By presenting such a sentiment, in a way Tacitus'
Paulinus makes it appear as if Boudica was correct all along: the Romans intend—as they always have—to treat conquered peoples without any inkling
of regard. This sentiment, which serves as the speech's finale, hardly seems
as emphatic as Boudica's aforementioned conclusion. It merely amounts to
an appeal to soldiers to wait before despoiling the Britons. Paulinus' reasoning, moreover, remains essentially practical: the Roman troops can defeat the
rebels more easily if they are not distracted by plunder.

Overall, then, Tacitus' Paulinus oration does not seem particularly strong.[41]
Although it connects with a few issues Boudica directly addressed in her exhortation—the noise of the Britons and the gender of their commander—
it fails to answer any of Boudica's charges pertaining to Roman misrule. It
avoids a defense of the Romans and their empire, unlike, for example, that
offered in Cerialis' speech in the *Historiae* (4.73-74).[42] It does not argue,
furthermore, that the gods are on Rome's side, or that the Romans act with
justice. Instead it presents a workmanlike appeal to Roman valor and superior
military tactics. It highlights the "barbarian" qualities of the Britons, but fails
to do so at length, in a manner that might imply Rome's inclination to "civilize" these "savages." This does not mean that Tacitus aimed at vilifying Paulinus—or, more generally, the Romans—through such an appeal. Still, it fails
to amount to a compelling speech.

Tacitus could have used Paulinus' oration as an opportunity to refute (or
at least attempt to refute) the arguments his Boudica presents. This seems a
particularly glaring omission, since Paulinus' speech echoes some of the general themes in Boudica's harangue. Instead, he gave the Roman commander
an uninspired, generic retort. Perhaps this serves to reinforce the differences
between the emotional Boudica and the disciplined Paulinus. It also could
be faithful to Paulinus' character: his speech in the *Historiae* (2.32) appears

rather workmanlike, too. Either way, though, the challenges Boudica offers to Roman rule in the provinces go unmet.

## ECHOES OF BOUDICA?
## CIVILIS CONDEMNS COLONIALISM

Is the Boudica oration typical of Tacitus' discussions of Roman imperial mal-feasance? As we mentioned at the start of this chapter, Tacitus presents a fair number of enemy speeches in his historical works. These offer us the opportunity to determine whether sentiments in Tacitus' Boudica oration are echoed in other compositions critical of Rome in his oeuvre. If so, this could speak to Tacitus' personal attachment to the sorts of strictures found in these speeches. At the very least, they might imply that Tacitus had particular ways of censuring Roman imperialism and colonialism. It will prove useful, then, to turn to a few of these other "anti-Roman" orations in Tacitus' histories.

In the *Historiae*, Tacitus grants two speeches to the Batavian nobleman and Roman citizen C. Iulius Civilis, both of which appear in *oratio obliqua* (4.14.2–4, 17.2–6).[43] Having gathered his tribesmen in a sacred grove in order to persuade them to revolt from Roman control in A.D. 69,[44] Tacitus' Civilis says:

> (2) . . . neque enim societatem, ut olim, sed tamquam mancipia haberi. (3) Quando legatum, gravi quidem comitatu et superbo, cum imperio venire? Tradi se praefectis centurionibusque; quos ubi spoliis et sanguine expleverint, mutari, exquirique novos sinus et varia praedandi vocabula. Instare dilectum, quo liberi a parentibus, fratres a fratribus velut supremum dividantur. (4) Numquam magis adflictam rem Romanam nec aliud in hibernis quam praedam et senes: attollerent tantum oculos et inania legionum nomina ne pavescerent. At sibi robur peditum equitumque, consanguineos Germanos, Gallias idem cupientes. Ne Romanis quidem ingratum id bellum; cuius ambiguam fortunam Vespasiano imputaturos: victoriae rationem non reddi. (4.14.2–4)[45]

> (2) ". . . for we are not considered allies, as was previously the case, but as property: (3) when does even a legate, vested with authority, come, albeit with an oppressive and arrogant retinue?" He says that, "We are handed over to prefects and centurions. When we have filled up one group with spoils and blood, new men take their place and new purses and pretexts for plundering are discovered. A levy presses upon us according to which children are separated from their parents and brothers from brothers, just like death. (4) The Roman state has never been more distressed, and there

is nothing in their winter quarters except loot and old men: merely lift up your eyes and do not fear the hollow reputation of their legions. But at our disposal is the elite of foot soldiers and cavalry, our relatives the Germans, and the Gallic provinces, which desire what we desire. This war is not even unwelcome to the Romans; if its outcome is not clear, we shall argue that we undertook it on Vespasian's behalf, and no one expects a rationale for a victory."

Before the start of this speech, Tacitus mentions that the Romans enraged the Batavians in part through the sexual defilement of their children (4.14.1). Although Civilis does not refer to this detail in his speeches, we should recognize that it offers a link to other Tacitean orations put in the mouths of anti-Roman leaders. As we have already seen, Tacitus' Boudica excoriates the Romans for engaging in sexual aggression in Briton (14.35.1). Calgacus does the same (*Ag.* 31.1). Tacitus had a penchant, then, for viewing the excesses of Roman provincial administration through the lens of sexual misconduct. To Tacitus, both stemmed, it seems, from a species of unrestrained lust.[46]

According to Tacitus' Civilis, the Romans' rapacity is so rampant and unbridled that they treat the Batavians as property (*mancipia*)—as mere opportunities for slaughter and booty. And this maltreatment, Civilis contends, occurs repeatedly, since the rotation of troops allows various portions of the Roman army to get their fill of killing and plunder. Thus Civilis rouses his fellow Batavians not only by complaining about a levy, but also by emphasizing the Romans' provincial misconduct. On its own, conscription was a likely source of discontent.[47] Roman maladministration would only serve to make it worse. Civilis' remarks, then, dramatically remind the reader of the sort of mischief that could plague Rome's subordinates.

It must be admitted, however, that the oration seems less impressive when it turns to pragmatic and expedient matters. Civilis calls into question the effectiveness of Roman forces. This proved wrongheaded, given the ultimate failure of his revolt. Further, Tacitus' Civilis speech closes with an equivocation: if the rebellion becomes unsuccessful, the Batavians can claim that they undertook it on Vespasian's behalf. This serves to highlight Civilis' own duplicity; in reality, Tacitus informs us, Civilis decided to rebel from Roman rule because of Fonteius Capito's murder of his brother as well as Civilis' personal maltreatment at the hands of the Romans (4.13.1, 32.2), and he was determined to mask his revolt by pretending to be allied to Vespasian (4.13). Civilis, then, exploited his fellow Batavians' grievances, and Tacitus reminds the reader of this in the speech's conclusion.

Soon after presenting these words from Civilis, Tacitus grants the Batavian leader another *oratio obliqua* harangue. In between the two addresses, Tacitus stresses the (typically Germanic) disloyalty of Civilis and the Batavians, who gain a victory against the Romans through treachery (4.15–16). Even so, Tacitus tells us that those in the German and Gallic provinces deemed the Batavians and their co-conspirators *auctores libertatis* ("progenitors of freedom"; 4.17.1).[48] After their initial victory, with aid flowing in from various Germans and Gauls, Tacitus again has Civilis attack Rome's conduct:

> (2) Simul secretis sermonibus admonebat malorum, quae tot annis perpessi miseram servitutem falso pacem vocarent. Batavos, quamquam tributorum expertis, arma contra communes dominos cepisse; prima acie fusum victumque Romanum. Quid si Galliae iugum exuant? Quantum in Italia reliquum? Provinciarum sanguine provincias vinci. (3) Ne Vindicis aciem cogitarent: Batavo equite protritos Aeduos Avernosque; fuisse inter Verginii auxilia Belgas, vereque reputantibus Galliam suismet viribus concidisse. Nunc easdem omnium partes, addito, si quid militaris disciplinae in castris Romanorum viguerit; esse secum veteranas cohortes, quibus nuper Othonis legiones procuberint. (4) Servirent Syria Asiaque et suetus regibus Oriens: multos adhuc in Gallia vivere ante tributa genitos. Nuper certe caeso Quintilio Varo pulsam e Germania servitutem, nec Vitellium principem, sed Caesarem Augustum bello provocatum. (5) Libertatem natura etiam mutis animalibus datam, virtutem proprium hominum bonum; deos fortioribus adesse: proinde adriperent vacui occupatos, integri fessos. Dum alii Vespasianum, alii Vitellium foveant, patere locum adversus utrumque. (4.17.2–5)

> (2) At the same time, he [Civilis] was reminding them in private discussions of the evils that they had suffered for so many years, when they had falsely labeled their wretched slavery "peace." He said that the Batavians, although free from paying tribute, have taken up arms against their common masters; the Romans have been scattered and overcome in the first battle. He asked, "What if the Gallic provinces should take off the yoke? How many men remain in Italy? The provinces have been conquered through their own blood. (3) Do not contemplate Vindex's battle: the Aedui and Averni were crushed by the Batavian cavalry; Belgians were in Virginius' auxiliary cohorts, and those reckoning correctly know that Gaul was struck down by its own might. Now everyone is on the same side; moreover, we have grown stronger from the military discipline of the Roman camps. There are veteran cohorts with us to whom Otho's legions recently fell prostrate. (4) Let Syria, Asia, and the East—which is accustomed to kings—be slaves: many men still alive in Gaul were born before the advent of tribute. Recently, of

course, slavery was driven away from Germany with the murder of Quintilius Varus, and Caesar Augustus—not Vitellius—was the emperor challenged in war. (5) Nature has given freedom even to mute animals, but courage is the particular excellence of men. The gods assist those who are braver: accordingly, let us advance, the free against the beleaguered, the fresh against the exhausted. While some show favor to Vespasian and others to Vitellius, the way lies open to oppose them both."

These remarks contain a mixture of vigorous anti-Roman commentary and ineffective appeals to expedient military matters. As was the case with the Boudica oration, Civilis' speech introduces the theme of freedom and slavery. In fact, he offers a few elaborations on this idea: even animals possess freedom; men from the vigorous West ought to have liberty. Interestingly, Tacitus' Civilis contends that monarchy is the natural condition of Easterners. He presents, then, the same sort of associations between the East and kingship as Sallust's and Trogus' Mithridates proffers.[49] The continued focus on slavery and freedom demonstrates that Tacitus' Civilis oration depicts Roman imperialism—or any imperialism, perhaps—starkly. Conquerors qua conquerors treat the vanquished more roughly than chattel. It is worse than dehumanizing to be under the colonialist's yoke.

Despite these powerful sentiments, we must admit that much of this Civilis speech seems distinctly weaker than Tacitus' Boudica oration. Most importantly, perhaps, Civilis expounds on tactical matters that are unconnected to criticisms of Roman colonialism. His historical *exempla*, though attuned to the vicissitudes of the Roman West in the early Imperial period, do not pertain to Roman injustices in foreign affairs. Rather, they aim—speciously, as it turns out—to highlight Rome's purported martial weaknesses. The mention of the disaster of Varus of A.D. 9, for instance, would not compel many Roman readers to question their nation's provincial conduct. It would be more likely to provoke anger. Civilis' speech concludes, moreover, with a reference to the civil war of Vitellius and Vespasian. Through this conclusion, Tacitus may call to mind Civilis' duplicity: if his revolt proved unsuccessful, he hoped to take advantage of the situation in Rome to protect himself from harm (cf. *Hist.* 4.14.4).

Overall then, and despite their severe criticism of colonial servitude, these two Civilis speeches appear less potent than Boudica's harangue. Even so, this need not detract from the justice of Civilis' accusations. Although they do not present a consistent excoriation of Roman provincial misconduct, Civilis' speeches offer Tacitus an opportunity to ruminate on the possibilities of Roman imperial malfeasance and the plight of Rome's subjects. Tacitus may have had limited sympathy for Civilis' revolt—less sympathy, in fact, than he perhaps betrays in his discussion of the Boudica rebellion in the *Annales*—yet he still manages to use the speeches to question colonial malefactions that loom large in his other orations of Rome's enemies.

## MORE ECHOES OF BOUDICA? ARMINIUS ON COLONIALISM AS SLAVERY

The Civilis orations are not the only examples of Tacitus' tendencies in his speeches critical of Roman rule. Tacitus also granted an anti-Roman harangue to Arminius (*Ann.* 1.59), chieftain of the German Cherusci tribe and victor in the Battle of the Teutoburg Forest (A.D. 9).[50] The dramatic date for the oration is A.D. 15.[51]

Germanicus, having invaded northern Germany, captured Arminius' pregnant wife, Thusnelda, thanks to the efforts of her father, Segestes, a pro-Roman Cherusci chieftain and her husband's bitter enemy (1.57–58). Tacitus, portraying Arminius as a hotheaded and implacable foe of Rome, offers Arminius' response to these vicissitudes in *oratio obliqua*:[52]

> (2) Neque probris temperabat: egregium patrem, magnum imperatorem, fortem exercitum, quorum tot manus unam mulierculam avexerint. Sibi tres legiones, totidem legatos procubisse; (3) non enim se proditione neque adversus feminas gravidas, sed palam adversus armatos bellum tractare: cerni adhuc Germanorum in lucis signa Romana, quae dis patriis suspenderit. (4) Coleret Segestes victam ripam, redderet filio sacerdotium †hominum†: Germanos numquam satis excusaturos, quod inter Albim et Rhenum virgas et securis et togam viderint. (5) Aliis gentibus ignorantia imperii Romani inexperta esse supplicia, nescia tributa: quae quondo exuerint, inritusque discesserit ille inter numina dicatus Augustus, ille delectus Tiberius, ne imperitum adulescentulum, ne seditiosum exercitum pavescerent. (6) Si patriam parentes antiqua mallent, quam dominos et colonias novas, Arminium potius gloriae ac libertatis quam Segestem flagitiosae servitutis ducem sequerentur. (1.59.2–6)

> (2) And he [Arminius] was not moderate in his reproaches: "A distinguished father, a great commander, a brave army—their great powers have taken away a single little woman!" He said that three legions—and the same number of generals—had fallen before him. (3) For he openly, not through treachery, waged wars against armed men, not pregnant women. Roman standards could still be seen in the groves of the Germans—standards that he had hung up for their ancestral gods. (4) Let Segestes dwell on a con-

quered bank and surrender his son to a priesthood that worships men: the Germans would never forgive that completely, since they had seen the rods and the axes and the togas between the Elbe and the Rhine. (5) Other nations, ignorant of Roman rule, had not experienced her humiliations and did not know of tribute: since they had shaken off these things, and since Augustus, consecrated as a god, and his chosen Tiberius had left without any victory, may they not tremble at a callow youth, at a seditious army! (6) If they preferred their fatherland, parents, and ancient ways to masters and new colonies, let them follow the lead of Arminius to glory and freedom, rather than Segestes to shameful slavery!

Even before the start of this speech, Tacitus had highlighted the cardinal import of the situation in which Arminius found himself. His wife, we are told, was carried off (*rapta*) and his child—though unborn—was already subjected to slavery (*subiectus servitio*) (1.59). As was the case with the Tacitean orations of Boudica and Civilis, Arminius' complaints hinge on the notion that Rome's empire amounts to servitude for its vanquished subjects. In Arminius' exhortation, this sentiment remains the speaker's main focus— even though the chieftain of the Cherusci also points out perceived Roman military weakness. According to Arminius, in the speech's powerful conclusion, his fellow Germans should not join up with the traitorous Segestes, but fight valiantly for *libertas*. It is not surprising that this call to German freedom and autonomy roused not only the Cherusci but also their neighbors to repel Roman forces (1.60.1). In addition, we should mention that Tacitus speaks flatteringly of Arminius elsewhere in his narrative, deeming him the Germans' liberator (*Ann.* 2.88.2).[53]

All the same, it must be admitted that Tacitus' Arminius harangue seems less compelling than its corollary from Boudica. Although the German chieftain likens life as a Roman colonial subject to slavery, he presents little in the way of specific justifications for his contentions, save for a jibe at the expense of Imperial cult more appropriate to the perspective of a traditionalist Roman senator than an outraged tribal leader (1.59). In Arminius' eyes, the Germans were simply too manly to endure the disgraces of colonial control; their martial history with the Romans proved as much. Notably, Germanicus' capture of Thusnelda allowed Tacitus to view Arminius' resistance to Rome through the eyes of gender—much as the Iceni's female leadership offered Tacitus' Boudica the opportunity to cast her rebellion as a matter of masculine fortitude. Overall, Tacitus seems interested in exploiting gender matters when commenting on Roman imperialism.

We should note, additionally, that Arminius musters antipathy not only for Rome's exactions of tribute from conquered people, but also for its un-specified *supplicia* ("humiliations"; 1.59). Moreover, Tacitus concludes the speech with a rousing appeal to liberty, rather than continuing his focus on the military matters with which it begins. The speech revels in the highly charged language of *flagitiosa servitus* ("shameful slavery"), *domini* ("mas-ters"), and *libertas* ("freedom"). Though Tacitus' taunts about the disaster of Varus may have been more likely to incite Roman anger than self-reflection, his continued interest in casting expansionism as an extension of courage and fortitude could serve to highlight his nervousness about the plight of a deca-dent and demoralized Imperial Rome. This may not seem as compelling as the specific complaints against Roman misrule Tacitus' Boudica musters, but it is not toothless.

## CONCLUSIONS

Overall, Tacitus' speech of Boudica amounts to a withering indictment of Roman misrule in Britain. It is a pointed attack on Roman character: the oration asserts that Roman administrators, soldiers, and colonists have acted with unrestrained lust for riches. Though brief, the oration presents forceful examples of Roman malefactions, focused chiefly on the family of Boudica herself. Its concision renders it even more potent.[54] Tacitus' Boudica spends little time ridiculing the purported pusillanimity of the Roman military, pre-ferring to harp on the degenerate character of Rome's colonial administra-tion. Through her remarks, Boudica comes across as both a wronged Roman matron and a hyper-masculine Celtic chieftain. By highlighting the gender of the Britons' leader on multiple occasions during Boudica's short speech, Tacitus simultaneously treats both Britain *and* Rome as the "Other." As men-tioned above, Tacitus' account of the rebellion underscores the foreignness of the barbarians, who are sufficiently unaccustomed to Roman mores as to allow a woman to lead a military endeavor. Further, Boudica's focus on the Britons' lack of orderliness (14.35.2) perhaps emphasizes their supposed "femininity," since, as Shumate has stressed, the Romans perceived that self-control was a masculine trait.[55]

Yet the attention Tacitus grants to Boudica's gender also serves to associate then-contemporary Rome with effeteness, decadence, and servility. As the re-sult of Boudica's pugnacious rhetoric, Rome becomes a feminized, Oriental monarchy. Tacitus' Boudica links the Romans' greed to the sexual defilement of their colonial subjects (*Ann.* 14.35.1). This serves to make the Romans seem incapable of self-restraint—and thus, somewhat paradoxically, more "feminine" in the Romans' eyes. Although one detects in Tacitus' account of the Iceni revolt the typical Roman appraisal of supposedly "feminine" characteristics, his portrayal suggests that feminine associations are not merely the preserve of Rome's colonial subjects. Rather, the Roman Empire comes across as every bit as stereotypically feminine. To suppose that Tacitus only demonizes Britons through associations with femininity unduly simplifies Tacitus' use of gendered language in his Boudica oration.[56]

The downcast quality of the speech—which veritably forecasts a Roman victory and belies Boudica's bluster about Celtic military might—ennobles the Iceni, making it appear as if they, conscious of their fate, knowingly chose death over a life of subhuman conditions under the thumb of unscrupulous and louche masters. Interestingly, Tacitus' decision to grant speeches to figures well aware of Roman imperial malefactions by virtue of their personal histories allowed him to present numerous attacks on the perceived evils of Roman colonial machinations, rather than mere rousing calls to arms.[57] His Boudica speech offers just one potent example of such attacks.

Tacitus' emphasis on colonial maladministration may be part of a change in enemy addresses in Roman historiography. As we have detected in earlier chapters, Roman historians from the Republic and the age of Augustus tended to concentrate the brunt of their anti-Roman orations on discussions of Roman aggression and failure to engage in morally justifiable warfare. Yet Tacitus, in his corresponding speeches, instead stresses the malignancies of Roman colonial administration. Perhaps this signals a shift during the course of the Empire from historians' elaborations on "just wars" to their deliberations on the failures of Rome's colonial policies.

This is not entirely surprising: the Iceni rebellion, after all, occurred as the result of Roman maltreatment of a client kingdom, and Boudica is a more reasonable conduit for criticisms of Roman colonial malefactions than, say, Hannibal. Still, we have seen that Tacitus repeatedly gives voice to anti-Roman figures who chiefly home in on Roman colonial vices. It is possible that, as Roman expansion slowed during the course of the early Empire, historians' second thoughts about imperialism naturally began to surround colonial policy rather than fetial law.[58]

Even as the focus shifts to Roman colonialism, however, the portrait of Roman behavior remains substantively the same. Tacitus' Boudica and Civilis complain about the ways in which greed fomented hardships for Rome's subordinates, much like, say, Sallust's Mithridates argues that rapaciousness drives Roman expansionism. In the eyes of Tacitus' Civilis, Roman rule was so malignant that the Romans looked upon their subjects as mere property—

yet more objects to appease the Romans' insatiable lusts (*Hist.* 4.14.2). Accordingly, Tacitus describes Roman colonial control in much the same manner as earlier historians depicted Rome's entries into various conflicts.

In Tacitus' work, both Boudica (*Ann.* 14.35.1) and Civilis (*Hist.* 4.14.3) stress the ways in which Roman rule subverts its subjects' families. This may not prove striking in the case of Boudica, since Tacitus could have focused on such a topic as the result of his perceptions of likely female complaints. Yet his Civilis echoes these sentiments. All the same, however, Tacitus' Arminius seems to suggest that Roman colonialism was not necessarily more horrific than that of any other imperial power; thus he decries the paying of tribute whole cloth (*Ann.* 1.59). This offers the possibility that Tacitus, as much as he may have been interested in reflecting on the potential sins of Roman rule, was also intent on demonstrating the humiliations forced upon all subjects of conquest.

To be sure, Tacitus' portrayal of Boudica does not remain unmoored from Tacitus' senatorial preoccupations and outlook.[59] His Celtic leader seems unrealistically "Roman" in some of her traits. One also spies more than a hint of primitivism in Tacitus' representation of the Iceni as heroic and uncorrupted tribesmen aghast at the degenerate behavior of the Romans in their midst.[60] Although one might conclude that a society boasting a female leader was, to the Romans, naturally corrupted and degenerate, Tacitus' depiction of Boudica as manly instead serves to make the Britons seem like primitives. After all, even their women come across as rugged and hardy. This surely relates to a vision of the Britons as Noble Savages—tribesmen un-effeminized by the trappings of civilization.

Additionally, anti-Roman figures in Tacitus' work underscore Roman stereotypes about Western barbarians. Tacitus' Civilis, for instance, offers typical sentiments about Easterners as accustomed to slavery and contrasts them with the freedom-loving Germans (*Hist.* 4.17.4).[61] Yet Tacitus has not entirely distanced his barbarian speakers from Roman traits. After all, the partial equation of Boudica with a Roman matron gainsays a simplistic assessment of the Britons as stereotypical Westerners in the Roman imagination. And the focus on matters of *servitus* and *libertas* in the context of the revolt also demonstrates that Tacitus has connected the Boudica rebellion with then-contemporary senatorial reactions to Imperial authoritarianism.

Even so, Tacitus' Boudica is neither an unenlightened brute nor a mirror image of a righteous and helpless Roman matron. Rather, Tacitus' characterization offers the reader a more sensitive portrait. It is a picture partly aimed at criticizing Roman imperial misconduct yet also seemingly tied up in highlighting the disenchanting foreignness of the Britons. Although harping on the strangeness of the female leadership of the Britons' revolt, Tacitus also couches his speech in the language of the senatorial Stoic resistance to the Roman government—an inclination we also detected in the Tacitean orations of Civilis and Arminius. Overall, this is no dehumanizing portrait from the pen of an unreflective colonizing power.

How does another member of the Greco-Roman Imperial elite characterize Boudica and the Britons' rebellion? In the next chapter, which examines Cassius Dio's speech of Boudica, we shall take up this question.

## CASSIUS DIO'S "NEO-THUCYDIDEAN" ORATIONS; THE HISTORICITY OF THE BOUDICA ORATION

Though the crafting of orations was clearly one of Cassius Dio's major pre-occupations in his history, comparatively little attention has been paid to most of them. As we mentioned above,[1] modern scholars have proved unlikely to conclude that Dio's speeches are concerned with much more than ostentatious displays of philosophical musings and oratorical commonplaces.[2] Accordingly, Dio's orations directly pertaining to Roman behavior in the provinces—unlike Tacitus' corollaries in his historical works—have not merited much attention. Rather, the great weight of scholarship on Dio's speeches focuses on the orations of Agrippa (52.2-13) and Maecenas (52.14-40), which contemplate the best way to rule an empire.[3]

As we shall see in this chapter, however, Dio's Boudica speech (62.3-6), though a pell-mell creation, presents some powerful indictments of Roman rule more specific than the generalities that Tacitus' Boudica musters. Although reflecting upon the nature of Roman rule was not a chief concern for him, we shall see that Dio was capable of calling into question the justness of Rome's foreign policy. Additionally, through an analysis of this address we can detect how Dio portrayed Roman colonialism and Western barbarians, among other topics. In this case, at least, it seems incorrect to assume that Dio's orations merely reflect an interest in rhetorical showmanship.

This remains an important argument to convey, since far more attention has been paid to the literary influences detectable in Dio's speeches. In addition, it has bearing on the potential historicity of Dio's Boudica oration, to which we now turn. First, we must note that Dio's account of Boudica's revolt—which includes Boudica's speech—has survived from antiquity only in the form of an eleventh-century Byzantine epitome penned by Ioannes Xiphilinus.[4] Although it was once assumed that Xiphilinus was a fairly comprehensive and accurate copyist,[5] this no longer seems tenable. In fact, it appears likely that Xiphilinus drastically shortened the material he excerpted from

Dio by excising what he found uninteresting.[6] Although it is possible—perhaps even likely—that Xiphilinus copied Dio's speech of Boudica verbatim (or close to verbatim), it seems even more probable that he has cut and/or altered the context in which this oration appears. This is important, since the context can drastically change our conclusions concerning the strength and efficacy of a given oration.

Nor is this the only issue that has an effect on our conclusions about the historicity of Dio's Boudica oration. As was the case with Tacitus,[7] we lack sufficient evidence to present supportable conclusions regarding the (now lost) source(s) Dio consulted when crafting his version of the Iceni rebellion. With Dio's source(s) not extant, their naming amounts to educated guesswork.[8] As we shall highlight below, too many discrepancies between Tacitus' and Dio's versions of the Boudica revolt exist for the former to be the ultimate source of the latter.[9] Accordingly, it appears as if these two authors had at least one differing history at their fingertips for their respective discussions of the Iceni rebellion.

Naturally, it would be foolhardy to assume that the sentiments in these compositions necessarily reflect their authors' opinions on the topics discussed. This may be particularly the case regarding Dio's speech, since his devotion to the literary strictures of the Second Sophistic led him to punctuate his orations with stylistic imitations of Attic writers,[10] particularly Thucydides.[11] As such, perhaps we have even more reason to conclude that Dio's Boudica oration is essentially the invention of its author and does not attempt to reflect sentiments the Iceni leader may have mustered in addressing her fellow rebels.

## DIO ON BOUDICA'S REVOLT

Before turning to the speech itself—or to the counterpoised orations Dio puts in the mouth of Suetonius Paulinus (62.8.3–11.5)—we must consider Dio's account of the rebellion (62.1–12). Xiphilinus/Dio introduce the narrative of the revolt by noting that it included the sack of two cities and the deaths of 80,000 Romans and allies (62.1.1).[12] One immediately notes a discrepancy between Tacitus' and Dio's accounts: the former posited the sack of three cities (Camulodunum, Londinium, Verulamium), the latter one fewer.[13] Again unlike Tacitus, who mentions the female leader of the uprising only midway through his narrative, Dio quickly highlights that a woman was the primary instigator, which he presents as a mark of shame.

Directly after offering this opinion, Dio launches into a list of omens that foretold the revolt's occurrence: barbarian babble was audible in the Senate house; clamor unuttered by human beings could be heard in the theater; there was a vision of homes underwater in the Thames; the English Channel was blood-red. Although there are some differences between the portents presented by Tacitus and Dio (in addition to Dio's characteristic wordiness), one may reasonably assume that this list stems from a common source.[14]

More importantly, Dio next discusses what he calls the πρόφασις ("explanation," "pretext") for the uprising (62.2.1).[15] According to Dio, the reasons for the rebellion were threefold: the procurator Decianus Catus' confiscation of money that the emperor Claudius had previously bestowed on prominent Britons; Seneca the Younger's recalling of forty million sesterces he loaned to the islanders; and the entreaties of Boudica herself, which Dio considered the fundamental cause of the revolt (62.2.1–2). Perhaps we can distinguish a different attitude toward the rebellion on Dio's part from the one we detected in Tacitus' *Annales*.[16] Dio, for instance, offers financial causes for the uprising, eschewing discussion of Prasutagus' family's personal grievances.[17] In addition, Dio's use of the term πρόφασις (which can mean "excuse") when discussing the revolt's cause may signal limited sympathy for the rebels (62.2.1).[18] One can make too much of this terminology, however. This word could signal nothing more than an example of Dio's employment of Thucydidean terminology. Even so, we must mention that Dio believed that Boudica's exhortations were the key element inciting the uprising (62.2.1–2); obviously, this implies that Dio does not imbue the natives' grievances with the import that Tacitus aimed to elicit.[19]

Having deemed Boudica the principal cause of the rebellion, Dio then describes this woman in detail, as she stands before an army of about 120,000 men (62.2.2–3). Dio accords Boudica with μεῖζον ἢ κατὰ γυναῖκα φρόνημα ("greater intelligence than befits a woman"; 62.2.2). He then offers a physical description of her.[20] She was tall, Dio informs us, with a frightening countenance and a harsh voice; she had long blonde hair and wore a great necklace and a multicolored frock. While speaking to the assembled throng, Boudica brandished a spear (62.3.3–4). By describing Boudica's physical characteristics at the start of his narrative of the revolt, Dio, unlike Tacitus, reinforces both Boudica's gender and her Amazonian characteristics.[21] Her great height, for instance, seems more often a distinguishing feature of men than women.

Dio next offers his version of Boudica's speech (62.3–6), which we shall discuss at length below. This address appears in Dio's narrative before the outbreak of the rebellion, not before the final battle, as it does in Tacitus' *Annales*. This is unlikely to impact readers' perceptions of the strength of the respective Boudica orations, and it probably tells us nothing about the source(s) the authors employed. It could signal, however, that both Tacitus and Dio felt free to add speeches in their narratives where they saw fit, rather than relying on their sources for the proper placement of their addresses.[22]

After finishing this declamation, Dio's Boudica leads her troops into war with the Romans, who were leaderless, since Suetonius Paulinus, the Roman governor, was at Mona (62.7.1).[23] As a result, the rebels were able to sack two Roman cities. According to Dio, the Britons treated the inhabitants with unspeakable cruelty. For example, Dio informs us that the rebels cut off the breasts of their female captives, hung these women upside-down, and stitched their breasts to their mouths (62.7.2–3). As if this were insufficiently inhumane, the Britons then skewered the women on stakes. This brutality, Dio claims, was committed to the accompaniment of sacrifices in the grove of Andate, apparently a Celtic victory goddess.[24]

Clearly, by relating this torture in vivid detail, Dio leaves the reader with less sympathy for the Britons and their plight. Tacitus, as we discussed in the last chapter, mentioned that the rebels were capable of treating their captives in an unsavory manner, but did not relate any specifics. Dio, moreover, associates these malefactions with Celtic religion—more specifically, with a female warrior goddess. Accordingly, he keeps the reader's focus on the foreignness of the Britons and the female leadership of their rebellion. We should keep in mind, however, that Dio may have simply enjoyed presenting such macabre details, and thus offered them for entertainment purposes.[25] P. A. Brunt's useful description of Xiphilinus' *modus scribendi*, moreover, could leave us with the impression that Dio's epitomator would have savored the addition of such material.[26] We need not, then, conclude that the inclusion of these details demonstrates Dio's disenchantment with the Britons. Even so, it seems clear that Dio does not offer a portrayal of the rebels as sympathetic as that found in Tacitus' *Annales*.

After relating these brutalities, Dio then discusses Paulinus' actions. Departing from Mona, the Roman governor feared the Britons' forces; a shortage of supplies, however, compelled him to engage the enemy (62.8.1). This suggests another difference from Tacitus' account: the *Annales* lead the reader to believe that Paulinus willingly entered combat with the rebels (14.36.3).[27] Gravely outnumbered, Dio tells us, Paulinus divided his forces into three units, so that the Britons could not swarm and surround their foes (62.8.2–3). Through this device, Dio establishes three distinct groups of Roman soldiers, to which Paulinus will deliver separate orations before the final battle (62.9; 62.10; 62.11), as we shall discuss anon.

At the completion of these speeches, the battle commences (62.12.1). From the start, Dio contrasts the Roman troops and the rebellious Britons: whereas the Romans remain silent in their formations, the barbarians shout and sing cacophonously. Much like Tacitus before him, Dio presents a fundamental distinction between the Britons, who represent an uncivilized lack of discipline, and the Romans, who come across as their orderly opposites. Clearly, both Tacitus and Dio deemed organization and military discipline key elements differentiating these two groups.[28] We need not make too much of this distinction, however. Although modish readings might suggest otherwise, it was not entirely a construct in the minds of Tacitus and Dio. As Graham Webster correctly asserts, the Roman forces were tactically superior to the Britons and far more organized in their mode of combat.[29] After all, Paulinus' troops were greatly outnumbered in this final battle and still managed to attain victory—even if Tacitus and Dio exaggerated the scope of this victory in their accounts. Thus the counterpoise Tacitus and Dio offer between the Romans and the Britons is not entirely a rhetorical construct or a demonization of foreignness.[30] Some of this must be based on reality, not Greco-Roman primitivism.

Though Dio expands on the undisciplined nature of the Celtic forces, he stresses that the battle between the two sides was hard-fought, and claims that the Romans prevailed only after much hardship (62.12.5). The Britons, he says, prepared to regroup, but Boudica became ill and died, thus ending the revolt (62.12.6). This amounts to a different view of the conflict's end from what Tacitus presented in the *Annales*; Tacitus claims that Boudica deliberately killed herself with poison (14.37.3). Perhaps these are merely different ways of presenting the same story: the poison could have caused her sickness.[31] If these are not variants of an identical tale, however, it seems more likely that Dio's version is correct.[32] Why would a historian—particularly Dio—alter the story of Boudica's death to make it appear *less* dramatic?[33] Either way, this abruptly concludes Dio's discussion of the revolt, or at least Xiphilinus' excerpts from it.[34]

Regardless of concerns for historical accuracy, as we have already suggested, we must conclude that Tacitus' narrative of the rebellion in the *Annales* appears at least subtly more sympathetic to the Britons than does Dio's account. It may be true that Dio's description of the financial underpinnings of the revolt is more substantial than Tacitus' focus on personal slights.[35] Still, Dio's harping on the Britons' savagery—among other details found in his version of the rebellion—renders Boudica and her followers less attractive characters. The greater pathos in Tacitus' account is not overwhelming, however: Dio, as we shall see, presents the reader with a narrative in which an address that vigorously attacks Rome and its foreign policy does not appear incongruent.

## DIO'S BOUDICA EXHORTATION

### On Freedom and Slavery (62.3)

It is to Boudica's speech that we now turn. It begins as follows:

(1) πέπεισθε μὲν τοῖς ἔργοις αὐτοῖς ὅσον ἐλευθερία τῆς δουλείας διαφέρει, ὥστ' εἰ καὶ πρότερόν τις ὑμῶν ὑπὸ τῆς τοῦ κρείττονος ἀπειρίας ἐπαγωγοῖς ἐπαγγέλμασι τῶν Ῥωμαίων ἠπάτητο, ἀλλὰ νῦν γε ἑκατέρου πεπειραμένοι μεμαθήκατε μὲν ὅσον ἡμαρτήκατε δεσποτείαν ἐπισπαστὸν πρὸ τῆς πατρίου διαίτης προτιμήσαντες, ἐγνώκατε δὲ ὅσῳ καὶ πενία ἀδέσποτος πλούτου δουλεύοντος προφέρει. (2) τί μὲν γὰρ οὐ τῶν αἰσχίστων, τί δ' οὐ τῶν ἀλγίστων, ἐξ οὗπερ ἐς τὴν Βρεττανίαν οὗτοι παρέκυψαν, πεπόνθαμεν; οὐ τῶν μὲν πλείστων καὶ μεγίστων κτημάτων ὅλων ἐστερήμεθα, τῶν δὲ λοιπῶν τέλη καταβάλλομεν; (3) οὐ πρὸς τῷ τἄλλα πάντα καὶ νέμειν καὶ γεωργεῖν ἐκείνοις, καὶ τῶν σωμάτων αὐτῶν δασμὸν ἐτήσιον φέρομεν; καὶ πόσῳ κρεῖττον ἦν ἅπαξ τισὶ πεπρᾶσθαι μᾶλλον ἢ μετὰ κενῶν ἐλευθερίας ὀνομάτων κατ' ἔτος λυτροῦσθαι; πόσῳ δὲ ἐσφάχθαι καὶ ἀπολωλέναι μᾶλλον ἢ κεφαλὰς ὑποτελεῖς περιφέρειν; (4) καίτοι τί τοῦτο εἶπον; οὐδὲ γὰρ τό τελευτῆσαι παρ' αὐτοῖς ἀζήμιόν ἐστιν, ἀλλ' ἴστε ὅσον καὶ ὑπὲρ τῶν νεκρῶν τελοῦμεν· παρὰ μὲν γὰρ τοῖς ἄλλοις ἀνθρώποις καὶ τοὺς δουλεύοντάς τισιν ὁ θάνατος ἐλευθεροῖ, Ῥωμαίοις δὲ δὴ μόνοις καὶ οἱ νεκροὶ ζῶσι πρὸς τὰ λήμματα. (5) τί δ' ὅτι, κἂν μὴ ἔχῃ τις ἡμῶν ἀργύριον (πῶς γὰρ ἢ πόθεν), ἀποδυόμεθα καὶ σκυλευόμεθα ὥσπερ οἱ φονευόμενοι; τί δ' ἂν προϊόντος τοῦ χρόνου μετριάσαιεν, οὕτως ἡμῖν κατὰ τὴν πρώτην εὐθύς, ὅτε πάντες καὶ τὰ νεάλωτα θεραπεύουσι, προσενηνεγμένοι; (62.3.1-5)[36]

(1) You have found out how much freedom differs from slavery through real experiences, so that, even if earlier some of you, through ignorance of what was superior, were tricked by the tempting promises of the Romans, now that you have tried both, you have learned how great a mistake you made in preferring an imported tyranny to your ancient way of life, and you know how much penury without a master surpasses wealth as a slave. (2) For what of the most shameful, the most distressing sort have we not experienced since these people have taken themselves to Britain? Have we not been robbed entirely of most of our greatest possessions, and do we not pay taxes on the rest? (3) Besides pasturing and farming for them, do we not pay yearly tribute for our own bodies? How much better would it have been to be sold once and for all, rather than to be held ransom each year with the empty titles of freedom? How much better would it have been to be slain and die than to endure while subject to a head tax? And yet why did I say this? (4) For, among them not even dying is scot-free, but you know how

much we pay even for our dead; with other people, death frees even those who are enslaved, but with the Romans alone the dead live on for ill-gotten gain. (5) And why is it that, even though none of us has money (for how would we get it, and from where?), we are sold and stripped like victims of a homicide? And why should they be moderate in the time to come, when they have treated us in this fashion from the start, although all men treat even newly caught beasts well?

Although we noted a lesser degree of sympathy for the rebellion on Dio's part, we must admit that his speech of Boudica commences with a comparatively potent point. Dio's Boudica first remarks that her troops, having suffered the indignities of Roman rule, now understand the difference between freedom (ἐλευθερία) and slavery (δουλεία); accordingly, she continues, ἐγνώκατε δὲ ὅσῳ καὶ πενία ἀδέσποτος πλούτου δουλεύοντος προφέρει ("you know how much penury without a master surpasses wealth as a slave"; 62.3.1). Dio thus starts the oration by discussing the Britons' loss of autonomy, rather than focusing on the gender of the speaker.[37] In this instance—as well as many others in the speech—Dio casts Boudica and the Britons as what Arthur Lovejoy and George Boas termed "hard primitives": "Noble Savages" unaccustomed to the slothful and effete ways of the civilized.[38] Boudica claims to prefer ancestral hardiness and penury to life under the Romans. From the start, then, Dio portrays Boudica (and, through her, the Britons) as only recently tainted by the more "advanced" society of Rome.

Having commenced with a mention of Roman imperial misrule, Dio's Boudica turns to expanding on this theme. No treatment is worse, she says, than that which the Britons have suffered under the Romans. They have been robbed of most of their possessions, paying taxes all the while (62.3.2). Unlike Tacitus, Dio focuses on the fiscal aspects of the revolt, just as he had in his own discussion of the uprising's causes. This echo in his oration thus adds weight to the argument that Dio did not lift this speech from any of his sources, but crafted it himself. It demonstrates the same preoccupations Dio presents in the narrative.

We pasture and till for the Romans, Dio's Boudica continues. It would be better for us if we sold ourselves once and for all, instead of living under the pretence of freedom. In fact, she claims, it would be better to die than to have a tax on our heads (62.3.3). Some of this seems like very strong criticism. Dio has Boudica stress the notion that the Romans have not allowed any autonomy to the Britons. This does not imply that Dio was entirely sympathetic to the Britons' plight; he may well merely have been making an attempt to depict Boudica as a "hard primitive," and thus unaccustomed to taxation. In fact, Dio appears to have imagined here an idyllic pre-Roman Celtic society without taxation of any sort. It is difficult to determine whether Dio considered this a dystopia or utopia. Regardless, the economic arguments he presents (even if overstated) might have caused some ancient readers to reflect on the potential injustices of Roman rule. Dio's Boudica maintains her focus on Roman provincial taxation. Britons must even pay a tax when they die, she continues. The Romans also profit from their death (62.3.4). Since Dio's oration is far longer than Tacitus', it offers its author the opportunity to delve into specific criticisms of Roman rule. Thus Dio has mixed economic complaints with a strong moral appeal, which is aimed at vilifying the Romans.

## A Humanized Boudica (62.4–5.1)

Yet Dio's Boudica then changes her argument. In Dio's version of the speech, Boudica even takes responsibility for the vicissitudes of the Britons' situation. She claims:

> ἡμεῖς δὲ δὴ πάντων τῶν κακῶν τούτων αἴτιοι, ὥς γε τἀληθὲς εἰπεῖν, γεγόναμεν, οἵτινες αὐτοῖς ἐπιβῆναι τὴν ἀρχὴν τῆς νήσου ἐπετρέψαμεν, καὶ οὐ παραχρῆμα αὐτούς, ὥσπερ καὶ τὸν Καίσαρα τὸν Ἰούλιον ἐκεῖνον, ἐξηλάσαμεν· οἵτινες οὐ πόρρωθέν σφισιν, ὥσπερ καὶ τῷ Αὐγούστῳ καὶ τῷ Γαίῳ τῷ Καλιγόλᾳ, φοβερὸν τὸ καὶ πειρᾶσαι τὸν πλοῦν ἐποιήσαμεν. (62.4.1)

> To speak the truth, we are responsible for all these evils, as some of us entrusted them to set foot on the island to begin with, and did not immediately drive them off, as we expelled the famous Julius Caesar.

Although this sentiment is quixotic (for the Britons could hardly have driven off from the island a determined Roman force), it is ennobling: it allows the reader to conclude that the pitiable subject wants no pity, no special treatment. Taking responsibility, even though erroneously, is laudable; it amounts to a way of humanizing Boudica. For all of Dio's emphasis on her supposedly Amazonian qualities, his Boudica is not merely a monster or a barbarian.[39]

Boudica's speech continues with this line of reasoning. Though Britons inhabit a large island and are separated from the rest of mankind to such an extent that many wise men do not know them by name, still, she avers, they have been trampled on by men who know only how to steal from others (62.4.2). Here one can detect a telltale hybrid of denigration and championing of Rome—an amalgamation typical in ancient depictions of colonial subjects, which, in the words of Shumate, often "oscillate between self-righteousness and self-doubt."[40] Boudica's discussion of Britain's geography, naturally, stems from a Greco-Roman perspective, not a Celtic one.[41] A Celtic leader would be highly unlikely to discuss Britain's distance from the rest of the world; to the Britons, their land would be the center of their activity, and thus not the periphery. Still, Dio's placing of unrealistic geographical statements in the mouth of his Boudica—though demonstrating little regard for verisimilitude—magnifies the theme of Roman greediness by mentioning the distance of Britain from the heart of the Roman Empire. Having pillaged the known world, Dio's Boudica appears to be saying, the Romans now find themselves in far-flung Britain. Yet there may also be a bit of Roman boasting contained in this sentiment: the Romans have conquered a territory so far from their home that many cannot even name the people who inhabit it.

Boudica then turns to rallying her troops. Fellow Britons, she exclaims, let us now do what is necessary while we still recognize what freedom is, so that our children may know it. For what hope, she asks rhetorically, do people born in servitude have in realizing their liberty (62.4.3)? Through these sentiments, Dio's Boudica returns to the theme with which she began her address—slavery versus freedom. She continues: I am not mentioning this to inspire hatred and fear. After all, you have already experienced them. Rather, she claims, she recommends cooperation among the Britons (62.5.1). Interestingly, Dio appears here to demonstrate some understanding that there were disparate tribes of Britons that would join forces against the Romans, whereas Tacitus views them as one indistinguishable group. This seems particularly noteworthy since Dio is commonly deemed responsible for offering a more "barbarized" portrait of the Britons. It is he, however, who recognizes (however simplistically) the logistics surrounding the Britons' struggle against the Romans.

## Do Not Fear the Romans (62.5.2–6.2)

Dio's Boudica then exhorts her fellow Celts not to fear the Romans. The Romans, she claims, require armor, defensive walls, and trenches to protect themselves, whereas the Britons do not. According to her, this demonstrates that the Romans are terrified of them (62.5.2). For the first time in the oration, Dio's Boudica has touched on the topic of Roman cowardice, instead of continuing to craft an argument critical of Roman rule in the provinces. Still, the sentiment echoes earlier parts of the oration; as before, Dio focuses on the Britons as "hard primitives": they do not require any of the trappings of civilization to win their wars. Dio's depiction of the Celts seems linked to a vision of pre-Roman Britain as an idyllic golden age, free from the vicissitudes of "civilized" life. All the same, Boudica's boast regarding Celtic military might proves utterly wrongheaded: the Britons were ultimately no match for Suetonius Paulinus' Roman forces.

Still, the leader of the Iceni rebellion continues with the same theme. They are braver than the Romans, Dio's Boudica tells her soldiers, and thus can capture and elude their Roman enemies by concealing themselves in places inaccessible to the enemy (62.5.3). Further, she claims that the Romans' heavy armor inhibits them from flight (62.5.4). And the Romans cannot endure hunger, cold, thirst, or heat as the Celts can (62.5.5). Again, Dio focuses on the Britons as "hard primitives." His discussion seems indicative of the (false) nostalgia a "civilized" person might harbor for those whose societies are not as "advanced." Dio's vision of a pre-Roman Celtic Valhalla seems connected to his complaints about supposed Roman decadence. As such, it could have been linked to earnest—if foolish—criticism of the Roman Empire (and, more generally, perhaps, of comparatively advanced societies).

Boudica next turns to a strategic point. They themselves are familiar with the area, she informs her soldiers, whereas the Romans are not. Thus, she opines, let us trust boldly in fortune. Let us demonstrate to the Romans that they are hares and foxes, and we are dogs and wolves (62.5.6). Taking a short break from the text of the speech, Dio describes how Boudica, as part of some form of Celtic divination, here allows a rabbit to escape from her dress, thus referring back to her animal metaphor about the Britons and Romans. Dio mentions that this theatrical gesture—which likens the Iceni's leader to a conjurer—whips up particular excitement among the ranks of the Britons (62.6.1). Despite "humanizing" Boudica at times, here Dio appears to stress her monstrous, barbarian qualities.

Dio then has Boudica continue with the oration. She gives thanks to the goddess Andraste, as one woman speaking to another. As we have learned from the Romans, she says, I do not rule over the Egyptians as Nitocris, nor over the Assyrians as Semiramis (62.6.2). For the first time, Dio's Boudica makes an explicit reference to her gender. And Dio further connects the Britons with femininity, by compelling his Boudica to pray to a female goddess.[42] All the same, Dio's Amazonian portrait of a foreboding and resolute Boudica qualifies these associations between the Iceni and femininity. Dio's Boudica would surely come across as ominously alien to many ancient readers. Still, her courage serves to highlight the absence of valor among elite Roman males in Neronian Rome.[43] The bookish mention of female rulers seems to be a way for Dio to impress the reader with his own erudition. Even if Boudica had somehow managed to obtain this information, there would be little reason to offer it to her troops. The nod to the idea of the Romans schooling the Britons in the history of other societies is a particularly clunky and unrealistic touch.

## Nero, Queen of the Romans (62.6.3–5)

This bookish reference nevertheless allows Dio's Boudica to transition into another argument. She claims that she does not rule over the Romans, as did Messalina, then Agrippina, and now Nero (62.6.2). Although Nero is in name a man, Boudica argues, his theatrical bent proves that he is actually a woman (62.6.3). Elsewhere in his history, Dio offers numerous comments that suggest a profound antipathy to the spectacle of an emperor taking part in theatrical activities.[44] In fact, throughout his work, Dio appears particularly concerned about the circus, the arena, and the stage; further, his discussions of this topic make it seem as if Dio perceives that an emperor's conduct can be measured by his reaction to the games.[45] Thus Boudica's viewing of Nero through the lens of his stage performances and the concomitant denigration of his masculinity seem to fit Dio's preoccupations.

The commentary Boudica presents also allows Dio to continue with his focus on the Britons as primitives; here he posits that the Britons, before Roman involvement on the island, lived in a communistic society—even a sexually communistic society, à la Aristophanes' *Ecclesiazusae* (62.6.3). Naturally, these details are the invention of Dio: the Britons were not proto-communists, and Dio's vision of sexual communism may be a typical way for men to picture female visions of society. Importantly, the argument is damaging not only to Nero himself, but also to Roman society, which is supposedly allowing such a weak, "feminine" emperor to rule over it.[46] This does not imply that Dio was opposed to monarchy.[47] Yet Dio could have intuited the problems that monarchies entail—at least under a bad ruler. Dio, after all, had witnessed his fair share of unreasonable emperors during his tenure in the Senate. For this reason, we should not be surprised that Dio's Boudica oration concludes with this piquant exhortation:

μὴ γάρ το μήτ' ἐμοῦ μήθ' ὑμῶν ἔτι βασιλεύσειεν ἡ Νερωνὶς ἡ Δομιτία, ἀλλ' ἐκείνη μὲν Ῥωμαίων ᾄδουσα δεσποζέτω (καὶ γὰρ ἄξιοι τοιαύτῃ γυναικὶ δουλεύειν, ἧς τοσοῦτον ἤδη χρόνον ἀνέχονται τυραννούσης), ἡμῶν δὲ σὺ ὦ δέσποινα ἀεὶ μόνη προστατοίης. (62.6.5)

Truly may Ms. Domitia-Nero no longer rule over us, but let that singing girl be lord over the Romans, for surely they are deserving of being slaves to such a woman, since they have already put up with her playing the tyrant for so long; but, mistress [sc. Andraste], may you always be our only leader.

The speech certainly demonstrates an intense hatred of Nero, which fits the overall impression Dio gives of him in this work.[48] This does not disqualify the broader criticism of Roman society offered in this passage, but it does suggest that such criticism was not his only concern. Even so, Dio intertwines his abuse of Nero with explicit condemnation of the Romans: in addition to claiming in the conclusion of her speech that the Romans deserve such an effete ruler, Dio's Boudica also criticizes the Roman soldiers whom the Britons face. She says:

> τοιούτων οὖν ἀνδρῶν καὶ τοιούτων γυναικῶν βασιλεύουσα προσεύχομαί τέ σοι καὶ αἰτῶ νίκην καὶ σωτηρίαν καὶ ἐλευθερίαν κατ᾽ ἀνδρῶν ὑβριστῶν ἀδίκων ἀπλήστων ἀνοσίων, εἴ γε καὶ ἄνδρας χρὴ καλεῖν ἀνθρώπους ὕδατι θερμῷ λουμένους, ὄψα σκευστὰ ἐσθίοντας, οἶνον ἄκρατον πίνοντας, μύρῳ ἀλειφομένους, μαλθακῶς κοιμωμένους, μετὰ μειρακίων, καὶ τούτων ἐξώρων, καθεύδοντας, κιθαρῳδῷ, καὶ τούτῳ κακῷ, δουλεύοντας. (62.6.4)

Ruling over such men and women, then, I both pray to you and ask for victory, safety, and freedom against unjust, insatiate, and profane men—if, at any rate, one should even call people "men" who bathe in warm water, eat artificial dainties, imbibe unmixed wine, anoint themselves with myrrh, sleep on soft beds with boys—even ones past their prime—and are slaves to a bad lyre-player.

This remark demonstrates Dio's ambiguous stance regarding the Britons' rebellion that one can detect throughout the oration. The criticism of Roman society both dramatically calls into question the potentially decadent nature of the Roman world, and also casts the Britons as primitive and, by extension, inferior. Dio has not simply penned a blistering attack on Roman foreign policy; the speech is a hodgepodge of ideas and appears to present an ambiguous take on the Celtic revolt. Still, Dio, like Tacitus, seems capable of valorizing barbarian complaints pertaining to Roman provincial misconduct.

## PAULINUS' RETORTS

Before we offer any conclusions regarding Dio's Boudica oration, it is necessary to discuss the three shorter addresses Dio attributes to Suetonius Paulinus, which he delivers to three separate Roman units directly before the final battle between the Romans and the rebels (62.8.3–11.5). Paulinus' first address (62.9) commences with an exhortation to courage:

(1) ἄγετε ἄνδρες συστρατιῶται, ἄγετε ἄνδρες Ῥωμαῖοι, δείξατε τοῖς ὀλέθροις τούτοις ὅσον καὶ δυστυχοῦντες αὐτῶν προφέρομεν· αἰσχρὸν γάρ ἐστιν ὑμῖν, ἃ μικρῷ πρόσθεν ὑπ᾽ ἀρετῆς ἐκτήσασθε, νῦν ἀκλεῶς ἀπολέσθαι. πολλάκις τοι τῶν νῦν παρόντων ἐλάττους ὄντες πολὺ πλείονας ἀντιπάλους καὶ ἡμεῖς αὐτοὶ καὶ οἱ πατέρες ἡμῶν ἐνίκησαν. (2) μήτ᾽ οὖν τὸ πλῆθος αὐτῶν φοβηθῆτε καὶ τὴν νεωτεροποιίαν (ἐκ γὰρ ἀόπλου καὶ ἀμελετήτου προπετείας θρασύνονται), μήθ᾽ ὅτι πόλεις τινὰς ἐμπεπρήκασιν· οὐ γὰρ κατὰ κράτος οὐδὲ ἐκ μάχης, ἀλλὰ τὴν μὲν προδοθεῖσαν τὴν δὲ ἐκλεφθεῖσαν εἷλον. ἀνθ᾽ ὧν νῦν τὴν προσήκουσαν παρ᾽ αὐτῶν δίκην λάβετε, ἵνα καὶ τοῖς ἔργοις αὐτοῖς ἐκμάθωσιν οἵους ὄντας ἡμᾶς οἷοι ὄντες ἠδικήκασι. (62.9.1–2)

(1) Come on, fellow soldiers, come on, Roman men! Show these accursed men how much we surpass them, even though fairing badly; for it is shameful for you now to lose disgracefully those things that you recently won by your valor. Many times now have both we and our fathers, although far fewer in number, defeated more antagonists. (2) Do not fear their multitude or their rebellion (for they are bold because of unarmored and unpracticed rashness) nor the fact that they have burned some cities; for they did not take them by force or after a battle, but they took one that was betrayed and another that was abandoned. And so now extract from them a fitting penalty, so that they who have wronged us may learn from experience what sort of men we are.

It would be shameful to lose, the Roman general asserts, since the Romans have previously tasted victory. He further informs the troops that they have no reason to fear their enemies, who, in their rashness, lack both weapons and training. For all their insolence, they deserve a proper punishment, which demonstrates the difference between the Romans and the Britons. In short, during the course of this brief harangue, Paulinus has asked for revenge—a topic Tacitus' Paulinus, more concerned with tactical matters, does not discuss. In this instance, however, Dio's Paulinus does not seem much concerned with justice; rather, he attempts to rouse courage in his troops. Thus he highlights the notion that the Britons' sacking of two cities was not the result of Celtic military might. In this regard, Dio's Paulinus unwittingly questions the Romans' valor. He makes it appear as if the Roman troops, outnumbered in a distant land, require encouragement to disregard their fears and face their foes. Hence his speech is divorced from the sorts of moral appeals Dio's Boudica presents.

Paulinus' second oration (62.10) seems even more removed from ethical commentary on the conflict:

(1) ταῦτά τισιν εἰπὼν ἐφ᾽ ἑτέρους ἦλθε, καὶ ἔφη "νῦν καιρὸς ὦ συστρατιῶται προθυμίας, νῦν τόλμης. ἂν τήμερον ἄνδρες ἀγαθοὶ γένησθε, καὶ τὰ προειμένα ἀναλήψεσθε· ἂν τούτων κρατήσητε, οὐκέτ᾽ οὐδεὶς ἡμῖν οὐδὲ τῶν ἄλλων ἀντιστήσεται. διὰ μιᾶς τοιαύτης μάχης καὶ τὰ ὑπάρχοντα βεβαιώσεσθε καὶ τὰ λοιπὰ προσκαταστρέψεσθε· (2) πάντες γὰρ καὶ οἱ ἄλλοθί που ὄντες στρατιῶται ζηλώσουσιν ὑμᾶς καὶ ἐχθροὶ φοβηθήσονται. ὥστε ἐν ταῖς χερσὶν ἔχοντες ἢ πάντων ἀνθρώπων ἀδεῶς ἄρχειν ὧν καὶ οἱ πατέρες ὑμῶν κατέλιπον καὶ αὐτοὶ ὑμεῖς προσεπεκτήσασθε, ἢ πάντως αὐτῶν στερηθῆναι, ἕλεσθε ἐλεύθεροι εἶναι, ἄρχειν πλουτεῖν εὐδαιμονεῖν μᾶλλον ἢ τἀναντία αὐτῶν ῥᾳθυμήσαντες παθεῖν." (62.10.1–2)

After saying these words to them, he [Paulinus] went to another group and said "Now, fellow soldiers, is the right time for fighting spirit and boldness. If you are brave men today, you will take back the things you have lost; if you prevail over them, no one will stand against us. Through one such battle you will secure your possessions and will subdue all that remains; (2) for elsewhere all our fellow soldiers will admire you, and our enemies will be afraid. Thus, since it is in your hands either to rule over all people fearlessly (over those places your father left behind for you and those you yourselves acquired in addition), or to be robbed of them entirely, choose to be free, to rule, to be wealthy, to be fortunate, rather than, through faintheartedness, the opposite."

The Roman governor exhorts his soldiers to be brave, and stresses that they can recover lost territory and subdue all that remains. This generic-seeming argument could strike the reader as unapologetically imperialistic. Paulinus does not question the value of further subjugating the Britons. Thus, he claims, if the Romans win this battle, they can rule all mankind without fear. The only alternative, he suggests, is to lose and suffer. So, he concludes, Romans ought to rule in prosperity and freedom. Dio's Paulinus here offers a starkly Thucydidean argument: one either rules or is ruled—there is no middle ground. The oration, then, is wholeheartedly imperialistic, albeit in a manner that divorces expansionism from the moral realm. Paulinus' overwrought argument necessitates nothing short of world empire for anyone aiming for autonomy and well-being.

In this historical context, the speech seems manifestly absurd: the Roman abandonment of Britain would hardly amount to Roman slavery. Additionally, this address appears removed from the specifics that Dio's Boudica mustered in her exhortation. Whereas Dio's Boudica complains about Roman colonial injustices, his Paulinus waxes philosophic on the nature of states.

The Roman commander's third address (62.11), however, begins on a more moralistic note:

(1) τοιαῦτα δὲ καὶ τούτοις εἰπὼν ἐπὶ τοὺς τρίτους ἐπιπαρῆλθε, καὶ ἔλεξε καὶ ἐκείνοις "ἠκούσατε μὲν οἷα ἡμᾶς οἱ κατάρατοι οὗτοι δεδράκασι, μᾶλλον δὲ ἔνια αὐτῶν καὶ εἴδετε· (2) ὥσθ' ἕλεσθε πότερον καὶ αὐτοὶ τὰ αὐτὰ ἐκείνοις παθεῖν καὶ προσέτι καὶ ἐκπεσεῖν παντελῶς ἐκ τῆς Βρεττανίας, ἢ κρατήσαντες καὶ τοῖς ἀπολωλόσι τιμωρῆσαι καὶ τοῖς ἄλλοις ἀνθρώποις ἅπασι παράδειγμα ποιῆσαι καὶ πρὸς τὸ πειθαρχοῦν εὐμενοῦς ἐπιεικείας καὶ πρὸς τὸ νεωτερίζον ἀναγκαίας τραχύτητος." (62.11.1–2)

When he had finished an address like this to those men, he went to the third group, and said to them, "You have heard what sort of things these damnable men have done to us—rather, you have even seen some of them. (2) Thus choose whether you yourselves want to suffer the same things our fellow Romans did, and, moreover, to be driven out of Britain entirely, or by victory to avenge those who died and to make an example for all other people regarding both the equitable treatment of those who are obedient and the requisite harshness to the rebellious."

He informs his troops that they have witnessed the outrages the Britons had committed at the Romans' expense. This sentiment appears to demonstrate more concern for the disrespect the Celts have shown to the Romans in the course of their rebellion than for the intrinsic injustice of the natives' behavior. Given Paulinus' casting of the conflict through the lens of Realpolitik, one might conclude that the Britons were merely fighting for their own autonomy. Yet Paulinus dismissively regards Boudica's revolt as outrageous insolence. And Dio's Paulinus next turns to another Thucydidean sentiment. Either choose to be driven out of Briton, he counsels his soldiers, or avenge those who have perished, thereby offering a reason for mankind to be obedient. Such an argument is equally rooted in Realpolitik and machismo. Some ancient readers may have delighted in this appeal to Roman fortitude. But the appeal is both nakedly and unapologetically imperialistic, as if Roman maltreatment of colonial subjects is the equitable price the subjugated pay for their insufficient valor.

From here Dio's Paulinus presents his most morally charged argument. He claims that justice is on the Roman side. Interestingly, though, in this same address, the Roman governor claims that the Britons are δούλοις ἡμετέροις ("our slaves"; 63.11.3). This proves Boudica's earlier argument: the Romans have treated the Britons as slaves, and Paulinus does not perceive this as problematic. This leaves Paulinus' address looking like an odd mix of Thucydidean notions and half-hearted moral appeals. If we lose, Paulinus continues, it would be better to die on the battlefield, since the Britons would treat us like animals. This sentiment harkens back to Dio's discussion of the horrid tortures of Roman captives performed by the Britons (cf. 62.7.2–3), and thus potentially grants Paulinus' argument a degree of power. Yet Dio's Paulinus ends the oration by claiming that if the Romans lose the forthcoming battle, their bodies can possess Britain (62.11.5). Although this manages to proffer a victory-or-death salvo similar to Boudica's, Paulinus' conclusion is blatantly imperialistic—even in death the Romans will occupy the natives' lands.

Overall, then, one detects a Thucydidean cast to Paulinus' three addresses. At the same time, however, the Roman general attempts to fashion a moral appeal stemming from the perceived injustices of the Britons' rebellion.[49] These features of the speeches do not mesh well together: Realpolitik should leave little room for moral considerations.

### DIO AND THUCYDIDES: CAESAR'S SPEECH ON WAR WITH ARIOVISTUS

The degree to which we deem Paulinus' orations persuasive (or at least potentially persuasive) depends to a great extent on our impression of Dio's views regarding Thucydidean notions of foreign policy and human nature. Thankfully, we possess a test case on these issues in the form of Dio's speech of Caesar regarding war with Ariovistus (38.36–46).[50] In this oration, Caesar addresses his lieutenants and offers a brutal defense of Roman imperialism. It is shameful, Caesar argues, for Rome to have such a rich inheritance and not to augment it (38.38.1). Further, Dio's Caesar casts the life of Roman subjects as one of safety and ease (38.39.2). One must constantly acquire more territory, Caesar claims, in order to thwart the plans of those who aim to destroy your empire (38.40.2–3).

Caesar's appeal has much in common with Paulinus' orations. After all, both characters stress the necessity of Roman expansionism in stark terms. According to Emilio Gabba, Dio himself endorsed Caesar's view of imperialism—a decidedly Thucydidean defense of the practice.[51] Yet this seems wrongheaded.[52] Caesar, for one thing, offers the flimsiest of pretexts for the war: he claims that Ariovistus is an enemy of Rome merely because he refused to meet with Caesar when summoned (38.42–43). Moreover, Caesar, in the course of his apologia for imperialism, offers a truncated history of Roman conquests in order to persuade his subordinates of the justice of his actions (38.38). Among the nations Caesar proudly declares an object of Rome's conquest is Bithynia, Dio's homeland (38.38.2).[53] If we are to assume that Dio agrees wholeheartedly with Caesar's vision of imperialism, we must posit that he harbored no concern for his fatherland's loss of autonomy. In fact, we need to assume that Dio blithely made an example of his own homeland in Caesar's speech. Although some modern scholars have downplayed Dio's sympathy for and attachment to the Greek world,[54] it is unlikely that he would champion Bithynia's defeat—especially since there were so many other conquests he could have mentioned instead.

The reaction of Caesar's lieutenants in Dio's narrative also offers a key to the author's view of the oration. No one objected to Caesar's arguments, Dio says, even though some believed the complete opposite (38.47.1). In this case, Dio—unlike with the Boudica speech or the Paulinus addresses—informs the reader that at least some of Caesar's audience disagreed with the speaker's rationale.[55] Dio further casts doubt on the saliency of Caesar's remarks by noting that Caesar delivered this speech because some Romans believed that he had challenged Ariovistus merely because of personal ambition (38.35.2). None of this can assure us that Dio was utterly opposed to Caesar's arguments in favor of Roman imperialism. Still, these points, taken together, lead us to believe that Dio had his reservations concerning Caesar's viewpoint.[56]

This fits our picture of Dio as an author. Throughout his speeches (and, to a lesser extent, in his narrative), Dio appears more interested in Thucydides' style than in Thucydidean views of state power and foreign policy. Accordingly, Marie-Laure Freyburger-Galland considers Thucydides to be Dio's chief literary model, but posits Livy as his main historical model.[57] Regarding Demosthenes' influence on Dio, furthermore, N. P. Vlachos posits that Dio proved more interested in mimicking the great orator's style than his messages.[58] All in all, then, Dio's speeches may be peppered with Thucydidean turns of phrase and sentiments,[59] but this does not imply that Dio was himself a steadfast devotee of Thucydidean Realpolitik.

Further, it is simplistic to assume that Dio remained wholly pragmatic and amoral in his approach to conquest and foreign policy.[60] To be sure, in regard to the establishment of the Roman Empire, Dio appears to demonstrate more sympathy for Maecenas' pragmatic (or pseudo-pragmatic) speech than for Agrippa's moralistic oration.[61] But Dio has M. Antonius, before the Battle of Actium, deliver an address to his soldiers that seems quite pragmatic (when it does not boast about Antonius' own generalship) (50.16–22). Octavian's oration before the selfsame battle (50.24–30), on the other hand, is more moralistic: justice, he says, is on his side (50.24.1–2). Whereas Dio viewed Augustus as the ideal ruler,[62] his Antonius speech, for all its pragmatism and disregard for moralistic sentiments, proved ineffective.

Thus a sprinkling of Thucydideanisms in an oration does not imply Dio's sympathy with the general tenor of that address. Accordingly, we need not conclude that Paulinus' orations represent Dio's own views on Roman imperialism merely because they reflect some sentiments and language found in the work of the great Athenian historian. We can, in fact, find much in Dio's Boudica speech that leads us to believe that Dio was at least partially sympathetic to the rebels. Many of Boudica's criticisms relate to Roman maladministration during the rule of an emperor Dio detested.[63] And while this does not imply that Dio was in complete agreement with Boudica and the Britons, it does mean that he likely had some understanding of and respect for the complaints of Rome's colonial subjects.

One can, moreover, find anti-imperialistic commentary in Dio's speeches. Maecenas' oration, purportedly a blueprint for Dio's vision of the perfect government, offers one, for example. During the course of his long discussion, Dio's Maecenas comments that nothing good has happened to Rome since it expanded beyond Italy (52.16.1–2). Tiberius' funeral oration for Augustus (56.35–41), in addition, praises its departed subject for treating provincials well (56.41.4). Perhaps this demonstrates that Dio was aware of the possibility of Roman misconduct outside of Italy. All this should lead us to conclude that Dio was capable of at least partially valorizing Boudica's arguments about Roman exploitation in the provinces.

## CONCLUSIONS

This leaves us with some general conclusions regarding Dio's speech of Boudica. In comparison with its Tacitean corollary, Dio's version seems garrulous and pell-mell. Even so, it is replete with arguments missing from Tacitus' address—arguments that occasionally condemn Roman misrule in strong terms. Dio's oration is specific in its examination of provincial exploitation—far more specific than is Tacitus', which proffers no details, save the personal maltreatment of Boudica and her daughters. If anything, Dio's exhortation appears less impressive than Tacitus' to our modern sensibilities because it is rambling and unfocused, not because Dio lacks sympathy for Boudica and the Iceni.

Both Tacitus' and Dio's Boudica orations focus on colonial maladministration as their chief criticism of Rome. This may suggest that by the mid-Imperial period the Greco-Roman elite had become more concerned with the potential injustices of its rule over colonial subjects and less troubled by matters associated with fetial law. Yet Dio's speech proffers denunciations of Roman rule different from those Tacitus' Boudica advances. As we have seen, Dio's version of the address musters far more detailed complaints, which tend to underscore the financial misery Roman colonial rule promoted. Whereas Tacitus' account of the Iceni revolt mainly harped on the maltreatment of Prasutagus' family, Dio concentrates his Boudica address on the burdens of Roman taxation.

Criticisms concerning the Romans' cultivation of fiscal chaos in Britain found in Dio's narrative of the rebellion (62.2.1) suggest that the sentiments his Boudica presents were not anathema to him. Still, one detects both a valorization and a demonization of the Iceni for their leader's excoriation of Roman colonial practices. Dio's Boudica disapproves of taxation so strenuously that we can imagine Greek and Roman readers scoffing at her ignorance of "civilized" societies. Even so, one could argue that Dio approved of the Britons' decision to rebel as a valorous response to an unjust colonizer and its effete emperor. Dio's discussion of Roman colonial maladministration, then, demonstrates a sense of ambiguity different from Tacitus' portrayal of the Iceni revolt.

All the same, Tacitus' and Dio's criticisms of colonialism correspond in the ultimate object of their reproofs: Roman greed. In more explicit terms than Tacitus musters, Dio makes clear that lust for riches animated Roman conquest and colonial control. The Romans, Dio's Boudica would assert, did not expand their empire due to a desire to "civilize" foreign nations. Nor did strategic concerns compel them to advance as far as Britain. Rather, they hungered to exploit their pitiable subjects. Dio's Boudica address, like Tacitus', essentially eschews the topic of Roman martial aggression. Even so, both authors' portrayals of Roman colonial administration echo themes found in earlier historians' elaborations on fetial law.

More so than Tacitus, whose Boudica partly comes across as a maltreated Roman matron, Dio harps on the "primitive" society the Britons inhabit. This leads Dio's Boudica contradictorily to complain about the specifics of Roman taxation and yet claim not to possess any money in the first place (62.3.5). As a result, Dio's Britons call to mind more stereotypical representations of Western barbarians. Still, in his version of the Boudica speech, Dio largely characterizes the Romans as indolent Easterners—emasculated by tyranny, weakened by sloth. To be certain, we need not take Boudica's description entirely at face value. Her chastising of the Romans as cowardly for wearing armor (62.5.2) seems ridiculous. Yet Dio's animus toward the decadence of Neronian Rome is sufficiently palpable to discount the notion that he merely held up his Boudica's views to ridicule. The Britons surely are the victims of Dio's ethnic stereotyping. But Dio's Boudica also offers an unflattering assessment of Roman mores.

Dio's depiction of gender relations among the Britons also differs from

Tacitus'. Whereas Tacitus' Boudica amounts to an amalgamation of a wronged Roman noblewoman and a virile avenger, Dio's version seems more cartoonishly hyper-masculine. In order to fashion a potent contrast between the Iceni's leader and the debauched, effete Nero, Dio plays up his Boudica's pugnacity and resolve. Further, Dio's Boudica makes clear that her society's sexual communalism breeds Celtic females who are as valorous as men (62.6.3). All Celtic women, Dio appears to suggest, share traits with his Boudica. In this way, Dio casts both Britain and Rome as promoting a pernicious gender imbalance: the former is too masculine, the latter too feminized. To Dio, it seems, conquest emasculates the colonizer, not, initially at least, the colonized.[64]

All this suggests that classical scholars have been incorrect to deem all (or almost all) of Dio's speeches as amounting to little more than rhetorical commonplaces and quasi-philosophical generalities.[65] In light of our examination of Dio's Boudica address, such a view seems overstated. Although histrionic, Dio's Boudica oration grapples directly with the financial aspects of Roman control of the provinces and touches on Nero's misrule. Dio's speeches of Boudica and Paulinus, combined with his version of Caesar's exhortation regarding war with Ariovistus, demonstrate that Dio had some interest in the subject of Roman expansionism and colonialism, and did not compose all of his orations merely to offer apothegms in Attic prose.

Moreover, Dio, like Tacitus, betrays at least partial sympathy for Boudica and the Britons. Neither author's Boudica oration, to be sure, presents an unambiguous condemnation of Roman imperialism entirely free from the cultural baggage associated with the outlook of the Greco-Roman elite. To a certain extent, it is unreasonable to assume that Tacitus or Dio—or any other Roman historian—would be capable of offering a portrayal of a Celtic rebellion utterly divorced from a Greco-Roman perspective on native revolts. After all, Tacitus and Dio were not Britons; they likely did not possess much firsthand knowledge of the Iceni.[66] As a result, we can safely presume that Dio, by likening Boudica and her tribesmen to "hard primitives," partly used the Iceni revolt to comment on the nature of Roman society.

It is true that Greco-Roman discourses on the Noble Savage, as they appear in such places as Dio's speech of Boudica, demonstrate acute cultural anxiety. For this reason, discussions of the Noble Savage point to introspection on the part of ancient Greek and Roman authors as much, if not more, than to attempts at accurate depictions of the "Other."[67] Even so, we need not agree with Shumate that this anxiety denotes a sense of superiority among an imperial elite. Why, for example, cannot Dio's portrayal of the Iceni as in part Noble Savages not demonstrate an ability to recognize the failings of

Roman civilization and the (admittedly idealized) virtues of other ways of life? Similarly, as we saw in the previous chapter, Tacitus' take on Boudica demonstrates an inclination to use a barbarian enemy to question the justice of Roman colonialism.

It would be foolish, of course, to assert that Tacitus and Dio, on the basis of their respective Boudica speeches, were stalwart anti-imperialists. Still, a discussion of these orations based on a perception of the authors as "abettors in the colonial process" (to borrow Stephen Rutledge's phrase discussed in the introduction of this book)[68] will lead to a failure to grasp their nuances and ambiguities. Dio's Boudica oration, like Tacitus', seems trapped between a condemnation of Roman society tied to romanticizing a "primitive" Celtic culture and a denigration of non-Romans. Dio also offers a few distinctly Roman touches to his Amazonian portrait of Boudica. And there is something moral about Dio's Boudica—even if this morality is largely encased in alien garb. If anything, Dio's exhortation appears less impressive because it seems undisciplined, not because Dio lacks regard for Boudica's plight.

## A SMALL—BUT DISPARATE—GROUP
## OF ANCIENT HISTORIANS

The close scrutiny of oratorical and epistolary compositions that we have undertaken in the previous chapters suggests a number of conclusions about the work and thought of the six Roman historians who were the focus of our examinations.

Before turning to them, however, we should note that the differences among these authors potentially render our conclusions broader and more significant in regard to the intellectual history of the Greco-Roman elite than might otherwise be the case. The earlier chapters focused, for instance, on historians whose *floruit* ranged from the mid-second century B.C. (Polybius) to the early third century A.D. (Cassius Dio). This means that we can chart some of the intellectual predilections of ancient historians from the mid-Republican period to the mid-Empire.

Further, our survey—though naturally confined to wealthy, well-connected, and educated types—encompasses figures of disparate backgrounds: Greeks living under Roman rule (Polybius, Cassius Dio); Italians (Sallust, Livy, possibly Tacitus); non-Italians (Pompeius Trogus, Cassius Dio); senators (Sallust, Tacitus, Cassius Dio); and non-senators (Polybius, Pompeius Trogus, Livy). To be certain, our sample size is quite small, and thus we cannot presume that these authors' views represent those of similar ethnic and social groups. Nor, we should add, ought we to assume that these ancient historians' backgrounds influence their thought in the same ways they might shape the *Weltanschauung* of contemporary human beings. One's ethnic profile, for instance, likely betokened different associations from those of people inhabiting the modern "multicultural" West. We need not presume, then, that Pompeius Trogus' Gallic ancestry compelled him to deem himself a Gaul, or a Gallic-Roman. He was, after all, a Roman citizen, the scion of Roman citizens, and though in chapter 2 we have seen reasons to conclude that Trogus possessed some affinity for his Gallic homeland, he did not necessarily experience a sense of ethnic kinship similar to that felt by some contemporary peoples.

## ROMAN HISTORIOGRAPHY AND
## SOCIETAL "SELF-CRITICISM"

These important caveats notwithstanding, our examination suggests some conclusions pertaining to matters associated with ancient intellectual history and Greco-Roman historiography. As we have seen throughout this book, far from incessantly offering patriotic sentiments in their speeches, the ancient historians whose texts we have discussed all—to a greater or lesser degree— possessed the ability to present readers with portraits of Roman imperialism and colonialism that are at least partly negative in their tenor. The speeches of ostensible enemies of Rome, as they appear in Roman historiography, then, can go some way to demonstrate the nuanced opinions on expansionism that their authors promoted. In most cases, these historians provide texts that present readers with the opportunity to criticize Roman foreign policy. Although in some instances an author may have downplayed the efficacy of anti-Roman polemic, all the historians we have examined provide enemy addresses that one can reasonably construe as potential evidence against the justice of Roman imperialism and colonial rule. In short, most of these enemy orations can be seen as both flattering and insulting by staunch defenders of Rome's foreign policy.

This sort of criticism, moreover, does not merely pertain to episodes in Roman history from the first century B.C. onward—from the period, that is to say, that coincides with many ancient historians' views of Roman moral collapse. Rather—as we have seen, for example, in the case of Livy's speeches of the Samnite C. Pontius—ancient Roman historians were willing to present potentially withering arguments about their society's failings well before Roman conduct supposedly degenerated in the late Republic. This penchant to advertise both the benefits and the pitfalls of Roman imperialism presents itself early on, since Polybius, as we have seen in chapter 3, employs it to some effect in his Hannibalic orations. By the time Polybius composed his history, however, Rome's expansionary inclinations were already manifest. Still, as far back as we can find complete orations put in the mouths of Rome's adversaries, we can detect an inclination to observe—if not expound upon— the potentially negative aspects associated with the acquisition of an empire. Since, as we have concluded in chapter 1, Sallust demonstrates the same abilities one notices in Polybius' speeches, we can also assert that this interest in highlighting both the perceived blessings and the perceived curses of Roman foreign policy exists in the earliest Roman accounts of Roman history that survive in toto from antiquity.

Nor does the ancient historians' criticism of Roman expansion appear only in the time periods when Rome's military dominance over its neighbors was obvious (at least in hindsight). Rather, the work of the latest historian whose speeches we have discussed at length, Cassius Dio, demonstrates a similar inclination to touch upon the downsides of Roman territorial acquisition and mismanagement. Accordingly, we can safely conclude that the inclusion of speeches at least partially critical of Rome's imperialism was part of a historiographical tradition—a tradition that, as far as we can discern, had an effect on generations of ancient Roman historians.

It must be admitted, however, that we possess insufficient evidence to present conclusions on this topic with great confidence. It would be foolhardy, for instance, to assert that the existence of partially compelling orations opposed to aspects of Roman expansionism and colonialism in ancient historiography indicates a widespread inclination on the part of Greco-Roman elites throughout antiquity to criticize Roman imperialism. Even so, it seems reasonable to aver that speeches critical of Rome were an integral part of the Roman historiographical tradition.

Additionally, we have detected sufficient evidence in the previous chapters to suggest that the impulse to offer orations critical of Rome's expansion and misrule is not confined to Greek or Romano-Gallic historians (Polybius, Cassius Dio, Pompeius Trogus), but remains detectable in the works of Italian-born historians as well. In fact, both Sallust and Livy offer anti-Roman arguments—some of which appear more compelling than the corresponding sentiments found in the matching speeches of Pompeius Trogus and Polybius. We can conclude, then, that criticism of Rome's empire was not confined to those historians supposedly on the periphery of the Roman world, but appeared throughout the entire Roman historiographical tradition.

Perhaps this makes some sense. Numerous classical scholars have supposed that the impulse to criticize the Roman world was more pronounced in those ancient historians who purportedly had less attachment to it. In some sense, Rome was supposedly not *their* culture, and thus they felt less restrained in their castigations of Roman failings. Hence, as we saw in chapters 1 and 2, for example, many modern scholars have believed that Pompeius Trogus, due to his Gallic ancestry, was genuinely anti-Roman.[1] This seems entirely plausible. Yet the reverse may have been true as well. Maybe those lacking an impressive Roman pedigree felt less inclined to criticize Rome, given their lack of unimpeachable Latin roots. The ancient "bluebloods," if you will, could contemn Rome; others were not as comfortable with such arguments. Thus

Sallust, the Sabine senator, and the Italian-born Livy felt little need to water down the anti-Roman polemic in their respective orations, whereas Trogus, the comparative outsider, needed to pull most of his punches.

Admittedly, this highly speculative argument has its share of short-comings. Sallust, for instance, as a *novus homo*, was in some ways an outsider in the milieu of the Roman Senate; his Sabine birth does not suggest that he could trace his family ancestry back to Romulus. Further, it seems fool-ish to assume that ancient ties to one's ethnic and geographical background possessed the same associations as they do in the modern world. Even so, this contention is not without interest. It also questions the presumptions that ancient historians with supposedly less attachment to Rome—say, Polybius—were most capable of and interested in criticizing it.

Just as we cannot detect a greater degree of hostility to Roman foreign policy and provincial administration among the speeches by historians born outside of Italy, we have not seen a stronger impetus to include criticism of empire among those ancient authors whom modern scholars often deem more competent. As we noted in chapter 6, Cassius Dio, whom many consider a second-rate historian (at best), appears as capable of crafting enemy orations that harp on Roman failings as was Tacitus. Our examination, then, does not present evidence allowing us to conclude that those historians typically con-sidered more sophisticated or self-aware craftsmen were necessarily more able or inclined to criticize aspects of Roman imperialism.

Nor does an ancient historian's chronological remove from a particular enemy's threat appear to affect the penchant to find fault with Roman fail-ures. As we have seen in chapters 3 and 4, for example, Livy's Hannibalic ad-dresses seem more passionate than their Polybian corollaries, despite the fact that Polybius' lifetime was far closer to the events of the Second Punic War. Similarly, we detected evidence to conclude that Cassius Dio's incendiary Boudica oration owes some of its firepower to Dio's distaste for Nero, even though Dio lived at a far remove from the Julio-Claudian dynasty. Overall, the passage of time does not appear to have diminished historians' interest in employing enemy addresses to ruminate on the nature of Roman expansion and rule. Perhaps this speaks to, inter alia, the import to Roman historians of emulating earlier works. Thus Pompeius Trogus, for example, sensing the gravity of Sallust's *Epistula Mithridatis*, chose to grant Mithridates a promi-nent oration in his world history. This helped signal Trogus' connection to the Roman historiographical tradition.

As far as we can discern, the inclination to present speeches that offer a complex portrait of Roman expansion is not confined to any specific subgenre of Roman historiography. Although most of the histories we have examined in this book essentially stem from an annalistic tradition of composition (Sallust's *Historiae*, Livy's *Ab urbe condita*, Tacitus' *Annales*, Cassius Dio's *Historiae Romanae*), Pompeius Trogus' "anti-Roman" orations prove that such addresses were equally at home in so-called world histories. In addition, our briefer discussions of speeches found in, for example, Sallust's *Bellum Iugurthinum* and Tacitus' *Agricola* lead us to believe that ancient historical monographs showed an equal regard for the inclusion of such orations.

Having demonstrated that speeches partly critical of Roman territorial acquisition and provincial exploitation can be found throughout the Roman historiographical tradition, we must discuss some reasons why these compositions appeared in the first place. The existence of these addresses does not imply that ancient historians were proto-postcolonialists, or even possessed great sympathy for anti-Roman sentiments. In fact, there appears to be no reason to posit that any of the historians whose work we have considered in this book can be accurately described as anti-imperialist.

There were likely numerous factors that contributed to the penchant to include such orations. Since speeches of generals loomed large in Greek historiographical traditions, it is unsurprising that the historians of Rome offer them as well. Accordingly, pre-battle exhortations were a stock element of Roman historiography, and thus the appearance of speeches by foreign generals does not necessarily suggest that their authors sympathized with the sentiments they presented. In addition, oratory could help break the monotony of historical accounts, and we may suppose that speeches of Rome's enemies before important battles added a degree of dramatic tension desirable to many ancient authors.

All this could lead us to speculate that many of the arguments put in the mouths of Rome's adversaries were essentially pro forma, or at least do not represent their composers' views. To be sure, the preceding chapters have gone some way toward demonstrating that rhetorical considerations loomed large in the inclusion of strong sentiments attributed to enemies in orations appearing in Roman historiography. As Lucian noted (although, we can safely presume, at least partially in jest) in his tongue-in-cheek essay aimed at aspiring historians, the inclusion of speeches offered their authors a chance to delight the world with oratorical fireworks and purple passages.[2] Rhetorical prowess, after all, was a key attribute for an educated Greek or Roman in antiquity. As far back as Herodotus, it was important for full-scale histories to include numerous speeches.

But this does not gainsay the potential efficacy of the sentiments contained within enemy orations in Roman historiography. Rather, these points suggest that for many ancient Roman historians, rhetorical strictures were of greater import than a desire to promote pro-Roman sentiments in their works. As we saw in chapter 4, for example, the purportedly jingoistic Livy allowed his regard for crafting lofty addresses to trump his typical concern for hewing to a Rome-friendly reading of the past. Thus his Hannibalic orations demonstrate pathos one might expect Livy to confine to his Roman speakers.

All the same, we cannot rule out the possibility that some of the sentiments found in these orations could be close to the views harbored by their authors. At the very least, we cannot deny the chance that these speeches offer criticisms of aspects of Rome's expansion and colonialism that troubled ancient historians. The connection between Dio's concerns about the financial underpinning of the Iceni revolt against Rome, for instance, more or less parallel the criticisms voiced by Dio's Boudica.[3] This suggests that ancient historians could very well have felt some sympathy for those enemies of Rome whom they make outspoken critics of Roman imperialism.

In general this implies that ancient Roman historians took fetial law more seriously than many contemporary scholars contend.[4] It speaks, furthermore, to the importance of "just war" considerations on the part of the Roman elite. At present, it is common to view Roman recourse to fetial law with a jaundiced eye—its import and application supposedly withered fairly early in the Republican period. In a similar vein, it appears modish to discount Roman regard for waging "just wars." After all, a quasi-systematic, philosophical approach to this topic originated rather late in Rome's history—more specifically, with Cicero, whose own views on imperialism often appear strikingly incongruous and perhaps fail to merit the label of a theory.[5] Much of this contemporary skepticism regarding *ius fetiale* and *iustum bellum* may well be warranted. To be sure, ample proof exists to conclude that, for many, following the dictates of fetial law amounted to a thoughtless exercise in Roman self-exoneration. Despite the purportedly declining importance of fetial law in the late Republic and Empire, however, we have seen that some Roman historians in their enemy orations regularly focused great attention on complaints against Roman pretensions to engage in justifiable warfare on the basis of proper cause. Even if fetial law itself became a dead letter early on in Roman history, the concerns that it encompassed appear to have remained important to Roman historians for generation after generation. Additionally, though the Romans may have lacked satisfying philosophical treatises on the nature of "just wars," this need not imply that they were unconcerned about the ethics and morals of warfare. All the boasting about military might and valor notwithstanding, many ancient historians of Rome seem attuned to the potential moral failings associated with Roman foreign policy's pugnacity.

This leads us to an important conclusion. It is possible that the ancient

readership of these histories was not disconcerted by criticism of Roman society. Although this need not imply that this audience agreed with such critiques, it was presumably not adverse to the inclusion of numerous "anti-
Roman" remarks in the works of Roman historians. On the contrary: as we
discussed in chapter 2, the incorporation of Sallust's *EM* in a collection of
speeches serving as examples of oratorical skill suggests that Roman audiences were not offended by criticism of Rome's actions. Further, as we also
noted in chapter 2, Justin's great attention to anti-Roman addresses found
in Pompeius Trogus' world history leads us to the same conclusion. Many
Romans, it appears, were not disconcerted by the addition of speeches critical of Roman expansion and maladministration, even when these addresses
excoriated Rome for its purported lapses and congenital flaws.

In this regard, we should not be surprised by the fact that in the preceding chapters some of the arguments offered in such compositions have struck
us as convincing. All the orations of Rome's adversaries we have scrutinized
contain at least a hint of questioning of Roman expansionism. To be certain,
the strength of this criticism varies greatly. Additionally, the pro-Roman harangues that often accompany these speeches tend to vitiate some of their
force. In some cases, furthermore, various details scattered throughout the
narratives of the histories in which such critical speeches are found can speak
against the conclusion that their authors were ultimately in sympathy with
them. Yet even this is not necessarily true in all cases. As we saw in chapter 1,
Sallust presents his readers with some clues that he was partially sympathetic
to some of Mithridates' criticisms in the *EM*. Cassius Dio's detestation of
Nero, moreover, may have compelled him to craft a particularly powerful
Boudica address.[6]

## THE NATURE OF ROMAN "SELF-CRITICISM"

In addition to highlighting the power of various criticisms found in enemy
orations in Roman historiography, our examination allows us to present conclusions about the forms these criticisms take. We can offer assessments, that
is to say, about Roman elite reflections on Roman foreign affairs and colonial
administration, and discuss matters pertaining to gender, ethnicity, sexuality,
greed, and aggression as they appear in such speeches. Overall, our analysis
of anti-Roman addresses demonstrates the prominence most ancient historians granted to moral or quasi-moral arguments. Ethically charged complaints
dominate many enemy speeches, often at the expense of tactical concerns that
might have seemed more realistic additions to pre-battle exhortations.[7]

This is not the case, interestingly enough, in regard to the speeches of Polybius we have discussed. In fact, in many ways, Polybius' enemy orations make their author seem like a singular figure in the annals of Roman historiography. As we saw in chapter 3, moral matters hardly play a part in Polybius' Scipionic and Hannibalic addresses. Perhaps this is due to their author's greater regard for verisimilitude. Thus Polybius' pre-battle speeches focus much attention on instilling courage in soldiers and kindred pragmatic concerns. Yet it remains possible that Polybius' Thucydidean take on the expansion of powerful states left little room in his orations for moral considerations. In the non-Polybian enemy orations we have surveyed, however, moral considerations loom large.

Polybius also appears anomalous in his anti-Roman speeches' disinclination to harp on Roman rapacity and desire for plunder. In many of the enemy addresses we have examined, greed comes across as the primary motivating factor in Roman foreign policy and colonialism. In the works of various Roman historians, barbarians excoriate Rome for its preternatural cupidity and its concomitant lack of self-control. Even in speeches less focused on the topic, greed shines through as the implicit inducement for Roman imperialism. This is the case despite the fact that their authors could have stressed other concerns, such as various tactical matters or the Roman elite's insatiable desire for martial status. All the same, the ancient historians whose works we have surveyed often failed to produce specific examples of this purported Roman inclination. Rather, the historians presuppose that greed is the quintessential Roman trait. This is in striking contrast to Roman historians' elaborations on issues pertaining to fetial law. As we have seen, their enemy addresses often contain elaborate ruminations on Roman foreign affairs, conjuring precise historical examples of Roman pugnacity and bad faith. Roman lapses from ethical foreign policy concerns appear to warrant detailed examinations, whereas Roman rapacity typically earns generalized hectoring.

These conclusions correspond with Catharine Edwards' helpful work on the Roman inclination to moralize political and martial failures.[8] On this topic, for example, Edwards writes:

> Issues which for many in the present day might be "political" or "economic" were moral ones for Roman writers, in that they linked them to the failure of individuals to control themselves. It was the weakness or perversity of individuals, their lack of self-control, on this view, which caused undesirable events. Problems could be solved only if individuals embraced virtue. Thus what might be seen as, for instance, political problems were explained in terms of the ambition of individuals, economic ones in terms of their greed.[9]

Overall, this assessment fits well with tendencies we have detected in numerous enemy speeches in Roman historiography—as we have seen, Roman historians often focus on moral failures as key to Roman imperial and colonial malefactions. This should also serve to emphasize the technique whereby ancient historians used enemy speeches to pronounce upon criticisms dear to Roman elites. After all, as Edwards stresses, claims of superior moral virtue and self-control remained an essential means for the elite to justify its position and perquisites.[10] Enemy orations, then, often focus on themes that were key to Roman elite anxieties and correspond in important ways with domestic rhetoric surrounding the hurly-burly of Roman politics.

In a sense, such speeches in Roman historiography—given their criticisms of character traits fundamental to Roman elite self-definition—turn the tables on the Romans. If foreign adversaries charge Romans with an utter lack of self-restraint, in essence they contend that the Romans possess the characteristics typically associated with barbarians. Rome becomes home to the greedy, the lusty, the profligate. Perhaps such opprobrium contains particular force when put in the mouth of an Eastern monarch such as Mithridates, given Roman associations of the Greek East with luxuriousness and decadence. Although the enemy addresses we have examined often appear to produce anachronistically Roman critiques of Roman behavior, they also serve to expand the rhetorical insults lobbed at elites domestically into an excoriation of Rome tout court.

Despite the obvious import of matters pertaining to martial aggression in many of the anti-Roman speeches we have discussed, one notes a shift over the course of the Roman Empire from an emphasis on Roman pugnacity and "just wars" to a keener focus on Roman administrative corruption. Although this appears true especially in the case of Tacitus, we should not make too much of this realization. Obviously, if more of Dio's earlier books survived or we had the opportunity to reflect on, say, Appian's orations, this change would not seem nearly so dramatic. Furthermore, even passing acquaintance with the history of the Roman Republic suggests that provincial misconduct played a key role in political affairs and was the focus of much elite attention. In regard to speeches offered to anti-Roman figures from the Imperial period, however, one detects a greater interest in Roman colonial malfeasance and less focus on Roman bellicosity. As the pace of the empire's expansion halted, perhaps, Roman historians placed greater stress on matters pertaining to Roman misrule.

All the same, we have seen evidence to suggest that this shift did not entail dramatic reappraisals of the nature of Roman imperialism and colonialism on the part of Roman historians crafting enemy addresses. Rather, historians from the mid-Imperial period still chose to use barbarian speeches to criticize Roman colonial rule in ways similar to earlier reproofs of Roman martial aggression. In the case of both topics, enemy orations portray Roman lapses as examples of insatiate and rampant greed, and occasionally condemn Roman actions through sexual metaphors, as if Roman pugnacity and colonial misrule were examples of the Romans' unbridled lusts.[11]

These orations also offer us an opportunity to examine Roman views of other cultures. We have seen, for example, that Sallust highlights Eastern and African hostility to political freedom in his enemy speeches, and appears to separate his barbarian addresses from those of Rome's internal critics partly on the basis of the formers' complaints about Roman hostility to monarchies. In Sallust's works, another view separating barbarians' sentiments from the rebukes of Romans irked by aspects of Roman society pertains to what Lovejoy and Boas label "chronological primitivism."[12] Sallust's barbarian critics prove incapable of detecting Rome's decline from erstwhile glory, whereas his internal critics underscore this notion in their addresses. No other enemy speech we have encountered, furthermore, stresses Rome's fall from former greatness. Perhaps "chronological primitivism," as it pertains to the Roman world, comes across as a uniquely Roman outlook. Some prejudices appearing in Sallust's work, furthermore, are notable in other historians' speeches as well. If anything, for example, Pompeius Trogus plays up the decadence of the East and its supposed incompatibility with political freedom even more than does Sallust.

As so often is the case in his enemy orations, however, Polybius seems quite different from other ancient historians in his disinclination to promote stereotypical portrayals of barbarians. Little signifies his Hannibal as quintessentially Punic, at least as far as typical Greco-Roman prejudices pertaining to Carthaginians are concerned.[13] But this seems anomalous: the previous chapters have demonstrated many examples of ethnic bias in other Roman historians' portraits of enemy leaders, much of which appears compatible with Greco-Roman stereotypes of specific cultures.

Not all examples of ethnic bias are so straightforward, however. In the course of our examination, we have detected numerous examples of striking incongruities in Roman historians' portrayals of foreign leaders. Livy's P. Scipio, for instance, labels Hannibal both a menacing foe and an impotent novice. Similarly, Tacitus depicts Boudica as both a wronged Roman matron and a hyper-masculine Celtic barbarian. These sorts of inconsistencies point to Roman historians' use of foreign kings and generals as opportunities to peer inward at the perceived glories and faults of Roman society. We need not assume, however, that this self-reflection on the part of Roman historians in-eluctably aimed at denigrating foreigners and lauding Roman achievements.

Incongruities in ancient historians' depictions of foreign leaders also per-tain to the realm of gender. As we noted in chapters 5 and 6, both Tacitus and Cassius Dio created a hybrid Boudica whose foreboding Amazonian qualities are partly vitiated by at least a few feminine touches. Further, Tacitus and Dio use the gender of the Iceni leader to contemn the Britons themselves. They stress, for example, the disorderliness of the Britons—thus linking the Celts as a whole to a trait associated with femininity in the Greco-Roman world. All the same, it is clear that the Boudica speeches also use issues of gender to castigate the purported decadence of the Roman Empire. In some ways, Rome, notwithstanding its military superiority, is characterized as weak and effeminate—an Oriental monarchy of sorts.

Despite the predominance of stereotypical views of barbarians in many of the addresses we have examined, at times Roman historians paradoxically seem to stress a sense of kinship between ancient peoples. As we determined in chapters 3 and 4, for example, Polybius and Livy occasionally allow their speeches on imperialism to underscore the pandemic support for expansion among citizens of strong states and the omnipresent acquisitiveness lurking behind such support. In this instance, it appears, views on imperialism and colonialism associated with Realpolitik led Roman historians to highlight the similarities between all peoples.

Still, in many orations we have analyzed one detects typical Greco-Roman prejudices regarding foreigners. Thus Eastern kings often appear decadent and conniving, and Western leaders come across as rambunctious, undisci-plined, and uncivilized. Even so, in these speeches foreigners are not the only objects of ethnic prejudice. On the contrary: in examining enemy speeches in Roman historiography, we see numerous negative appraisals of Romans recur with great frequency. In the words of foreign enemies, as they were composed by Roman historians, the Romans seem chronically untrustworthy, treach-erous, insatiably avaricious, lusty, and utterly lacking in self-restraint. These traits reappear so often as to suggest that Roman historians had very similar notions of likely foreign complaints regarding Romans. And they allow us to cobble together a strikingly consistent stereotype of the Roman people and their misbehavior.

## ROMAN HISTORY'S POSTCOLONIAL FUTURE

All in all, we have seen throughout this book that almost from the dawn of Roman historiography to a time when Rome's might was teetering, ancient historians were intent on questioning Roman power—its acquisition, its use, and its consequences. To be sure, there are many reasons Roman historians—and their ancient audiences—could show some sympathy for critiques of Roman society. Much like Sallust or Livy, for instance, a given reader may have felt that Rome's halcyon days were long since past. Personal failures in public life may have attracted other readers to delight in anti-Roman sentiments found in Roman historiography. But we should not discount the notion that ancient historians of Rome were capable of and interested in portraying their society's failures. This inclination, detectable as far back in the Western intellectual tradition as Herodotus, can be gleaned in the works of all the ancient authors we have examined in this study. It also may partially account for, mutatis mutandis, the popularity of postcolonial theory in segments of Western academia. Ancient historians of Rome, much like contemporary classical scholars influenced by postcolonial theory, were interested in imagining the criticisms of the people whom Rome conquered.

All the same, we have also seen reason to contend that Roman historians did not shelve their own intellectual preoccupations when crafting enemy orations. Rather, the speeches of Rome's adversaries often echo criticisms of great import to members of the Roman elite. In this way, the enemies become mouthpieces for Roman anxieties one detects in much Roman moralistic rhetoric. We need not, of course, presume that Roman historians agreed with such critiques, either in part or in whole. After all, in the previous chapters we have seen numerous reasons to qualify the efficacy of this criticism, or at least to question whether it corresponds to the sentiments of its authors. In this context, however, we should be mindful of Don Fowler's discussion of "deviant focalization," which was mentioned briefly in the introduction.[14] Ancient historians, of course, were not compelled to give lengthy orations to Rome's adversaries. Their attempt to do so—regardless of the many rhetorical and historiographical reasons that may have suggested their inclusion— was an ideological act. As Fowler suggests, the incorporation of a character's viewpoint adds that viewpoint to the text; regardless of the author's intention, the reader retains the option of seeing matters from the character's perspective.[15]

This is not to say, of course, that modern scholars have been blind to Roman authors' ability to criticize the vicissitudes of the Roman world. Only the most myopic reader could conclude, for example, that Tacitus was a stalwart supporter of the Roman Empire, and was immune to its deficiencies. All the same, as we pointed out in the introduction, in recent years one can detect a tendency on the part of numerous classical scholars to minimize the import of this Roman "self-criticism." In a major work that offers a fundamental reassessment of Greco-Roman views of other cultures, Benjamin Isaac, for instance, argues that the Greeks and Romans were "proto-racists" and downplays their desire to engage in auto-critiques.[16] Further, he connects Greco-Roman anti-"barbarian" sentiments to imperialism.[17] Nor is Isaac alone in circumscribing—if not delegitimizing—the Romans' abilities to find fault with their own society.[18]

This does not imply that Roman historians were obsessive about Rome's missteps or that criticism of the Roman world amounted to their chief intellectual preoccupation. Contemporary scholars are correct to detect haughty and supercilious perspectives on foreigners in the works of ancient Roman historians. Furthermore, one can often glean a connection between Roman authors' xenophobic sentiments and their support for imperial expansion. As such, the application of postcolonial theory to the Roman world has been a fruitful enterprise. Yet a danger exists that the excitement associated with gainsaying earlier scholars' sometimes rosy views of Roman attitudes toward foreigners could blind us to other intellectual tendencies detectable in Roman historiography—and, more broadly, in Roman literature as a whole.

SALLUST'S *Epistula Mithridatis* (*Hist.* 4.69) [KURFESS 1976]

(4.69.1) Rex Mithridates regi Arsaci salutem. Omnes, qui secundis rebus suis ad belli societatem orantur, considerare debent, liceatne tum pacem agere, dein, quod quaesitur, satisne pium tutum gloriosum an indecorum sit. (2) Tibi si perpetua pace frui licet, nisi hostes opportuni et scelestissumi, egregia fama, si Romanos oppresseris, futura est, neque petere audeam societatem et frustra mala mea cum bonis tuis misceri sperem. (3) Atque ea, quae te morari posse videntur, ira in Tigranem recentis belli et meae res parum prosperae, si vera existumare voles, maxume hortabantur. (4) Ille enim obnoxius qualem tu voles societatem accipiet; mihi fortuna multis rebus ereptis usum dedit bene suadendi et, quod florentibus optabile est, ego non validissumus praebeo exemplum, quo rectius tua conponas.

(5) Namque Romanis cum nationibus populis regibus cunctis una et ea vetus causa bellandi est: cupido profunda imperi et divitiarum. Qua primo cum rege Macedonum Philippo bellum sumpsere, (6) dum a Carthaginiensibus premebantur, amicitiam simulantes. Ei subvenientem Antiochum concessione Asiae per dolum avortere, ac mox fracto Philippo Antiochus omni cis Taurum agro et decem milibus talentorum spoliatus est. (7) Persen deinde, Philippi filium, post multa et varia certamina apud Samothracas deos acceptum in fidem callidi et repertores perfidiae, quia pacto vitam dederant, insomniis occidere. (8) Eumen<en>, quoius amicitiam gloriose ostentant, initio prodidere Antiocho pacis mercedem; post, habitum custodiae agri captivi, sumptibus et contumeliis ex rege miserrumum servorum effecere, simulatoque inopio testamento filium eius Aristonicum, quia patrium regnum petiverat, hostium more per triumphum duxere; Asia ab ipsis obsessa est. (9) Postremo Bithyniam Nicomede mortuo diripuere, quom filius Nysa, quam reginam appellaverat, genitus haud dubie esset.

(10) Nam quid ego me appellem? Quem diiunctum undique regnis et tetrarchiis ab imperio eorum, quia fama erat divitem neque serviturum esse, per Nicomedem bello lacessiverunt, sceleris eorum haud ignarum et ea, quae adcidere, testatum antea Cretensis, solos omnium liberos ea tempestate, et regem Ptolemaeum. (11) Atque ego ultus iniurias Nicomedem Bithynia expuli Asiamque, spolium Regis Antiochi, recepi et Graeciae dempsi grave servitium. (12) Incepta mea postremus servorum Archelaus exercitu prodito inpedivit. Illique, quos ignavia aut prava calliditas, ut meis laboribus tuti essent, armis abstinuit, acerbissumas poeanas solvunt, Ptolemaeus pretio in dies bellum prolatans, Cretenses inpugnanti semel iam neque finem nisi excidio habitur<i>.

(13) Equidem quom mihi ob ipsorum interna mala dilata proelia magis quam pacem datam intellegerem, abnuente Tigrane, qui mea dicta sero probat, te remoto procul, omnibus aliis obnoxiis, rursus tamen bellum coepi, Marcumque Cottam, Romanum ducem, apud Calchedona terra fudi, mari exui classe pulcherruma. (14) Apud Cyzicum magno cum exercitu in obsidio moranti frumentum defuit, nullo circum adnitente; simul hiems mari prohibebat. Ita sine vi hostium regredi conatus in patrium regnum naufragiis apud Parium et Heracleam militum optumos cum classibus amisi. (15) Restituto deinde apud Caberam exercitu et variis inter me atque Lucullum proeliis inopia rursus ambos incessit. Illi suberat regnum Ariobarzanis bello intactum, ego vastis circum omnibus locis in Armeniam concessi. Secutique Romani non me, sed morem suom omnia regna subvortundi, quia multitudinem artis locis pugna prohibuere, inprudentiam Tigranis pro Victoria ostentant.

(16) Nunc quaeso considera, nobis oppressis utrum firmiorem te ad resistundum an finem belli fururum putes? Scio equidem tibi magnas opes virorum, armorum et auri esse; et ea re a nobis ad societatem. Ab illis ad praedam peteris. Ceterum consilium est, Tigranis regno integro meis militibus <belli prudentibus> procul ab domo [parvo labore] per nostra corpora bellum conficere, quo[m] neque vincere neque vinci sine tuo periculo possumus. (17) An ignoras Romanos, postquam ad occidentem pergentibus finem Oceanus fecit, arma huc convortisse? Neque quicquam a principio nisi raptum habere, domum coniuges agros imperium? Convenas olim sine patria parentibus, peste conditos orbis terrarum; quibus non humana ulla neque divina obstant, quin socios amicos. Procul iuxta sitos, inopes potentisque trahant excindant, omniaque non serva et maxume regna hostilia ducant? (18) Namque pauci libertatem, pars magna iustos dominos volunt; nos suspecti sumus aemuli et in tempore vindices adfuturi. (19) Tu vero, quoi Seleucea, maxuma urbium, regnumque Persidis inclutis divitiis est, quid ab illis nisi dolum in praesens et postea bellum expectas? (20) Romani arma in omnis habent, acerruma in eos. Quibus victis spolia maxuma sunt; audendo et fallundo et bella ex bellis serundo magni facti: (21) per hunc morem extinguent omnia aut occident. . . .quod haud difficile est. Si tu in Mesopotamia, nos Armenia circumgredimur exercitum sine frumento, sine auxiliis, fortuna aut nostris vitiis adhuc incolumem. (22) Teque illa fama sequetur, auxilio profectum magnis regibus latrones gentium oppressisse. (23) Quod uti facias, moneo hortorque, neu malis pernicie nostra tuam prolatare quam societate victor fieri.

(4.69.1) King Mithridates to King Arsaces, Greetings. Everyone who is entreated to enter a war alliance when his circumstances are good must consider whether it is right to keep the peace, and then whether what is sought from him is sufficiently reverent, safe, honorable, or disgraceful. (2) If it is right for you to enjoy enduring peace, if there were not a susceptible and vicious enemy, and there would not be extraordinary fame if you should overcome the Romans, I would not dare to seek your alliance and hope in vain to entangle your good situation with my bad one. (3) And this anger directed toward Tigranes because of the recent war and the fact that my affairs have been insufficiently favorable—which might seem to give you reason to pause—will most especially urge you on, if you wish to consider them truly. (4) For Tigranes, obedient, will accept whatever sort of alliance you demand; although many things have been taken from me, fortune gave to me the skill of advising well, and, because I am not at the height of my powers, I offer an example desirable to those who are flourishing by which you may arrange your affairs more properly.

(5) Indeed, for the Romans there is a single age-old cause for instigating war on all nations, people, and kings: a deep-seated lust for empire and riches. As a result, they first took up a war with Philip, the king of the Macedonians, (6) while pretending friendship with him as long as they were hard pressed by the Carthaginians. By insincerely giving up Asia they dissuaded Antiochus, who was assisting him, but soon, with Philip crushed, Antiochus was plundered of all the land on this side of the Taurus, and of ten thousand talents. (7) Then Perseus, the son of Philip, was accepted into a protective alliance after various struggles among the gods of Samothrace, and the shrewd devisors of treachery, because they had promised life to him in their pact, killed him by not letting him sleep. (8) They betrayed Eumenes, whose friendship they boastfully exhibited, first to Antiochus as a price of peace; afterward they transformed him, as guardian of a captured territory, from a king to the most wretched of slaves through charges and insults, and they led his son Aristonicus in a triumph in the manner of enemies, after a dishonest will was counterfeited, because he aimed at his ancestral realm; Asia was besieged by them. (9) Finally, with Nicomedes dead they snatched up Bithynia, although a son had no doubt been born by Nysa, whom Nicomedes had called queen.

(10) Truly, why should I mention myself? They provoked me, separated on all sides by kingdoms and tetrarchies from their empire, into war through Nicomedes, because of the rumor that I was rich and would not be a slave; I was not ignorant of their crimes, and I previously appealed to the Cretans — the only free people at that time — and to King Ptolemy about the things that had happened. (11) But I avenged the wrongs, driving Nicomedes from Bithynia, and I recovered Asia, the spoil of king Antiochus, and I took Greece from the harsh servitude. (12) Archelaus, the basest of slaves, impeded my attempts by betraying my army. And those men whose ignorance or perverse slyness held me back from arms, so that they might be safe in my travails, are paying a very bitter penalty. Ptolemy is delaying a war day by day through money, and the Cretans, already having been attacked once, will have no end except by their destruction. (13) Indeed, since I understood that their internal strife postponed war rather than offered peace, although Tigranes (who now appreciates my advice too late) declined to join me, and you were far away, and everyone else spineless, nevertheless I began war anew. On land I vanquished Marcus Cotta, the Roman commander at Calchedon, and at sea I deprived him of a most superb fleet. (14) At Cyzicus, since my army was large, grain failed as the siege dragged on, because no one from the area came to my aid; at the same time winter was keeping me from the sea. Thus, without enemy action, having attempted to go back to my ancestral kingdom, I lost my best soldiers and ships at Parium and Heraclea due to shipwrecks. (15) Then, after my army revived at Cabira, scarcity hindered both Lucullus and me in various battles.

The kingdom of Ariobarzanes, untouched by war, was at Lucullus' disposal; since all the places around me were devastated, I went to Armenia. And the Romans followed me—or, rather, followed their custom of subverting all monarchies—and paraded the bad judgment of Tigranes as a victory, since they kept a great number of troops from battle by hemming them in.

(16) Now I ask you to consider whether, when we have been overwhelmed, you will be more able to resist the Romans or if there will be an end of war. Indeed, I know that you have great abundances of men, of weapons, and of gold; and for this reason we have sought you as an ally, they as a spoil. Yet the plan is to finish the war far from home at the expense of our bodies while Tigranes' kingdom is intact, with my soldiers skilled in war—a war in which we are not able to conquer or be conquered without it being a danger to you. (17) Do you not know that the Romans only turned their weapons in this direction after the Ocean put an end to their western wanderings? And that they possess nothing from their beginning except that which they seized—their home, wives, fields, and empire? That once they were stragglers, without a fatherland and ancestors, produced as a pestilence to the world; for whom no human or divine laws stand in the way of their annihilating allies and friends, near and far alike, weak and powerful, and from considering all those who are not their slaves—particularly monarchies—as enemies? (18) Truly, few people desire freedom; the great majority want just rulers; we have been looked upon as rivals and in time as future avengers. (19) What do you await—you who have Seleuces, the greatest of cities, and the kingdom of Perseus with its famous riches—from them except deception in the present and war in the future? (20) The Romans take up arms against all men, most fiercely when they can win the greatest spoils from the defeated; by daring and deceit and instigating war after war they have become mighty: (21) by this custom they will destroy everything or die . . . which is hardly difficult, if you in Mesopotamia and we in Armenia surround their unprovisioned army, without auxiliaries, up to this point unharmed due to good fortune or our mistakes. (22) And a particular fame will be yours, if you help great kings by crushing the robbers of mankind. (23) I advise and exhort you to do this, and not to prefer to postpone your downfall through ours, but to become a victor through an alliance.

## POMPEIUS TROGUS' SPEECH OF MITHRIDATES (JUSTIN 38.4–7) [SEEL 1972A]

(38.4.1) Optandum sibi fuisse ait, ut de eo liceret consulere, bellumne sit cum Romanis an pax habenda; (2) quin vero sit resistendum inpugnantibus, ne eos quidem dubitare, qui spe victoriae careant; quippe adversus latronem, si nequeant pro salute, pro ultione tamen sua omnes ferrum stringere. (3) Ceterum quia non id agitur, an liceat quiescere non tantum animo hostiliter, sed etiam proelio congressis, consulendum, qua ratione ac spe coepta bella sustineant. (4) Esse autem sibi victoriae fiduciam, si sit illis animus; Romanosque vinci posse cognitum non sibi magis quam ipsis militibus, qui et in Bithynia Aquilium et † Malthinum in Cappadocia fuderint. (5) Ac si quem aliena

magis exempla quam sua experimenta moveant, audire se a Pyrro, rege Epiri, non am-
plius quinque milibus Macedonum instructo fusos tribus proeliis Romanos. (6) Audire
Hannibalem sedecim annis Italiae victorem inmoratum, et quin ipsam caperet urbem,
non Romanorum illi vires restitisse sed domesticae aemulationis atque invidiae stu-
dium. (7) Audire populos transalpinae Galliae Italiam ingressos maximis eam pluri-
busque urbibus possidere et latius aliquanto solum finium, quam in Asia, quae dicatur
inbellis, idem Galli occupavissent. (8) Nec victam solum dici sibi Romam a Gallis,
sed etiam captam, ita ut unius illis montis tantum cacumen relinqueretur; nec bello
hostem, sed pretio remotum. (9) Gallorum autem nomen, quod semper Romanos ter-
ruit, in partem virium suarum ipse numeret. Nam hos, qui Asiam incolunt, Gallos ab
illis, qui Italiam occupaverant, sedibus tantum distare, (10) originem quidem ac virtu-
tem genusque pugnae idem habere; tantoque his acriora esse quam illis ingenia, quod
longiore ac difficiliore spatio per Illyricum Thraciamque prodierint, paene operosius
tansitis eorum finibus quam ubi consedere possessis. (11) Iam ipsam Italiam audire se
numquam, ut Roma condita sit, satis illi pacatam, sed adsidue per omnes annos pro
libertate alios, quosdam etiam pro vice imperii bellis continuis perseverasse; (12) et a
multis civitatibus Italiae deletos Romanorum exercitus ferri, a quibusdam novo contu-
meliae more sub iugum missos. (13) Ac ne veteribus inmoremur exemplis, hoc ipso
tempore universam Italiam bello Marsico consurrexisse, non iam libertatem, sed con-
sortium imperii civitatisque poscentem; (14) nec gravius vicino Italiae bello quam domesticis principium factionibus urbem premi, multoque periculosius esse Italico civile
bellum. (15) Simul et a Germania Cimbros, immensa milia ferorum atque inmitium
populorum, more procellae inundasse Italiam; (16) quorum etsi singula bella sustinere
Romani possent, universis tamen obruantur, ut ne vacaturos quidem bello suo putet.

(5.1) Utendum igitur occasione et rapienda incrementa virium, ne, si illis occupatis
quieverint, mox adversus vacuos et quietos maius negotium habeat. (2) Non enim
quaeri, an capienda sint arma, sed utrum sua potius occasione an illorum. (3) Nam
bellum quidem iam tunc secum ab illis geri coeptum, cum sibi pupillo maiorem Phrygiam ademerint, quam patri suo praemium dati adversus Aristonicum auxilii conces-
serant, gentem quam et proavo suo Mithridati Seleucus Callinicus in dotem dedisset. (4) Quid, cum Paphlagonia se decedere iusserint, non alterum illud genus belli
fuisse? Quae non vi, non armis, sed adoptione testamenti et regum domesticorum
interitu hereditaria patri suo obvenisset. (5) Cum inter hanc decretorum amaritudi-
nem parendo non tamen eos mitigaret, quin acerbius in dies gerant, non obtinuisse.
(6) Quod enim a se non praebitum illis obsequium? Non Phrygiam Paphlagoniamque
dimissas? Non Cappadocia filium eductum, quam iure gentium victor occupaverat?
(7) Raptum tamen sibi esse victoriae ius ab illis, quorum nihil est nisi bello quaesitum.
(8) Non regem Bithyniae Chreston, in quem sentatus arma decreverat, a se in gratiam
illorum occisum? Tamen nihilo minus inputari sibi, si qua Gordius aut Tigranes faciat.
(9) Libertatem etiam in contumeliam sui a senatu ultro delatam Cappadociae, quam
reliquis gentibus abstulerunt; dein populo Cappadocum pro libertate oblata Gordium
regem orante ideo tantum, quoniam amicus suus esset, non obtinuisse. (10) Nicomeden praecepto illorum bellum sibi intulisse; quia ultum ierit se, ab ipsis ventum

obviam in eo; et nunc eam secum bellandi illis causam fore, quod non inpune se Nicomedi lacerandum, saltatricis filio, praebuerit.

(6.1) Quippe non delicta regum illos, sed vires ac maiestatem insequi, neque in uno se, sed in aliis quoque omnibus hac saepe arte grassatos. (2) Sic et avum suum Pharnacen per cognitionum arbitria succidaneum regi Pergameno Eumeni datum; (3) sic rursus Eumenen, cuius classibus primo in Asiam fuere transiecti, cuius exercitu magis quam suo et Magnum Antiochum et Gallos in Asia et mox in Macedonia regem Perseum domuerant, (4) et ipsum pro hoste habitum eique interdictum Italia, et quod cum ipso deforme sibi putaverant, cum filio eius Aristonico bellum gessisse. Nullius apud eos maiora quam Masinissae, regis Numidarum, haberi merita; (5) huic inputari victum Hannibalem, huic captum Syphacem, huic Karthaginem deletam, hunc inter duos illos Africanos tertium servatorem urbis referri: (6) tamen cum huius nepote bellum modo in Africa gestum adeo inexpiabile, ut ne victum quidem patris memoriae donarent, quin carcerem ac triumphi spectaculum experiretur. (7) Hanc illos omnibus regibus legem odiorum dixisse, scilicet quia ipsi tales reges habuerint, quorum etiam nominibus erubescant, aut pastores Aboriginum, aut aruspices Sabinorum, aut exules Corinthiorum, aut servos vernasque Tuscorum, aut, quod honoratissimum nomen fuit inter haec, Superbos; atque ut ipse ferunt conditores suos lupae uberibus altos, (8) sic omnem illum populum luporum animos inexplebiles sanguinis, atque imperii divitiarumque avidos ac ieiunos habere.

(7.1) Se autem, seu nobilitate illis conparetur, clariorem illa conluvie convenarum esse, qui paternos maiores suos a Cyro Darioque, conditoribus Persici regni, maternos a magno Alexandro ac Nicatore Seleuco, conditoribus imperii Macedonici, referat, seu populus illorum conferatur suo, earum se gentium esse, quae non modo Romano imperio sint pares, sed Macedonico quoque obstiterint. (2) Nullam subiectarum sibi gentium expertam peregrina imperia; nullis umquam nisi domesticis rebigus paruisse, Cappadociam velint an Paphlagoniam recensere, rursus Pontum an Bithyniam, itemque Armeniam maiorem minoremque; quarum gentium nullam neque Alexander ille, qui totam pacavit Asiam, nec quisquam successorum eius aut posterorum attigisset. (3) Scythiam duos umquam ante se reges non pacare, sed tantum intrare ausos, Darium et Philippum, aegre inde fugam sibi expedisse, unde ipse magnam adversus Romanos partem virium haberet. (4) Multoque se timidius ac diffidentius bella Pontica ingressum, cum ipse rudis ac tiro esst, Scythiae praeter arma virtutemque animi locorum quoque solitudinibus vel frigoribus instructae, per quae denuntiaretur ingens militiae periculum ac labor. (5) Inter quas difficultates ne spes quidem praemii foret ex hoste vago nec tantum pecuniae, sed etiam sedis inope. (6) Nunc se diversam belli condicionem ingredi. Nam neque caelo Asiae esse temperatius aliud, nec solo fertilius nec urbium multitudine amoenius; magnamque temporis partem non ut militiam, sed ut festum diem acturos bello dubium facili magis an ubere, (7) si modo aut proximas regni Attalici opes aut veteres Lydiae Ioniaeque audierint, quas non expugnatum eant, sed possessum; (8) tantumque se avida expectat Asia, ut etiam vocibus vocet: adeo illis odium Romanorum incussit rapacitas proconsulum, sectio publicanorum, calumniae litium. (9) Sequantur se modo fortiter et colligant, quid se duce posit efficere tantus exercitus, quem sine cuiusquam militum auxilio suamet unius opera viderint Cappadociam caeso rege cepisse, qui solus mortalium Pontum omnem Scythiamque pacaverit, quam nemo ante transire tuto atque adire potuit. (10) Nam iustitiae atque liberalitatis suae ne ipsos milites quin experiantur testes refugere et illa indicia habere, quod solus regum non paternum solum, verum etiam externa regna hereditatibus propter munificentiam adquisita possideat, Colchos, Paphlagoniam, Bosphorum.

(38.4.1) He said that it would have been desirable for him to consider whether it might be permissible to be at peace or in war with the Romans; (2) yet not even those who lack the hope of victory doubt that attackers must be resisted—since everyone draws his sword against a robber, if not for his own safety, at least for revenge. (3) Otherwise, since it is not a question of whether it is permissible to keep quiet, since they have come not only with hostile intentions but also fighting as they go, it must now be considered by what rationale and hope they may sustain the war that has been begun. (4) There is, however, confidence in victory, if they should have the fighting spirit; that the Romans are capable of being beaten is not more known to him, he said, than to the soldiers themselves, who had vanquished Aquilius in Bithynia and Malthinus in Cappadocia. (5) And if foreign examples may move anyone more than their own experiences, he heard that the Romans were beaten in three battles by Pyrrhus, the king of Epirus, who had no more than five thousand Macedonians. (6) He heard that Hannibal remained as the victor of Italy for sixteen years, and that it was not Roman strength but the jealousy and malice of his own people that had stopped him from seizing Rome. (7) He heard that the people of Transalpine Gaul had invaded Italy and possessed most of the greatest of its cities, and that the same Gauls had seized a somewhat broader territory than that in Asia, a place that is called unwarlike. (8) And it was said to him that Rome had not only been conquered by the Gauls, but even captured, so that only the top of a single hill was left for them; and that the enemy was removed by a bribe, not by war. (9) The name of the Gauls, moreover, which always frightened the Romans, he himself could count as part of his strength. For those Gauls who inhabit Asia are different from those who had seized Italy only in their location; (10) they have the same origin, courage, and manner of fighting; and the former's disposition is by far more fierce than the latter's, because they advanced in a longer and more difficult trek through Illyricum and Thrace, almost more energetic in crossing these boundaries than in occupying the places where they now live. (11) He heard that Rome, since it had been founded, never had sufficiently pacified Italy itself, but that Italy had through all its years persisted continuously in perpetual wars, some of its people fighting for their liberty, others for the sake of power; (12) and he heard that the armies of the Romans had been destroyed by many states in Italy, and that they had even been sent under the yoke by some of them, in a new kind of insult. (13) And lest we get bogged down in ancient examples, at this very time all Italy has risen up in the Marsic War, demanding not only freedom, but even their share of power and citizenship; (14) and the city was pressed with war by its Italian neighbors no more gravely than by strife among its elite—and civil war is by far more dangerous than an

Italian one. (15) At the same time the Cimbri from Germany—immense thousands of savage, harsh people—inundated Italy like a storm; (16) even if the Romans could maintain individual wars with them, nevertheless they would be overwhelmed by all of them, so that he did not think that the Romans would even be free for his war.

(5.1) Thus his army must seize this opportunity and become stronger, lest if they rested while the Romans were occupied, soon they would have greater difficulty when the enemy was unhindered and rested. (2) For there was no question of whether arms should be taken up, but whether at an opportunity that was better for them or for the Romans. (3) For indeed, a war was already begun by the Romans against him when they took away, while he was an orphan, Greater Phrygia (which they had granted to his father for the aid he gave against Aristonicus), a country that Seleucus Callinicus had given to his great-grandfather Mithridates as a dowry. (4) What else was it than another kind of war when they had ordered him to depart from Paphlagonia? This country was allotted to his father not by force, not by arms, but by the adoption of a will and the ruin of native kings. (5) He did not soften them amidst this bitterness of decrees by being obedient, and he did not stop them from becoming even harsher day by day. (6) For what act of submission did he not offer them? Had he not let go of Phrygia and Paphlagonia? Was his son not removed from Cappadocia, which he had taken by the right of nations? (7) Even so, the right of his victory had been stolen by those who have sought everything by war. (8) Had not Chreston, the king of Bithynia, against whom the Senate had declared war, been murdered by him as a favor to them? Nevertheless, he was blamed if Gordius or Tigranes did anything in response. (9) Besides, freedom was granted to Cappadocia by the Senate as an insult to him—freedom that they had taken away from all other races; then, with the people of Cappadocia begging for Gordius to be the king instead of the freedom that was granted, they did not obtain this, because he was his friend. (10) Nicomedes waged war against him at the behest of the Romans; and because he had come to take revenge, they were coming after him; and now their reason for going to war with him would be that he had not surrendered himself without resistance to be torn to pieces by Nicomedes, the son of a dancing girl.

(6.1) They do not reproach the crimes of kings, but their strength and majesty, and do not just attack Mithridates himself, but all others as well in this way. (2) Thus they had made Pharnaces, his own grandfather, through the judgment of a trial, a substitute for Eumenes, the king of Pergamum; (3) on the other hand, they had vanquished Eumenes, on whose fleets they had first crossed into Asia, and by whose army, more than their own, they had conquered Antiochus the Great, the Gauls in Asia, and soon after King Perseus in Macedonia, (4) and they considered him an enemy and barred him from Italy, and because they had thought it unbecoming to wage a war with him, waged it with his son Aristonicus. No one had favor with the Romans more than Masinissa, king of Numidia; (5) they ascribe the conquering of Hannibal, the capture of Syphaces, and the destruction of Carthage to him; they consider him, along with the two famous Africani, a third savior of the city: (6) even so, the war they waged with his grandson was so merciless that they did not even grant a concession to the memory of his father when he was conquered, so that he wouldn't have to endure imprisonment and the spectacle of a triumph. (7) They affirmed this law of the hatred for every king, of course, because they had such kings that they even blush at their names: either Aboriginal shepherds, or Sabine soothsayers, Corinthian exiles, or Etruscan slaves, or—that name that was most honored among them—the Superbi; and they themselves say that their founders were nourished by the teats of a wolf, (8) and thus their whole population has the spirit of wolves, insatiably bloodthirsty and sordidly greedy for power and riches.

(7.1) Moreover, if he were compared to them in regard to nobility, he would be more distinguished than these dregs of refugees—he who traced back his paternal ancestors from Cyrus and Darius, founders of the Persian kingdom, and his mother's ancestors from Alexander the Great and Seleucus Nicator, founders of the Macedonian Empire; or if the Roman people were compared with his stock, he was from people who not only were the equal of Roman power, but even withstood the Macedonian Empire. (2) None of the people who were his subjects had ever experienced foreign rule; they had never obeyed any kings other than their own—whether they wished to consider Cappadocia or Paphlagonia, or, on the other hand, Pontus and Bithynia, likewise Greater and Lesser Armenia; not even did the famous Alexander, who pacified all of Asia, take control over any of these people, nor did any of his successors or descendants. (3) Before him only two kings, Darius and Philip, had dared, not to pacify Scythia, but merely to enter it; and they had made their getaway with difficulty from the place where he was drawing the great part of his strength against the Romans. (4) He said that he entered the Pontic Wars with much more fear and diffidence, because he was inexperienced and a tyro; Scythia, besides its weapons and military spirit, was equipped with deserts and cold places, through which huge danger and labor of military service threatened. (5) Among these difficulties there would be no hope for booty from a wandering enemy lacking not only money but even a fixed habitation. (6) Now he was entering a war under different circumstances. For there is nothing more clement than the Asian sky, and nothing more fertile than its ground, nor more charming than its great many cities; and the great part of the time would not be spent as military service but as a festival day, in a war it is difficult to call more easy or more fruitful, (7) if only they had heard of the nearby riches of the kingdom of Attalus or the ancient wealth of Lydia and Ionia, which they would not capture, but own; (8) so eagerly was Asia awaiting him that it was even calling with its voices; the greed of the proconsuls, the public auctioning of forfeited goods by the publicans, and the trickery of lawsuits have excited such hatred for the Romans among them. (9) Only let them follow him bravely and consider what so great an army could do with him as a leader—whom they had seen seize Cappadocia without the aid of any soldiers by the work of him alone, with its king slaughtered, who alone of all mortals had subdued all of Pontus and Scythia, which no one had ever been able to cross and enter safely. (10) As for his fairness and generosity, he did not object to his soldiers being called as witnesses to give evidence that he not only possessed his paternal territory, but also external land that he had obtained through inheritance on account of his munificence, namely Colchis, Paphlagonia, and the Bosporus.

## POLYBIUS' SPEECH OF HANNIBAL BEFORE THE BATTLE OF TICINUS (3.63.1-13) [FOUCAULT 1971]

(3.63.1) Ἀννίβας δὲ διὰ τῶν προειρημένων τὴν προκειμένην διάθεσιν ἐνεργασάμενος ταῖς τῶν δυνάμεων ψυχαῖς, (2) μετὰ ταῦτα προελθὼν αὐτὸς τούτου χάριν ἔφη παρεισάγειν τοὺς αἰχμαλώτους, ἵν' ἐπὶ τῶν ἀλλοτρίων συμπτωμάτων ἐναργῶς θεασάμενοι τὸ συμβαῖνον, βέλτιον ὑπὲρ τῶν σφίσι παρόντων βουλεύωνται πραγμάτων. (3) εἰς παραπλήσιον γὰρ αὐτοὺς ἀγῶνα καὶ καιρὸν τὴν τύχην συγκεκλεικέναι καὶ παραπλήσια τοῖς νῦν ἆθλα προτεθεικέναι. (4) δεῖν γὰρ ἢ νικᾶν ἢ θνήσκειν ἢ τοῖς ἐχθροῖς ὑποχειρίους γενέσθαι ζῶντας. εἶναι δ' ἐκ μὲν τοῦ νικᾶν ἆθλον οὐχ ἵππους καὶ σάγους, ἀλλὰ τὸ πάντων ἀνθρώπων γενέσθαι μακαριωτάτους, κρατήσαντας τῆς Ῥωμαίων εὐδαιμονίας, (5) ἐκ δὲ τοῦ μαχομένους τι παθεῖν, διαγωνιζομένους ἕως τῆς ἐσχάτης ἀναπνοῆς ὑπὲρ τῆς καλλίστης ἐλπίδος μεταλλάξαι τὸν βίον ἐν χειρῶν νόμῳ, μηδενὸς κακοῦ λαβόντας πεῖραν, (6) τοῖς δ' ἡττωμένοις καὶ διὰ τὴν πρὸς τὸ ζῆν ἐπιθυμίαν ὑπομένουσι φεύγειν ἢ κατ' ἄλλον τινὰ τρόπον ἑλομένοις τὸ ζῆν παντὸς κακοῦ καὶ πάσης ἀτυχίας μετασχεῖν. (7) οὐδένα γὰρ οὕτως ἀλόγιστον οὐδὲ νωθρὸν αὐτῶν ὑπάρχειν ὃς μνημονεύων μὲν τοῦ μήκους τῆς ὁδοῦ τῆς διηνυσμένης ἐκ τῶν πατρίδων, μνημονεύων δὲ τοῦ πλήθους τῶν μεταξὺ πολεμίων, εἰδὼς δὲ τὰ μεγέθη τῶν ποταμῶν ὧν διεπέρασεν ἐλπίσαι ποτ' ἂν ὅτι φεύγων εἰς τὴν οἰκείαν ἀφίξεται. (8) διόπερ ᾤετο δεῖν αὐτούς, ἀποκεκομμένης καθόλου τῆς τοιαύτης ἐλπίδος, τὴν αὐτὴν διάληψιν ποιεῖσθαι περὶ τῶν καθ' αὑτοὺς πραγμάτων ἥνπερ ἀρτίως ἐποιοῦντο περὶ τῶν ἀλλοτρίων συμπτωμάτων. (9) καθάπερ γὰρ ἐπ' ἐκείνων τὸν μὲν νικήσαντα καὶ τεθνεῶτα πάντες ἐμακάριζον, τοὺς δὲ ζῶντας ἠλέουν, οὕτως ᾤετο δεῖν καὶ περὶ τῶν καθ' αὑτοὺς διαλαμβάνειν καὶ πάντας ἰέναι πρὸς τοὺς ἀγῶνας μάλιστα μὲν νικήσοντας, ἂν δὲ μὴ τοῦτ' ᾖ δυνατόν, ἀποθανουμένους. (10) τὴν δὲ τοῦ ζῆν ἡττημένους ἐλπίδα κατὰ μηδένα τρόπον ἠξίου λαμβάνειν ἐν νῷ. (11) τούτῳ γὰρ χρησαμένων αὐτῶν τῷ λογισμῷ καὶ τῇ προθέσει ταύτῃ, καὶ τὸ νικᾶν ἅμα καὶ τὸ σῴζεσθαι προδήλως σφίσι συνεξακολουθήσειν. (12) πάντας γὰρ τοὺς ἢ κατὰ προαίρεσιν ἢ κατ' ἀνάγκην τοιαύτῃ προθέσει κεχρημένους οὐδέποτε διεψεῦσθαι τοῦ κρατεῖν τῶν ἀντιταξαμένων. (13) ὅταν δὲ δὴ καὶ τοῖς πολεμίοις συμβαίνῃ τὴν ἐναντίαν ἐλπίδα ταύτης ὑπάρχειν, ὃ νῦν ἐστι περὶ Ῥωμαίους, ὥστε φεύγουσι πρόδηλον εἶναι τοῖς πλείστοις τὴν σωτηρίαν, παρακειμένης αὐτοῖς τῆς οἰκείας, δῆλον ὡς ἀνυπόστατος γίνοιτ' ἂν ἡ τῶν ἀπηλπικότων τόλμα.

(3.63.1) Hannibal, having produced the present disposition in the minds of his forces through this means, (2) came forward after these things and said he set up the prisoners before them so that, having seen manifestly in the fortunes of others what might befall them, they might take better counsel regarding the present matters. (3) He says that Fortune has enclosed them in a similar and opportune contest, and has now put forward similar prizes. (4) For it is necessary either to conquer, die, or become living subjects of the enemy. For the prize for winning the contest is not horses and cloaks, but to become the most blessed of all people, having power over Roman prosperity; (5) and the prize of death is to depart from life fighting, struggling for the most beautiful hope until your last breath, experiencing nothing evil; (6) but those who are beaten and who, through eagerness for life, submit to flight, or choosing to live by some other means, must endure every evil and every misfortune. (7) For no one among you is so irrational or slow that, remembering the length of the journey he has accomplished from his fatherland, and recalling the number of enemies in between and knowing the size of the rivers he crossed, he thought that he could arrive home by fleeing. (8) Therefore Hannibal thought, since all such hope had been knocked out of them, that it was necessary to take the same distinction concerning their own situation that they readily made regarding the others' chances. (9) For as everyone considered both the victorious and the dead blessed and pitied the living, thus he thought it necessary to believe this about themselves, and all go to the battles to conquer, and if this was not possible, to die. (10) He considered it to be in no way worthy to contemplate the hope of living defeated. (11) For those using reason and calculation will clearly be attended by victory and safety together. (12) Truly everyone either by preference or necessity using such calculation was not cheated in victory in prevailing over the opposition. (13) And whenever the opposite hope exists for the enemy, as was then the case among the Romans, that clearly most of those who fled would be safe since their homes were nearby, it becomes obvious that the courage of those despairing of safety is irresistible.

## POLYBIUS' SPEECH OF P. SCIPIO BEFORE THE BATTLE OF TICINUS (3.64.3–10) [FOUCAULT 1971]

(3.64.3) ἔφη γὰρ δεῖν, καὶ μηδεμίαν μὲν εἰληφότας πεῖραν ἐπὶ τοῦ παρόντος τῶν ὑπεναντίων, αὐτὸ δὲ τοῦτο γινώσκοντας ὅτι μέλλουσι πρὸς Καρχηδονίους κινδυνεύειν, ἀναμφισβήτητον ἔχειν τὴν τοῦ νικᾶν ἐλπίδα, (4) καὶ καθόλου δεινὸν ἡγεῖσθαι καὶ παράλογον, εἰ τολμῶσι Καρχηδόνιοι Ῥωμαίοις ἀντοφθαλμεῖν, πολλάκις μὲν ὑπ᾿ αὐτῶν ἡττημένοι, πολλοὺς δ᾿ ἐξενηνοχότες φόρους, μόνον δ᾿ οὐχὶ δουλεύοντες αὐτοῖς ἤδη τοσούτους χρόνους. (5) "ὅταν δέ, χωρὶς τῶν προειρημένων, καὶ τῶν νῦν παρόντων ἀνδρῶν ἔχωμεν ἐπὶ ποσὸν πεῖραν ὅτι μόνον οὐ τολμῶσι κατὰ πρόσωπον ἰδεῖν ἡμᾶς, τίνα χρὴ διάληψιν ποιεῖσθαι περὶ τοῦ μέλλοντος τοὺς ὀρθῶς λογιζομένους; (6) καὶ μὴν οὔτε τοὺς ἱππεῖς συμπεσόντας τοῖς παρ᾿ αὐτῶν ἱππεῦσι περὶ τὸν Ῥοδανὸν ποταμὸν ἀπαλλάξαι καλῶς, ἀλλὰ πολλοὺς ἀποβαλόντων αὐτῶν φυγεῖν αἰσχρῶς μέχρι τῆς ἰδίας παρεμβολῆς, (7) τόν τε στρατηγὸν αὐτῶν καὶ τὴν σύμπασαν δύναμιν ἐπιγνόντας τὴν παρουσίαν τῶν ἡμετέρων στρατιωτῶν φυγῇ παραπλησίαν ποιήσασθαι τὴν ἀποχώρησιν καὶ παρὰ τὴν αὐτῶν προαίρεσιν διὰ τὸν φόβον κεχρῆσθαι τῇ διὰ τῶν Ἄλπεων πορείᾳ." (8) παρεῖναι δὲ καὶ νῦν ἔφη τὸν Ἀννίβαν, κατεφθαρκότα μὲν τὸ πλεῖστον μέρος τῆς δυνάμεως, τὸ δὲ περιλειπόμενον ἀδύνατον καὶ δύσχρηστον ἔχοντα διὰ τὴν κακουχίαν, ὁμοίως δὲ καὶ τῶν ἵππων τοὺς μὲν πλείστους ἀπολωλεκότα, τοὺς δὲ λοιποὺς ἠχρειωκότα διὰ τὸ μῆκος καὶ τὴν δυσχέρειαν τῆς ὁδοῦ. (9) δι᾿ ὧν ἐπιδεικνύειν ἐπειρᾶτο διότι μόνον ἐπιφανῆναι δεῖ τοῖς πολεμίοις. (10) μάλιστα δ᾿ ἠξίου θαρρεῖν αὐτοὺς βλέποντας εἰς τὴν αὐτοῦ παρουσίαν·

οὐδέποτε γὰρ ἂν ἀπολιπὼν τὸν στόλον καὶ τὰς ἐν Ἰβηρίᾳ πράξεις, ἐφ᾽ ἃς ἀπεστάλη, δεῦρο μετὰ τοιαύτης ἐλθεῖν σπουδῆς, εἰ μὴ καὶ λίαν ἐκ τῶν κατὰ λόγον ἑώρα τὴν πρᾶξιν ταύτην ἀναγκαίαν μὲν οὖσαν τῇ πατρίδι, πρόδηλον δ᾽ ἐν αὐτῇ τὴν νίκην ὑπάρχουσαν.

(3.64.3) He said that, even if they had not recently experienced the enemies, knowing this thing alone, namely that they intended to venture against the Carthaginians, it was necessary to have an indisputable hope of victory, (4) and it is necessary for them to consider it overall outrageous and unexpected that the Carthaginians had the audacity to meet the Romans face-to-face, because they have many times been worsted by them, to whom they have paid so much tribute, and whom for so long a time they had served as all but slaves. (5) "And when, apart from what has been said beforehand, we can determine essentially by our own experiences that the men who are present now do not dare to look us in the face, what distinction should we make about the future, if we compute it correctly? (6) In fact, by the Rhone River not even their cavalry came off well against ours, but many of them, thrown off, fled shamefully to their own encampment, and their general and all his forces, seeing our soldiers upon them, made a retreat rather like a flight, and, on account of their fear, they journeyed on a route through the Alps, against their own choice." (8) He said that Hannibal was now present, having lost the greatest part of his forces, the remnants of which were weak and nearly useless because of hardship; he had similarly lost most of his horses, and the remaining ones he had rendered useless on account of the length and difficulty of the journey. (9) Through these remarks he tried to show that it was merely necessary to be seen by the enemy. (10) And he demanded that they take heart in seeing him present; for never would he have left behind his fleet and business in Spain on which he was sent, to come here with such haste if he did not see that it was crystal clear that this was a necessary matter for the fatherland, and that victory was manifest.

## POLYBIUS' SPEECH OF HANNIBAL TO SCIPIO AFRICANUS BEFORE THE BATTLE OF ZAMA (15.6.4–7.9) [FOULON 1995]

(15.6.4) δεξιωσάμενος δὲ πρῶτος Ἀννίβας ἤρξατο λέγειν ὡς ἐβούλετο μὲν ἂν μήτε Ῥωμαίους ἐπιθυμῆσαι μηδέποτε μηδενὸς τῶν ἐκτὸς Ἰταλίας μήτε Καρχηδονίους τῶν ἐκτὸς [τῆς] Λιβύης· (5) ἀμφοτέροις γὰρ εἶναι ταύτας καὶ καλλίστας δυναστείας καὶ συλλήβδην ὡς ἂν εἰ περιωρισμένας ὑπὸ τῆς φύσεως. (6) "ἐπεὶ δὲ πρῶτον μὲν ὑπὲρ τῶν κατὰ Σικελίαν ἀμφισβητήσαντες ἐξεπολεμώσαμεν ἀλλήλους, μετὰ δὲ ταῦτα πάλιν ὑπὲρ τῶν κατ᾽ Ἰβηρίαν, τὸ δὲ τέλος ὑπὸ τῆς τύχης οὔπω νουθετούμενοι μέχρι τούτου προβεβήκαμεν ὥστε καὶ περὶ τοῦ τῆς πατρίδος ἐδάφους τοὺς μὲν κεκινδυνευκέναι, τοὺς δ᾽ ἀκμὴν ἔτι καὶ νῦν κινδυνεύειν, (7) λοιπόν ἐστιν, εἴ πως δυνάμεθα δι᾽ αὐτῶν παραιτησάμενοι τοὺς θεοὺς διαλύσασθαι τὴν ἐνεστῶσαν φιλοτιμίαν. (8) ἐγὼ μὲν οὖν ἕτοιμός εἰμι τῷ πεῖραν εἰληφέναι δι᾽ αὐτῶν τῶν πραγμάτων ὡς <εὐ>μετάθετός ἐστιν ἡ τύχη καὶ παρὰ μικρὸν εἰς ἑκάτερα ποιεῖ μεγάλας ῥοπάς, καθάπερ εἰ νηπίοις παισὶ χρωμένη·

(7.1) "σὲ δ᾽ ἀγωνιῶ, Πόπλιε, λίαν᾽ ἔφη καὶ διὰ τὸ νέον εἶναι κομιδῇ καὶ διὰ τὸ πάντα σοι κατὰ λόγον κεχωρηκέναι καὶ τὰ κατὰ τὴν Ἰβηρίαν καὶ τὰ κατὰ τὴν Λιβύην καὶ μηδέπω μέχρι γε τοῦ νῦν εἰς τὴν τῆς τύχης ἐμπεπτωκέναι παλιρρύμην, μήποτε οὐ πεισθῇς διὰ ταῦτα τοῖς ἐμοῖς λόγοις, καίπερ οὖσι πιστοῖς. (2) σκόπει δ᾽ ἀφ᾽ ἑνὸς τῶν λόγων τὰ πράγματα, μὴ τὰ τῶν προγεγονότων, ἀλλὰ τὰ καθ᾽ ἡμᾶς αὐτούς. (3) εἰμὶ τοιγαροῦν Ἀννίβας ἐκεῖνος ὃς μετὰ τὴν ἐν Κάνναις μάχην σχεδὸν ἁπάσης Ἰταλίας ἐγκρατὴς γενόμενος μετά τινα χρόνον ἧκον πρὸς αὐτὴν τὴν Ῥώμην, καὶ στρατοπεδεύσας ἐν τετταράκοντα σταδίοις ἐβουλευόμην ὑπὲρ ὑμῶν καὶ τοῦ τῆς ὑμετέρας πατρίδος ἐδάφους πῶς ἐστί μοι χρηστέον, (4) ὃς νῦν ἐν Λιβύῃ πάρειμι πρὸς σὲ Ῥωμαῖον ὄντα περὶ τῆς ἐμαυτοῦ καὶ τῶν Καρχηδονίων σωτηρίας κοινολογησόμενος. (5) εἰς ἃ βλέποντα παρακαλῶ σε μὴ μέγα φρονεῖν, ἀλλ᾽ ἀνθρωπίνως βουλεύεσθαι περὶ τῶν ἐνεστώτων· τοῦτο δ᾽ ἐστὶ τῶν μὲν ἀγαθῶν ἀεὶ τὸ μέγιστον, τῶν δὲ κακῶν τοὐλάχιστον αἱρεῖσθαι. (6) τίς οὖν ἂν ἕλοιτο νοῦν ἔχων πρὸς τοιοῦτον ὁρμᾶν κίνδυνον οἷος σοὶ νῦν ἐνέστηκεν; ἐν ᾧ νικήσας μὲν οὔτε τῇ σαυτοῦ δόξῃ μέγα τι προσθήσεις οὔτε τῇ τῆς πατρίδος, ἡττηθεὶς δὲ πάντα τὰ πρὸ τούτου σεμνὰ καὶ καλὰ δι᾽ αὑτὸν ἄρδην ἀναιρήσεις. (7) τί οὖν ἐστιν ὃ προτίθεμαι τέλος τῶν νυνὶ λόγων; (8) πάντα περὶ ὧν πρότερον ἠμφισβητήσαμεν, Ῥωμαίων ὑπάρχειν — ταῦτα δ᾽ ἦν Σικελία, Σαδρώ, τὰ κατὰ τὴν Ἰβηρίαν — καὶ μηδέποτε Καρχηδονίους Ῥωμαίοις ὑπὲρ τούτων ἀντᾶραι πόλεμον· ὁμοίως δὲ καὶ τὰς ἄλλας νήσους ὅσαι μεταξὺ κεῖνται τῆς Ἰταλίας καὶ Λιβύης, Ῥωμαίων ὑπάρχειν. (9) ταύτας γὰρ πέπεισμαι τὰς συνθήκας καὶ πρὸς τὸ μέλλον ἀσφαλεστάτας μὲν εἶναι Καρχηδονίοις, ἐνδοξοτάτας δὲ σοὶ καὶ πᾶσι Ῥωμαίοις."

(15.6.4) Hannibal, having greeted Scipio, first began to speak, saying that he wished that neither the Romans had ever desired anything outside of Italy nor the Carthaginians outside of Libya; (5) for these were perfect empires for both, and empires that are held together as if nature had marked their boundaries. (6) "But since first we have gone to war over Sicily and afterwards over Spain, finally, ignoring the lessons of Fortune, we have gone so far that your fatherland was formerly in danger and ours is still even now, (7) what we are left with is the matter of through what means we are able to prevail upon the gods to put an end to our present rivalry. (8) And so I am ready, having learned through actual experiences how capricious Fortune is, and how by the slightest move either way she tips the scales the most, as if she were playing with silly children.

(7.1) "But I am exceedingly distressed, Publius," he says, "on account of your youth and because success has constantly been by your side in both Spain and Libya, and you have not yet fallen into the ebb tide of Fortune, and will not be convinced of my words on account of this, although they are trustworthy. (2) Consider matters in light of one example, not ancient, but from our own times. (3) Look now, I am that famous Hannibal who, after the Battle of Cannae, nearly was the master of all Italy, and not long after I came to Rome itself, and bivouacking at forty stades, was considering how I should treat you and your native land; (4) now I am present in Libya, about to take counsel with you, a Roman, regarding my safety and that of the Carthaginians. (5) I ask you to look upon these things and not to be overconfident, but to take counsel regarding the present circumstances humanely: always to choose the greatest good and the least evil. (6) And what sane person would choose to rush into so great a danger as now threatens you? If you win, you will neither add much at all to your own repute or that of your fatherland, but if you lose, you will utterly annul all your awesome and noble accomplishments. (7) What end, then, do I put forward for this meeting? (8) That all the places concerning which we previously fought—namely Sicily, Sardinia, and Spain—belong to the Romans, and that the Carthaginians will never do battle with the Romans on behalf of them; likewise that the other islands that lie between Italy and Libya belong to the Romans. (9) For I am certain that these agreements will be most safe for the Carthaginians and most honorable to you and all the Romans."

POLYBIUS' SPEECH OF SCIPIO AFRICANUS TO HANNIBAL
BEFORE THE BATTLE OF ZAMA (15.8) [FOULON 1995]

(15.8.1) Ἀννίβας μὲν οὖν ταῦτ᾽ εἶπεν. ὁ δὲ Πόπλιος ὑπολαβὼν οὔτε τοῦ περὶ Σικελίας ἔφη πολέμου Ῥωμαίους οὔτε τοῦ περὶ τῆς Ἰβηρίας αἰτίους γεγονέναι, Καρχηδονίους δὲ προφανῶς· (2) ὑπὲρ ὧν κάλλιστα γινώσκειν αὐτὸν τὸν Ἀννίβαν. μάρτυρας δὲ καὶ τοὺς θεοὺς γεγονέναι τούτων, περιθέντας τὸ κράτος οὐ τοῖς ἄρχουσι χειρῶν ἀδίκων, ἀλλὰ τοῖς ἀμυνομένοις. (3) βλέπειν δὲ καὶ τὰ τῆς τύχης οὐδενὸς ἧττον καὶ τῶν ἀνθρωπίνων στοχάζεσθαι κατὰ δύναμιν. (4) "ἀλλ᾽ εἰ μὲν πρὸ τοῦ τοὺς Ῥωμαίους διαβαίνειν εἰς Λιβύην αὐτὸς ἐξ Ἰταλίας ἐκχωρήσας προύτεινας τὰς διαλύσεις ταύτας, οὐκ ἂν οἴομαί σε διαψευσθῆναι τῆς ἐλπίδος. (5) ἐπεὶ δὲ σὺ μὲν ἄκων ἐκ τῆς Ἰταλίας ἀπηλλάγης, ἡμεῖς δὲ διαβάντες εἰς τὴν Λιβύην τῶν ὑπαίθρων ἐκρατήσαμεν, δῆλον ὡς μεγάλην εἴληφε τὰ πράγματα παραλλαγήν. (6) τὸ δὲ δὴ μέγιστον ἤλθομεν ἐπὶ τί πέρας; (7) ἡττηθέντων καὶ δεηθέντων τῶν παρὰ πολιτῶν σοῦ, ἐθέμεθα συνθήκας ἐγγράπτους, ἐν αἷς ἦν πρὸς τοῖς ὑπὸ σοῦ νῦν προτεινομένοις τοὺς αἰχμαλώτους ἀποδοῦναι χωρὶς λύτρων Καρχηδονίους, τῶν πλοίων παραχωρῆσαι τῶν καταφράκτων, πεντακισχίλια τάλαντα προσενεγκεῖν, ὅμηρα δοῦναι περὶ τούτων. (8) ταῦτ᾽ ἦν ἃ συνεθέμεθα πρὸς ἀλλήλους· ὑπὲρ τούτων ἐπρεσβεύσαμεν ἀμφότεροι πρός τε τὴν σύγκλητον τὴν ἡμετέραν καὶ πρὸς τὸν δῆμον, ἡμεῖς μὲν ὁμολογοῦντες εὐδοκεῖν τοῖς γεγραμμένοις, Καρχηδόνιοι δὲ δεόμενοι τούτων τυχεῖν. (9) ἐπείσθη τὸ συνέδριον τούτοις, ὁ δὲ δῆμος συγκατένευσε. τυχόντες ὧν ἠξίουν, ἠθέτησαν ταῦτα Καρχηδόνιοι παρασπονδήσαντες ἡμᾶς. (10) τί λείπεται ποιεῖν; σὺ τὴν ἐμὴν χώραν μεταλαβὼν εἰπόν. (11) ἀφελεῖν τὰ βαρύτατα τῶν ὑποκειμένων ἐπιταγμάτων; ἵνα δὴ λαβόντες ἆθλα τῆς παρανομίας διδαχθῶσι τοὺς εὖ ποιοῦντας εἰς τὸ λοιπὸν παρασπονδεῖν· ἀλλ᾽ ἵνα τυχόντες ὧν ἀξιοῦσι, χάριν ὀφείλωσιν ἡμῖν; (12) ἀλλὰ νῦν μεθ᾽ ἱκετηρίας τυχόντες ὧν παρεκάλουν, ὅτι βραχείας ἐλπίδος ἐπελάβοντο τῆς κατὰ σέ, παρὰ πόδας ὡς ἐχθροῖς ἡμῖν κέχρηνται καὶ πολεμίοις. (13) ἐν οἷς βαρυτέρου μέν τινος προσεπιταχθέντος δυνατὸν ἀνενεγκεῖν τῷ δήμῳ περὶ διαλύσεως, ὑφαίρεσιν δὲ ποιουμένοις τῶν ὑποκειμένων οὐδ᾽ ἀναφορὰν ἔχει τὸ διαβούλιον. (14) τί πέρας οὖν πάλιν τῶν ἡμετέρων λόγων; ἢ τὴν ἐπιτροπὴν ὑμᾶς διδόναι περὶ σφῶν αὐτῶν καὶ τῆς πατρίδος ἢ μαχομένους νικᾶν."

(15.8.1) And so Hannibal said these things. Scipio, retorting, said that the Romans were responsible neither for the war around Sicily nor for that around Spain, but clearly the Carthaginians were; (2) Hannibal knew this especially well. He said that the gods were witnesses of these matters, conferring the victory not upon those beginning the war unjustly, but upon those warding off attackers. (3) He said that he gave way to no one in foreseeing the whims of Fortune and aimed at things suitable to men according to his ability. (4) "But," he said, "if you, having departed from Italy and crossed into Libya, proposed this cessation of hostilities, I do not think that you would have been mistaken in your hope. (5) Yet since you have been compelled unwillingly from Italy, and we, having crossed into Libya, have control over the open country, it is clear that matters have greatly changed. (6) The most important thing is: What end have we reached? (7) With your fellow citizens worsted and begging for peace, we made a written agreement in which it was stipulated, in addition to the requests you have put forward now, the Carthaginians should give away their prisoners without ransom, that they should give up decked vessels, and that they should pay five thousand talents, and that they should give hostages for these things. (8) These are the conditions concerning which we agreed with one another; we both sent ambassadors to our Senate and our people; we were granting that we approved of the agreement, and the Carthaginians were entreating to get it approved. (9) The Senate was persuaded by it, and the people consented. The Carthaginians, having gained their terms, broke faith with us. (10) What is left to do? Having exchanged places with me, tell me. (11) Take away the most grievous of the injunctions proposed? That would give prizes for your treachery, and teach them hereafter to betray those who treat you well; (12) but agreeing to the terms will they owe thanks to us? Yet now, having happened upon these things through supplication, because they were encouraged that they laid hold of a scant hope from you, they treated us immediately as enemies and foes. (13) With something more grievous added among these conditions, I can report on the settlement to the Roman people, but if we removed some of the terms, the *fait accompli* would allow them no opportunity for deliberation. (14) So, once more, what end is there for our conference? Either give yourselves and your fatherland to us, or beat us in battle."

## LIVY'S SPEECH OF P. SCIPIO BEFORE THE BATTLE OF TICINUS (21.40–41) [DOREY 1971]

(21.40.1) Si eum exercitum, milites, educerem in aciem, quem in Gallia mecum habui, supersedissem loqui apud vos; (2) quid enim adhortari referret aut eos equites, qui equitatum hostium ad Rhodanum flumen egregie vicissent, aut eas legiones, cum quibus fugientem hunc ipsum hostem secutus confessionem cedentis ac detractantis certamen pro victoria habui? (3) Nunc, quia ille exercitus, Hispaniae provinciae scriptus, ibi cum fratre Cn. Scipione meis auspiciis rem gerit, ubi eum gerere senatus populusque Romanus voluit, (4) ego, ut consulem ducem adversus Hannibalem ac Poenos haberetis, ipse me huic voluntario certamini obtuli, novo imperatori apud novos milites pauca verba facienda sunt. (5) Ne genus belli neve hostem ignoretis, cum iis est vobis, milites, pugnandum, quos terra marique priore bello vicistis, a quibus stipendium per viginti annos exegistis, <a> quibus capta belli praemia Siciliam ac Sardiniam habetis. (6) Erit igitur in hoc certamine is vobis illisque animus, qui victoribus et victis esse solet. Nec nunc illi, quia audent, sed quia necesse est, pugnaturi sunt; (7) nisi creditis, qui exercitu incolumi pugnam detractavere, eos duabus paene partibus peditum equitumque in transitu Alpium amissis, cum plures perierint quam supersint, plus spei nactos esse. (8) "At enim pauci quidem sunt, sed vigentes animis corporibusque, quorum robora ac vires vix sustinere vis ulla possit." (9) Effigies immo, umbrae hominum, fame frigore inluvie, squalore enecti, contusi ac debilitati inter saxa rupesque; ad hoc praeusti artus, nive rigentes nervi, membra torrida gelu, quassata fractaque arma, claudi ac debiles equi: (10) cum hoc equite, cum hoc pedite pugnaturi estis; reliquias extremas hostis, non hostem habetis; ac nihil magis vereor quam ne cui, vos cum pugnaveritis, Alpes vicisse Hannibalem videantur. (11) Sed ita forsitan decuit, cum foederum ruptore duce ac populo deos ipsos sine ulla humana ope committere ac profligare bellum, nos, qui secundum deos violati sumus, commissum ac profligatum conficere.

(41.1) Non vereor, ne quis me haec vestri adhortandi causa magnifice loqui existimet, ipsum aliter animo adfectum esse. (2) Licuit in Hispaniam, provinciam meam, quo iam profectus eram, cum exercitu ire meo, ubi et fratrem consilii participem ac periculi socium haberem et Hasdrubalem potius quam Hannibalem hostem et minorem haud dubie molem belli; (3) tamen, cum praeterveherer navibus Galliae oram, ad famam huius hostis in terram egressus praemisso equitatu ad Rhodanum movi castra. (4) Equestri proelio, qua parte copiarum conserendi manum fortuna data est, hostem fudi; peditum agmen, quod in modum fugientium raptim agebatur, quia adsequi terra [non poteram] nequieram, regressus ad navis [erat], quanta maxime potui celeritate, tanto maris terrarumque circuitu in radicibus prope Alpium huic timendo hosti obvius fui. (5) Utrum, cum declinarem certamen, inprovidus incidisse videor, an occurrere in vestigiis eius, lacessere ac trahere ad decernendum? (6) Experiri iuvat, utrum alios repente Carthaginienses per viginti annos terra ediderit, an idem sint, qui ad Aegatis pugnaverunt insulas et quos ab Eryce duodevicenis denariis aestimatos emisistis, (7) et utrum Hannibal hic sit aemulus itinerum Herculis, ut ipse fert, an vectigalis stipendiariusque et servus populi Romani a patre relictus. (8) Quem nisi Saguntinum scelus agitaret, respiceret profecto, si non patriam victam, domum certe patremque et foedera Hamilcaris scripta manu, (9) qui iussus ab consule nostro praesidium deduxit ab Eryce, qui graves inpositas victis Carthaginiensibus leges fremens maerensque accepit, qui decedens Sicilia stipendium populo Romano dare pactus est. (10) Itaque vos ego, milites, non eo solum animo, quo adversus alios hostes soletis, pugnare velim, sed cum indignatione quadam atque ira, velut si servos videatis vestros arma repente contra vos ferentes. (11) Licuit ad Erycem clausos ultimo supplicio humanorum, fame, interficere; licuit victricem classem in Africam traicere atque intra paucos dies sine ullo certamine Carthaginem delere: (12) veniam dedimus precantibus, emisimus ex obsidione, pacem cum victis fecimus, tutelae deinde nostrae duximus, cum Africo bello urgerentur. (13) Pro his impertitis furiosum iuvenem sequentes oppugnatum patriam nostram veniunt. Atque utinam pro decore tantum hoc vobis et non pro salute esset certamen! (14) Non de possessione Siciliae ac Sardiniae, de quibus quondam agebatur, sed pro Italia vobis est pugnandum. (15) Nec est alius ab tergo exercitus, qui, nisi, nos vincimus, hosti obsistat, nec Alpes aliae sunt, quas dum superant, comparari nova possint praesidia. Hic est obstandum, milites, velut si ante Romana moenia pugnemus. (16) Unus quisque se non corpus suum sed coniugem ac liberos parvos armis protegere putet; nec domesticas solum agitet curas, sed identidem hoc animo reputet, nostras nunc intueri manus senatum populumque Romanum; (17) qualis nostra vis virtusque fuerit, talem deinde fortunam illius urbis ac Romani imperii fore.

(21.40.1) If, soldiers, I were leading into battle formation the army that I had with me in Gaul, I would have refrained from addressing you; (2) for what advantage would there be to exhort those horsemen who had brilliantly conquered the cavalry of the enemy at the Rhone River, or those legions with whom I followed after the routed enemy, whose withdrawal and flight from battle I considered a confession of our victory? (3) Now, since that army, conscripted in Spain, conducts operations there with my brother Gnaeus Scipio by my authority, where the Senate and the Roman people wished him to serve, (4) I, so that you might have a consul as your leader against Hannibal and the Carthaginians, offered myself for this battle on my own initiative, and must speak a few words as a new commander to new soldiers. (5) First recognize the nature of this war and the enemy you face, soldiers. You must fight with those whom previously you have conquered on land and sea, from whom you have exacted tribute for twenty years, and from whom you hold Sicily and Sardinia as the spoils of war. (6) In this struggle, therefore, you and they will have the spirit that is usual for the victors and the defeated. And those men will not fight you because they are daring, but because they must, (7) unless you believe that those who declined battle when their army was whole became more hopeful when they lost two thirds of their infantry and cavalry in crossing the Alps. (8) [Someone may claim,] "Truly they are few, but strong in mind and body, whose vigor and strength hardly any force could withstand." (9) No indeed: they are imitations, specters of men, plagued by hunger, cold, filth, and squalor, battered and crippled among rocks and cliffs; in addition to this, their limbs are frostbitten, their muscles stiffened by the snow, their bodies sluggish with ice, their battle gear flimsy and broken, their horses limping and frail. (10) You will have to do battle with this cavalry, with this infantry; you have the leftover vestiges of an enemy, not an enemy. And I fear nothing more than that it may seem as if the Alps conquered Hannibal, even though you fought him. (11) But perhaps it was right that the gods themselves without any human aid should begin and end a war with a leader and a people who break treaties, and that we, who have been wronged second only to the gods, finish the war that has been begun and all but won.

(41.1) I do not fear that anyone thinks I say these things grandiosely in order to encourage you, but that I think otherwise. (2) I could have gone with an army to Spain, my own province, towards which I had already set out, where I would have had my brother as a participant in my plans and an ally in my danger, and Hasdrubal rather than Hannibal as an enemy, and surely a less difficult war; (3) even so, when I was sailing by the coast of Gaul with my fleet, as soon as the report of the enemy reached me I landed, set out with the cavalry, and moved my forces to the Rhone. (4) I scattered the enemy in a cavalry battle (for this was the part of my army that fortune gave me for fighting at close quarters), and because I had not been able to overtake by land the enemy line that suddenly was withdrawing as if in flight, I returned to the ships and with as much speed across as great a compass of sea and land as I could I came to confront this fearful enemy almost at the foot of the Alps. (5) Do I seem to have avoided battle and then to have blundered blindly into it, or rather to have tracked the enemy down to challenge him and draw him into a fight? (6) It would please me to test whether the earth suddenly produced another kind of Carthaginian in the last twenty years, or if they are the same men who fought at the Aegatian islands and whom you released from Eryx for a ransom of eighteen denarii a head, (7) and whether this Hannibal is a rival of the wandering Hercules, as he himself says, or has been left behind by his father as a tributary, tax payer, and slave of the Roman people. (8) If he were not disturbed by the crime at Saguntum, he would certainly respect, if not his conquered country, at least his home, his father, and the treaties written by the hand of Hamilcar, (9) who, at the command of our consul, led his garrison away from Mount Eryx, and who, raging and lamenting, accepted the strict conditions imposed upon the defeated Carthaginians and as he left Sicily agreed to pay tribute to the Roman people. (10) Thus I could wish you, soldiers, to fight not only with that courage with which you are accustomed against other enemies, but also with indignation and a certain wrath, as if you were seeing your slaves suddenly taking up arms against you. (11) We had them trapped at Mount Eryx and could have starved them to death—the most extreme punishment of human beings. We could have transferred our victorious fleet to Africa, and within a few days destroyed Carthage without any struggle; (12) yet we pardoned them when they begged us to do so, we discharged them from a siege, we made peace with the conquered, and, when they were burdened with the African war, we at last considered them as under our guardianship. (13) For these favors, they, following their young firebrand, come to attack our fatherland! And I wish that this battle were only for your honor and not for your safety; (14) you must fight not for the possession of Sicily and Sardinia, which were once in dispute, but for Italy. (15) And there is no other army at your back that can resist the invaders if we are not victorious, nor are there other Alps, which will obstruct them as we prepare new defenses. Soldiers, we must stop them here, as if we were fighting before the walls of Rome. (16) Let each one of you think that you protect not only your own body, but also your wife and little children; let each one not be absorbed by his personal worries, but again and again reflect upon this, that now the Senate and the Roman people look to our hands. (17) The fortune of this city and the Roman empire will stand or fall with our might and courage.

## LIVY'S SPEECH OF HANNIBAL BEFORE THE BATTLE OF TICINUS (21.43–44) [DOREY 1971]

(21.40.1) Cum sic aliquot spectatis paribus adfectos dimisisset, contione inde advocata ita apud eos locutus fertur: (2) "Si, quem animum in alienae sortis exemplo paulo ante habuistis, eundem mox in aestimanda fortuna vestra habueritis, vicimus, milites; neque enim spectaculum modo illud, sed quaedam veluti imago vestrae condicionis erat. (3) Ac nescio an maiora vincula maioresque necessitates vobis quam captivis vestris fortuna circumdederit; (4) dextra laevaque duo maria claudunt nullam ne ad effugium quidem navem habentis, circa Padus amnis maior [Padus] ac violentior Rhodano, ab tergo Alpes urgent, vix integris vobis ac vigentibus transitae. (5) Hic vincendum aut moriendum, milites, est, ubi primum hosti occurristis. Et eadem fortuna, quae necessitatem pugnandi imposuit, praemia vobis ea victoribus proponit, quibus ampliora homines ne ab diis quidem immortalibus optare solent. (6) Si Siciliam tantum ac Sardiniam parentibus nostris ereptas nostra virtute reciperaturi essemus, satis tamen ampla pretia essent: quidquid Romani tot triumphis partum congestumque possident, id omne vestrum cum ipsis dominis futurum est. (7) In hanc tam opimam mercedem, agite dum, diis bene iuvantibus arma capite. (8) Satis adhuc in vastis Lusitaniae Celtiberiaeque montibus pecora consectando nullum emolumentum tot laborum periculorumque vestrorum vidistis; (9) tempus est iam opulenta vos ac ditia stipendia facere et magna operae pretia mereri, tantum itineris per tot montes fluminaque et tot armatas gentes emensos. (10) Hic vobis terminum laborum fortuna dedit; hic dignam mercedem emeritis stipendiis dabit. (11) Nec, quam magni nominis bellum est, tam difficilem existimaritis victoriam fore: saepe et contemptus hostis cruentum certamen edidit et incluti populi regesque perlevi momento victi sunt. (12) Nam dempto hoc uno fulgore nominis Romani quid est, cur illi vobis comparandi sint? (13) Ut viginti annorum militiam vestram cum illa virtute, cum illa fortuna taceam, ab Herculis columnis, ab Oceano terminisque ultimis terrarum per tot ferocissimos Hispaniae et Galliae populos vincentes huc pervenistis; (14) pugnabitis cum exercitu tirone, hac ipsa aestate caeso victo circumsesso a Gallis, ignoto adhuc duci suo ignorantique ducem. (15) An me in praetorio patris, clarissimi imperatoris, prope natum, certe eductum, domitorem Hispaniae Galliaeque, victorem eundem non Alpinarum modo gentium sed ipsarum, quod multo maius est, Alpium, cum semenstri hoc conferam duce, desertore exercitus sui? (16) Cui si quis demptis signis Poenos Romanosque hodie ostendat, ignoraturum certum habeo, utrius exercitus sit consul. (17) Non ego illud parvi aestimo, milites, quod nemo est vestrum, cuius non ante oculos ipse saepe militare aliquod ediderim facinus, cui non idem ego virtutis spectator ac testis notata temporibus locisque referre sua possim decora. (18) Cum laudatis <a> me miliens donatisque, alumnus prius omnium vestrum quam imperator, procedam <in> aciem adversus ignotos inter se ignorantesque.

(44.1) "Quocumque circumtuli oculos, plena omnia video animorum ac roboris, veteranum peditem, generosissimarum gentium equites frenatos infrenatosque, (2) vos socios fidelissimos fortissimosque, vos Carthaginienses, cum <pro> patria tum ob iram iustissimam pugnaturos. (3) Inferimus bellum infestisque signis descendimus in Italiam, tanto audacius fortiusque pugnaturi quam hostis, quanto maior spes, maior est animus inferentis vim quam arcentis. (4) Accendit praeterea et stimulat animos dolor iniuria indignitas. Ad supplicium depoposcerunt me ducem primum, deinde vos omnes, qui Saguntum oppugnassetis; deditos ultimis cruciatibus adfecturi fuerunt. (5) Crudelissima ac superbissima gens sua omnia suique arbitrii facit. Cum quibus bellum, <cum> quibus pacem habeamus, se modum imponere aequum censet. Circumscribit includitque nos terminis montium fluminumque, quos non excedamus, neque eos quos statuit terminos obseruat. (6) 'Ne transieris Hiberum! Ne quid rei tibi sit cum Saguntinis!' Ad Hiberum est Saguntum? 'Nusquam te vestigio moveris!' (7) Parum est, quod veterrimas provincias meas Siciliam ac Sardiniam, <ademisti?> Adimis etiam Hispanias, et, inde <si de>cessero, in Africam transcendes. <Transcendes> autem? Duos transcendisse dico; duos consules huius anni, unum in Africam, alterum in Hispaniam miserunt. Nihil usquam nobis relictum est, nisi quod armis vindicarimus. (8) Illis timidis et ignavis esse licet, qui respectum habent, quos sua terra, suus ager per tuta ac pacata itinera fugientes accipient: vobis necesse est fortibus viris esse et, omnibus inter victoriam mortemve certa desperatione abruptis, aut vincere aut, si fortuna dubitabit, in proelio potius quam in fuga mortem oppetere. (9) Si hoc bene fixum omnibus, <si> destinatum in animo est, iterum dicam, vicistis; nullum contemptu m<ortis incitamentum> ad vincendum homini ab dis immortalibus acrius datum est."

(21.40.1) After his troops had been stirred by watching several dueling pairs, he dismissed them. It is said that he then spoke to them in an assembly. (2) "If, soldiers, you presently will have the same spirit in contemplating your fortune that you had a bit before in others fighting for theirs, then we have won; for that was not merely a spectacle but a clear representation of your own condition. (3) And I do not know whether fortune has locked you up in greater chains and greater constraints than your captives. (4) On the right and left two seas enclose you, and you do not even have a ship for flight; the Po River is around you—a greater and more turbulent river than the Rhone; at your back the Alps press upon you, which you barely crossed when you were unwounded and strong. (5) Here, soldiers, you must conquer or die, where first you met the enemy. And the same fortune that has imposed the necessity of fighting on you offers prizes for victory no less than those that men venture to seek only from the gods. (6) If we were only going to recover by our courage Sicily and Sardinia (which were torn from our parents), these would be precious enough; whatever the Romans possess, taken and heaped up in numerous triumphs—it all will be yours, along with the masters themselves. (7) Come now, for the sake of this greatest of recompenses, take up arms with the gods as your helpers! (8) Up till now you have long enough followed your herds in the barren mountains of Lusitania and Celtiberia, and have seen no profit for so much work and danger; (9) it is now time for you to acquire lavish and rich tribute and to earn a great reward for your work, a journey passing through so many mountains, and rivers, and through so many armed tribes. (10) Here fortune put an end to your labors; here it will pay out a treasure well worth campaigns well done. (11) You must not think that victory will prove difficult in proportion to the war's great name; often a scorned enemy has mounted a bloody struggle, and famous people and kings have been conquered with scant effort. (12) With the one glory of the Romans—their name—taken from them, how can they be compared to you? (13) I shall pass over in silence your brave and successful military service of twenty years. You have now come here from the Pillars of Hercules, from the ocean and the outermost boundaries of the world through the most ferocious people of Spain and Gaul as conquerors; (14) you will be fighting with an unseasoned army, which has been cut down, defeated, and besieged by Gauls this very summer—an unknown quantity to their own leader, and who is no more familiar to them. (15) Should I compare myself, all but born and wholly reared in the headquarters of my father (that most distinguished commander), the master of Spain and Gaul, the very conqueror of not only the Alpine tribes, but also—which is much more—of the Alps, with this six-month leader, a deserter from his own army? (16) If anyone should show him today the Carthaginians and the Romans with the standards taken away, I am sure that he could not tell of which army he was the consul. (17) I do not consider it of little value, soldiers, that there is no one of you before whose eyes I have not often myself fought in battle, nor anyone of whose courage there I have not likewise been a spectator and witness, able to recount in detail the splendid things they did and when and where they did them. (18) I shall proceed into battle with those praised and decorated a thousand times, in whose midst I was first of all their foster child and then their commander, against those unknown by and ignorant of one another.

(44.1) "Wherever I have turned my eyes, I see a wealth of eagerness and vigor, a veteran army, and bridled and unbridled cavalry of the most noble stock, (2) you most faithful and brave allies, you Carthaginians, who will do battle for your fatherland on account of a most righteous wrath. (3) We are beginning the war, and we are descending into Italy with hostile standards, where we will fight more boldly and bravely than the enemy to the extent that our hope is greater, and the courage of attackers is greater than those who are attacked. (4) In addition, outrage, wrongs, and insults inflame and goad our spirits. First they demanded I, your leader, be punished, then of all of you who attacked Saguntum; they were going to set upon those who surrendered with the most brutal tortures. (5) This most cruel and arrogant nation considers all things its own and for its own pleasure. This nation thinks it fair that only they should decide with whom we should have war, with whom we should have peace. This nation circumscribes and confines us by the boundaries of mountains and rivers from which we may not depart; yet it does not observe those boundaries that they established. (6) 'Do not cross the Ebro! The Saguntines are not your concern!' Is Saguntum on the Roman side of the Ebro? 'Never move a step!' (7) Is it not enough that you have taken away my most ancient provinces of Sicily and Sardinia? You even take away Spain? And then, if I depart from these places, will you cross into Africa? Are you going to cross? I say that two men have crossed; they have sent two consuls of this year, one into Africa, the other into Spain. Nothing at all has been left for us, except that which we defend with arms. (8) Those who have refuge can be timid and sluggish, those whom their own country and their own fields will receive fleeing through safe and peaceful routes: it is necessary for you men to be brave and, with sure desperation, to reject everything save victory or death, either to conquer or, if fortune falters, to seek death in battle rather than in flight. (9) If this has been well fixed in all of you and determined in your minds, let me say one more time: you have conquered; no more fierce an incentive has been bestowed on men by the immortal gods than the contempt for death."

## LIVY'S SPEECH OF HANNIBAL TO SCIPIO AFRICANUS BEFORE THE BATTLE OF ZAMA (30.30.3–30) [WALSH 1986]

(30.30.3) Si hoc ita fato datum erat, ut qui primus bellum intuli populo Romano quique totiens prope in manibus victoriam habui, is ultro ad pacem petendam venirem, laetor te mihi sorte potissimum datum a quo peterem. (4) Tibi quoque inter multa egregia non in ultimis laudum hoc fuerit, Hannibalem, cui de tot Romanis ducibus victoriam di dedissent, tibi cessisse, teque huic bello vestris prius quam nostris cladibus insigni finem imposuisse. (5) Hoc quoque ludibrium casus ediderit fortuna, ut cum patre tuo consule ceperim arma, cum eodem primum Romano imperatore signa contulerim, ad filium eius inermis ad pacem petendam veniam.

(6) Optimum quidem fuerat eam patribus nostris mentem datam ab dis esse, ut et vos Italiae et nos Africae imperio contenti essemus. (7) Neque enim ne vobis quidem Sicilia ac Sardinia satis digna pretia sunt pro tot classibus, tot exercitibus, tot tam egregiis amissis ducibus; sed praeterita magis reprehendi possunt quam corrigi. (8) Ita aliena appetivimus ut de nostris dimicaremus, nec in Italia solum nobis bellum, vobis in Africa esset; sed et vos in portis vestris prope ac moenibus signa armaque hostium vidistis, et nos ab Carthagine fremitum castrorum Romanorum exaudimus. (9) Quod igitur nos maxime abominaremur, vos ante omnia optaretis, in meliore vestra fortuna de pace agitur. Agimus ii quorum et maxime interest pacem esse, et qui quodcumque egerimus ratum civitates nostrae habiturae sunt; animo tantum nobis opus est non abhorrente a quietis consiliis.

(10) Quod ad me attinet, iam aetas senem in patriam revertentem unde puer profectus sum, iam secundae iam adversae res ita erudierunt ut rationem sequi quam fortunam malim; (11) tuam et adulescentiam et perpetuam felicitatem, ferociora utraque quam quietis opus est consiliis, metuo. Non temere incerta casuum reputat quem fortuna nunquam decepit. (12) Quod ego fui ad Trasumennum, ad Cannas, id tu hodie es. Vixdum militari aetate imperio accepto, omnia audacissime incipientem nusquam fefellit fortuna. (13) Patris et patrui persecutus mortem, ex calamitate vestrae domus decus insigne virtutis pietatisque eximiae cepisti. Amissas Hispanias reciperasti, quattuor inde Punicis exercitibus pulsis; (14) consul creatus, cum ceteris ad tutandam Italiam parum animi esset, transgressus in Africam, duobus hic exercitibus caesis, binis eadem hora captis simul incensisque castris, Syphace potentissimo rege capto, tot urbibus regni eius, tot nostri imperii ereptis, me sextum decimum iam annum haerentem in possessione Italiae detraxisti.

(15) Potest victoriam malle quam pacem animus. Novi spiritus magnos magis quam utiles; et mihi talis aliquando fortuna adfulsit. (16) Quod si in secundis rebus bonam quoque mentem darent di, non ea solum quae evenissent sed etiam ea quae evenire possent reputaremus. Ut omnium obliviscaris aliorum, satis ego documenti in omnes casus sum; (17) quem modo, castris inter Anienem atque urbem vestram positis, signa inferentem ac iam prope scandentem moenia Romana videras, hic cernas duobus fratribus, fortissimis viris, clarissimis imperatoribus orbatum, ante moenia prope obsessae patriae quibus terrui vestram urbem ea pro mea deprecantem.

(18) Maximae cuique fortunae minime credendum est. In bonis tuis rebus, nostris dubiis, tibi ampla ac speciosa danti est pax, nobis petentibus magis necessaria quam honesta. (19) Melior tutiorque est certa pax quam sperata victoria; haec in tua, illa in deorum manu est. Ne tot annorum felicitatem in unius horae dederis discrimen. (20) Cum tuas vires tum vim fortunae Martemque belli communem propone animo; utrimque ferrum, utrimque corpora humana erunt. Nusquam minus quam in bello eventus respondent. (21) Non tantum ad id quod data pace iam habere potes, si proelio vinces, gloriae adieceris, <abieceris> quantum, si quid adversi eveniat. Simul parta ac sperata decora unius horae fortuna evertere potest. (22) Omnia in pace iungenda tuae potestatis sunt, P. Corneli; tunc ea habenda fortuna erit quam di dederint. (23) Inter pauca felicitatis virtutisque exempla M. Atilius quondam in hac eadem terra fuisset, si victor pacem petentibus dedisset patribus nostris; sed non statuendo felicitati modum nec cohibendo efferentem se fortunam, quanto altius elatus erat, eo foedius corruit.

(24) Est quidem eius qui dat, non qui petit, condiciones dicere pacis; sed forsitan non indigni simus qui nobismet ipsi multam inrogemus. (25) Non recusamus quin omnia propter quae ad bellum itum est vestra sint, Sicilia Sardinia Hispania, quidquid insularum toto inter Africam Italiamque continetur mari. (26) Carthaginienses, inclusi Africae litoribus vos—quando ita dis placuit—externa etiam terra marique videamus regentes imperio. (27) Haud negaverim propter non nimis sincere petitam aut exspectatam nuper pacem suspectam esse vobis Punicam fidem; multum per quos petita sit ad fidem tuendae pacis pertinet, Scipio. (28) Vestri quoque, ut audio, patres nonnihil etiam ob hoc, quia parum dignitatis in legatione erat, negaverunt pacem. (29) Hannibal peto pacem, qui neque peterem nisi utilem crederem, et propter eandem utilitatem tuebor eam propter quam petii; (30) et quemadmodum, quia a me bellum coeptum est, ne quem eius paeniteret quoad ipsi invidere di praestiti, ita adnitar ne quem pacis per me partae paeniteat.

(30.30.3) If it is fated that I, who have first waged war on the Roman people and who have so often had victory nearly in my hands, come to seek peace, I am glad that chance has given me you, a man of the first order, as the person from whom I sue for peace. (4) This will also be one of your most outstanding accomplishments, and by no means the least praised, that Hannibal, to whom the gods have given victory over so many Roman leaders, yielded to you, and that you have made an end to this war, a war that was remarkable for your disasters and then our own. (5) Fortune also made a laughingstock of our expectations, so that, although I took up arms when your father was consul, and though I first went to battle with him as the Roman general, unarmed I come to his son in order to seek peace.

(6) Indeed it would have been best if the gods had put into our fathers' minds that you should be content to rule over Italy and we to rule over Africa; (7) for not even for you have Sicily and Sardinia been a worthy exchange for the loss of so many fleets, so many armies, and so many excellent leaders. But it is easier to blame the past than correct it. (8) Thus we sought after others' possessions and ended up contending over our own, and for us it was not only a war in Italy, and for you not only one in Africa, but you have seen the standards and weapons of the enemy near by your gates and walls, and we hear from Carthage the rumblings of the Roman camp. (9) Thus we discuss peace when Fortune smiles on you—something we should most detest, and you desire above all else. We, for whom peace is of the greatest interest, are seeking it out, and whatever terms we have made, our states will approve. All we need is a state of mind that does not abhor calm deliberations.

(10) As for me, age, the return to my fatherland from which I set out as a boy, and favorable and unfavorable experience have taught me to prefer to follow reason rather than fortune; (11) I fear both your youth and your incessant luck, both of which are too fierce to grasp the need for calm deliberations. He does not easily reflect upon the uncertainties of chance whom fortune has never deceived. (12) What I was at Trasumenus, at Cannae, you are today. Although you received a command when scarcely of military age, fortune never cheated you as you undertook everything with the greatest boldness. (13) When you avenged the death of your father and uncle you took from the calamity of your home the signal distinction of courage and uncommon filial piety; you recovered the lost Spanish provinces after you had driven out four Punic armies. (14) In your subsequent consulship, when the rest did not even have the courage to defend Italy, you crossed into Africa and cut down two armies here, seized and burned two camps at the same hour, captured the great ruler, King Syphax, and took by force many cities of his kingdom and many of yours. Thus you drew me back from Italy, which I had tenaciously held for sixteen years.

(15) The heart can prefer victory rather than peace. I know that these spirits are great more than they are useful; such fortune once shown on me too. (16) But if the gods should also give sound reason in fortunate circumstances, we should be pondering not only those things that have occurred, but also those things that are able to occur. Though you have forgotten everything else, I am sufficient proof of all that can befall one. (17) The man whom you had seen pitching my camp not long ago between the Anio and the city, advancing my standards and then almost scaling Rome's walls, here you can see deprived of my two brothers, the bravest of men, the most distinguished commanders, before the walls of my nearly bested fatherland, seeking to avert from my land those things with which I terrified your city.

(18) Each person must trust the greatest fortune least. In your good circumstances, in our dubious ones, peace is glorious and splendid for you, should you grant it, and necessary more than honorable for us who seek it. (19) A sure peace is better and safer than a hoped for victory; the former is in your hands, the latter in those of the gods.

Do not expose the good fortune of so many years to the test of one hour. (20) Keep in mind not only your strength, but also the power of Fortune and the impartial god of war. On both sides there will be the sword and human bodies; nowhere less than in war do outcomes match expectations. (21) You cannot gain as much in glory if you conquer in battle as you will lose if you do not. The fortune of one hour is able to overturn at once honors gained and hoped for. (22) The power to make peace is in your hands, Publius Cornelius; otherwise you must endure the fortune that the gods give. (23) Among the few examples of good luck and courage would have been Marcus Atilius formerly in this same land, if he, as a victor, had granted peace to our fathers who were seeking it; but by not establishing a limit to his good luck, and not restraining unruly fortune, the higher he rose, the more shamefully he fell.

(24) It is, in fact, he who gives peace, not the one seeking it, who sets the conditions; but perhaps we might not be unworthy of inflicting a penalty on ourselves. (25) We accept the term that all the possessions for which we went to war are to be yours: Sicily, Sardinia, Spain, and all the islands between Africa and Italy that are bound by the sea. (26) Let us Carthaginians, restricted to the shores of Africa, behold you ruling even lands and seas, since it so pleased the gods. (27) I would not deny that, due to the fact that we recently sought or anticipated peace without real sincerity, Punic trustworthiness is suspect in your view. Much of the credibility of the peace depends on the quality of those through whom it has been sought, Scipio. (28) Your senators too, as I hear, denied the peace in part because there was a lack of men of stature in the embassy. (29) I, Hannibal, seek peace, I who would not seek it unless I believed it beneficial, and I shall maintain it on account of the same benefit that led me to seek it. (30) And in the same way, since I began the war, I saw to it that that no one faulted my conduct of the war (until the gods themselves grew hostile), so I shall take pains that no one will regret the peace gained through me.

## LIVY'S SPEECH OF SCIPIO AFRICANUS TO HANNIBAL BEFORE THE BATTLE OF ZAMA (30.31.1–9) [WALSH 1986]

(30.31.1) Adversus haec imperator Romanus in hanc fere sententiam respondit: "Non me fallebat, Hannibal, adventus tui spe Carthaginienses et praesentem indutiarum fidem et spem pacis turbasse; (2) neque tu id sane dissimulas, qui de condicionibus superioris pacis omnia subtrahas praeter ea quae iam pridem in nostra potestate sunt. (3) Ceterum ut tibi curae est sentire cives tuos quanto per te onere leventur, sic mihi laborandum est ne, quae tum pepigerunt, hodie subtracta ex condicionibus pacis praemia perfidiae habeant. (4) Indigni quibus eadem pateat condicio, etiam ut prosit vobis fraus petitis. Neque patres nostri priores de Sicilia, neque nos de Hispania fecimus bellum; et tunc Mamertinorum sociorum periculum et nunc Sagunti excidium nobis pia ac iusta induerunt arma. (5) Vos lacessisse et tu ipse fateris et di testes sunt, qui et illius belli exitum secundum ius fasque dederunt et huius dant et dabunt.

(6) "Quod ad me attinet, et humanae infirmitatis memini et vim fortunae reputo et omnia quaecumque agimus subiecta esse mille casibus scio. (7) Ceterum quemad-

modum superbe et violenter me faterer facere si, priusquam in Africam traiecissem, te tua voluntate cedentem Italia et imposito in naves exercitu ipsum venientem ad pacem petendam aspernarer, (8) sic nunc, cum prope manu conserta restitantem ac tergiversantem in Africam attraxerim, nulla sum tibi verecundia obstrictus. (9) Proinde si quid ad ea in quae tum pax conventura videbatur, quasi multa navium cum commeatu per indutias expugnatarum legatorumque violatorum, adicitur, est quod referam ad consilium; sin illa quoque gravia videntur, bellum parate, quoniam pacem pati non potuistis."

(30.31.1) In answer to these words, the Roman commander offered essentially this judgment: "I was not deceived, Hannibal, that the Carthaginians, in hope of your arrival, confounded both the present pledge of the armistice and the hope of peace; (2) and of course you do not conceal it, when you withdraw all the elements of the former terms for peace except those that have been in our power for some time. (3) Still, as it is a concern to you by how much you free your citizens from a burden, thus I must make sure that they are not rewarded for their treachery through remission of peace terms to which they had previously agreed. (4) Unworthy of the terms that lie open to you, you even hope to profit from your deceit. Our fathers were not the aggressors in Sicily, and we did not incite the war in Spain; then the danger to our allies the Mamertines and now the destruction of Saguntum clad us in holy and righteous arms. (5) You yourself admit and the gods are our witnesses that you provoked us, who gave a favorable, just, and lawful end to the former war, and give and will give one to the latter one.

(6) "As for me, I remember human weakness, and I think about the force of fortune and know that all the things we do are exposed to a thousand chances; (7) still, I would admit that I would be acting in an arrogant and violent way if after you had withdrawn from Italy by your own volition and embarked your army in ships before I came to Africa, I should spurn your overtures of peace; (8) as things stand, since I have dragged you back to Africa resisting almost to the point of blows and equivocating besides, I have been bound by no reverence for you. (9) Thus if anything is added to the terms of a peace treaty that seemed imminent, like compensation for our supply ships seized during the armistice or our mistreated ambassadors, I could bring this to the council, but if those additions also seem too harsh, prepare for war, since you have not been able to stomach peace."

## TACITUS' SPEECH OF BOUDICA (*Ann.* 14.35.1–2) [WELLESLEY 1986]

(14.35.1) Boudicca curru filias prae se vehens, ut quamque nationem accesserat, solitum quidem Britannis feminarum ductu bellare testabatur, sed tunc non ut tantis maioribus ortam regnum et opes, verum ut unam e vulgo libertatem amissam, confectum verberibus corpus, contrectatam filiarum pudicitiam ulcisci. Eo provectas Romanorum cupidines, ut non corpora, ne senectam quidem aut virginitatem impollutam relinquant. (2) Adesse tamen deos iustae vindictae; cecidisse legionem, quae proelium ausa sit; ceteros castris occultari aut fugam circumspicere. Ne strepitum quidem et clamorem tot milium, nedum impetus et manus perlaturos. Si copias armatorum, si causas belli secum expenderent, vincendum illa acie vel cadendum esse. Id mulieri destinatum: viverent viri et servirent.

(14.35.1) Boudica, riding in a chariot with her daughters before her, said as she approached each tribe that it was customary for the Britons to wage war under the leadership of women; but then, she said, she was avenging not her kingdom and her power as a woman born from noble ancestors, but rather her lost freedom, her body worn out by whips, and the defiled chastity of her daughters as one of the people. The rapaciousness of the Romans had advanced so far, she said, that they do not even leave bodies, old age, or maidenhood unsoiled. (2) Nevertheless, the gods of just revenge were present: a legion that dared battle had fallen; others hid in the camp or searched intently for an escape. She said that the Romans would not even be able to endure the roar and clamor of so many thousands, much less their fury and violence: if the Britons considered the abundance of troops and the motives of the war, they would know that their battle line must either conquer or fall. That was the resolve of a woman: the men might live and be slaves.

## TACITUS' SPEECH OF PAULINUS (*Ann*. 14.36.1–2) [WELLESLEY 1986]

(14.36.1) Quamquam confideret virtuti, tamen exhortationes et preces miscebat, ut spernerent sonores barbarorum et inanes minas: plus illic feminarum quam iuventutis adspici. Imbelles inermes cessuros statim, ubi ferrum virtutemque vincentium totiens fusi agnovissent. (2) Etiam in multis legionibus paucos, qui proelia profligarent; gloriaeque eorum accessurum, quod modica manus universi exercitus famam adipiscerentur. Conferti tantum et pilis emissis post umbonibus et gladiis stragem caedamque continuarent, praedae immemores: parta victoria cuncta ipsis cessura.

(14.36.1) Although he [Paulinus] trusted his soldiers' courage, he nevertheless mixed exhortations and entreaties that they should scorn the clamor of the barbarians and their empty threats: in their ranks there were more women than young men to be seen. Unwarlike and unarmed, they would give up immediately when, so often routed, they recognized the iron and courage of the conquerors. (2) Even in many legions, he said, there are a few people who win battles; that a small band would win the fame of an entire army would add to their glory. Only let them cast their javelins from a tight formation and, indifferent to plunder, carry on with the havoc and slaughter with shield-bosses and swords: when they had won, everything would be theirs.

## CASSIUS DIO'S SPEECH OF BOUDICA (62.3–6)
## [BOISSEVAIN, SMILDA, AND NAWIJN 1895–1931]

(62.3.1) "πέπεισθε μὲν τοῖς ἔργοις αὐτοῖς ὅσον ἐλευθερία τῆς δουλείας διαφέρει, ὥστ᾽ εἰ καὶ πρότερόν τις ὑμῶν ὑπὸ τῆς τοῦ κρείττονος ἀπειρίας ἐπαγωγοῖς ἐπαγγέλμασι τῶν Ῥωμαίων ἠπάτητο, ἀλλὰ νῦν γε ἑκατέρου πεπειραμένοι μεμαθήκατε μὲν ὅσον ἡμαρτήκατε δεσποτείαν ἐπισπαστὸν πρὸ τῆς πατρίου διαίτης προτιμήσαντες, ἐγνώκατε δὲ ὅσῳ καὶ πενία ἀδέσποτος πλούτου δουλεύοντος προφέρει. (2) τί μὲν γὰρ οὐ τῶν αἰσχίστων, τί δ᾽ οὐ τῶν ἀλγίστων, ἐξ οὗπερ ἐς τὴν Βρεττανίαν οὗτοι παρέκυψαν, πεπόνθαμεν; οὐ τῶν μὲν πλείστων καὶ μεγίστων κτημάτων ὅλων ἐστερήμεθα, τῶν δὲ λοιπῶν τέλη καταβάλλομεν; (3) οὐ πρὸς τῷ τἆλλα πάντα καὶ νέμειν καὶ γεωργεῖν ἐκείνοις, καὶ τῶν σωμάτων αὐτῶν δασμὸν ἐτήσιον φέρομεν; καὶ πόσῳ κρεῖττον ἦν ἅπαξ τισὶ πεπρᾶσθαι μᾶλλον ἢ μετὰ κενῶν ἐλευθερίας ὀνομάτων κατ᾽ ἔτος λυτροῦσθαι; πόσῳ δὲ ἐσφάχθαι καὶ ἀπολωλέναι μᾶλλον ἢ κεφαλὰς ὑποτελεῖς περιφέρειν; (4) καίτοι τί τοῦτο εἶπον; οὐδὲ γὰρ τὸ τελευτῆσαι παρ᾽ αὐτοῖς ἀζήμιόν ἐστιν, ἀλλ᾽ ἴστε ὅσον καὶ ὑπὲρ τῶν νεκρῶν τελοῦμεν· παρὰ μὲν γὰρ τοῖς ἄλλοις ἀνθρώποις καὶ τοὺς δουλεύοντάς τισιν ὁ θάνατος ἐλευθεροῖ, Ῥωμαίοις δὲ δὴ μόνοις καὶ οἱ νεκροὶ ζῶσι πρὸς τὰ λήμματα. (5) τί δ᾽ ὅτι, κἂν μὴ ἔχῃ τις ἡμῶν ἀργύριον (πῶς γὰρ ἢ πόθεν), ἀποδυόμεθα καὶ σκυλευόμεθα ὥσπερ οἱ φονευόμενοι; τί δ᾽ ἂν προϊόντος τοῦ χρόνου μετριάσαιεν, οὕτως ἡμῖν κατὰ τὴν πρώτην εὐθύς, ὅτε πάντες καὶ τὰ νεάλωτα θεραπεύουσι, προσενηνεγμένοι;

(4.1) "ἡμεῖς δὲ δὴ πάντων τῶν κακῶν τούτων αἴτιοι, ὥς γε τἀληθὲς εἰπεῖν, γεγόναμεν, οἵτινες αὐτοῖς ἐπιβῆναι τὴν ἀρχὴν τῆς νήσου ἐπετρέψαμεν, καὶ οὐ παραχρῆμα αὐτούς, ὥσπερ καὶ τὸν Καίσαρα τὸν Ἰούλιον ἐκεῖνον, ἐξηλάσαμεν· οἵτινες οὐ πόρρωθέν σφισιν, ὥσπερ καὶ τῷ Αὐγούστῳ καὶ τῷ Γαΐῳ τῷ Καλιγόλᾳ, φοβερὸν τὸ καὶ πειρᾶσαι τὸν πλοῦν ἐποιήσαμεν. (2) τοιγαροῦν νῆσον τηλικαύτην, μᾶλλον δὲ ἤπειρον τρόπον τινὰ περίρρυτον νεμόμενοι καὶ ἰδίαν οἰκουμένην ἔχοντες, καὶ τοσοῦτον ὑπὸ τοῦ ὠκεανοῦ ἀφ᾽ ἁπάντων τῶν ἄλλων ἀνθρώπων ἀφωρισμένοι ὥστε καὶ γῆν ἄλλην καὶ οὐρανὸν ἄλλον οἰκεῖν πεπιστεῦσθαι, καί τινας αὐτῶν καὶ τοὺς σοφωτάτους γε μηδὲ τὸ ὄνομα ἡμῶν ἀκριβῶς πρότερον ἐγνωκέναι, κατεφρονήθημεν καὶ κατεπατήθημεν ὑπ᾽ ἀνθρώπων μηδὲν ἄλλο ἢ πλεονεκτεῖν εἰδότων. (3) ἀλλ᾽ εἰ καὶ μὴ πρότερον, νῦν ἔτι, ὦ πολῖται καὶ φίλοι καὶ συγγενεῖς (πάντας γὰρ ὑμᾶς συγγενεῖς, ἅτε καὶ μιᾶς νήσου οἰκήτορας ὄντας καὶ ἓν ὄνομα κοινὸν κεκλημένους, νομίζω), τὰ προσήκοντα πράξωμεν, ἕως ἔτι τῆς ἐλευθερίας μνημονεύομεν, ἵνα καὶ τὸ πρόσρημα καὶ τὸ ἔργον αὐτῆς τοῖς παισὶ καταλίπωμεν. ἂν γὰρ ἡμεῖς τῆς συντρόφου εὐδαιμονίας παντελῶς ἐκλαθώμεθα, τί ποτε ἐκεῖνοι ποιήσουσιν ἐν δουλείᾳ τραφέντες;

(5.1) "λέγω δὲ ταῦτα οὐχ ἵνα μισήσητε τὰ παρόντα (μεμισήκατε γάρ), οὐδ᾽ ἵνα φοβηθῆτε τὰ μέλλοντα (πεφόβησθε γάρ), ἀλλ᾽ ἵνα ἐπαινέσω τε ὑμᾶς ὅτι καὶ καθ᾽ ἑαυτοὺς πάνθ᾽ ὅσα δεῖ προαιρεῖσθε, καὶ χάριν ὑμῖν γνῶ ὅτι καὶ ἐμοὶ καὶ ἑαυτοῖς ἑτοίμως συναίρεσθε. φοβεῖσθε δὲ μηδαμῶς τοὺς Ῥωμαίους· (2) οὔτε γὰρ πλείους ἡμῶν εἰσιν οὔτ᾽ ἀνδρειότεροι. τεκμήριον δὲ ὅτι καὶ κράνεσι καὶ θώραξι καὶ κνημῖσιν ἐσκέπασθε καὶ προσέτι καὶ σταυρώμασι καὶ τείχεσι καὶ τάφροις ἐσκεύασθε πρὸς τὸ μήτι πάσχειν ἐξ ἐπιδρομῆς τῶν πολεμίων. τοῦτο γὰρ αἱροῦνται μᾶλλον ὑπὸ τῶν φόβων ἢ τὸ καὶ δρᾶσαί τι προχείρως ὥσπερ ἡμεῖς. (3) τοσαύτη γὰρ περιουσία ἀνδρίας χρώμεθα ὥστε καὶ τὰς σκηνὰς ἀσφαλεστέρας τῶν τειχῶν καὶ τὰς ἀσπίδας πολυαρκεστέρας τῆς ἐκείνων πανοπλίας νομίζειν. ἐξ οὗπερ ἡμεῖς μὲν καὶ

κρατοῦντες αἱροῦμεν αὐτοὺς καὶ βιασθέντες ἐκφεύγομεν, κἂν ἄρα καὶ ἀναχωρῆσαί ποι
προελώμεθα, ἐς τοιαῦτα ἕλη καὶ ὄρη καταδυόμεθα ὥστε μήτε εὑρεθῆναι μήτε ληφθῆναι·
(4) ἐκεῖνοι δὲ οὔτε διῶξαί τινα ὑπὸ τοῦ βάρους οὔτε φυγεῖν δύνανται, κἂν ἄρα καὶ
ἐκδράμωσί ποτε, ἔς τε χωρία ἀποδεδειγμένα καταφεύγουσι, κἀνταῦθα ὥσπερ ἐς γαλεάγρας
κατακλείονται. (5) ἔν τε οὖν τούτοις παρὰ πολὺ ἡμῶν ἐλαττοῦνται, καὶ ἐν ἐκείνοις, ὅτι
οὔτε λιμὸν οὔτε δίψος, οὐ ψῦχος οὐ καῦμα ὑποφέρουσιν ὥσπερ ἡμεῖς, ἀλλ' οἱ μὲν καὶ σκιᾶς
καὶ σκέπης σίτου τε μεμαγμένου καὶ οἴνου καὶ ἐλαίου δέονται, κἂν ἄρα τι τούτων αὐτοὺς
ἐπιλίπῃ διαφθείρονται, ἡμῖν δὲ δὴ πᾶσα μὲν πόα καὶ ῥίζα σῖτός ἐστι, πᾶς δὲ χυμὸς ἔλαιον,
πᾶν δὲ ὕδωρ οἶνος, πᾶν δὲ δένδρον οἰκία. (6) καὶ μὴν καὶ τὰ χωρία ταῦτα ἡμῖν μὲν συνήθη
καὶ σύμμαχα, ἐκείνοις δὲ δὴ καὶ ἄγνωστα καὶ πολέμια· καὶ τοὺς ποταμοὺς ἡμεῖς μὲν γυμνοὶ
διανέομεν, ἐκεῖνοι δὲ οὐδὲ πλοίοις ῥᾳδίως περαιοῦνται. ἀλλ' ἴωμεν ἐπ' αὐτοὺς ἀγαθῇ τύχῃ
θαρροῦντες. δείξωμεν αὐτοῖς ὅτι λαγωοὶ καὶ ἀλώπεκες ὄντες κυνῶν καὶ λύκων ἄρχειν
ἐπιχειροῦσιν."

(6.1) ταῦτα εἰποῦσα λαὼν μὲν ἐκ τοῦ κόλπου προήκατο μαντείᾳ τινὶ χρωμένη, καὶ ἐπειδὴ
ἐν αἰσίῳ σφίσιν ἔδραμε, τό τε πλῆθος πᾶν ἡσθὲν ἀνεβόησε, καὶ ἡ Βουδουῖκα τὴν χεῖρα ἐς
τὸν οὐρανὸν ἀνατείνασα εἶπε (2) "χάριν τέ σοι ἔχω, ὦ Ἀνδράστη, καὶ προσεπικαλοῦμαί
σε γυνὴ γυναῖκα, οὐκ Αἰγυπτίων ἀχθοφόρων ἄρχουσα ὡς Νίτωκρις, οὐδ' Ἀσσυρίων τῶν
ἐμπόρων ὡς Σεμίραμις (καὶ γὰρ ταῦτ' ἤδη παρὰ τῶν Ῥωμαίων μεμαθήκαμεν), (3) οὐ μὴν
οὐδὲ Ῥωμαίων αὐτῶν ὡς πρότερον μὲν Μεσσαλῖνα ἔπειτ' Ἀγριππῖνα νῦν δὲ Νέρων (ὄνομα
μὲν <γὰρ> ἀνδρὸς ἔχει, ἔργῳ δὲ γυνή ἐστι· σημεῖον δέ, ᾄδει καὶ κιθαρίζει καὶ καλλωπίζεται),
ἀλλὰ ἀνδρῶν Βρεττανῶν, γεωργεῖν μὲν ἢ δημιουργεῖν οὐκ εἰδότων, πολεμεῖν δὲ ἀκριβῶς
μεμαθηκότων, καὶ τά τε ἄλλα πάντα κοινὰ καὶ παῖδας καὶ γυναῖκας κοινὰς νομιζόντων, καὶ
διὰ τοῦτο καὶ ἐκείνων τὴν αὐτὴν τοῖς ἄρρεσιν ἀρετὴν ἐχουσῶν. (4) τοιούτων οὖν ἀνδρῶν
καὶ τοιούτων γυναικῶν βασιλεύουσα προσεύχομαί τέ σοι καὶ αἰτῶ νίκην καὶ σωτηρίαν καὶ
ἐλευθερίαν κατ' ἀνδρῶν ὑβριστῶν ἀδίκων ἀπλήστων ἀνοσίων, εἴ γε καὶ ἄνδρας χρὴ καλεῖν
ἀνθρώπους ὕδατι θερμῷ λουμένους, ὄψα σκευαστὰ ἐσθίοντας, οἶνον ἄκρατον πίνοντας,
μύρῳ ἀλειφομένους, μαλθακῶς κοιμωμένους, μετὰ μειρακίων, καὶ τούτων ἐξώρων,
καθεύδοντας, κιθαρῳδῷ, καὶ τούτῳ κακῷ, δουλεύοντας. (5) μὴ γάρ τοι μήτ' ἐμοῦ μήθ' ὑμῶν
ἔτι βασιλεύσειεν ἡ Νερωνὶς ἢ Δομιτία, ἀλλ' ἐκείνη μὲν Ῥωμαίων ᾄδουσα δεσποζέτω (καὶ
γὰρ ἄξιοι τοιαύτῃ γυναικὶ δουλεύειν, ἧς τοσοῦτον ἤδη χρόνον ἀνέχονται τυραννούσης),
ἡμῶν δὲ σὺ ὦ δέσποινα ἀεὶ μόνη προστατοίης."

(62.3.1) "You have found out how much freedom differs from slavery through real experiences, so that, even if earlier some of you, through ignorance of what was superior,
were tricked by the tempting promises of the Romans, now that you have tried both,
you have learned how great a mistake you made in preferring an imported tyranny to
your ancient way of life, and you know how much penury without a master surpasses
wealth as a slave. (2) For what of the most shameful, the most distressing sort have
we not experienced since these people have taken themselves to Britain? Have we not
been robbed entirely of most of our greatest possessions, and do we not pay taxes on
the rest? (3) Besides pasturing and farming for them, do we not pay yearly tribute
for our own bodies? How much better would it have been to be sold once and for all,
rather than to be held ransom each year with the empty titles of freedom? How much

better would it have been to be slain and die than to endure while subject to a head tax? And yet why did I say this? (4) For, among them not even dying is scot-free, but you know how much we pay even for our dead; with other people, death frees even those who are enslaved, but with the Romans alone the dead live on for ill-gotten gain. (5) And why is it that, even though none of us has money (for how would we get it, and from where?), we are sold and stripped like victims of a homicide? And why should they be moderate in the time to come, when they have treated us in this fashion from the start, although all men treat even newly caught beasts well?

(4.1) "To speak the truth, we are responsible for all these evils, as some of us trusted them to set foot on the island to begin with, and did not immediately drive them off, as we expelled the famous Julius Caesar; and we did not, as we did with both Augustus and Gaius Caligula, make an attempt at a formidable voyage. (2) Thus, though we inhabit so large an island—rather a continent surrounded by water—and though we have our own world and are cut off by the ocean from all other people to such an extent that we have been believed to inhabit another land and sky, and even some of their wisest men have not previously known our exact name, we have been disdained and trampled on by people who know nothing other than greed. (3) But although we have not done what we ought beforehand, let us, my countrymen and friends and kinsmen (for I consider you kinsmen, since you inhabit one island and are called by a common name), do it now, so that we may leave behind to our children both the name and reality of freedom, while we still remember it. For if we utterly forget our natural state of happiness, what will our children do, nursed in slavery?

(5.1) "I do not say these things so that you will hate your present circumstances (for you already do), nor so that you will fear what is to come (for you already do), but so that I may laud you, because you have by yourselves chosen all the necessary steps, and thank you for readily working together with me and each other. Do not fear the Romans at all; (2) for they are neither more numerous than we nor more brave. And the proof is that they are covered with helmets and breastplates and greaves and besides prepared with stockades and walls and trenches so as not to suffer from an attack of the enemy. For they are overpowered by fears, unlike us, who are nonchalantly bold. (3) We truly enjoy such a wealth of bravery that we consider our tents more secure than their walls and our shields far more suitable than their full suits of armor. Thus when we beat them, we capture them, but when we are bested, we escape, and if we decide to withdraw somewhere, we slink away and hide in such marshes and hills that we can't be found or captured; (4) but the Romans, because of their heavy armor, are neither able to chase anyone nor to flee, and if they ever run away, they flee to appointed places, and are enclosed there as if trapped. (5) And in these respects they are by far inferior to us: they can also not endure hunger, thirst, cold, or heat as we can, but requiring shade, shelter, and bread, they need wine and oil, and if any of these things runs dry, they perish; for us, all grasses and roots serve as bread, all liquids serve as oil, all water serves as wine, and all trees serve as a house. (6) Indeed, these lands are familiar to us and our allies, but are unknown and adverse to them; and we swim the rivers naked, whereas they cannot get to the other side of them easily with boats. But let us go against them trusting in good fortune. Let us show them that they are hares and foxes attempting to rule over dogs and wolves."

(6.1) After she said this, employing some sort of divination, she let a hare escape from a fold of her dress, and when it ran in an auspicious direction, the whole multitude shouted out with delight and Boudica, lifting her hand toward the sky, said (2) "I give thanks to you, Andraste, and I call upon you as a woman to a woman, as one who does not rule over burden-bearing Egyptians as Nitocris, or over the tradesmen Assyrians as Semiramis (for even we have already learned these things from the Romans), (3) or over the Romans themselves, as did Messalina, then Agrippina, and now Nero (for though he has the name of a man, he is in fact a woman, as one can tell from his singing, his lyre playing, and his make up); rather, I rule over the Britons, who don't know how to farm or practice a trade, but have learned how to be consummate fighters, and consider all things common—including children and wives—and as a result the women have the same valor as men. (4) Ruling over such men and women, then, I both pray to you and ask for victory, safety, and freedom against insolent, unjust, insatiate, and profane men—if, at any rate, one should even call people men who bathe in warm water, eat artificial dainties, imbibe unmixed wine, anoint themselves with myrrh, sleep on soft beds with boys—even ones past their prime—and are slaves to a bad lyre-player. (5) Truly may Ms. Domitia-Nero no longer rule over us, but let that singing girl be lord over the Romans, for surely they are deserving of being slaves to such a woman, since they have already put up with her playing the tyrant for so long; but, mistress [sc. Andraste], may you always be our only leader."

## CASSIUS DIO'S SPEECH OF SUETONIUS PAULINUS (62.8.3–11.5) [BOISSEVAIN, SMILDA, AND NAWIJN 1895–1931]

(62.8.3) συντάττων δ' αὐτοὺς καὶ καθιστὰς προσπαρῄνει, λέγων

(9.1) "ἄγετε ἄνδρες συστρατιῶται, ἄγετε ἄνδρες Ῥωμαῖοι, δείξατε τοῖς ὀλέθροις τούτοισ ὅσον καὶ δυστυχοῦντες αὐτῶν προφέρομεν· αἰσχρὸν γάρ ἐστιν ὑμῖν, ἃ μικρῷ πρόσθεν ὑπ' ἀρετῆς ἐκτήσασθε, νῦν ἀκλεῶς ἀπολέσθαι. πολλάκις τοι τῶν νῦν παρόντων ἐλάττους ὄντες πολὺ πλείονας ἀντιπάλους καὶ ἡμεῖς αὐτοὶ καὶ οἱ πατέρες ἡμῶν ἐνίκησαν. (2) μήτ' οὖν τὸ πλῆθος αὐτῶν φοβηθῆτε καὶ τὴν νεωτεροποιίαν (ἐκ γὰρ ἀόπλου καὶ ἀμελετήτου προπετείας θρασύνονται), μήθ' ὅτι πόλεις τινὰς ἐμπεπρήκασιν· οὐ γὰρ κατὰ κράτος οὐδὲ ἐκ μάχης, ἀλλὰ τὴν μὲν προδοθεῖσαν τὴν δὲ ἐκλεφθεῖσαν εἷλον. ἀνθ' ὧν νῦν τὴν προσήκουσαν παρ' αὐτῶν δίκην λάβετε, ἵνα καὶ τοῖς ἔργοις αὐτοῖς ἐκμάθωσιν οἵους ὄντας ἡμᾶς οἷοι ὄντες ἠδικήκασι."

(10.1) ταῦτά τισιν εἰπὼν ἐφ' ἑτέρους ἦλθε, καὶ ἔφη "νῦν καιρὸς ὦ συστρατιῶται προθυμίας, νῦν τόλμης. ἂν τήμερον ἄνδρες ἀγαθοὶ γένησθε, καὶ τὰ προειμένα ἀναλήψεσθε· ἂν τούτων κρατήσητε, οὐκέτ' οὐδεὶς ἡμῖν οὐδὲ τῶν ἄλλων ἀντιστήσεται. διὰ μιᾶς τοιαύτης μάχης καὶ τὰ ὑπάρχοντα βεβαιώσεσθε καὶ τὰ λοιπὰ προσκαταστρέψεσθε· (2) πάντες γὰρ καὶ οἱ ἄλλοθί που ὄντες στρατιῶται ζηλώσουσιν ὑμᾶς καὶ ἐχθροὶ φοβηθήσονται. ὥστε ἐν ταῖς χερσὶν ἔχοντες ἢ πάντων ἀνθρώπων ἀδεῶς ἄρχειν ὧν καὶ οἱ πατέρες ὑμῶν κατέλιπον καὶ αὐτοὶ ὑμεῖς προσεπεκτήσασθε, ἢ πάντως αὐτῶν στερηθῆναι, ἕλεσθε ἐλεύθεροι εἶναι, ἄρχειν πλουτεῖν εὐδαιμονεῖν μᾶλλον ἢ τἀναντία αὐτῶν ῥαθυμήσαντες παθεῖν."

(11.1) τοιαῦτα δὲ καὶ τούτοις εἰπὼν ἐπὶ τοὺς τρίτους ἐπιπαρῆλθε, καὶ ἔλεξε καὶ ἐκείνοις "ἠκούσατε μὲν οἷα ἡμᾶς οἱ κατάρατοι οὗτοι δεδράκασι, μᾶλλον δὲ ἔνια αὐτῶν καὶ εἴδετε· (2) ὥσθ' ἕλεσθε πότερον καὶ αὐτοὶ τὰ αὐτὰ ἐκείνοις παθεῖν καὶ προσέτι καὶ ἐκπεσεῖν παντελῶς ἐκ τῆς Βρεττανίας, ἢ κρατήσαντες καὶ τοῖς ἀπολωλόσι τιμωρῆσαι καὶ τοῖς ἄλλοις ἀνθρώποις ἅπασι παράδειγμα ποιῆσαι καὶ πρὸς τὸ πειθαρχοῦν εὐμενοῦς ἐπιεικείας καὶ πρὸς τὸ νεωτερίζον ἀναγκαίας τραχύτητος. (3) μάλιστα μὲν οὖν ἔγωγε νικήσειν ἡμᾶς ἐλπίζω καὶ τῇ παρὰ τῶν θεῶν συμμαχίᾳ (τοῖς γὰρ ἀδικουμένοις ὡς τὸ πολὺ συναίρονται) καὶ τῇ πατρῴᾳ ἡμῶν ἀνδρίᾳ, Ῥωμαίους τε ὄντας καὶ ταῖς ἀρεταῖς ἁπάντων ἀνθρώπων κεκρατηκότας, καὶ ταῖς ἐμπειρίαις (καὶ γὰρ αὐτοὺς τούτους τοὺς νῦν ἀντικαθεστῶτας ἡττήσαντες κεχειρώμεθα), τῷ τε ἀξιώματι (οὐ γὰρ ἀντιπάλοις τισὶν ἀλλὰ δούλοις ἡμετέροις συμβαλοῦμεν, οὓς καὶ ἐλευθέρους καὶ αὐτονόμους ὄντας εἰάσαμεν)· (4) ἂν δὲ δὴ παρ' ἐλπίδα τι συμβῇ (οὐδὲ γὰρ <οὐδὲ> τοῦτ' εἰπεῖν ὀκνήσω), ἄμεινόν ἐστι μαχομένους ἡμᾶς ἀνδρείως πεσεῖν ἢ ἁλόντας ἀνασκολοπισθῆναι, τὰ σπλάγχνα τὰ ἑαυτῶν ἐκτμηθέντα ἰδεῖν, πασσάλοις διαπύροις ἀναπαρῆναι καὶ ὕδατι ζέοντι τηκομένους ἀπολέσθαι, καθάπερ ἐς θηρία τινὰ ἄγρια ἄνομα ἀνόσια ἐμπεπτωκότας. (5) ἢ οὖν περιγενώμεθα αὐτῶν, ἢ ἐνταῦθα ἀποθάνωμεν. καλὸν τὸ μνημεῖον τὴν Βρεττανίαν ἕξομεν, κἂν πάντες οἱ λοιποὶ Ῥωμαῖοι ἐξ αὐτῆς ἐκπέσωσι· τοῖς γὰρ σώμασι τοῖς ἡμετέροις πάντως αὐτὴν ἀεὶ καθέξομεν."

(62.8.3) Ordering and placing the men, he [Paulinus] exhorts them, saying,

(9.1) "Come on, fellow soldiers, come on, Roman men! Show these accursed men how much we surpass them, even though fairing badly; for it is shameful for you now to lose disgracefully those things that you recently won by your valor. Many times now have both we and our fathers, although far fewer in number, defeated more antagonists. (2) Do not fear their multitude or their rebellion (for they are bold because of unarmored and unpracticed rashness) nor the fact that they have burned some cities; for they did not take them by force or after a battle, but they took one that was betrayed and another that was abandoned. And so now take from them a fitting penalty, so that they who have wronged us may learn from experience what sort of men we are."

(10.1) After saying these words to them, he went to another group and said "Now, fellow soldiers, is the right time for fighting spirit and boldness. If you are brave men today, you will take back the things you have lost; if you prevail over them, no one will stand against us. Through one such battle you will secure your possessions and will subdue all that remains; (2) for elsewhere all our fellow soldiers will admire you, and our enemies will be afraid. Thus, since it is in your hands either to rule over all people fearlessly (over those places your father left behind for you and those you yourselves acquired in addition), or to be robbed of them entirely, choose to be free, to rule, to be wealthy, to be fortunate, rather than, through faintheartedness, the opposite."

(11.1) When he had finished an address like this to those men, he went to the third group, and said to them "You have heard what sort of things these damnable men have done to us—rather, you have even seen some of them. (2) Thus choose whether you yourselves want to suffer the same things our fellow Romans did, and, moreover, to be driven out of Britain entirely, or by victory to avenge those who died and to make an example for all other people regarding both the equitable treatment of those who are obedient and the requisite harshness to the rebellious. (3) And so now I especially hope that we shall be victorious, since the gods are our allies (for they most often side with those who have been treated unjustly), and because of our ancestral valor, as we are Romans and have conquered all men by our courage, and due to our experience (for we have subdued all these inferior characters who now oppose us), and because of our prestige (for we do not engage some rivals, but rather our slaves, whom we defeated when they were free and independent); (4) and if the result goes against our hope (for I will not shrink from saying this), it is better for us to fall while fighting bravely than to be captured and impaled, to see our innards cut out, to be spitted on fiery skewers, to die consumed by boiling water, as if we had been thrown to some wild, lawless, and unholy beasts. (5) And so let us either prevail over them or die here. We shall have Britain as a beautiful memorial, even if the rest of the Romans will be deprived of it; for with our very bodies we shall always entirely possess it."

## INTRODUCTION

1. Rutledge 2000:75.

2. Ibid. For criticism of Rutledge's position, see Shumate 2006:83.

3. E.g., Webster 1994 and 1996a (esp. 116-119); Alston 1996; Rutledge 2000; Clarke 2001. See also O'Gorman (1993), who, though at points discussing the ways in which the *Germania* criticizes contemporary Rome (146-148), views Tacitus as ultimately engaging in a sort of textual possession of the Germans: "The very study of Germany represents that country as passive, subject to scrutiny by the powerful, invasive Rome" (139). Cf. Rose (1995:396), who, in elaborating on Cicero, detects a link between support for imperialism and impressions of the colonized as both inferior and destined for servitude. For a discussion of the link between Roman stereotyping of foreigners and Roman imperial expansion, see Isaac 2004:304-323.

4. E.g., Rutledge 2000; Clarke 2001:103; Fincham 2001 (esp. 31).

5. Isaac 1990:27-28.

6. E.g., Woolf 1998:24-76; Mattern 1999:70-80; Allen 2006:34: "In talking about hostages, the Romans seem to congratulate themselves on their imperial accomplishment, perpetually glancing over the hostage's shoulder at the world that he might someday help them to control." Yet note that Allen sees Tacitus as an unrepresentative example of a Roman author who did not use hostages as a means to glorify the Empire (224-244); Phang 2008:79-81.

7. See Mommsen 1894; Frank 1912 and 1929; Holleaux 1921; Badian 1968; Errington 1972 (esp. 3-5). Badian (1958) has been associated with the notion of "defensive imperialism," due to the recurring argument that Rome shunned annexing foreign territories in favor of a loose-ended patron-client relationship between itself and the states it had conquered. Yet Badian's thesis is more nuanced than the label "defensive imperialism" allows: he argues that for strategic purposes Rome preferred nebulous bonds of patronage with its defeated enemies to enable it to assess its own obligations and lack of obligations to the conquered areas in question.

8. E.g., Harris 1971 and 1979; Brunt 1978; North 1981; Hingley 1982 and 1993; Jal 1982; Miles 1990; De Souza 1996; Freeman 1996 and 1997; Mattingly 1996 and 1997b; Hanson 1997; Whittaker 1997. For important criticism of more recent approaches to Roman expansion, see Eckstein 2006. For a survey of scholarly approaches to Roman imperialism, see Frézouls 1983.

9. For discussions of this topic, see Hingley 1993 and 2000; Freeman 1996.

10. On this topic, see Vasunia 2003:93–96.

11. E.g., Freeman 1997; Whittaker 1997; Fincham 2001; Hingley 2005:49–71. For some perceptive comments on the often broad and unspecific influence of post-colonial theory on classicists, see Vasunia 2003:88. For a general discussion of post-colonial theory in the context of Roman imperialism, see Webster 1996b.

12. Said [1978] 2003. For Said's discussion of Orientalism as it pertains to the ancient world, see 21, 56–57.

13. See Adler 2008a and 2008b.

14. Frank 1929:7. On Frank's life, see DeWitt 1939.

15. Frank 1929:8–10, 324–325: "Pompey seems to be the first general frankly sent out for the purposes of extending Rome's borders" (325). On fetial law, see Frank 1912; Gelzer 1964; Brunt 1978; Wiedemann 1986; Watson 1993.

16. On Haverfield's life, see Macdonald 2004.

17. Haverfield 1911:xviii.

18. Ibid. xviii–xix.

19. Cf. Haverfield [1910] 1915:11: "Our civilization seems firmly set in many lands; our task is rather to spread it further and develop its good qualities than to defend its life. If war destroy it in one continent, it has other homes. But the Roman Empire was the civilized world. Outside roared the wild chaos of barbarism. . . . Had Rome failed to civilize, had the civilized life found no period in which to grow firm and tenacious, civilization would have perished utterly."

20. For criticism of Said's work, see Kerr 1980; Young 1990:119–140; al-'Azm 1991; Ahmad 1992; Lewis 1993:99–118; MacKenzie 1995:xii–39; Kramer 2001; Fraiman 2003:36–53; Figuera 2004; Irwin 2006; Warraq 2007. For more positive impressions of Said's oeuvre, see Prakash 1995; Moore-Gilbert 1997:34–73; Ashcroft and Ahluwalia 1999; Huggan 2002.

21. Al-'Azm 1991.

22. Said [1978] 2003:204. According to MacKenzie (1995:xix), "Said's books are profoundly polemical, both because scholarship and ideology are seen to be so inseparably intertwined and because he insists upon the necessity of the scholar being involved in the hurly-burly of politics."

23. For a discussion of the influence of Third Worldism on postcolonial theory, see Gordon 1989:51–57; Adler 2005:41–47.

24. For examples of interesting works that at least partly pertain to Roman imperialism and elite Roman perceptions of foreigners, see above, n. 6.

25. Hingley 1994:12.

26. The text of Tac. *Ag.* used in this book is that of Winterbottom and Ogilvie 1975.

27. It has not proved possible throughout to assess the historians' works according to chronological order, since the book compares and contrasts two authors' approaches to similar speeches. Thus the chapters on Sallust's and Trogus' Mithridatic compositions appear before those of Polybius and Livy on Hannibal.

28. This is, however, not entirely the case, since Trogus—or any other Roman historian, for that matter—could have chosen to eschew such enemy orations in his work. The desire to include the *ipsissima verba* orations of foreign rivals would itself demonstrate an author's preferences, even if other considerations compelled him to relate them.

29. For examples of extremely divergent conclusions on this issue, contrast the skepticism regarding the historicity of speeches of Hansen (1993), Yunis (2002), and Damon (2007:440) with the optimism of Fornara (1983:142–168) and Pritchett (2002:1–80). See also Avenarius 1956:40–53; Russell 1967:135–136; Wiseman 1981; Brock 1995; Adler 2005:4–33.

30. Overall, it should be noted that in recent decades scholars have tended to focus on the poetic and rhetorical aspects of Greco-Roman historiography and have proved skeptical of its supposedly proto-"scientific" nature; e.g., Wiseman 1979; Woodman 1988. As a result, one detects a general aversion to concluding that any set speeches in works from this tradition correspond to historical orations; e.g., Brock 1995.

31. As Burgess (1902:209–214) noted. Cf. Marincola 1997:17: "Certain types of incidents common in war, such as the capture of a city, or the speech of a commander before battle, were particularly subject to imitation [in Greco-Roman historiography]."

32. On this topic, see Hansen 1993. Cf. Daly 2002:139–143. Note, however, Pritchett (2002:52–65), who disagrees with Hansen's position.

33. As Taine (1874:291–292) noted. Marincola (2007:128) doubts that generals gave lengthy speeches to their troops prior to battles.

34. Given his lineage and education, it is possible that Mithridates addressed his troops in Greek. The same is true—though far less probable—in the case of Hannibal; see below. Mithridates would not have composed a letter to Arsaces, the Persian king, in Greek, however, and this would naturally affect the quality of firsthand information Sallust possessed for his *Epistula Mithridatis*.

35. See below: on Polybius, chapter 3; on Livy, chapter 4; on Sallust, chapter 1; on Pompeius Trogus, chapter 2.

36. See below.

37. Laird 1999:121–152.

38. For a discussion of the purposes of such orations in Greco-Roman historiography, see Keitel 1987:159–160, 167; Laird 2009:206–209.

39. For ancient discussion of deliberative oratory, see Cic. *Inv.* 2.155–176; *Rhet. Her.* 3.1–9; Quint. *Inst.* 3.8. For a modern assessment of the basics of Roman deliberative oratory, see Kennedy 1972:18–21; Levene 1999:198–202.

40. On this topic, see Marincola 1997:19–33.

41. See ibid. 20–21.

42. For a variety of views on this topic, see Harris 1989; Humphrey 1991. In general, scholars do not suppose that literacy rates in Roman antiquity were ever very high.

43. Marincola 1997:30–31.

44. Ibid. 24–25.

45. To give a modern example: Mamet (2006), for instance, specifically addresses "self-loathing" Jews as both the target and the target audience for his polemic. It is far more likely, however, that the majority of the book's readers largely agrees with its thesis, and thus do not consider themselves part of this group. This is, admittedly, a particularly pointed example, but it does speak to the difficulties inherent in assuming a work's readership.

46. An example from modern publishing: Bloom's Straussian tract *The Closing of the American Mind* (1987) found itself atop the *New York Times*' bestseller lists despite its ponderousness.

47. Arist.: τέλος δὲ ἑκάστοις τούτων ἕτερόν ἐστι, καὶ τρισὶν οὖσι τρία, τῷ μὲν συμβουλεύοντι τὸ συμφέρον καὶ βλαβερόν ("There is a different goal for each of these [kinds of orations], and there are three goals, since there are three kinds of orations; for the deliberative kind, the goal is the expedient and the harmful"). The text of Aristotle used here is that of Ross 1959. In *Rh.* 1.6.1, however, Aristotle equates the expedient with the good, thereby offering a morally charged notion of expediency. *Rhet. Her.*: <O>mnem orationem eorum, qui sententiam dicent, finem sibi conveniet utilitatis proponere, ut omnis eorum ad eam totius orationis ratio conferatur ("It is proper for every speech of those who consider official opinion to set forth expediency as their goal, so that the entire plan of their whole speech may be directed toward this end"). The text of the *Rhet. Her.* used here is that of Marx and Trillitzsch 1964.

48. Quint. *Inst.* 3.8.1: *Deliberativas quoque miror a quibusdam sola utilitate finitas. Ac si quid in his unum sequi oporteret, potior fuisset apud me Ciceronis sententia, qui hoc materiae genus dignitate maxime contineri putat* ("I am also amazed that deliberative orations have been restricted by some people to expediency alone. And if it were necessary to pick one of these goals, I would have agreed with Cicero, who thinks that this kind of oratory is chiefly comprised of what is honorable"). The text of Quintilian used in this book is that of Winterbottom 1970. Cic. *De orat.* 2.82.334: *Ergo in suadendo nihil est optabilius quam dignitas; nam qui utilitatem petit, non quid maxime velit suasor, sed quid interdum magis sequatur, videt* ("Thus in an advisory speech nothing is more desirable than that which is honorable; for he who seeks expediency does not see what the advisor wants above all but what suffices for the time being"). The text of *De orat.* used here is that of Wilkins 1902. Cf. *Inv.* 2.173. On these differing assessments of deliberative oratory among ancient critics and their potential influence on ancient historians, see Levene 1999.

49. See, e.g., Kennedy 1959, which discusses the development of Greek deliberative oratory during the fifth and fourth centuries B.C. Kennedy argues that Thucydides focused on a single form of argument, whereas Isocrates preferred to present a variety.

50. Cf. Quint. *Inst.* 8.1.3; 10.1.32. Cf. D.H. *Th.* 42 for equally unspecific praise of Pericles' speech in Th. 1.140–144.

51. Cf. Lucian *Hist. conscr.* 15, which criticizes one Crepereius Calpurnianus for creating an oration that copies Thucydides' Corcyrean speech (1.32–36). Even if

Lucian's comment is a joke (which strikes this author as likely), it demonstrates the importance of offering believable addresses in Greco-Roman historiography.

52. D.H. *Th.* 36, 40–41. Cf. D.H. *Pomp.* 5 on the merits of Philistus' orations.

53. Cf. Demetr. *Eloc.* 227, which relates that epistolary compositions should abound in glimpses of the author's character.

54. The text of Lucian used is that of Macleod 1980.

55. Plb. 2.56.10; 12.25a5; 29.12. Elsewhere, however, he appears to consider verisimilitude a proper—if not *the* proper—guide to the presenting of speeches in historical works (12.25i; 12.25k; 36.1). For a useful discussion of this apparent inconsistency in Polybius' methodological criticisms regarding speechifying, see Mohm 1977:53–62.

56. Andersen 2001.

57. Ibid. 5–6.

58. For Dionysius' criticisms of Thucydides' speechifying, see *Th.* 34, 40–41.

59. Cf. Levene 1999:204: "Where the historian's standpoint may emerge is not simply from the role of morality in the actual content of the speeches, but from the part which the narrator shows the speech playing in the narrative as a whole . . . , and in particular from the way in which the characters in the work are presented as responding—or failing to respond—to the moral topics in it." This may not prove as straightforward or easy to discern, however, as Levene suggests.

60. See above.

61. E.g., 21.4.9; 22.6.12.

62. Cf. Quint. *Inst.* 7.1.10–11. Both Cicero and Quintilian discuss this topic in the context of judicial oratory, but their comments also seem applicable to deliberative speeches.

63. Fowler 1990.

64. Cf. ibid. 47: "One way of looking at the way that cultural hegemony is imposed through language is to think of *enforced* focalisation shifts. People are forced to use expressions which do not 'really' represent their point of view because no others are available to them" (emphasis in original).

65. Ibid. 57.

## PART ONE INTRODUCTION

1. *Chron.* 151 H.

2. Justin 43.5.11. Justin specifies that Trogus was of Vocontian origin.

3. Some manuscripts of Justin offer the reading "*avum*" in 43.5.11, and thus claim that Trogus' grandfather received citizenship from Pompey the Great. Others read "*proavum*" ("great-grandfather"). From a chronological standpoint, it is more likely that "*avum*" is correct. See Klotz 1952:2301.

4. E.g., von Gutschmid [1882] 1894b:223; Mazzolani [1972] 1976:172; Santi-Amantini 1981:30–31; Alonso-Núñez 1987:68. Some scholars claim that Trogus' choice of sources is chiefly to blame for his history's anti-Romanism. A few scholars

believe that Trogus did his best to limit the anti-Romanism he found in these sources (e.g., Jacoby [1926:221]). Still, Trogus selected these sources—and not others—for his world history, and thus remains implicated in the supposed anti-Roman elements in his speech of Mithridates.

5. Those scholars who believe that Sallust has sympathy to a certain extent for the arguments offered in the *EM* posit that the letter criticizes only specific elements of Roman society—not Roman society wholesale. E.g., Bickerman (1946:148–151); Pasoli (1965:139); Mazzarino (1968:374–375); Mazzolani ([1972] 1976:41); Sherwin-White (1984:181 n. 82); Vázquez (1989:151).

6. For an extended discussion of this topic, see Earl 1966.

7. Lovejoy and Boas [1935] 1997:1–7.

8. See above, n. 4. Rambaud (1948:182–184) is an exception and does link Trogus' view of Mithridates to "chronological primitivism." Yet Rambaud sees Sallust as Trogus' intellectual influence regarding this idea.

9. See Justin 43, esp. 1.1–2; 2.5. Admittedly, Justin's book 43 discusses only early Italy and the Roman kingship. It is possible that Trogus believed Rome began to decay earlier than Sallust thought.

### CHAPTER ONE

1. In the *EM* (1), Sallust refers to Phraates simply as Arsaces. This prompted von Carosfeld (1888:75) to claim that the *EM* was addressed to Sinatruces, Phraates' predecessor. Phlegon 12.7, however, informs us that Phraates succeeded Sinatruces in 70/69 B.C., before the Battle of Tigranocerta; it is to the former, then, that the *EM* must be addressed. For the dramatic date of the letter, see below, n. 2.

2. Debevoise (1938:70) dates the *EM* to shortly *before* the Battle of Tigranocerta in 69 B.C. Von Carosfeld (1888:75) and Pasoli (1965:136) claim that the *EM* was composed after Tigranocerta. In view of the ancient evidence regarding Mithridates' and Tigranes' diplomatic contact with the Parthians, however, it is unlikely that Sallust had Mithridates write the *EM* before the battle.

3. For contradictory views regarding Mithridates', Tigranes', and Lucullus' diplomacy with Phraates after the Battle of Tigranocerta, see App. *Mith.* 87; D.C. 36.1; Plu. *Luc.* 30.1–2; Memnon 38.7–8. For opposing modern assessments of this situation, see van Ooteghem 1959:136; Keaveney 1981:203 and 1992:116; Dabrowa 1982:24–25 (Dabrowa mistakenly believes that Sinatruces is part of the negotiations); Bulin 1983:81–85; Sherwin-White 1984:180.

4. For the date at which the collection was made, see McGushin 1992:6; Geckle 1995:12, 21.

5. E.g., Sanford 1937:438–439; Stier 1969:447.

6. See Richter 1987:178–179.

7. E.g., Volkmann (1964:10–11); Mazzarino (1968:374); Raditsa (1969:6–9, 310–314); McGing (1986:154–161); Vázquez (1989:148).

8. This in fact appears to be the majority view. See Büchner 1960:229; Earl

1966:109–110; Mazzolani [1972] 1976:60; Sherwin-White 1984:180–181; Ahlheid 1988:67; McGushin 1994:174; Geckle 1995:v, 68.

9. Fronto *Ad Verum* 2 (p. 124 van den Hout 1988): *Ex<s>tant epistulae utraque lingua partim ab ipsis ducibus conscriptae, partim a scriptoribus historiarum vel annalium compositae, ut illa Thucydidi nobilissima Niciae ducis epistula ex Silicia missa; item apud C. Sallustium ad Arsacen regem Mithridatis auxilium inplorantis litterae criminosae* ("There are letters in both languages partly written by the leaders themselves, partly composed by the writers of histories or annals, such as Thucydides' most dignified epistle of the commander Nicias that was sent from Sicily; likewise the reproachful letter of Mithridates to King Arsaces asking for help in the work of C. Sallustius").

10. Welles 1934:297.

11. D.C. 36.1; Cic. *Man.* 23; Posidonius *FGrH* 87 F 36 = fr. 253 Edelstein-Kidd (Ath. 5.211d–215b).

12. In the inscription, Mithridates refers to the Romans as τοὺς κοινοὺς πολεμίους ("the common enemies [of mankind]"; 6–7). In *Jug.* 81.1, Jugurtha calls the Romans *communis omnium hostis* ("the common enemy of all men"). Are we to assume that Sallust studied Pontic propaganda in order to craft a short speech by the Numidian Jugurtha? Hardly. More likely this phrase is a rhetorical commonplace. For more discussion of *Jug.* 81.1, see below.

13. For a more thorough discussion of the historicity of the *EM*, and the problems with considering it the product of an in-depth analysis of a pro-Pontic tradition, see Adler 2005:106–119.

14. The text of Sallust's work used in this chapter is that of Kurfess 1976. For the full text and translation of the *EM*, see the appendix to the current volume.

15. Bickerman 1946:134–137. See also McGushin 1994:174.

16. Cf. Leeman 1963:246; Ahlheid 1988:69; Geckle 1995:153. According to Bickerman (1946:135–136) and Raditsa (1969:50), however, the *EM*'s introduction follows standard rhetorical guidelines for rhetorical compositions, and thus, it seems, need not be adapted from Thucydides.

17. The text of Thucydides used here is that of Jones 1942.

18. Memnon 38.8 mentions the return of these lands to Parthia as essential to a potential alliance between Mithridates, Tigranes, and Phraates.

19. On Roman fetial law, see Frank 1912; Gelzer 1964; Brunt 1978; Wiedemann 1986. Admittedly, Roman regard for fetial law may have waned by the time Sallust wrote. See Watson 1993:54–61. Yet, as McGushin (1994:180) notes in regard to this section of the *EM*, "according to Livy (38.45.3–6) the eastern wars which Mithridates uses to illustrate his statement of motive were declared in strict compliance with fetial procedure." As a result, McGushin concludes that "this explanation for Roman reasons for going to war is in sharp contradiction to Roman pretensions." Some recent scholarship has suggested that deeply skeptical attitudes toward the import of fetial law—and, more expansively, Roman concern for waging "just wars"—may be mistaken: e.g., Riggsby 2006:157–189; Ager 2009; Yakobson 2009.

20. As Raditsa (1969) 73–74 notes.

21. Above all, see Stier 1969, offering the most thorough criticism of the view that the *EM* was composed to denounce Rome and its foreign policy.

22. We know of the existence of such sources, however: Metrodorus of Scepsis, Aesopus, Teucerus of Cyzicus, Heraclides of Magnesia, Hypsicrates of Amisus, Apollonides. For a fuller discussion of pro-Pontic sources concerning Mithridates, see Richter 1987:179–182. On Metrodorus, see Alonso-Núñez 1984.

23. This is particularly important in regard to Sallust, who was even capable of informing the reader that he knew that some details he had recorded were not generally accepted as true (*Jug.* 17.7).

24. According to Bickerman (1946:137–141), section 5 is the first part of the letter's *argumentatio*. Ahlheid (1988:72–74), however, views sections 5–15 as a *narratio*. See also McGushin 1994:177–178.

25. See Stier 1969:442–443.

26. See Liv. 31.2.1–4, 18.1–3; Plb. 16.27; Justin 30.3.5.

27. As Bickerman (1935) and (1945) suggested. Cf. Justin 29.4.11, 30.3.6; App. *Mac.* 2–4; Paus. 7.7.3–7; Zonar. 9.15.1–2.

28. Bickerman 1935:60 and 1945:144.

29. See Bickerman 1945:145. Raditsa (1969:87–90), moreover, reasonably points out that Mithridates' description of Philip as a trustworthy friend of the Romans is far-fetched.

30. Raditsa (1969:94) agrees with this assessment.

31. Liv. 33.39.5. For this reason, Stier (1969:442–443) considers the argument in section 6 to be distorted.

32. Sallust's speech of Julius Caesar also brings up Perseus (*Cat.* 51.5), albeit in a different context.

33. As Raditsa (1969:123) mentions.

34. *Pace* Stier (1969:443).

35. Raditsa 1969:131–132.

36. See Raditsa 1969:141–142.

37. Ibid. 139.

38. Stier 1969:445.

39. Cic. *Agr.* 2.40; Liv. *Per.* 93; Vell. 2.4.1, 39.2; App. *Mith.* 7 and 71; *BC* 1.111.

40. Magie 1950:209–210. Raditsa (1969:179–180) also finds fault with the Romans and argues in favor of Mithridates' view. App. *Mith.* 11 refers to Cassius' *praenomen* as "Lucius." The correct *praenomen*, however, is Gaius: see Broughton 1951–1986:2.38 n. 6. Glew (1977:398) believes that Mithridates was acting defensively against Aquilius and Cassius.

41. It is peculiar that Mithridates specifically mentions the Cretans and Ptolemy in section 10. Perhaps Sallust discussed them because they played a key part in earlier portions of the narrative that are now lost.

42. For a more thorough discussion of Greek animosity toward Roman control of the East, see Raditsa 1969–1970a, which views Mithridates' criticisms of Roman conduct in Asia Minor as valid.

43. As in section 10 of the *EM*, Mithridates offers the examples of Crete and the Ptolemaic kingdom. Raditsa (1969:200–202) believes that Mithridates' summation of Cretan affairs is accurate. Still, one wonders why Sallust mentioned these two examples but not others.

44. App. *Mith.* 64. For a more thorough discussion of this topic, see Raditsa 1969–1970b.

45. Plu. *Luc.* 30.2.

46. See Plb. 21.11.2, 5–6; Liv. 42.52.16, 44.24.1–6; Plu. *Cat. Mai.* 8.8; Rawson 1975:150–152.

47. *Pace* Raditsa (1969:221).

48. See, e.g., Liv. 1.59–60, 2.1; Tac. *Ann.* 1.1; D.C. 44.11.1–3.

49. Contra Plu. *Luc.* 30.2.

50. See Bickerman 1946:148–151 and below.

51. Raditsa (1969:287), who usually perceives arguments in the *EM* to be reflections of genuine Pontic propaganda, believes that section 20 could comment on the vicissitudes of Roman foreign policy in Sallust's own day.

52. For a discussion of Memmius' oration in Sallust, see Ullmann 1927:35–37; Syme 1964:156, 166–167; Earl 1966:68–69; Paul (1984:97–103) believes that Sallust "uses the speech (like the excursus and Marius' speech) as a vehicle for his own reflections on political life" (97).

53. According to Paul (1984:100), this sentence contains "typical political invective."

54. *Jug.* 30.3–4. See also 27.2. Earl (1966:68) notes that both Memmius' speech and Sallust's discussion of "party strife" in the Republic "refer to the control of the state by the nobility in very similar terms."

55. On this speech, see Ullmann 1927:37–40; Pöschl 1940:48–58; Syme 1964:168–169; Paul 1984:207–215.

56. On the speech of Adherbal, see Pöschl 1940:88–89; Paul 1984:201, which links the speech to "Carneades' lectures on justice"; and Dué 2000, which focuses on the tragic character of Adherbal in the *Bellum Iugurthinum*.

57. Paul (1984:201) correctly points out that "Carthage, of course, was not ruled by kings." For this reason, perhaps Jugurtha's mention of it amounts to a less potent example.

58. Some scholars have noted the similarities between the *EM* and *Jug.* 81.1: e.g., Büchner (1960:229); La Penna (1968:291–292); Leggewie (1975:59); Mazzolani ([1972] 1976:60).

59. For a discussion of Sallust's notion of post-146 B.C. Roman decline, see Earl 1966:41–59.

60. On this speech, see Earl 1966:96–98; McGushin 1977:257–268. Earl writes (97): "Many passages in both speeches [i.e., those of Caesar and Cato in the *Bellum Catilinae*], but especially that of Cato, show close resemblance to views elsewhere put forward as Sallust's own."

61. On this point, see McDonnell 2006:378–379.

62. App. *Mith.* 63; Plu. *Luc.* 20. Syme (1964:250–251) saw a direct connection between Cato's criticisms of contemporary Roman colonial rule in Sallust and the *EM*.

63. On this passage, see McGushin 1977:103–104.

64. Cf. *Cat.* 11–12.

65. E.g., *Romanos iniustos, profunda avaritia, communis omnium hostis esse* ("Romans, he said, were unjust on account of their boundless greed and the common enemies of mankind"; *Jug.* 81.1).

66. E.g., *namque Romanis cum nationibus populis regibus cunctis una et ea vetus causa bellandi est: cupido profunda imperi et divitiarum* ("Indeed, for the Romans there is a single age-old cause for instigating war on all nations, people, and kings: a deep-seated lust for empire and riches"; 5).

67. For this reason, it is unfortunate that many scholars who have examined the *EM* appear to have missed its nuances. To Stier (1969: passim, esp. 449), for example, the distortions in the letter prove that Sallust had no sympathy for Mithridates' position. Schneider (1913:449) and Mazzarino (1968:374) hold similar views. At the other extreme, Bickerman (1946:148–151), Leggewie (1975:59), and Mazzolani ([1972] 1976:60–61) conclude that Sallust had sympathy with the arguments expressed in the *EM*, even though these scholars do not agree on what Sallust was criticizing.

68. As mentioned in the introduction to the current volume, *Rhet. Her.* 3.18 states that the strongest arguments in an oration should be placed at the beginning and end. And Quint. *Inst.* 7.1.10–11 offers essentially the same advice, albeit in regard to judicial oratory.

69. Cf. Pasoli 1965:139.

70. Bickerman (1946:147–148) claims that Sallust composed the *EM* ca. 35 B.C. La Penna (1968:291) agrees.

71. On this topic, see Morstein-Marx 2001 (esp. 189–192), which links the *Bellum Iugurthinum* to then-contemporary concerns about Parthia.

72. Geckle 1995:156–157. Cf. von Carosfeld 1888:75; Büchner 1960:234–235; Vázquez 1989:150–151.

73. Isaac (2004:62–64, 72, 188–189) demonstrates that the Greco-Roman perception of Asiatics as weakened by their monarchies has a long pedigree.

74. On Mithridates' philhellenism, see App. *Mith.* 112; McGing (1986:64, 89, 91–94). On Greek elaborations on imperialism and "just wars," see Hasebroek 1926; de Romilly 1963.

75. According to Geckle (1995:v), Sallust's speeches and letters aim to illustrate the "moral degeneration of the Roman state." As such, his speakers employ the sort of moral terminology that Sallust himself uses.

## CHAPTER TWO

1. Our evidence for the full name of Justin comes to us only in the genitive form, and thus his *nomen* could be either "Iunianius" or "Iunianus." See Syme 1988:369, where he prefers "Iunianius."

2. Perhaps Jal (1987:196–197) offers the best description of this "epitome": "une sorte d'adaptation abrégée."

3. Goodyear (1982a) sees Justin's abridgment as being around one-seventh the size of Trogus' history. Syme (1988:358 n. 1) and Yardley and Heckel (1997:2 n. 3) consider it around one-tenth the size. Jal (1987:197) posits that Justin has reduced the size of Trogus' books by at least one third apiece.

4. Only two speeches in Justin's abridgment are in *oratio recta*: 14.4.2 and 18.7.10. On Trogus' use of *oratio obliqua*, see Schlicher 1933:293.

5. In 38.4.4 Trogus has Mithridates refer to his victories against M'. Aquilius in Bithynia and Mallius Maltinus in Cappadocia (whom Justin refers to as "Malthinus" both here and in 38.3.8). Whereas Maltinus was driven from Cappadocia in 89 B.C. (Justin 38.3.8; App. *Mith.* 15), Mithridates did not ultimately put Aquilius to flight until 88 B.C. (see Broughton [1951–1986]: 2.43; App. *Mith.* 17, 19). Although it is possible that Mithridates refers merely to an earlier defeat of Aquilius, it is far more likely that Trogus has conflated the fates of the two Romans, since Justin mentions their defeats in tandem in 38.3.8. The speech, then, belongs to the dramatic date of 88 B.C., not 89 B.C., although Justin may not have realized this when he presented it in his text.

6. The following offer a second-century date for Justin's life: Seel (1972c:41); Alonso-Núñez (1987:56 and 1990:72) (pre-226 A.D.); Yardley and Develin (1994:4); Yardley and Heckel (1997:11–12). The following offer a third-century date: Seel (1955:37 and 1972a:iii) (late third or early fourth century). The following offer a fourth-century date: Syme (1988:365 and 1992:15); Vázquez (1989:148); Barnes (1991:343). Barnes (1988) argues that Justin's abridgment must have been composed post-260 A.D.; Yardley (2000) criticizes this argument. For an overview of scholarly support for various dates, see Pendergast 1961:14–16; Santi-Amantini 1981:10–11; and Syme 1988:359–360.

7. Steele (1917:28–35) supposed that Justin was African, on the basis of a now-outdated view of "African Latin." Syme (1988:369–370) tentatively suggested Africa as Justin's homeland, mentioning that Justin appears interested in Carthage. Yardley and Heckel (1997:10) proposed either Africa or Gaul. Goodyear (1984:177) suggested Spain. Yet these are mere guesses.

8. Most scholars have assumed that Justin's contribution was quite limited; e.g., Klotz (1952:2304); Pendergast (1961:18–21); Lytton (1973:7); Goodyear (1982a:1–3 and 1984:168–169); Syme (1992:14). More recently this view has been questioned, although without general approval; e.g., Jal (1987:199–200); Yardley (1994); Yardley and Heckel (1997:12–15).

9. It is true, however, that the issue of this speech's historicity has not been as widely discussed as that of the *EM*. This is most likely because scholars are more inclined to presume that Trogus' speech is a free invention.

10. E.g., McGing (1986:160); Richter (1987:178–182).

11. E.g., Sellge (1882:27); Kaerst (1897:654–656); Schneider (1913:54).

12. Numerous scholars have noted the similarities in the two compositions;

e.g., Rambaud (1948:182, 186); Leeman (1963:245–246); Syme (1964:284); Nicolet (1978:905); McGing (1986:160); Vázquez (1989:149); Geckle (1995:153).

13. Aetolians' speech: 28.2.4–7; speech of Mithridates: 38.4.7–10.

14. Speech of Demetrius: 29.2.2; speech of Mithridates: 38.6.7.

15. E.g., Fuchs (1964:42–43); Lytton (1973:8); Glew (1977); Urban (1982:1433–1440); Hammond (1983:164); Syme (1986:357).

16. E.g., Klotz (1952:2308); Seel (1972b:26–27 and 1972c:210, 251–252), who perceives that this criticism is very slight, and in league with other Roman historians' criticisms of Rome; Mazzolani (1976 [1972]:122, 172); Nicolet (1978:884–885); Santi-Amantini (1981:30–31); Alonso-Núñez (1987:63, 65–69) and (1990:77, 79); Jal (1987:202–204, 208); Vázquez (1989:150); Yardley and Develin (1994:8); Yardley and Heckel (1997:29–30) contend that this criticism of Rome is slight, and does not amount to anti-Romanism.

17. Von Gutschmid originally offered this suggestion at [1872] 1894a:352. He developed this thesis in [1882] 1894b. Among those supportive of von Gutschmid's contention were Kaerst (1897:655–656); Jacoby (1926:220–222); Schanz and Hosius (1935:322). Wachsmuth (1891) proved critical of the thesis soon after von Gutschmid presented it. In later years, numerous scholars have dismissed the idea: e.g., Büdinger (1895:192–194); Lamarre (1907:687–689); Momigliano (1934a:56); Klotz (1952:2305); Seel (1955:71); Pendergast (1961:11); Fuchs (1964:43); Santi-Amantini (1891:37); Hammond (1983:163–165); Alonso-Núñez (1987:61 and 1990:79); Jal (1987:204 n. 45); Shrimpton (1991:121); Yardley and Develin (1994:9). Sanford (1937:440–441) believed that Trogus used Timagenes "extensive[ly]." Hornblower (1981:66–67) is not certain whether Timagenes is the lone source for Trogus.

18. It is highly unlikely that von Gutschmid's thesis is correct. We know, for instance, that Timagenes and Trogus had different opinions of Augustus: Seneca tells us that the former was extremely hostile toward the first emperor (*De ira* 3.23); Justin 44.5.8, which praises Augustus' efforts at Romanization in Spain, demonstrates that the latter had a far more positive view. Justin, moreover, considered Trogus a learned figure who had expended a great deal of effort to compose his world history (*Praef.* 1). The author of the *HA* appears to have agreed: cf. *Aur.* 2.2; *Prob.* 2.7. It appears, then, that Justin did not deem Trogus' *Historiae Philippicae* a mere Latin adaptation of Timagenes. There is little reason for us to doubt him.

19. Quoted in Wistrich 2001:202.

20. Cf. 36.3.9, which criticizes Romans for being lavish with other people's belongings.

21. In this case, Justin is praising Macedonian expansionism. Cf. 8.2.11, which seems uncharacteristically positive concerning Athenian imperialism. See also 9.3.11, which lauds Greek supremacy and independence. And see 13.1.14, which commends Alexander's underlings and their conquests. There is a possibility that Trogus viewed empire as glorious for the successful imperialist and as detestable slavery for the subjugated.

22. One also detects primitivism in Sallust's work. See Green 1993.

23. This seems reminiscent of Sallust's view of post-146 B.C. Roman depravity (cf. *Cat.* 10).

24. The text of Justin used in this chapter is that of Seel 1972a.

25. Some scholars believe that the importance of *fortuna* to Rome's success in Justin's eyes demonstrates an anti-Roman bias: e.g., Momigliano (1934a:52); Alonso-Núñez (1982:135, 1987:66, and 1990:79). Others disagree: e.g., Pendergast (1961:130); Fuchs (1964:43); Urban (1982:1453); Yardley and Heckel (1997:29).

26. For a thorough discussion of this topic, see the unjustly neglected work of Schneider (1913). This work, to a certain extent akin to Stier's article on the *EM* (1969), offers a debunking of the notion that the speech of Mithridates is anti-Roman. Although Schneider offers overly strong conclusions, his argument is sounder than Stier's.

27. See chapter 1 above.

28. Justin refers to Maltinus as "Malthinus," both here and in 38.3.8. Cf. *Prol.* 38. See above, n. 5.

29. But cf. 24.4.4 and 25.2.1, in which Justin seems uncharacteristically critical of the Gauls.

30. It is possible that Trogus had Mithridates argue that the Romans were preoccupied and thus this was the best time to fight them (4.16) because it was a key argument in the *EM* (cf. 13). This could be, then, a nod to Sallust's *Letter of Mithridates*.

31. For instance, the speech mentions the Samnites (4.11-12), whom Justin discusses in 18.1.1 and 20.1.14. And the speech discusses the causes of the Jugurthine War (6.4-6), which Justin touches on in 33.1.12.

32. Cf. 5.2 and *EM* 2, 23.

33. Schneider 1913:53.

34. See ibid.

35. See Magie 1950:205.

36. See chapter 1 on *EM* 10. Cf. App. *Mith.* 11.

37. Interestingly, Eumenes was involved in border disputes with Pharnaces I. Naturally, Mithridates leaves out this detail.

38. Schneider 1913:52.

39. The wording is close to that of the *EM*. Cf. *atque imperii divitiarumque avidos ac ieiunos habere* (Justin 38.6.8) and *cupido profunda imperi et divitiarum* (*EM* 5). Trogus appears to have made a deliberate nod to the Sallustian letter.

40. It is possible that Trogus' research for his forty-third book, which focused on early Rome, provided him with the fodder for this line of argument.

41. E.g., 18.2.7; 31.8.8-9; 43.1.3.

42. See Schneider 1913:54. This does not, however, amount to much in the way of a negation of Mithridates' boasts. Book 39, after all, is far removed from book 13, and Roman readers would have had to possess a very good memory and a keen interest in the veracity of Mithridates' statements to see through this fib.

43. For a discussion of this (potentially invented) delegation and its likely date, see Oost 1954:92-97.

44. Cf. 31.5.9, in which Hannibal, offering advice to Antiochus, mentions the Gallic sack of Rome.

45. Contra Rimbaud (1983:136), who sees the speech as pro-Gaul and anti-Rome. See Pendergast 1961:57.

46. Justin's abridgment highlights the Roman victory over the Aetolians (32.1.1-3), which demonstrates that their speech is wrongheaded. The Aetolians, after all, proved to be no match for Rome.

47. Cf. 30.4.6-7, in which Philip V offers a short *oratio obliqua* speech to his troops before battling Rome. For discussion of Demetrius' speech, see Pendergast 1961:61.

48. Cf. Plb. 3.16, 18-19.

49. By mentioning Hannibal's inveterate hatred for Rome (29.1.7), Justin seems to disagree with the notion that Rome was responsible for the inauguration of hostilities. Cf. Hannibal's speech of counsel to Antiochus (31.5.2-9).

50. Admittedly, such a sentiment might have had darker resonances during Trogus' lifetime, since Augustus had effectively ended senatorial *libertas*. Justin's abridgment, however, seems supportive of the Augustan regime (cf. 42.5.11-12; 44.5.8), and we need not suppose that Pompeius Trogus harbored Tacitean opinions regarding the Republic's downfall.

51. On the topic of Roman perceptions of Germans, see Isaac 2004:427-439.

52. On the use of the collection of Sallustian speeches and letters from which the *EM* comes (Vatican Lat. 3864) as a pedagogical text, see Boese 1874:7. Quint. *Inst.* 2.5.19 recommends studying Sallust's speeches. In 3.8.67 he seems to suggest that Sallust's orations were studied in school.

53. E.g., *Jug.* 35.10; 81.1.

54. Scholars attracted to the so-called defensive imperialism thesis believed that Rome maintained a "defensive-minded" foreign policy until the early to mid-first century B.C., when the Republic became more openly aggressive; e.g., Ferrero and Barbagallo (1918:375-376); Frank (1929:316-325); Badian (1958:59). For a fuller discussion of this impression, see Adler 2008a:187-188.


PART TWO INTRODUCTION

1. E.g., Hoffmann (1942:101); Walsh (1954:110; 1982:1060-1062); Luce (1977:276-277, 284-287); Händl-Sagawe (1995:256); Lancel ([1995] 1998:26). Leeman (1963:193) doubts that vigorous patriotic sentiments affected Livy's entire oeuvre, noting that we have lost the later portions of his work, which cover the more modern history that Livy himself, in his preface (4-5), considered morally inferior in comparison with early Rome. See also the work of Twyman (1987), who attempts to exonerate the Roman annalistic tradition, in part at least, for its supposedly vigorous patriotism. Regarding the dangerous business of assuming knowledge about works (or portions of works) that have not survived from antiquity, see Brunt 1980.

2. E.g., Quint. *Inst.* 10.1.32, 101.101; Tac. *Ann.* 4.34; Suet. *Dom.* 10.3. For a modern discussion of this topic, see Kemper 1995:349–357.

3. E.g., Hoffmann (1942:101); Cavallin (1947:33–36); Burck (1950:158–160); Herrman (1979:95–96); Händl-Sagawe (1995:256).

4. E.g., Pédech (1964:217–218); Walbank (1972:162–182); Shimron (1979–1980:95, 104–105, 117); Gruen (1984:346–348); Eckstein (1989:12–13); Davidson (1991:22); Champion (2000). See also Walbank 1983.

5. As Burck (1950:156), Treptow (1964:33), and Kemper (1995:364) have noticed.

6. To some extent, this conclusion agrees with the portrait of Livy as subtly critical of Augustus and his regime that Miles (1995) advances.

## CHAPTER THREE

1. See Walbank 1957:26–35.

2. In regard to the former pair, Kahrstedt (1913:165) claimed that it is impossible to know. Burck (1950:72 n. 10) and Herrman (1979:95) concluded that these orations derive from the work of Fabius Pictor. In regard to the pre-Zama colloquy, Pédech (1958:440) considers Laelius the likely source. Pédech also—justly—doubts the efficacy of *Quellenforschung* in regard to Polybius' history.

3. See Wooten 1974, Wiedemann 1990, and below.

4. See below, chapter 4.

5. As Walbank (1957:397) and Seibert (1993:115–116) conclude.

6. As De Sanctis (1917:171) argues. Even Walbank (1985:253) asserts that Polybius' pre-Ticinus orations "are among the greatest stumbling blocks to the theory that Polybius is an honest man."

7. On this topic, see De Sanctis 1917:594–595, Walbank 1967:452. According to Lehmann (1896:515) and Groag (1929:99 n. 2), the pre-Zama conference never took place.

8. De Sanctis (1917:594–595) has debunked this view. Other scholars likewise assert that such a meeting between Hannibal and Scipio did take place: e.g., Scullard (1930:234–235; 1970:274 n. 107); Walbank (1967:451); Lancel ([1995] 1998:175).

9. Cic. *De orat.* 2.18.75; Nep. *Hann.* 13.2–3.

10. Zonar. 8.24.8. Daly (2002:142), however, deems Zonoras' claim that Hannibal knew Latin "unconvincing."

11. E.g., Ullmann (1927:49–50; 1929:12); Gries (1949:137–138); Walsh (1961:219–220, 231–232); Burck (1971:41–42); Händl-Sagawe (1995:256). For a short introduction to Livy's speechifying, see Treptow (1964:1–8).

12. Some scholars seem sanguine about the historical accuracy of Polybius' speeches: e.g., Ullmann (1932:57–58); Devroye (1956:92–106); Walbank (1957:13–14; 1963:10; 1985:249–261); Wooten (1974:235–236); Harris (1979:116–117). Others are less convinced: e.g., Pédech (1964:259); Mørkholm (1974); Händl-Sagawe (1995:256).

13. As Wiedemann (1990) suggested.

14. On this topic, see Walbank 1985:248.

15. See Wooten 1974; Wiedemann 1990:291–295.

16. Wooten (1974:250) notices that "striking metaphors" abound in Polybius' speeches.

17. For a summary discussion of this topic, see Dubisson 1990. Some consider Polybius to be largely supportive of Roman imperialism: e.g., Leeman (1963:197); Walbank (1972:171–181), who argues that Polybius became increasingly pro-Roman over the course of his work; Derow (1979:14–15); Dubisson (1990:243). Others believe that he was more critical: e.g., Shimron (1979–1980); Champion (2000:426, 441–442). Other scholars hold opinions that fall somewhere in between: e.g., Gruen (1984:346–348); Davidson (1991:22).

18. Jal 1982:148–149. Polybius introduces this question in 3.47.

19. For modern views on this topic, see Pédech 1964:217–219; Eckstein 1989, 1995:144–145; Erskine 1993:61–62; Seibert 1993; Daly 2002:118–119; Champion 2004:117–121.

20. This does not imply that Polybius necessarily thought Rome's desire for a world empire was malign, however.

21. See below.

22. For other pre-Ticinus speeches found in our ancient sources, see D.C. 14.57.4–6a; Silius 4.56–80; and possibly Coelius Antipater *HRR* fr. 16, who may have penned a Hannibalic oration before the battle.

23. Walbank (1957:397) deems the entire story "apocryphal." De Sanctis (1917:171) avers that at some point in the historiographical tradition orations by Scipio and Hannibal were added due to the dramatic character of the duel.

24. The text of Polybius book 3 used in this chapter is that of Foucault 1971.

25. For a discussion of the role of τύχη in Polybius' history, see Shorey 1921; Walbank 1957:16–26.

26. As Wooten (1974) and Wiedemann (1990:291–295) argue.

27. On this topic, see Ullmann 1932:57–58.

28. E.g., 3.63.5, 10, 12. More on this subject is given by Walbank (1967:451–452), who considers both pre-Ticinus addresses to be chockablock with commonplaces.

29. The fact that Polybius cut out part of what he appears to consider the actual speech of Scipio does not mean, of course, that Polybius offered a truncated version of any real address.

30. Ullmann (1927:89–90) offers the following rhetorical division of Scipio's pre-Ticinus speech in Polybius, which highlights its focus on a few themes alone: 3.64.2: *prooemium*; 3.64.3–10: *tractatio*, chiefly concerned with *facile*, but 10 with *necessarium*; 3.64.11: *conclusio*.

31. Ullmann 1927:92 and 1932:58.

32. See above, "Introduction," n. 62.

33. Treptow (1964:126–127) offers this argument in regard to the Livian versions of these speeches.

34. The text of Polybius book 15 used in this chapter is that of Foulon 1995.

35. See above, n. 25.

36. Walbank (1967:452) doubts that Hannibal said the following part of this sentence: μηδέπω μέχρι γε τοῦ νῦν εἰς τὴν τῆς τύχης ἐμπεπτωκέναι παλιρρύμην ("as long as you have not yet fallen into the ebb tide of Fortune"). Walbank does not specify why he disbelieves in the historicity of this remark, but it seems likely that he thinks Polybius here intentionally increases the import of fortune for the oration.

37. Cf. Plb. 15.8.7.

38. Perhaps not coincidentally, Polybius' Hannibal also put faith in the gods, not fortune, in his speech to his troops before the Battle of Cannae. Cf. 3.111.3.

39. Cf. Champion 2004:150: "In the interview with Hannibal before the decisive engagement [at Zama], Scipio constructs a picture in line with the large narrative trajectory of Rome and Roman enemies in books 1–5: Rome is on the defensive; Carthage is the treacherous aggressor (15.8.1–14)."

40. Walbank (1967:452) considers this a particularly strong argument.

41. Walbank (1967:453) points out that Cassius Dio 17.74 mentions that the Carthaginians actually gave money to the Romans at this time. Polybius might have expunged these details from his speech to make the Punic side appear more perfidious, yet this is unlikely to be the case. Rather, it is more probable that Dio's information comes from a different tradition.

42. Cf. Walbank 1957:442: "Aemilius' speech and that of Hannibal (III.2–11) are full of commonplaces and it is unlikely that they go back to a genuine record"; Davidson 1991:13. Contra Daly (2002:227 n. 50).

43. One detects echoes of this sentiment in Sallust's *EM* (16) and Tacitus' Calgacus speech (*Ag.* 31.1–2), which highlights Rome's maltreatment of Celtic women and children.

44. Erskine (1993), noting the absence of such Carthaginian propaganda regarding the freedom of Italy in Livy's account of the Second Punic War, concludes that it is likely a Polybian invention.

45. In the context of the Zama colloquy, however, it makes sense that Hannibal spoke first. See above.

## CHAPTER FOUR

1. On this topic, see above.

2. On the early Roman annalists, see Alföldi 1965; Badian 1966; Forsythe 1994; Frier [1979] 1999.

3. See, e.g., Miles 1995.

4. See above, chapter 3.

5. Those scholars who defend Livy's speechifying tend to argue that his orations offer insights into the characters who speak them and the situations in which they occur—not that they are in any way historically accurate; e.g., Walsh (1961:219–220; 1982:1068); Miller (1975:51). Contra Gries (1949:135), who does not consider Livy to be concerned primarily about the character of the speakers of his speeches, but rather

about "the character and destiny of . . . the city of Rome." For a short introduction to Livy's speechifying, see Treptow 1964:1-8.

6. E.g., Lambert (1946:8-9); Gries (1949:137-138); Walsh (1961:219-220, 231-232); Burck (1971:41-42); Händl-Sagawe (1995:256).

7. This would not mean, however, that we could dismiss Livy's potential preoccupations with this subject wholesale. Even the inclusions of such copying would still allow us to suppose that Livy was capable of finding fault with Rome. Livy, naturally, could have chosen to cut such sentiments out of his own compositions.

8. For a short summary of the major nineteenth-century opinions regarding Livian *Quellenforschung*, see Luterbacher 1875:1-3. For a more general discussion of Livy's sources for his Third Decade, see Walsh 1961:124-132. For a thorough discussion of Livy's potential use of Polybius for books 21 and 22, see Jumeau 1964.

9. This conclusion does not imply, as Ogilvie (1965:5-7) believes, that Livy essentially followed Nissen's Law, on which see below.

10. Nissen 1863:83-85. For a discussion of Nissen's impact on this question, see Briscoe 1993:39.

11. E.g., Walbank (1971:49); Tränkle (1972:15); Briscoe (1973:1; 1993:39); Luce (1977:178-179). Tränkle (1977:193) prematurely concludes that almost all experts agree that Livy did not use Polybius for books 21-23.

12. Some classical scholars think it probable (if not outright certain) that Polybius was a source for Livy's twenty-first book; e.g., Klotz (1941:118-119). De Sanctis (1917:180-184) contends that Livy used Polybius only sparingly for book 21, possibly for Scipio's pre-Ticinus speech. Walsh (1961:124-125, 232) deems Polybius a subsidiary source for books 21-23, but not for the pre-Ticinus addresses. Jumeau (1964:333) concludes that Livy did employ Polybius sparingly for books 21 and 22. Jal (1988:xix) believes that Livy used both (an) annalist(s) and Polybius for book 21. Erskine (1993:61) thinks that while Polybius was not a major source, Livy did consult him for books 21 and 22. Hine (1979:898-899) is not certain whether Livy has used Polybius directly for book 21.

13. E.g., Soltau (1891-1893:714; 1894:73-74), who appears somewhat certain of the Polybian provenance of these orations; Luterbacher (1875:52), in regard to Hannibal's speech before the battle, is even more certain. Consider Kahrstedt (1913:165), however, who claims that we cannot determine the sources for either address.

14. Nissen 1863:83-85.

15. E.g., Walsh (1961:125); Treptow (1964:209); Burck (1971:26).

16. E.g., Hoffmann (1942:99); Cavallin (1947:27); Treptow (1964:209).

17. For more information on these possibilities, see Jumeau 1964:325-330; Burck 1971:26-28; Walbank 1971:49; Tränkle 1977:193; Herrman 1979; Walsh 1982:1060-1065.

18. Numerous scholars have deemed Coelius at least a major direct source for the Third Decade; e.g., Hoffmann (1942:101); Jumeau (1964:345-346); Burck (1971:26); Luce (1977:179); Tränkle (1977:193); Walsh (1982:1065). There have been some disagreements over Livy's Greek proficiency. See Foucault 1968, where he concludes that

Livy was quite capable of translating Greek well. Although Livy must have preferred to use Latin source material for his work, Foucault is reasonable to conclude that he could have employed Greek sources rather easily.

19. *HRR* fr. 16. See Herrman 1979:94–97.

20. At 21.19.15 Livy claims that the Carthaginians were in the wrong regarding the siege of Saguntum.

21. On this topic, see Franko 1994:154; Isaac 2004:328–329, 335.

22. For further descriptions of Hannibal's religiosity, see 21.21.9 and 21.45.8.

23. For a discussion of Polybius' life, see Walbank 1957:1–6 and 1972:1–31. For a discussion of Livy's life, see Walsh 1961:1–19; Ogilvie 1965:1–5.

24. Perhaps, as Hesselbarth (1889:49) suggests, Livy changed the order of these addresses in order to grant the emphatic last place to the successful general's oration.

25. These introductory words to the speech, similar as they are to Thucydides' oft-used τοιάδε, insinuate that their author realizes that he did not offer *ipsissima verba*, or perhaps anything close to them. This is interesting to note in the context of Livy's orations, since so many modern scholars are quick to blame Livy for inventing such manifestly rhetorical orations. Here, at least, Livy does not appear to vouch for the speech's accuracy.

26. The text of Livy 21 used in this chapter is that of Dorey 1971.

27. Alternatively, Livy could have taken this remark (or the essence of this remark) from an earlier source. Without its appearance in Polybius' version, we cannot tell its originality in Livy.

28. As Händl-Sagawe (1995:257) correctly notes.

29. Kohl 1887:25–26; Ullmann 1927:89–90.

30. Ullmann (1927:89) labels this section of the oration the κατάστασις and Klotz (1941:25–26) considers it the beginning of the *tractatio* proper.

31. Klotz (1941) considers this argument *facile*, and believes that it extends through 21.40.9.

32. Ullmann (1927:90) believes that 21.40.5–6 resembles Plb. 3.63.3–5.

33. Ullmann (1927:89) deems the argument found in 7–10 to be expressing the τόπος of *facile*. Klotz (1941:25–26), as noted above (n. 31), considers 5–9 to be based on this τόπος.

34. Ullmann (1927:89–90) is correct to view the argument of this sentence as most consistent with the τόπος of *facile*. It is, at least, surely a continuation of the argument offered in the last few sentences. Klotz (1941:25–26), however, considers sentences 10–13 representative of the τόπος *indignatio*. Ullmann also sees 21.40.7–10 as resembling Plb. 3.63.8–9, albeit different in execution.

35. Ullmann (1927:89–90) correctly notices a change in argument here. In contrast to Klotz (1941:25–26), he labels this sentence *religiosum*. According to Treptow (1964:118), Scipio must know that his argument in 21.40.7–11 is weak.

36. According to Ullmann (1927:89–90), this marks the start of the *possibile* τόπος, which he sees as akin to Plb. 3.63.6–7.

37. Ullmann (1927:90) believes that 21.41.5 is similar to Plb. 3.63.10. This may be

an example of forcing a comparison between sentiments that are not very much alike, however.

38. According to Händl-Sagawe (1995:262), Livy mentions this comparison between Hannibal and Hercules in order to make the former appear foolish.

39. On the import of fetial law to Livy, see Gelzer 1964:91–92.

40. Ullmann (1927:89–90) deems this the start of the τόπος *pium*. To Klotz (1941:25–26), somehow, it remains part of *facile*.

41. Livy's Scipio here mentions Mount Eryx, which Polybius does not note in the passage that is most akin to this sentence (3.64.4). On this point, see Jumeau 1964:317.

42. Händl-Sagawe (1995:263) views 21.41.10–13 as akin to Plb. 3.64.4. There is much truth in this, but Livy's sentiments are far harsher and cast the Carthaginians as slaves more directly. According to Ullmann (1927:89–90), sentences 10 through 13 represent *dignum*—an assessment difficult to support for sentence 10. Klotz (1941:25–26) deems these same sentences (10–13) *indignatio*, perhaps more reasonably. For criticism of Ullmann's desire to label every Livian argument in his speeches according to a specific rhetorical τόπος, see Burck 1971:40–41; Briscoe 1973:19–22, 1981:43.

43. For an interesting elaboration on this point in relation to Tacitus' oeuvre, see Shumate 2006:81–127 (esp. 95–96).

44. According to Ullmann (1927:89–90) and Klotz (1941:25–26), sentences 21.41.14–15 demonstrate the τόπος *necessarium*.

45. Ullmann (1927:89–90) labels this the speech's *conclusio*.

46. Ullmann (1932:60–61) agrees with this conclusion.

47. As Treptow (1964:117) argues. This does not imply, however, as Ullmann (1932:58–59) asserts, that Polybius' Scipionic speech is the more realistic.

48. Händl-Sagawe (1995:257) also concludes that Livy adds to the speech an ethical dimension that is absent from Polybius' version.

49. Clearly, as Ullmann (1929) has demonstrated in detail, the Livian version of the Scipionic oration is far more rhetorical—even though Treptow (1964:118–119) claims that it is comparatively unadorned. For example, Ullmann (1929:16) sees 21.40.9 (*effigies . . . equi*) as an example of ἐνάργια. He also (33) notices the metaphor in 21.40.11 (*decuit . . . conficere*). He sees (42) synecdoche in 21.41.7. He perceives (47) irony in 21.41.4. To him (50–51), both 21.40.9–10 and 21.41.7 are examples of hyperbole. He notices (78–79) repetition in 21.40.4 (*novo—novos*), 21.40.10–11 (*hostium—hostem; committere ac profligare—commissum ac profligatum*), and 21.40.5 (*quos . . . quibus . . . quibus*). He (87) also detects a combination of *iteratio* and ὁμοιοτέλευτον in 21.40.10. He notes (88) antithesis in 21.40.11. And he detects (98) anaphora and chiasmus in 21.41.15, as well as asyndeton (103, 109) in 21.41.15–16, 21.40.9–10. In addition, Lambert (1946:27) notices alliteration in 21.41.17 (*vis virtusque*) and 21.40.9 (*fama frigore*).

50. Cf. Plb. 3.62.2–11. See above.

51. E.g., Walbank (1957:397); Seibert (1993:115–116).

52. Both Ullmann (1927:93) and Händl-Sagawe (1995:265–266) consider this oration's *prooemium*.

53. Ullmann (1927:93), Luce (1993:75), and Händl-Sagawe (1995:265–266) all consider this the start of the speech's *tractatio*. They all, furthermore, consider this an argument to be related to the τόπος *necessarium*. On the significance of Hannibal mentioning fortune here, see Erkell 1952:165–166; Walsh 1961:103–104.

54. Ullmann (1927:93) and Händl-Sagawe (1995:265–266) consider this the start of the τόπος *utile*, which extends through sentence 10. Luce (1993:75) oddly connects this sentence with the τόπος *magnum*.

55. Ullmann (1927:93) sees sentences 5–6 as akin to Polybius 3.63.4, although he correctly believes that Livy has developed this theme more than his predecessor did.

56. Ullmann (1927:93), Luce (1993:75), and Händl-Sagawe (1995:265–266) all consider this the start of the oration's *facile* τόπος.

57. Livy has Hannibal refer to himself as *domitorem Hispaniae Galliaeque, victorem eundem non Alpinarum modo gentium sed ipsarum, quod multo maius est, Alpium* ("the tamer of Spain and Gaul, the same conqueror not only of the Alpine races, but—that which is by far greater—the Alps themselves").

58. According to Ullmann (1927:93) and Händl-Sagawe (1995:265–266), 21.44.1 marks the change from the τόπος of *utile* to that of *possibile*. Yet this transition is not as cut-and-dried as they suggest, since there is very little difference between the arguments proffered in 21.43.18 and in 21.44.1. Perhaps for this reason Luce considers 21.43.11 to 21.44.3 *facile*—certainly an equally defensible contention.

59. Ullmann (1927:93) and Händl-Sagawe (1995:265–266) correctly consider the sentiments of sentences 4–7 as amounting to the τόπος *iustum*. Luce (1993:75) calls 4–6 *(in)dignum*.

60. Händl-Sagawe 1995:271.

61. See above, chapter 1.

62. Luce (1993:75) wrongly views this as the start of the speech's *conclusio*. To Ullmann (1927:93) and Händl-Sagawe (1995:265–266), it begins with the next sentence. On the topic of Roman interest in Spain before the Second Punic War, see Errington 1970 and Sumner 1972.

63. Ullmann (1927) considers this sentence akin to Plb. 3.63.11–12. To Händl-Sagawe (1995:273), it is similar to Plb. 3.63.11–13.

64. As Ullmann (1927:94) and Treptow (1964:120) note. *Pace* Händl-Sagawe (1995:265).

65. The text of Livy book 30 used in this chapter is that of Walsh 1986.

66. Ullmann (1927:128) considers this the start of the *prooemium* (which extends through sentence 5). Both Ullmann (1927:129) and Hoffmann (1942:98) recognize that this *prooemium*, which amounts to a *captatio benevolentiae*, is missing in Polybius' version of the oration.

67. See above.

68. Ullmann (1927:128) marks this off as the start of the *tractatio*, and labels sentences 6–9 *utile*.

69. See above.

70. Ullmann (1927:128–129) notices the similarities between sentences 8–9 and Plb. 15.6.6–7.

71. As Ullmann (1927:129) notes.

72. It remains possible, however, that these additions could derive from Livy's use of another source that he more-or-less copied.

73. Ullmann (1927:128–129) notes that sentences 16–17 stem from the τόπος *certum*. He also believes that these sentences are akin to Plb. 15.7.2–4.

74. Ullmann (1927:128–129) considers sentences 18–23 to be linked to the τόπος *tutum*. That is, perhaps, too schematic, given that 18 is in part a repetition of prior claims. Ullmann also notes the kinship of 18–23 and Plb. 15.7.5–6. In 30.30.21 Livy's Hannibal argues that Scipio will not gain much glory from defeating him—not much more, that is, than he would gain by granting peace. This sentiment, which is akin to Plb. 15.7.6, is more realistic than the Polybian argument upon which it is presumably based. Livy's Hannibal admits that Scipio will win more glory from a military victory than from agreeing to peace terms—something Polybius' Hannibal does not concede.

75. Ullmann (1927:128–129) considers this sentence part of the speech's extended conclusion, which he gives the title of *mandatum* (24–26). He deems the remaining part of the *conclusio "amplificationes."*

76. As Ullmann (1927:128–129) noticed.

77. Ullmann (1929:26) notes sundry examples: 30.30.7, 11, 16, 18, 19, 20, 21, 23, 24, and 27 all contain *sententiae*. Canter (1917:133) claims that Hannibal uses the most *sententiae* of any Livian speaker. To Ullmann, 30.30.15 and 16 both offer examples of personification (1929:31–32); 30.30.23 provides an example of metaphors (34–35); 30.30.8 contains an instance of hyperbole (50–51); 30.30.7, 8 present examples of repetition (77); 30.30.27 offers an instance of ὁμοιοτέλευτον (86); 30.30.5, 7, 8 present examples of a combination of *iteratio* and ὁμοιοτέλευτον (97–88); Ullmann detects chiasmus in 30.30.18 (97) and anaphora and chiasmus in 30.30.14 (99); and sees asyndeton in 30.30.7, 12–14 (102, 105). Canter (1918:53) notes that Hannibal is one of the Livian speakers who employ chiasmus a good deal.

78. Ullmann (1927:130) labels these sentences the oration's *prooemium*.

79. Ullmann (1927:130) considers this the *propositio* portion of the speech, which, to him, lasts through sentence 4a. Ullmann divides the fourth sentence of the oration in two parts, so that he can fit one of these parts into the *propositio*, and the other in the *tractatio*. See below, nn. 80–81.

80. Ullmann (1927:130) breaks this sentence into two parts. The former, which ends with the phrase *fraus petitis*, Ullmann labels part of the *propositio*. Walsh's text (1986) does not offer this division, but it makes sense here, since the second portion of this sentence pertains to a different argument from that of the first.

81. Ullmann (1927:130) believes that this sentence starts the *tractatio* of the speech with the τόπος of *dignum* (which extends through sentence 5). He furthermore posits that the text in 4b–5 is so similar to Plb. 15.8.1–2 that the two passages use almost the exact same expressions.

82. Ullmann (1927:130–131) considers this sentence to be the start of the τόπος

*iustum,* which extends through sentence 8. This seems very much akin to Plb. 15.8.3–5, Ullmann believes. Yet sentence 6 appears distinct from the arguments that follow in 7 and 8, and *iustum* is not an accurate label for it. Ullmann is guilty here of form-fitting all the sentences into neatly arranged τόποι.

83. Ullmann (1927:130) deems this the *conclusio.*

84. Ullmann (1927:131) rightly sees sentence 9 as a shortening of Plb. 15.8.6–14. As Ullmann demonstrates, Livy's Scipionic pre-Zama oration is also comparatively lacking in rhetorical figures. He notes merely two examples of metaphors in the speech: in 30.31.4, 8 (1929:37).

85. As Cavallin (1947:31–36; 1948) contends. See also the work of Kolár (1953:132), who argues that Livy makes Hannibal's plea much longer than Scipio's reply in order for it to be more effective.

86. As Ullmann (1927:129), Hoffmann (1942:101), Lambert (1948:58–59), Burck (1950:158), and Treptow (1964:137) assert.

87. As Walsh (1954:104–105) noted.

88. Contra Kolár (1953:132). This seems like a natural argument for scholars who contend that Hannibal's pre-Zama speech is weak.

89. Mader 1993. Catin (1944:58–59) also sees Hannibal as a tragic figure, although he does not expand on this subject as Mader does.

90. 21.4.1: *Pauci ac ferme optimus quisque Hannoni adsentiebantur* ("A few people, and almost all the best ones, were in agreement with Hanno").

91. Mader 1993.

92. As Treptow (1964:138–139) partly views the matter.

93. *Pace* Walsh (1982:1060).

94. On this point, see Catin 1944:158–159.

95. Our sources often refer to him as "Gavius Pontius." For numerous ancient references to his nomenclature, see Oakley 2005:40. For modern discussions of Pontius, see Salmon 1967:225–226; Oakley 2005:40–41. For a précis of the Caudine Forks disaster and its aftermath, see Salmon 1929. We also possess two Pontius speeches among the fragments of Appian (*Samn.* 4.4, 4.5). On this topic, see Adler (forthcoming).

96. Cf. 9.9.1–12.4. See Oakley 2005:121–137. Cf. Chaplin 2000:39–41.

97. The text of Livy books 8 and 9 used in this chapter is that of Walters and Conway 1919.

98. See Oakley 2005:17–19, 139–140. Ullmann (1927:76–77) labels these sentences as part of the τόπος *honestum.* Oakley (2005:137), however, considers Ullmann's analysis unnecessarily rigid.

99. Additionally, Livy elsewhere (9.15.8) gloats about the Roman capture of Pontius (likely invented). On the dubiousness of this episode, see Salmon 1967:74–75.

100. In the case of the Gallic ransoming of Rome ca. 390 B.C., however, this may not be entirely true, since L. Lentulus offers his own précis of it in 9.4.8–9. This episode, furthermore, was of such import to Romans that many of them might have possessed at least a general sense of it—much like, perhaps, contemporary American recollection of Abraham Lincoln's assassination. This parallel, however, should alert

us to the possibility that many Romans had little knowledge of Roman historians' discussions of the Gallic sack.

101. See above, chapter 1.

102. Livy also grants Annius a second speech (8.5.3–6), with which he counterposes two orations by the Roman consul T. Manlius Torquatus (8.5.8–10, 6.5–6).

103. According to Ullmann (1927:71–72), this portion of the address is part of the τόπος *iustum*.

104. Additionally, Livy labels Torquatus *parem ferociae huius* ("an equal to his [Annius'] spirit"; 8.5.7).

105. Oakley 1998:413.

106. As Oakley (1998:409–411) demonstrates.

107. Oakley (1998:410–411) suggests that this argument actually stemmed from Campanian demands after the Battle of Cannae (cf. 23.6.6–8; Cic. *Agr.* 2.95), though he also contends (411) that "it is attractive to argue that it reflects the events of 90 [B.C.]."

108. On the details of Patavium's subjection to Rome, see Livy 10.2.

109. On the date of this conference, see Briscoe 1973:17. Contra Burck (1967:452–453), who supports 200 B.C. For historical background, see Balsdon 1954. On the Aetolian League, see Larsen 1952.

110. The text used here is that of Weissenborn and Mueller 1966.

111. Cf. the opinion of Burck (1966:330–331), who believes that the Roman retort to the Macedonian ambassador demonstrates that the former speech is replete with propagandistic falsehoods. See also Burck 1967:452–463.

112. For a discussion of the stereotypes regarding Phoenicians and Carthaginians that appear in Greek and Roman authors, see Isaac 2004:324–335.

113. On this term and its associations in Greco-Roman literature, see Isaac 2004:329–332.

114. As Shumate (2006, esp. 95–96 and 104–115) argues.

115. For a discussion of this topic, see Isaac 2004:411–426, on Greco-Roman perceptions of the Gauls.

## PART THREE INTRODUCTION

1. For the rationale behind this spelling of the name (as opposed to Boudicca or Boadicea), see Jackson 1979.

2. E.g., Syme (1958:529); Walker (1968:30), who asserts that Tacitus "can appreciate the rival nationalisms of Arminius, Calgacus, Boudicca, and can admire the qualities of the northern barbarians; he can write with passion — not sentimentality — of the provincials' sufferings when Rome's task of Empire is abused."

3. Syme 1958:529.

4. Gordon 1936 (esp. 150); Syme 1958:614, 618.

5. See, e.g., Ullmann 1927:246; Syme 1958:701–703; Miller 1968:2–5; Martin 1981:230–233; Aubrion 1985:624; Mellor 1993:114; Pagán 2000.

6. On Dio's name, see Robert and Robert 1971; Ameling 1984:123; Gowing 1990; de Blois 1991:369; Edmondson 1992:15–16; Freyburger-Galland 1997:8, 8 n. 12; Swan 1997:2524 n. 1. The *agnomen* occasionally attributed to him, "Cocceianus," is almost certainly the result of Photius' confusion between Cassius Dio and Dio of Prusa (see Gowing 1990:49–50; *pace* Ameling [1984:125–126]). Thus Dio's full name could reasonably be L. Cassius Dio, Cl. Cassius Dio, or L. Claudius Cassius Dio. The latter is perhaps the most likely, but we cannot rule out the other possibilities.

7. Although some scholars consider this at least partly the case: e.g., Dubisson (1979:101); Swain (1996:401).

8. E.g., Syme 1958:763 n. 6; Millar 1961, 1964:73–74, 79, 81–83; Miller 1969:110; van Stekelenberg 1971:152–153, 1976:53–54, 57; Martin 1981:175, 259 n. 22; Edmondson 1992:40; Gowing 1992:244–245; Webster [1978] 1993:17.

9. The book numbers of Dio used in this work are those of Boissevain, who reformulated the numbering of Leunclavius, a sixteenth-century editor. See Boissevain, Smilda, and Nawijn 1895–1931:2.xxi–xxvii; Gowing 1997:2558–2559.

10. Not, perhaps, according to Photius (*Bib.* 71), however, who prefers Dio's speeches to those of Thucydides.

CHAPTER FIVE

1. Tac. *Ann.* 14.29.1 sets the revolt in A.D. 61. Asbach (1878:8–16) first argued that Tacitus was mistaken and that the rebellion actually broke out in A.D. 60. The basis for this contention is essentially twofold: first, the outbreak and quelling of the revolt took too long to have occurred during one year alone; second, the logistics of the appointments of various Roman statesmen related to this rebellion favor A.D. 60 over 61. Numerous scholars have agreed with and/or added rationales for this argument: e.g., Syme (1958:391); Townend (1964a:467); Ogilvie and Richmond (1967:192); Dudley (1968:43); Birley (1973:181 n. 16); Orsi (1973:531); Bradley (1978:236); Martin (1981:173); Frere (1987:57); Sealey (1997:12). Others conclude that 61 is the correct date: e.g., Collingwood and Myers (1936:99); Stevens (1951:4); Königer (1966:61); Harrington (1970:135); Braund (1996:133); Laederich (2001:308).

2. Suetonius briefly mentions the revolt in *Nero* 39; since this notice is bereft of detail and not placed in chronological context, it is of essentially no use to our examination.

3. See below. For more information on Xiphilinus, see Boissevain, Smilda, and Nawijn 1895–1931:2.i–xvii; Millar 1964:2; Brunt 1980:488–494; Edmondson 1992:29; Gowing 1997:2561–2563. Some scholars have blamed Xiphilinus for the purportedly poor quality of Dio's account of the Boudica revolt: e.g., Bulst (1961:508); Orsi (1973:531), who guesses that this is the case; Gowing (1997:2563).

4. Hence these accounts have failed to satisfy many modern historians. Regarding Tacitus, Mommsen (1968:190 n. 10) famously condemned the account in the *Annales*: "A worse narrative than that of Tacitus concerning this war, *Ann.* xiv.31–39, is hardly to be found even in this most unmilitary of all authors." For more criticism

of Tacitus' accounts, see Laistner 1947:130; Griffin 1976–1977:149–152. On the insufficiency of Dio's version, see Syme 1958:762–763; Townend 1964a:467.

5. The Iceni were based in modern-day Norfolk and Suffolk.

6. On Tacitus' meaning of *libertas* and its import to his work, see Wirszubski 1950:163–167; Jens 1956. For a discussion of *libertas* under the early Roman Empire, see Hammond 1963; Roller 2001:213–287.

7. *EM* 5: *Namque Romanis cum nationibus populis regibus cunctis una et ea vetus causa bellandi est: cupido profunda imperi et divitiarum* ("For the Romans, there is a single age-old cause for instigating war on all nations, people and kings: a deep-seated lust for empire and riches").

8. The texts of the *Annales* used in this chapter are those of Wellesley 1986 and Borzsák 1992.

9. Scholars disagree about the import of Mona as a center of the revolt. Dyson (1971:260), Fraser (1988:69), and Nice (1993:16–17) do not think that the Druids on Mona inspired the uprising. Crawford (2002:23) doubts that it served as a stronghold for the rebellion. Dudley and Webster (1962:52) disagree, viewing Mona as a lodestone of "Celtic nationalism." Kostermann (1968:82) perceives that Mona was a potential threat to Roman rule in Britain. Laederich (2001:307 n. 12) sees Mona's potential as a center of resistance to the Romans, without remarking on its precise importance to the revolt.

10. As Dyson (1971:263) correctly notes. Tacitus may have intended to juxtapose Paulinus' conduct with that of Corbulo, his supposed rival (*Ann.* 14.29.2). See Gilmartin 1973.

11. On this favoritism, see Orsi 1973:535; Griffin 1976–1977:151; Martin 1981:173–174; Devillers 1994:99.

12. On Roman relations with client kings, see Dudley and Webster 1962:42–43; Braund 1983.

13. Ogilvie and Richmond (1967:198) posit that the following tribes were involved in the uprising: the Iceni, Trinovantes, Coritani, Cornovii, Durotriges, Brigantes, and probably the Catuvellauni. Laederich (2001:310) believes that a smaller number of tribes were involved: the Iceni, Trinovantes, Catuvellauni, and Coritani.

14. *Rapiunt arma, commotis ad rebellationem Trinovantibus et qui alii nondum servitio fracti resumere libertatem occultis coniurationibus pepigerant* ("they [the Iceni] seized arms, with the Trinovantes stirred up for a revolt, and others, who, not yet broken by slavery, had determined to resume their freedom by hidden conspiracies"; 14.31.2).

15. See Braund 1983 (esp. 43–44). Braund correctly concludes that Tacitus does not blame Rome for the confiscation of the king's property; rather, he seems irked by the manner in which it was accomplished. Dyson (1975:167–168) sees the Roman treatment of the Iceni as typical of abuses in the "early stages of Romanization."

16. In Dio's account of the rebellion, as we shall see in the next chapter, Catus helped incite the revolt by reclaiming financial gifts formerly bestowed upon the Britons by Claudius (62.2.1). Tacitus' mention of Catus' culpability supports the reasons Dio offers for the revolt's occurrence.

17. As Dyson (1971:262) mentions, it is not clear why Boudica, who was left out of her late husband's inheritance, held such a dominant position in the uprising. Were her daughters too young to play a prominent part? Certainly other members of the Iceni were involved in rousing the rebellion—especially since the Romans had not only maltreated Boudica's family, but also confiscated property belonging to nobles among the tribe. Neither Tacitus nor Dio, however, mentions anyone who conspired with her.

18. Fuentes (1983:314, 316) believes that the final battle could have occurred in Virginia Water, a suburb of Surrey in southeast England. Webster (1984:412; [1978] 1993:97, 111–112) thinks it possible that it took place in Mancetter.

19. Tacitus claims that almost 80,000 Britons were killed, along with some 400 Romans.

20. See above. There is even no consensus regarding the Lyon Tablet (*ILS* 212), which presents the official version of a Claudian speech that Tacitus included in the *Annales* (11.24). Cf. Syme 1958:703–708; Momigliano 1961:10, 16; Leeman 1963:355; Laird 1999:134. The same is true for the *Senatus consultum de Cn. Pisone patre*, which offers insight into a Tiberian speech that also appears in the *Annales* (3.12). Cf. Woodman and Martin 1996:138–139; Damon 1999; Talbert 1999:96.

21. Scholars have supported various (lost) historical works as Tacitus' main source for his discussion of the Boudica revolt in the *Annales*: Fabius Rusticus (Walser [1951:132]; Burn [1969:45], who deems Rusticus a likely source; Reed [1974:930–932]; contra Syme [1958:765], who claims that Rusticus was not used); Cluvius Rufus (Fabia [1893:402–404]; Kostermann [1968:85]); Pliny the Elder (Sickel [1876:44], who states that Tacitus occasionally used Pliny for his account of Nero's reign; Momigliano [1934b:702]; Walser [1951:135], who believes that Tacitus employed Pliny for the omens related at the start of the Boudica revolt [14.32.1]). A large number of classicists have concluded that Tacitus used manifold sources for his account of Nero's reign: e.g., Syme (1958:289–300); Questa (1967:153); Goodyear (1970:26, 28); Cizek (1972:18–19); Morford (1990:1588); Sage (1990:1015); consider also Tresch (1965), who tends toward Rusticus and Cluvius as sources. There has also been some discussion of Tacitus' potential use of the oral testimony of his father-in-law, Agricola: e.g., Townend 1964b:478 n. 5; Orsi 1973:532; Webster [1978] 1993:15–16. (Tacitus informs us that Agricola served under Paulinus [*Ag.* 5.2].) Some have speculated about the possibility of Tacitus employing the *acta senatus*: e.g., Syme (1958:278; 1982:73); Townend (1961:238–239); Cizek (1972:18); Goodyear (1982b:648).

22. On the memoirs of Paulinus, see Plin. *Nat.* 5.1.14. On the possibility of this work pertaining to Britain, see Syme 1958:297, 765; Peter 1967:2.cxxxviii–iv; Questa 1967:222–224; Wilkes 1972:187 n. 31; Griffin 1976–1977:149. Orsi (1973:532) thinks that Tacitus might have used the memoirs as a source; as does Reed (1974), who believes that both Tacitus' and Dio's accounts of the rebellion are ultimately based on the testimony of Paulinus. Contra Fabia (1893) 338–339, who doubts that Paulinus ever wrote about his experience in Britain. Jahn (1920:33) guesses that Dio's description of Boudica may come from Paulinus' memoirs.

23. Dio, in fact, cuts Paulinus' exhortation into three speeches (62.9; 62.10; 62.11).

24. See Miller 1969:110.

25. On Cartimandua, client queen of the Brigantes, see Tac. *Ann.* 12.36; *Hist.* 3.45.

26. Ogilvie and Richmond (1967:198) inform us that Tacitus' notion that the Celts did not discern between the sexes of their rulers is "exaggerated."

27. *Coniuges sororesque etiam si hostilem libidinem effugerunt, nomine amicorum atque hospitum polluuntur* ("even if our wives and sisters have escaped the lust of the enemy, they are defiled by so-called friends and guests"; *Ag.* 31.1).

28. As we shall discuss in chapter 7, linking political shortcomings to sexual transgressions is a commonplace of Roman moralizing rhetoric. On this topic, see the useful work in Edwards 1993.

29. Schürenberg (1975:77) offers a reasonable point when she notes the semi-paradoxical rationale Tacitus' Boudica presents: she claims to be acting in the capacity of an average Briton, yet still exploits her nobility by basing her exhortation to rebel on the maltreatment of her family. Such a rationale is not as hypocritical as Schürenberg suggests, however, since Boudica's loss of *libertas* is also the loss of the Iceni elite's *libertas*. She is, that is to say, far from the only one who is made to suffer by Roman misrule.

30. E.g., Schürenberg (1975:77); Crawford (2002:26–27).

31. On the rape of Lucretia, see Liv. 1.57.6–59; D.H. 4.64.4–67.4; Val. Max. 6.1.1.

32. In essence Tacitus' Boudica argues here that the maltreatment of her family and herself is typical. Her appeal to war, then, is not merely personal, as Schürenberg (1975:77) posits. See above, n. 29.

33. *Pace* Crawford (2002:26–27). In addition, though there is a kernel of truth in her argument, Crawford makes too much of Tacitus' granting Boudica supposedly "Roman" traits. This is one way in which the Romans (or any other people, for that matter) characterize those of other societies: they make them appear more like themselves. To some extent, Sallust and Trogus did so with Mithridates, as we have seen in the previous chapters. As Sallust in the *Bellum Jugurthinum* views Jugurtha in the light of Roman values, Tacitus does the same for Boudica. Crawford appears to believe that Tacitus belittles all those from other societies, and thus must cast Boudica as Roman in Tacitus' eyes, because Tacitus does not demonize Boudica.

34. For more discussion of this finale, see Kostermann 1968:95. Boudica's peroration seems to express a sentiment similar to that of Boiocalus, the German leader who denounces Rome in the *Annales: deese nobis terra *in qua vivamus*: in qua moriamur, non potest* ("we may lack a place to live, but not a place to die"; 13.56.1); I accept Wellesley's (1986) reading for these lines, but, for variants, see his *appendix critica*, 151.

35. As Aubrion (1985:625) suggests.

36. See above.

37. Shumate 2006:105–114.

38. Cf. Haynes 2003:155, describing the semi-barbarian Civilis: "What makes

Civilis such a threat is his status as both a civil and foreign foe; he embodies the prob-
lem facing the Romans of how to reestablish the boundaries of self and other after the
trauma of civil war." On Civilis, see below.

39. *Verum ut unam e vulgo libertatem amissam, confectum verberibus corpus, contrectatam filiarum pudicitiam ulcisci* ("but rather, as one of the people, she avenged her
lost freedom, her body worn out by whips, and the defiled chastity of her daughters";
14.35.1). According to Walser (1951:131), the Iceni's desire for freedom is the very cause
of the revolt. See Cizek 1972:20.

40. See *Ann.* 16.35. On Thrasea Paetus and the import of senatorial *libertas*, see
Wirszubski 1950:138–143, 165. One can witness Tacitus' use of such language elsewhere: e.g., in Percennius' stirring of a revolt among the Pannonian legions (*Ann.* 1.17);
in Calgacus' oration (*Ag.* 31.1–2); in Civilis' speech (*Hist.* 4.17).

41. Cf. the comment of Walker (1968:261), who sees Paulinus' retort as "distinctly
inferior" to Boudica's. According to Laederich (2001:318), this oration demonstrates
a good comprehension of Roman strategy.

42. Although some of Cerialis' arguments in this oration are weak, at least he attempts explicitly to justify Roman rule. Tacitus' Paulinus never bothers with such an
undertaking.

43. Tacitus describes Civilis' background and personality in *Hist.* 4.13. On Civilis,
see Syme 1958:172.

44. On the Batavian revolt, see Syme 1958:172–175; Brunt 1960; Haynes
2003:148–177.

45. The text is that of Wellesley 1989.

46. This sort of sentiment also appears in Sallust's *EM* (5); see above. On
the Romans' inclination to link political malefactions to sexual transgressions, see
Edwards 1993.

47. Cf. *Hist.* 4.26.1.

48. Tacitus tells us that the Batavians, Canninefates, and Frisians took part in the
revolt (4.16).

49. Cf. *EM* 5, 15, 17; Justin 38.6.7. See above, chapters 1 and 2.

50. For ancient discussion of Arminius' personality, see Vell. 2.118.2. On Arminius,
see Wells 2003. On Tacitus' use of Arminius, see Pagán 2000 (esp. 359–364).

51. See *Ann.* 1.55 for the consular year.

52. As we have seen, Tacitus seems to enjoy using indirect discourse to advertise
the sentiments of many of his anti-Roman characters. On *oratio obliqua* in Tacitus, see
Dangel 1994; Laird 1999:121–142.

53. See Syme 1958:531: "He [Tacitus] writes of Arminius as liberator *haud dubie
Germaniae*, and accords him a title of renown that belonged of old to the Roman
People itself, *proeliis ambiguus, bello non victus.*"

54. Aubrion (1985:619) argues that Tacitus' post-*Agricola* orations become more
succinct.

55. Shumate 2006:99.

56. Shumate (2006:103–104), otherwise a careful reader of Tacitean discussions of imperialism and colonialism, underplays the sharpness of Tacitus' criticisms of Rome in the description of the Boudica rebellion.

57. The Iceni, for example, had inhabited a client kingship of the Empire. Boioca-lus' Ampsivarii had been Rome's friends (*Ann.* 13.55). Arminius' Cherusci, by virtue of Segestes' good relations with Rome, had complex ties to the Empire. Arminius himself, moreover, was a Roman citizen of equestrian rank who had served in the Roman auxiliary forces (Vell. 2.118.2). All these figures possessed firsthand knowledge of Roman colonial practices.

58. This does not imply, of course, that the Romans were largely unconcerned with provincial maladministration until the Imperial period. Naturally, any acquaintance with mid and late Republican history—to say nothing of Cicero's orations—suggests that such misconduct was of crucial import to them.

59. On this topic, see the insightful criticism of Walser (1951:136).

60. According to Walker (1968:225), Boudica is just one example of the "Noble Savage" appearing in Tacitus' oeuvre.

61. Isaac (2004:439) stresses that the Germans in the Roman imagination should be the opposite of Easterners, and thus Civilis' remarks fit Roman stereotypes about both groups.

## CHAPTER SIX

1. Chapter 5.

2. E.g., Millar (1961; 1964:73–83); van Stekelenburg (1976:53–54). See, however, Gabba 1955:301–308 and van Stekelenburg 1971:38–39 on Caesar's speech regarding the war with Ariovistus (38.36–46), which directly pertains to the topic of Roman imperialism. For commentary on this speech, see below.

3. E.g., Meyer 1891; Hammond 1932; Millar 1964:102–118; Berrigan 1968; McKechnie 1981; Reinhold 1986:219–220; Rich 1989:98–100; Smyshlyaev 1991.

4. For information on Xiphilinus, see Boissevain, Smilda, and Nawijn 1895–1931:2.i–xvii; Millar 1964:2; Brunt 1980:488–494; Edmondson 1992:29; Gowing 1997:2561–2563.

5. E.g., Jahn 1920:5. Bartsch (1994:207 n. 3) still believes that Xiphilinus' excerpting presents few problems for those attempting to get an accurate assessment of Dio's narrative.

6. Sickel (1876:7) recognized this long ago. See Millar 1964:2; Brunt 1980:488–494; Edmondson 1992:29–30; Gowing 1997:2561.

7. See above, chapter 5.

8. Some have supposed that Pliny the Elder's *A fine Aufidii Bassi* was Dio's main source for the revolt: e.g., Cizek (1972:14–15); Reed (1974:932). Others have chosen Cluvius Rufus: e.g., Kostermann (1968:85), who sees this as a possibility, as does Braund (1996:144). Townend (1960:103) originally saw Cluvius as only a "subsidiary

source" for Dio; he later changed his mind (1964a:480), concluding that Cluvius was Dio's chief source. Questa (1967:91–93, 268) believes that Dio followed Nissen's Law (i.e., only used one source at a time), but asserts that it is impossible to determine which source he employed at any given time. Edmondson (1992:30–32) mentions all the known literary sources that Dio could have consulted, but does not choose between them.

9. Most scholars have assumed that Dio used Tacitus as a source for the revolt only sparingly, if at all: e.g., Heinz (1948:138); Syme (1958:690); Questa (1967:68); Burn (1969:44–45); Harrington (1970:57).

10. Dio's concern for mimicking Attic prose also qualifies the notion, put forward by Palm (1959:81–82), Cizek (1972:25), Orsi (1973:533), Bowie (1974:181), and Crawford (2002:22), that Dio, although a Bithynian Greek, was wholly Roman in his cast of mind. A splendid article by Aalders (1986) has justly criticized this view, and its shortcomings can be gleaned from an examination of various comments found in the work of Millar (1964:177–191), Harrington (1970:76), van Stekelenburg (1971:11–13), den Boer (1972:64), Ameling (1984:128), de Blois (1991:372), Edmondson (1992:17–18), Edwards (1994:96 n. 54), Swain (1996:248, 405–408), and Freyburger-Galland (1997:22). To be sure, as Walton (1929), Lambrechts (1936), and Hammond (1957) have demonstrated, Dio, as an Easterner in the Roman Senate of the second and third centuries A.D., would not have felt out of place. Still, it is unfathomable that Dio's birthplace and education had no effect, however subtle, on his outlook.

11. Dio's stylistic debt to Thucydides was noted by Photius (*Bibl.* 71). For modern assessments of this topic, see principally Litsch 1893 and Kyhnitzsch 1894. Numerous other scholars mention Dio's indebtedness to Thucydides: e.g., Gabba (1955:304); Millar (1961:11; 1964:42); Harrington (1970:126–127); Piatowski (1975:263); Ameling (1984:130–131); Aalders (1986:293); Rich (1989:88); Edmondson (1992:39–40); Hose (1994:367–369); Freyburger-Galland (1997:18–19). Dio claims that he read Greek authors to improve his style (55.12.5). Vlachos (1905) and Lintott (1997:2501) notice Dio's stylistic imitations of Demosthenes. Ameling (1984:128) discusses the influence of both Demosthenes and Aeschines on Dio's history. Freyburger-Galland (1997:20) claims that Dio was partly inspired by Demosthenes and/or Aeschines. Edmonson (1992:39–40) mentions both of these influences on Dio, and adds Lysias, Isocrates, and Plato.

12. For the sake of convenience, hereafter we refer to this narrative, which is found in Xiphilinus' epitome, as the work of Dio, instead of repeatedly alluding to "Xiphilinus/Dio." Bear in mind, however, that Xiphilinus is our source for this account, and our labeling of Dio as its author in no way assumes that Xiphilinus has offered a carbon copy of Dio's original. See above.

13. Suet. *Nero* 39, Eutrop. 7.14, and Oros. *Adv. pag.* 7.7 all agree with Dio on this matter. Since Tacitus names all three cities and Dio offers little in the way of detail, we may tentatively presume that Tacitus is correct. Dio's mention of 80,000 dead Romans and allies could be influenced by the number of Romans killed in Mithri-

dates' massacre before the First Mithridatic War, which, according to some of our ancient sources, had the same body count. See McGing 1986:113.

14. So argue Kostermann (1968:87), who posits Pliny the Elder as the source, and Nice (1993:16), who believes it was either Pliny or Cluvius.

15. For a thorough examination of the use of this word and its potential meanings, see Pearson (1952) and (1972).

16. See above.

17. On its own, this does not necessarily imply less sympathy for the rebellion on Dio's part, as Braund (1996:141) maintains. Tacitus also hints in the *Annales* at financial causes for the rebellion.

18. According to Pearson (1952:206), "It is frequently proper . . . to use the translation 'excuse' or 'pretext' [for the word πρόφασις] because we most commonly offer explanations for our behaviour if it appears reprehensible or if we wish to conceal our motives."

19. We ought not go as far as Walser (1951:131), though, who claims that Dio attributes the entire rebellion to Boudica's machinations. As Walser himself notes (128, 130), Dio proves quite critical of Nero, and thus has reason to allow the uprising to hint at the foibles of Rome's then-current emperor. Also, Dio admits the importance of Roman financial exploitation in Britain to the fomenting of the rebellion.

20. Some scholars consider this sketch historically valuable: e.g., Dudley and Webster (1962:54); Nice (1993:18). Others deem it specious: e.g., Jahn (1920:33); Macurdy (1937:104); Fraser (1988:60).

21. We should note that it is possible that Xiphilinus, not Dio, chose to present a physical description of Boudica at this point in his epitome's discussion of the rebellion. This, however, seems improbable.

22. Since we do not have sufficient information about the literary source(s) of either Tacitus or Dio, we cannot make this case with any certainty, however. It is conceivable that both Tacitus and Dio placed their Boudica speeches in the same places as their literary source(s) had done.

23. Dio, though not as biased in favor of Paulinus as was Tacitus, also offers no hint as to why the Roman governor was so unprepared for the uprising. See chapter 5.

24. Dio is the only author from antiquity who mentions this goddess. Dio has Boudica refer to Ἀνδράστη in 62.6.2. Perhaps this is the same goddess. For more information on her, see Nice 1993:17–18; Webster [1978] 1993:95.

25. As Webster [1978] 1993:94–95 suggests.

26. Brunt 1980:489–492.

27. This is one of a number of details that have led scholars to suggest Tacitus' comparatively favorable treatment of Paulinus. See Orsi 1973:535; Griffin 1976–1977:145–146; Martin 1981:173–174.

28. Numerous scholars have noted this juxtaposition: e.g., Walker (1968:225–228); Warmington (1969:75–76); Roberts (1988:120–122); Braund (1996:136, 138).

29. Webster [1978] 1993:28–29. Dudley and Webster (1962:18) also point out the Britons' military deficiencies.

30. *Pace* Rutledge (2000), whose article pertains to Tacitus' *Agricola*, but whose conclusions apply to Tacitus' and Dio's narratives of the Boudica rebellion.

31. As Townend (1964b:469), Fraser (1988:99), and Webster [1978] 1993:101 assert.

32. Contra Dudley and Webster (1962:76); Mommsen (1968:191); Warmington (1969:77). For opposing views, see Reed (1974:932-933); Fuentes (1983:316). Kostermann (1968:98) does not believe either version of Boudica's death.

33. On the influence of "tragic history" on Dio's work, see Piatowski 1975; Gowing 1992:216.

34. Gowing (1997:2563) blames Xiphilinus for the lack of "direction or depth" in Dio's examination of Nero. It is probable—though not certain—that Dio originally presented some discussion of the revolt's aftermath, which Xiphilinus chose not to excerpt.

35. Various scholars support the notion that fiscal considerations were of greater significance to the rebellion's outbreak: e.g., Bulst (1961:497, 500); Burn (1969:46); Overbeck (1969:140-141); Dyson (1971:254); Webster (1984:411). Not so Cizek (1972:138 n. 3). Webster ([1978] 1993) appears to believe that both Tacitus and Dio were correct about the causes for the uprising.

36. The text of Dio used in this chapter is that of Boissevain, Smilda, and Nawijn 1895-1931.

37. Dio perhaps felt free to do this because he had dwelled on Boudica's gender at such length in his description of her.

38. Lovejoy and Boas [1935] 1997:9-11. According to Lovejoy and Boas, "hard primitivism" is an attitude that uncritically lauds the uncivilized as living in austere conditions, and thus unblemished by the decadent trappings of civilization. For a discussion of the idea of the Noble Savage in antiquity, see Shumate 2006:81-88.

39. *Pace* Braund (1996:141-143); Crawford (2002:28).

40. Shumate 2006:96. On the hybridity of colonial subjects in ancient discourses, see Shumate 2006:105-114.

41. For a useful examination of how Tacitus' discussion of Britain's geography sheds light on his conception of Roman conquest, see Clarke 2001.

42. We need not make too much of this argument, however. The Greeks, after all, could pray to the goddess Athena for victory.

43. Cf. the opinions of Shumate (2006:91-92), who offers similar sentiments in regard to Tacitus' portrait of Boudica.

44. See 74.14.1; 78.13.7; 80.14.3. See also the comments on theatrical activity in the speech of Vindex, which encourages a revolt against Nero (63.22.4-5). For more on this subject, particularly regarding Nero, see Edwards 1994; Gowing 1997:2569.

45. See Newbold 1975.

46. *Pace* Jahn (1920:33), who believes that Boudica's harangue is intended merely to criticize the emperor.

47. As Millar (1964:74-118), Edmondson (1992:45-46), and Gowing (1992:25-26, 35, 91-92, 179, 212) demonstrate, contra Berrigan (1968).

48. For a discussion of Dio's attitude toward Nero, see Gowing 1997.

49. On the import of rebellions to the Roman historiographical tradition, and especially to Tacitus, see Manolaraki 2003; Fulkerson 2006; Woodman 2006.

50. For opposing views on this oration, see Gabba 1955:301-308; van Stekelenburg 1971:38-39.

51. Gabba 1955:302-308.

52. As van Stekelenburg (1971:38-39) argues. Also, Vlachos (1905:105) believes that in this speech Dio "deliberately perverted the truth with the sole object of obtaining an opportunity for displaying his rhetorical attainments." This is too strongly put, but Vlachos does realize that this speech does not likely represent Dio's own views on expansionism and colonialism.

53. Dio mentions in 75.15.3 and 80.5.3 that Bithynia was his homeland.

54. See above.

55. Cf. Levene 1999:204, asserting that the dramatic audience's response to a speech tells us a good deal about the historian's impression of its persuasiveness. Levene, however, may prove a bit too sanguine on this score.

56. Even Hose (1994:369), who believes that Dio is neo-Thucydidean in his outlook on foreign policy, does not think that Caesar's speech represents Dio's own views.

57. Freyburger-Galland 1997:16. Similarly, Manuwald (1979:282) concludes that Dio's imitations of Thucydides are chiefly aesthetic in nature, and not based on ideas.

58. Vlachos 1905:106.

59. For examples of this, see Litsch 1893; Kyhnitzsch 1894.

60. As does Hose (1994:370-373).

61. But Dio's Boudica speech, unlike Agrippa's, is not quixotic: there was no need for Roman representatives to mismanage Britain as much as they had, and no reason for Catus to act as poorly as he supposedly did.

62. On this topic, see Manuwald 1979; Rich 1989; Gowing 1992:58, 91-92, 254, 258, 267.

63. On Dio's hatred of Nero, see 61.1.2, 2.3, 4-5, 7.4-10, 11, 14.1-2, 17.1-2, 20.2; 62.13.3, 14, 15.1-16, 18.1, 18.3; 63.12.2, 13, 28.4-5.

64. Cf. Shumate 2006:63-64 on "the resurgent masculinity of native males subordinated under colonialism."

65. For this view, see Millar 1961, 1964:73-74; van Stekelenburg 1971:152-153, 1976:53-57; Gowing 1992:244-245.

66. As we discussed in the previous chapter, Tacitus might have had access to Suetonius Paulinus' memoirs—if they existed—and these in turn might have touched upon his career in Britain. See Plin. *Nat.* 5.1.14. On the possibility of the memoir pertaining to Britain, see Fabia 1893:338-339; Syme 1958:297, 765. Orsi (1973:532) thinks that Tacitus could have used them as a source; Reed (1974:926-933) believes that both Tacitus' and Dio's accounts of the rebellion are ultimately based on the testimony of Paulinus.

67. As Shumate (2006:84) suggests.

68. See above. For criticism of Rutledge's assessment, see Shumate 2006:83.

CONCLUSIONS

1. E.g., Klotz 1952:2308; Mazzolani [1972] 1976:122, 172; Nicolet 1978:884–885; Santi-Amantini 1981:30–31; Jal 1987:202–204, 208; Vázquez 1989:150.

2. *Hist. conscr.* 58.

3. See above, chapter 6.

4. See Brunt 1978; Watson 1983; Weidemann 1986. For a divergent—and at times powerful—contemporary assessment of fetial law in the late Republic, see Riggsby 2006:157–189.

5. On this topic, see Rose 1995; Riggsby 2006:158–161, 244 n. 5; Ager 2009 (esp. 17–23).

6. See above, chapter 6.

7. Cf. Levene (1999:201), who notes that ancient critics, despite their different assessments of proper rhetorical guidelines, all deemed moral matters an important category to include in deliberative orations.

8. Edwards 1993. See also Corbeill 1996.

9. Edwards 1993:4.

10. Ibid. 25: "In a sense, the rhetoric of moralising did play a key role in marking off the Roman elite (or at least male members of the elite) from the rest of society. The elite justified their privileged position by pointing to their superior morals."

11. Again, this seems consistent with the findings of Edwards (1993).

12. Lovejoy and Boas [1935] 1997:1–7.

13. For a discussion of these prejudices, see Isaac 2004:324–335.

14. Fowler 1990.

15. Ibid. 57.

16. Isaac 2004. For earlier views on Greco-Roman perceptions of other cultures, see Sherwin-White 1967 and Snowden 1983. For a useful extended review of Isaac 2004, see McCoskey 2006–2007.

17. See Isaac 2004 (esp. 304–323).

18. E.g., Webster 1994 and 1996a (esp. 116–119); Alston 1996; Rutledge 2000.

# WORKS CITED

Aalders, G. J. D. 1986. "Cassius Dio and the Greek World." *Mnemosyne* 39:282–304.

Adler, E. 2005. *The "Enemy" Speaks: Oratory and Criticism of Empire in Roman Historiography*. Diss. Duke University.

———. 2008a. "Late Victorian and Edwardian Views of Rome and the Nature of 'Defensive Imperialism.'" *IJCT* 15:187–216.

———. 2008b. "Post-9/11 Views of Rome and the Nature of 'Defensive Imperialism.'" *IJCT* 15:587–610.

———. Forthcoming. "Speeches of Enemies and Criticism of Empire in Early Imperial Historiography." In *Brill's Companion to Roman Imperialism*, ed. D. Hoyos. Leiden.

Ager, S. L. 2009. "Roman Perspectives on Greek Diplomacy." In *Diplomats and Diplomacy in the Roman World*, ed. C. Eilers, 15–43. Leiden.

Ahlheid, F. 1988. "Oratorical Strategy in Sallust's Letter of Mithridates Reconsidered." *Mnemosyne* 41:67–92.

Ahmad, A. 1992. *In Theory: Classes, Nations, Literatures*. London.

Al-'Azm, S. J. 1991. "Orientalism and Orientalism in Reverse." *Khamsin* 8:5–26.

Alföldi, A. 1965. *Early Rome and the Latins*. Ann Arbor.

Allen, J. 2006. *Hostages and Hostage-Taking in the Roman Empire*. Cambridge.

Alonso-Núñez, J. M. 1982. "L'opposizione contro l'imperialismo romano e contro il principato nella storiografia del tempo di Augusto." *RSA* 12:131–141.

———. 1984. "Un historien anti-romain: Métrodore de Skepsis." *DHA* 10:253–258.

———. 1987. "An Augustan World History: The *Historiae Philippicae* of Pompeius Trogus." *G&R* 34:56–72.

———. 1990. "Trogue-Pompée et l'impérialisme romain." *BAGB*: 72–86.

Alston, R. 1996. "Conquest by Text: Juvenal and Plutarch on Egypt." In Webster and Cooper 1996:99–109.

Ameling, W. 1984. "Cassius Dio und Bithynien." *EA* 4:123–138.

Andersen, Ø. 2001. "How Good Should an Orator Be?" In *The Orator in Action and Theory in Greece and Rome*, ed. C. W. Wooten, 3–16. Leiden.

Asbach, I. 1878. *Analecta historica et epigraphica latina*. Diss. Bonn University.

Ashcroft, B., and P. Ahluwalia. 1999. *Edward Said: The Paradox of Identity*. London.

Aubrion, E. 1985. *Rhétorique et histoire chez Tacite*. Metz.

Avenarius, G. 1956. *Lukians Schrift zur Geschichtsschreibung*. Meisenheim.

Badian, E. 1958. *Foreign Clientelae (264–70 BC)*. Oxford.

———. 1966. "The Early Historians." In *Latin Historians*, ed. T. A. Dorey, 1–38. New York.

———. 1968. *Roman Imperialism in the Late Republic*. Ithaca.

Balsdon, J. P. V. D. 1954. "Rome and Macedon, 205–200 B.C." *JRS* 44:30–42.

Barnes, T. D. 1988. "Two Passages of Justin." *CQ* 48:589–593.

———. 1991. "Latin Literature between Diocletian and Ambrose." *Phoenix* 45:341–355.

Bartsch, S. 1994. *Actors in the Audience: Theatricality and Doublespeak from Nero to Hadrian*. Cambridge, MA.

Berrigan, J. R. 1968. "Dio Cassius' Defense of Democracy." *CB* 44:42–45.

Bickerman, E. J. 1935. "Les préliminaires de la seconde guerre de Macédoine." *RPh* 61:59–81.

———. 1945. "*Bellum Philippicum*: Some Roman and Greek Views Concerning the Causes of the Second Macedonian War." *CP* 40:137–148.

———. 1946. "La lettre de Mithridate dans les 'Histoires' de Salluste." *REL* 24:131–151.

Birley, A. R. 1973. "Petillius Cerialis and the Conquest of Brigantia." *Britannia* 4:179–190.

Bloom, A. 1987. *The Closing of the American Mind: How Higher Education Has Failed Democracy and Impoverished the Souls of Today's Students*. New York.

Boese, G. 1874. *De fide et auctoritate codicis Sallustiani Vat. 3864*. Diss. University of Göttingen.

Boissevain, U. P., H. Smilda, and W. Nawijn, eds. 1895–1931. *Cassii Dionis Cocceiani historiarum romanorum quae supersunt*. 5 vols. Berlin.

Borzsák, S., ed. 1992. *Cornelii Taciti libri qui supersunt*, vol. 1.1. Leipzig.

Bowie, E. L. 1974. "Greeks and Their Past in the Second Sophistic." In *Studies in Ancient Society*, ed. M. I. Finley, 166–209. London.

Bradley, K. R. 1978. *Suetonius' Life of Nero: An Historical Commentary*. Brussels.

Braund, D. 1983. "Royal Wills and Rome." *PBSR* 51:16–57.

———. 1996. *Ruling Roman Britain: Kings, Queens, Governors, and Emperors from Julius Caesar to Agricola*. London.

Briscoe, J. 1973. *A Commentary on Livy, Books XXXI–XXXIII*. Oxford.

———. 1981. *A Commentary on Livy, Books XXXIV–XXXVII*. Oxford.

———. 1993. "Livy and Polybius." In *Livius: Aspekte seines Werkes*, ed. W. Schuller, 39–52. Konstanz.

Brock, R. 1995. "Versions, 'Inversions,' and Evasions: Classical Historiography and the 'Published' Speech." *PLLS* 8:209–224.

Broughton, T. R. S. 1951–1986. *The Magistrates of the Roman Republic*. 3 vols. New York.

Bruckner, P. 1986. *The Tears of the White Man: Compassion as Contempt*. Trans. W. R. Beer. New York.

Brunt, P. A. 1960. "Tacitus on the Batavian Revolt." *Latomus* 19:494–517 (= *Roman Imperial Themes* [Oxford, 1990], 33–52).

———. 1978. "Laus Imperii." In *Imperialism in the Ancient World*, ed. P. D. A. Garnsey and C. R. Whittaker, 159–191. Cambridge.

———. 1980. "On Historical Fragments and Epitomes." *CQ* 30:477–494.

Büchner, K. 1960. *Sallust*. Heidelberg.

Büdinger, M. 1895. *Die Universalhistorie im Alterthume*. Vienna.

Bulin, R. K. 1983. *Untersuchungen zur Politik und Kriegführung Roms im Osten von 100–68 v. Chr.* Frankfurt.

Bulst, C. M. 1961. "The Revolt of Queen Boudicca in A.D. 60." *Historia* 10:496–509.

Burck, E. 1950. *Einführung in die dritte Dekade des Livius*. Heidelberg.

———. 1966. *Vom Menschenbild in der römischen Literatur*. Heidelberg.

———. 1967. "Einzelinterpretation von Reden." In *Wege zu Livius*, ed. E. Burck, 430–463. Darmstadt.

———. 1971. "The Third Decade." In *Livy*, ed. T. A. Dorey, 21–46. London.

Burgess, T. C. 1902. "Epideictic Literature." *University of Chicago Studies in Classical Philology* 3:89–261.

Burn, A. R. 1969. "Tacitus on Britain." In *Tacitus*, ed. T. A. Dorey, 35–61. London.

Canter, H. V. 1917. "Rhetorical Elements in Livy's Direct Speeches, Part I." *AJP* 38:125–151.

———. 1918. "Rhetorical Elements in Livy's Direct Speeches, Part II." *AJP* 39:44–64.

Catin, L. 1944. *En lisant Tite-Live*. Paris.

Cavallin, S. 1947. "Avant Zama: Tite-Live XXX 29–31." *Eranos* 45:25–36.

Champion, C. [B.] 2000. "Romans as BAPBAPOI: Three Polybian Speeches and the Politics of Cultural Indeterminacy." *CP* 95:424–444.

———. 2004. *Cultural Politics in Polybius's* Histories. Berkeley.

Chaplin, J. D. 2000. *Livy's Exemplary History*. Oxford.

Cizek, E. 1972. *L'époque de Néron et ses controversies idéologiques*. Leiden.

Clarke, C. 2001. "An Island Nation: Re-reading Tacitus' *Agricola*." *JRS* 91:94–112.

Collingwood, R. G., and J. N. L. Myers. 1936. *Roman Britain and the English Settlements*. Oxford.

Corbeill, A. 1996. *Controlling Laughter: Political Humor in the Late Republic*. Princeton.

Crawford, J. 2002. "Cartimandua, Boudicca, and Rebellion: British Queens and Roman Colonial Views." In *Women and the Colonial Gaze*, ed. T. L. Hunt and M. R. Lessard, 17–28. New York.

Dabrowa, E. 1982. *La politique de l'état Parthe à l'égard de Rome, d'Artaban II à Vologèse I (ca. 11–ca. 79 de n.è.) et les facteurs qui la conditionnaient*. Cracow.

Daly, G. 2002. *Cannae: The Experience of Battle in the Second Punic War*. London.

Damon, C. 1999. "*Relatio* vs. *Oratio*: Tacitus, *Ann.* 3.12, and the *Senatus consultum de Cn. Pisone patre*." *CQ* n.s. 49:336–338.

———. 2007. "Rhetoric and Historiography." In *A Companion to Roman Rhetoric*, ed. W. Dominik and J. Hall, 439–450. Malden, MA.

Dangel, J. 1994. "Syntaxe et stylistique du discours indirect chez Tacite: Une parole rhétorique." In *Linguistic Studies on Latin: Selected Papers from the 6th International Colloquium on Latin Linguistics*, ed. J. Herman, 211–226. Amsterdam.

Davidson, J. 1991. "The Gaze in Polybius' Histories." *JRS* 81:10–24.

Debevoise, N. C. 1938. *A Political History of Parthia*. Chicago.

De Blois, L. 1991. "Tacitus, Suetonius en Cassius Dio over Nero's laatste Jaren (62–68 na Chr.)" *Lampas* 24:359–374.

Den Boer, W. 1972. *Some Minor Roman Historians*. Leiden.

De Romilly, J. 1963. *Thucydides and Athenian Imperialism*. Trans. P. Thody. New York.

Derow, P. S. 1979. "Polybius, Rome, and the East." *JRS* 69:1–15.

De Sanctis, G. 1917. *Storia dei Romani*, vol. 3.2. Milan.

De Souza, P. 1996. "'They Are All Enemies of Mankind': Justifying Roman Imperialism in the Late Republic." In Webster and Cooper 1996:125–133.

Devillers, O. 1994. *L'art de la persuasion dans les Annales de Tacite*. Brussels.

Devroye, I. 1956. *Over de historische Methode van Polybios*. Brussels.

DeWitt, N. W. 1939. "Tenney Frank." *AJP* 60:273–287.

Dorey, T. A., ed. 1971. *T. Livius: Ab urbe condita libri XXI–XXII*. Leipzig.

Dorrien, G. 2004. *Imperial Designs: Neoconservatism and the New Pax Americana*. New York.

Dubisson, M. 1979. "Le latin des historiens grecs." *LEC* 47:89–106.

———. 1990. "La vision polybienne de Rome." In *Purposes of History: Studies in Greek Historiography from the 4th to the 2nd Centuries B.C.*, ed. H. Verdin, G. Schepens, E. de Keyser, 233–243. Leuven.

Dudley, D. R. 1968. *The World of Tacitus*. London.

Dudley, D. R., and G. Webster. 1962. *The Rebellion of Boudicca*. New York.

Dué, C. 2000. "Tragic History and Barbarian Speech in Sallust's *Jugurtha*." *HSCP* 100:311–325.

Dyson, S. L. 1971. "Native Revolts in the Roman Empire." *Historia* 20:239–274.

———. 1975. "Native Revolt Patterns in the Roman Empire." *ANRW* 2.3:138–175.

Earl, D. C. 1966. *The Political Thought of Sallust*. Amsterdam.

Eckstein, A. M. 1989. "Hannibal at New Carthage: Polybius 3.15 and the Power of Irrationality." *CP* 84:1–15.

———. 1995. *Moral Vision in the* Histories *of Polybius*. Berkeley.

———. 2006. *Mediterranean Anarchy, Interstate War, and the Rise of Rome*. Berkeley.

Edmondson, J. 1992. *Dio: The Julio-Claudians: Selections from Books 58–63 of the* Roman History *of Cassius Dio*. London.

Edwards, C. 1993. *The Politics of Immorality in Ancient Rome*. Cambridge.

———. 1994. "Beware of Imitations: Theatre and Subversion of Imperial Identity." In *Reflections of Nero: Culture, History, and Representation*, ed. J. Elsner and J. Masters, 83–97. Chapel Hill.

Erkell, H. 1952. *Augustus, Felicitas, Fortuna: Lateinische Wortstudien*. Göteborg.

Errington, R. M. 1970. "Rome and Spain before the Second Punic War." *Latomus* 29:25–57.

———. 1972. *The Dawn of Empire: Rome's Rise to World Power*. Ithaca.

Erskine, A. 1993. "Hannibal and the Freedom of the Italians." *Hermes* 121:58–62.

Fabia, P. 1893. *Les sources de Tacite dans les* Histoires *et les* Annales. Paris.

Ferrero, G., and C. Barbagallo. 1918. *A Short History of Rome: The Monarchy and the Republic.* Trans. G. W. Chrystal. New York.

Figuera, D. 2004. "False Consciousness and the Postcolonial Subject." *Journal X* 8:137–150.

Fincham, G. 2001. "Writing Colonial Conflict, Acknowledging Colonial Weakness." In *TRAC 2000: Proceedings of the Tenth Annual Theoretical Roman Archaeology Conference*, ed. G. Davies, A. Gardner, and K. Lockyear, 25–34. Oxford.

Fornara, C. W. 1983. *The Nature of History in Ancient Greece and Rome.* Berkeley.

Forsythe, G. 1994. *The Historian L. Calpurnius Piso Frugi and the Roman Annalistic Tradition.* Lanham, MD.

Foucault, J.-A. de. 1968. "Tite-Live traducteur de Polybe." *REL* 46:208–221.

———, ed. 1971. *Polybe: Histoires livre III.* Paris.

Foulon, E., ed. 1995. *Polybe: Histoires livres XIII–XVI.* Paris.

Fowler, D. 1990. "Deviant Focalisation in Virgil's *Aeneid.*" *PCPS* 36:42–63.

Fraiman, S. 2003. *Cool Men and the Second Sex.* New York.

Frank, T. 1912. "The Import of the Fetial Institution." *CP* 7:335–342.

———. 1929. *Roman Imperialism.* New York.

Franko, G. F. 1994. "The Use of *Poenus* and *Carthaginiensis* in Early Latin Literature." *CP* 89:153–158.

Fraser, A. 1988. *Boadicea's Chariot: The Warrior Queens.* London.

Freeman, P. 1996. "British Imperialism and the Roman Empire." In Webster and Cooper 1996:19–34.

———. 1997. "'Romanization'—'Imperialism': What Are We Talking About?" In *TRAC 96: Proceedings of the Sixth Annual Theoretical Roman Archaeology Conference*, ed. K. Meadows, C. Lemke, and J. Heron, 8–14. Oxford.

Frere, S. 1987. *Britannia: A History of Roman Britain.* 3rd ed. London.

Freyburger-Galland, M.-L. 1997. *Aspects du vocabulaire politique et institutionnel de Dion Cassius.* Paris.

Frézouls, E. 1983. "Sur l'historiographie de l'impérialisme romain." *Ktema* 8:141–162.

Frier, B. W. [1979] 1999. *Libri annales pontificum maximorum: The Origins of the Annalistic Tradition.* Ann Arbor.

Fuchs, H. 1964. *Der geistige Widerstand gegen Rom in der antiken Welt.* Berlin.

Fuentes, N. 1983. "Boudicca Re-visited." *London Archaeologist* 4:311–317.

Fukuyama, F. 2006. *America at the Crossroads: Democracy, Power, and the Neoconservative Legacy.* New Haven.

Fulkerson, L. 2006. "Staging a Mutiny: Competitive Role-Playing on the Rhine (Tacitus, *Annals* 1.31–51)." *Ramus* 35:169–192.

Gabba, E. 1955. "Sulla 'Storia Romana' di Cassio Dione." *RSI* 67:289–333.

Geckle, R. P. 1995. *The Rhetoric of Morality in Sallust's Speeches and Letters.* Diss. Columbia University.

Gelzer, M. 1964. "Römische Politik bei Fabius Pictor." In *Kleine Schriften*, 3:51–92. Wiesbaden.

Gilmartin, K. 1973. "Corbulo's Campaigns in the East: An Analysis of Tacitus' Account." *Historia* 22:583–626.

Glew, D. G. 1977. "Mithridates Eupator and Rome: A Study of the Background of the First Mithridatic War." *Athenaeum* 55:380–405.

Goodyear, F. R. D. 1970. *Tacitus*. Oxford.

———. 1982a. "On the Character and Text of Justin's Compilation of Trogus." *PACA* 16:1–24.

———. 1982b. "History and Biography." In *The Cambridge History of Classical Literature*, vol. 2, ed. E. J. Kenney and W. V. Clausen, 639–666. Cambridge.

———. 1984. "Virgil and Pompeius Trogus." In *Atti del Convegno mondiale scientifico di studi su Virgilio*, vol. 2, 167–179. Milan.

Gordon, D. C. 1989. *Images of the West: Third World Perspectives*. Totowa, NJ.

Gordon, M. L. 1936. "The *patria* of Tacitus." *JRS* 26:145–151.

Gowing, A. M. 1990. "Dio's Name." *CP* 85:49–54.

———. 1992. *The Triumviral Narratives of Appian and Cassius Dio*. Ann Arbor.

———. 1997. "Cassius Dio on the Reign of Nero." *ANRW* 2.34.3:2558–2590.

Green, C. M. C. 1993. "*De Africa et eius incolis*: The Function of Geography and Ethnography in Sallust's History of the Jugurthine War (*BJ* 17–19)." *AncW* 24:185–197.

Gries, K. 1949. "Livy's Use of Dramatic Speech." *AJP* 70:118–141.

Griffin, M. T. 1976–1977. "Nero's Recall of Suetonius Paullinus." *SCI* 3:138–152.

Groag, E. 1929. *Hannibal als Politiker*. Vienna.

Gruen, E. S. 1984. *The Hellenistic World and the Coming of Rome*, vol. 1. Berkeley.

Hammond, M. 1932. "The Significance of the Speech of Maecenas in Dio Cassius, Book LII." *TAPA* 63:88–102.

———. 1948. "Ancient Imperialism: Contemporary Justifications." *HSCP* 58:105–161.

———. 1957. "Composition of the Senate, A.D. 68–235." *JRS* 47:74–81.

———. 1963. "*Res olim dissociabiles: Principatus ac libertas*: Liberty under the Roman Empire." *HSCP* 67:93–113.

Hammond, N. G. L. 1983. *Three Historians of Alexander the Great: The So-called Vulgate Authors, Diodorus, Justin, and Curtius*. Cambridge.

Händl-Sagawe, U. 1995. *Der Beginn des 2. punischen Krieges: Ein historisch-kritischer Kommentar zu Livius Buch 21*. Munich.

Hansen, M. H. 1993. "The Battle Exhortation in Ancient Historiography: Fact or Fiction?" *Historia* 42:161–180.

Hanson, W. S. 1997. "Forces of Change and Methods of Control." In Mattingly 1997a:67–80.

Harrington, J. D. 1970. *Cassius Dio: A Reexamination*. Diss. University of Kentucky.

Harris, W. V. 1971. "On War and Greed in the Second Century B.C." *AHR* 76:1371–1385.

———. 1979. *War and Imperialism in Republican Rome: 327–70 B.C.* Oxford.

———. 1989. *Ancient Literacy*. Cambridge, MA.

Hasebroek, J. 1926. *Der imperialistische Gedanke im Altertum*. Stuttgart.

Haverfield, F. 1911. "An Inaugural Address Delivered before the First Annual General Meeting of the Society, 11th May, 1911." *JRS* 1:xi–xx.

———. [1910] 1915. *The Romanization of Roman Britain*. 3rd ed. Oxford.

Haynes, H. 2003. *The History of Make-Believe: Tacitus on Imperial Rome*. Berkeley.

Heilbrunn, J. 2008. *They Knew They Were Right: The Rise of the Neocons*. New York.

Heinz, K. 1948. *Das Bild Kaiser Neros bei Seneca, Tacitus, Sueton und Cassius Dio*. Diss. University of Berlin.

Herrman, W. 1979. *Die Historien des Coelius Antipater: Fragmente und Kommentar*. Meisenheim am Glan.

Hesselbarth, H. 1889. *Historisch-kritische Untersuchungen zur dritten Dekade des Livius*. Halle.

Hine, H. M. 1979. "Hannibal's Battle on the Tagus (Polybius 3.14 and Livy 21.5)." *Latomus* 38:891–901.

Hingley, R. 1982. "Roman Britain: The Structure of Roman Imperialism and the Consequences of Imperialism on the Development of a Peripheral Province." In *The Romano-British Countryside: Studies in Rural Settlement and Economy*, ed. D. Miles, 17–52. Oxford.

———. 1993. "Attitudes to Roman Imperialism." In *Theoretical Roman Archaeology: First Conference Proceedings*, ed. E. Scott, 17–52. Aldershot.

———. 1994. "Britannia, Origin Myths, and the British Empire." In *TRAC 94: Proceedings of the Fourth Annual Theoretical Roman Archaeology Conference*, ed. S. Cottam, D. Dungworth, S. Scott, and J. Taylor, 11–23. Oxford.

———. 2000. *Roman Officers and British Gentlemen: The Imperial Origins of Roman Archaeology*. London.

———. 2005. *Globalizing Roman Culture: Unity, Diversity, and Empire*. London.

Hoffmann, W. 1942. *Livius und der zweite punische Krieg*. Berlin.

Holleaux, M. 1921. *Rome, la Grèce et les monarchies hellénistiques au IIIe siècle avant J.-C. (273–205)*. Paris.

Hornblower, J. 1981. *Hieronymus of Cardia*. Oxford.

Hose, M. 1994. *Erneuerung der Vergangenheit: Die Historiker im Imperium romanum von Florus bis Cassius Dio*. Stuttgart.

Huggan, G. 2002. "Postcolonial Studies and the Anxiety of Interdisciplinarity." *Postcolonial Studies* 5:245–275.

Humphrey, J. H., ed. 1991. *Literacy in the Roman World*. Ann Arbor.

Irwin, R. 2006. *Dangerous Knowledge: Orientalism and Its Discontents*. Woodstock, NY.

Isaac, B. 1990. *The Limits of Empire: The Roman Army in the East*. Oxford.

———. 2004. *The Invention of Racism in Classical Antiquity*. Princeton.

Jackson, K. 1979. "Queen Boudicca?" *Britannia* 10:55.

Jacoby, F. 1926. *Die Fragmente der griechischen Historiker*, vol. 2 C (comm.). Berlin.

Jahn, J. N. H. 1920. *A Critical Study of the Sources of the History of the Emperor Nero*. Diss. New York University.

Jal, P. 1982. "L'impérialism romain: Observations sur les témoignages littéraires latin de la fin de la République romaine." *Ktema* 7:143–150.

———. 1987. "A propos des *Histoires Philippiques*: Quelques remarques." *REL* 65:194–209.

———. 1988. *Tite-Live: Histoire romaine*, vol. 11. Paris.

Jens, W. 1956. "Libertas bei Tacitus." *Hermes* 84:331–352.

Jones, H. S., ed. 1942. *Thucydidis Historiae*. Emended by J. E. Powell. Oxford.

Jumeau, R. 1964. "Un aspect significatif de l'exposé livien dans les livres XXI et XXII." In *Hommages à Jean Bayet*, ed. M. Renard and R. Schilling, 309–331. Brussles.

Kaerst, J. 1897. "Untersuchungen über Timagenes von Alexandria." *Philologus* 56:621–657.

Kahrstedt, U. 1913. *Geschichte der Karthager von Otto Meltzer*, vol. 3. Berlin.

Keaveney, A. 1981. "Roman Treaties with Parthia circa 95–circa 64 B.C." *AJP* 102:195–212.

———. 1992. *Lucullus: A Life*. London.

Keitel, E. 1987. "Homeric Antecedents to the *Cohortatio* in the Ancient Historians." *CW* 80:153–172.

Kemper, J. A. R. 1995. "Quo usque tandem? Livius de redenaar." *Lampas* 28:349–365.

Kennedy, G. A. 1959. "Focusing of Arguments in Greek Deliberative Oratory." *TAPA* 90:131–138.

———. 1972. *The Art of Rhetoric in the Roman World: 300 B.C.–A.D. 300*. Princeton.

Kerr, M. 1980. Review, Edward W. Said, *Orientalism*. *International Journal of Middle East Studies* 12:544–547.

Klotz, A. 1941. *Livius und seine Vorgänger*. Leipzig.

———. 1952. "Pompeius Trogus." *RE* 21.2:2300–2313.

Kohl, O. 1887. "Ueber Zweck und Bedeutung der livianischen Reden." *Jahresbericht über die Realschule I.O. und das Gymnasium zu Barmen*, 1–29. Barmen.

Kolár, A. 1953. "De orationum liviano operi insertarum numerositate." *Mnemosyne* ser. 4, 6:116–139.

Königer, H. 1966. *Gestalt und Welt der Frau bei Tacitus*. Diss. Nürnberg University.

Kostermann, E. 1968. *Cornelius Tacitus*: Annalen, vol. 4. Heidelberg.

Kramer, M. 2001. *Ivory Towers on Sand: The Failure of Middle Eastern Studies in America*. Washington, DC.

Kurfess, A., ed. 1976. *C. Sallusti Crispi Catilina, Iugurtha, fragmenta ampliora*. Leipzig.

Kyhnitzsch, E. 1894. *De contionibus, quas Cassius Dio historiae suae intexuit, cum Thucydideis comparatis*. Diss. University of Leipzig.

Laederich, P. 2001. *Les limites de l'empire: Les stratégies de l'impérialisme romain dans l'oeuvre de Tacite*. Paris.

Laird, A. 1999. *Powers of Expression, Expressions of Power: Speech Presentation and Latin Literature*. Oxford.

———. 2009. "The Rhetoric of Roman Historiography." In *The Cambridge Companion to the Roman Historians*, ed. A. Feldherr, 197–213. Cambridge.

Laistner, M. L. W. 1947. *The Greater Roman Historians*. Berkeley.

Lamarre, C. 1907. *Histoire de la littérature latine au temps d'Auguste*, vol. 3. Paris.

Lambert, A. 1946. *Die indirekte Rede als künstlerisches Stilmittel des Livius*. Diss. University of Zürich.

Lambrechts, P. 1936. "Trajan et le recrutement du sénat." *AC* 5:105–114.

Lancel, S. [1995] 1998. *Hannibal.* Trans. A. Nevill. Oxford.

La Penna, A. 1968. *Sallustio e la "rivoluzione" romana.* Milan.

Larsen, J. A. O. 1952. "The Assembly of the Aetolian League." *TAPA* 83:1–33.

Leeman, A. D. 1963. *Orationis ratio: The Stylistic Theories and Practice of Roman Orators, Historians, and Philosophers.* 2 vols. Amsterdam.

Leggewie, O. 1975. *Gaius Sallustius Crispus: Historiae Zeitgeschichte.* Stuttgart.

Lehmann, K. 1896. "Zur Geschichte des Feldzugs Hannibals gegen Scipio (202 vor. Ch.)." *Neue Jahrbücher für Philologie und Paedagogik* 42:573–576.

Levene, D. S. 1999. "Tacitus' *Histories* and the Theory of Deliberative Oratory." In *The Limits of Historiography: Genre and Narrative in Ancient Historical Texts,* ed. C. S. Kraus, 197–216. Leiden.

Lewis, B. 1993. *Islam and the West.* New York.

Lintott, A. 1997. "Dio Cassius and the History of the Late Roman Republic." *ANRW* 2.34.3:2497–2523.

Litsch, E. 1893. *De Cassio Dione imitatore Thucydidis.* Diss. University of Freiburg.

Lovejoy, A. O., and G. Boas. [1935] 1997. *Primitivism and Related Ideas in Antiquity.* Baltimore.

Luce, T. J. 1977. *Livy: The Composition of His History.* Princeton.

———. 1993. "Structure in Livy's Speeches." In *Livius: Aspekte seines Werkes,* ed. W. Schuller, 71–87. Konstanz.

Luterbacher, F. 1875. *De fontibus librorum XXI et XXII Titi Livii.* Diss. University of Strassbourg.

Lytton, R. H. 1973. *Justin's Account of Alexander the Great: A Historical Commentary.* Diss. Pennsylvania State University.

Macdonald, G. 2004. "Haverfield, Francis John (1860–1919)." Revised by P. W. M. Freeman. *Oxford Dictionary of National Biography* 25:856–857.

MacKenzie, J. M. 1995. *Orientalism: History, Theory, and the Arts.* Manchester.

Macleod, M. D., ed. 1980. *Luciani opera,* vol. 3. Oxford.

Macurdy, G. H. 1937. *Vassal-Queens and Some Contemporary Women in the Roman Empire.* Baltimore.

Mader, G. 1993. "ΆΝΝΙΒΑΣ ῾ΥΒΡΙΣΤΗΣ: Traces of a 'Tragic' Pattern in Livy's Hannibal Portrait in Book XXI?" *Anc. Soc.* 24:205–224.

Magie, D. 1950. *Roman Rule in Asia Minor.* 2 vols. Princeton.

Mamet, D. 2006. *The Wicked Son: Anti-Semitism, Self-Hatred, and the Jews.* New York.

Mann, J. 2004. *Rise of the Vulcans: The History of Bush's War Cabinet.* New York.

Manolaraki, E. 2003. *Seditio: Military Disintegration in Tacitus' Histories.* Diss. Cornell University.

Manuwald, B. 1979. *Cassius Dio und Augustus: Philologische Untersuchungen zu den Büchern 45–56 des dionischen Geschichtswerkes.* Wiesbaden.

Marincola, J. 1997. *Authority and Tradition in Ancient Historiography.* Cambridge.

———. 2007. "Speeches in Classical Historiography." In *A Companion to Greek and Roman Historiography,* vol. 1, ed. John Marincola, 118–132. Malden, MA.

Martin, R. H. 1981. *Tacitus.* Berkeley.

Marx, F., and W. Trillitzsch, eds. 1964. *Incerti auctoris De ratione dicendi; ad C. Herennium lib. IV.* Leipzig.

Mattern, S. 1999. *Rome and the Enemy: Imperial Strategy in the Principate.* Berkeley.

Mattingly, D. J. 1996. "From One Colonialism to Another: Imperialism and the Maghreb." In Webster and Cooper 1996:49–69.

———, ed. 1997a. *Dialogues in Roman Imperialism: Power, Discourse, and Discrepant Experience in the Roman Empire.* Portsmouth, RI.

———. 1997b. "Introduction: Dialogues of Power and Experience in the Roman Empire." In Mattingly 1997a:7–24.

Mazzarino, S. 1968. *Il pensiero storico classico,* vol. 2.1. Bari.

Mazzolani, L. S. [1972] 1976. *Empire without End.* Trans. J. McConnell and M. Pei. New York.

McCoskey, D. 2006–2007. "Naming the Fault in Question: Theorizing Racism among the Greeks and Romans." *IJCT* 13:243–267.

McDonnell, M. 2006. *Roman Manliness: Virtus and the Roman Republic.* Cambridge.

McGing, B. C. 1986. *The Foreign Policy of Mithridates VI Eupator, King of Pontus.* Leiden.

McGushin, P. 1977. *C. Sallustius Crispus: Bellum Catilinae, a Commentary.* Leiden.

———. 1992. *Sallust: The Histories,* vol. 1. Oxford.

———. 1994. *Sallust: The Histories,* vol. 2. Oxford.

McKechnie, P. 1981. "Cassius Dio's Speech of Agrippa: A Realistic Alternative to Imperial Government?" *G&R* 28:150–155.

Mellor, R. 1993. *Tacitus.* New York.

Meyer, P. 1891. *De Maecenatis oratione a Dione ficta.* Diss. University of Berlin.

Miles, G. B. 1990. "Roman and Modern Imperialism: A Reassessment." *CSSH* 32:629–659.

———. 1995. *Livy: Reconstructing Early Rome.* Ithaca.

Millar, F. 1961. "Some Speeches in Cassius Dio." *Mus. Helv.* 18:11–22.

———. 1964. *A Study of Cassius Dio.* Oxford.

Miller, N. P. 1968. "Tiberius Speaks: An Examination of the Utterances Ascribed to Him in the *Annals* of Tacitus." *AJP* 89:1–19.

———. 1969. "Style and Content in Tacitus." In *Tacitus,* ed. T. A. Dorey, 99–116. London.

———. 1975. "Dramatic Speech in the Roman Historians." *G&R* 22:45–57.

Mohm, S. 1977. *Untersuchungen zu den historiographischen Anschauungen des Polybios.* Saarbrüken.

Momigliano, A. 1934a. "Livio, Plutarco e Giustino su virtù e fortuna dei Romani: Contributo alla ricostruzione della fonte di Trogo Pompeo." *Athenaeum* n.s. 12:45–56.

———. 1934b. "Nero." *CAH*: 702–742.

———. 1961. *Claudius: The Emperor and His Achievement.* 2nd ed. Trans. W. D. Hogarth. New York.

Mommsen, T. 1894. *The History of Rome*, vol. 4. Trans. W. P. Dickson. New York.

———. 1968. *The Provinces of the Roman Empire: The European Provinces.* Ed. T. R. S. Broughton. Chicago.

Moore-Gilbert, B. 1997. *Postcolonial Theory: Contexts, Practices, Politics.* London.

Morford, M. 1990. "Tacitus' Historical Methods in the Neronian Books of the 'Annals.'" *ANRW* 2.33.2:1582–1627.

Mørkholm, O. 1974. "The Speech of Agelaus Again." *Chiron* 4:127–132.

Morstein-Marx, R. 2001. "The Myth of Numidian Origins in Sallust's African Excursus (*Iugurtha* 17.7–18.12)." *AJP* 122:179–200.

Newbold, R. F. 1975. "Cassius Dio and the Games." *AC* 44:589–604.

Nice, A. 1993. "Superstition and Religion in Tacitus' and Dio's Accounts of the Boudicca Revolt." *Pegasus* 36:15–18.

Nicolet, C. 1978. "L'impérialism romain." In *Rome et la conquête du monde Méditerranéen 264–27 avant J.-C.*, 2:883–920. Paris.

Nissen, H. 1863. *Kritische Untersuchungen über die Quellen der vierten und fünften Dekade des Livius.* Berlin.

North, J. A. 1981. "The Development of Roman Imperialism." *JRS* 71:1–9.

Oakley, S. P. 1998. *A Commentary on Livy: Books VI–X*, vol. 2. Oxford.

———. 2005. *A Commentary on Livy: Books VI–X*, vol. 3. Oxford.

Ogilvie, R. M. 1965. *A Commentary on Livy, Books 1–5.* Oxford.

Ogilvie, R. M., and I. Richmond, eds. 1967. *Cornelii Taciti: De vita Agricolae.* Oxford.

O'Gorman, E. 1993. "No Place Like Rome: Identity and Difference in the Germania of Tacitus." *Ramus* 22:135–154.

Oost, S. I. 1954. *Roman Foreign Policy in Epirus and Acarnania in the Age of the Roman Conquest of Greece.* Dallas.

Orsi, D. P. 1973. "Sulla rivolta di Boudicca." *AFLB* 16:529–535.

Overbeck, J. C. 1969. "Tacitus and Dio on Boudicca's Rebellion." *AJP* 90:129–145.

Pagán, V. E. 2000. "Distant Voices of Freedom in the *Annales* of Tacitus." *Studies in Latin Literature and Roman History* 10:358–369.

Palm, J. 1959. *Rom, Römertum und Imperium in der griechischen Literatur der Kaiserzeit.* Lund.

Pasoli, E. 1965. *Le Historiae e le opere minori di Sallustio.* Bologna.

Paul, G. M. 1984. *A Historical Commentary on Sallust's Bellum Jugurthinum.* Liverpool.

Pearson, L. 1952. "*Prophasis* and *Aitia*." *TAPA* 83:205–223.

———. 1972. "*Prophasis*: A Clarification." *TAPA* 103:381–394.

Pédech, P. 1958. "Un nouveau commentaire de Polybe." *REG* 71:438–443.

———. 1964. *La méthode historique de Polybe.* Paris.

Pendergast, J. S. 1961. *The Philosophy of History of Pompeius Trogus.* Diss. University of Illinois.

Peter, H. 1967. *Historicum Romanorum reliquiae*, vol. 2. Stuttgart.

Phang, S. E. 2008. *Roman Military Service: Ideologies of Discipline in the Late Republic and Early Principate.* Cambridge.

Piatowski, A. 1975. "L'influence de l'historiographie tragique sur la narration de Dion Cassius." In *Actes de la XIIe conférence internationale d'études classique 'Eirene,'* 263–270. Amsterdam.

Pöschl, V. 1940. *Grundwerte römischer Staatsgesinnung in den Geschichtswerken des Sallust.* Berlin.

Prakash, G. 1995. "Orientalism Now." *History and Theory* 34.3:199–212.

Pritchett, W. K. 2002. *Ancient Greek Battle Speeches and a Palfrey.* Amsterdam.

Questa, C. 1967. *Studi sulle fonti degli 'Annales' di Tacito.* 2nd ed. Rome.

Raditsa, L. F. 1969. *A Historical Commentary to Sallust's Letter of Mithridates.* Diss. Columbia University.

———. 1969–1970a. "The Historical Context of Mithridates' Description of the Status of Asia in Sallust's *Letter of Mithridates.*" *Helikon* 9–10:689–694.

———. 1969–1970b. "Mithridates' View of the Peace of Dardanus in Sallust's *Letter of Mithridates.*" *Helikon* 9–10:632–635.

Rambaud, M. 1948. "Salluste et Trogue-Pompée." *REL* 26:171–189.

Rawson, E. 1975. "Caesar's Heritage: Hellenistic Kings and Their Roman Equals." *JRS* 65:148–159.

Reed, N. 1974. "The Sources for Tacitus and Dio for the Boudiccan Revolt." *Latomus* 33:926–933.

Reinhold, M. 1986. "In Praise of Cassius Dio." *AC* 55:213–222.

Rich, J. W. 1989. "Dio on Augustus." In *History as Text: The Writing of Ancient History*, ed. A. Cameron, 86–110. Chapel Hill.

Richter, H.-D. 1987. *Untersuchungen zur hellenistischen Historiographie: Die Vorlagen des Pompeius Trogus für die Darstellung der nachalexandrischen hellenistischen Geschichte (Iust. 13–40).* Frankfurt.

Riggsby, A. M. 2006. *Caesar in Gaul and Rome: War in Words.* Austin.

Rimbaud, M. 1983. "Trogue-Pompée, un gaulois dans l'empire." In *La patrie gauloise: d'Agrippa au VIeme siècle,* 129–147. Lyon.

Robert, J., and L. Robert. 1971. "Bulletin épigraphique." *REG* 84:454–455 n. 400.

Roberts, M. 1988. "The Revolt of Boudicca (Tacitus, *Annals* 14.29–39) and the Assertion of *Libertas* in Neronian Rome." *AJP* 109:118–132.

Roller, M. B. 2001. *Constructing Autocracy: Aristocrats and Emperors in Julio-Claudian Rome.* Princeton.

Rose, P. 1995. "Cicero and the Rhetoric of Imperialism: Putting the Politics Back into Political Rhetoric." *Rhetorica* 13:359–399.

Ross, W. D., ed. 1959. *Aristotelis Ars rhetorica.* Oxford.

Russell, D. A. 1967. "Rhetoric and Criticism." *G&R* 14:130–144.

Rutledge, S. H. 2000. "Tacitus in Tartan: Textual Colonization and Expansionist Discourse in the *Agricola.*" *Helios* 27:75–95.

Sage, M. M. 1990. "Tacitus' Historical Works: A Survey and Appraisal." *ANRW* 2.33.2:851–1030.

Said, E. W. [1978] 2003. *Orientalism.* New York.

Salmon, E. T. 1929. "The Pax Caudina." *JRS* 19:12–18.

————. 1967. *Samnium and the Samnites.* Cambridge.

Sanford, E. M. 1937. "Contrasting Views of the Roman Empire." *AJP* 58:437–456.

Santi-Amantini, L. 1981. *Storie filippiche: Epitome da Pompeo Trogo/Giustino.* Milan.

Schanz, M., and C. Hosius. 1935. *Geschichte der römischen Litteratur bis zum Gesetzgebungswerk des Kaisers Justinian,* vol. 2. Munich.

Schlicher, J. J. 1933. "Non-Assertive Elements in the Language of the Roman Historians." *CP* 28:289–300.

Schneider, E. 1913. *De Pompei Trogi Historiarum Philippicarum consilio et arte.* Diss. University of Leipzig.

Schürenberg, D. 1975. *Stellung und Bedeutung der Frau in der Geschichtsschreibung des Tacitus.* Diss. University of Marburg.

Scullard, H. H. 1930. *Scipio Africanus in the Second Punic War.* Cambridge.

————. 1970. *Scipio Africanus: Soldier and Politician.* Ithaca.

Sealey, P. R. 1997. *The Boudican Revolt against Rome.* Princes Risborough.

Seel, O. 1955. *Die Praefatio des Pompeius Trogus.* Erlangen.

————. 1972a. *M. Iuniani Iustini Epitoma Historiarum Philippicarum Pompei Trogi.* 2nd ed. Stuttgart.

————. 1972b. *Pompeius Trogus: Weltgeschichte von den Anfängen bis Augustus im Auszug des Justin.* Zürich.

————. 1972c. *Eine römische Weltgeschichte: Studien zum Text der Epitome des Iustinus und zur Historik des Pompejus Trogus.* Nürnberg.

Seibert, J. 1993. *Hannibal.* Darmstadt.

Sellge, J. 1882. *Symbola ad historiam librorum Sallustianorum condendam datur. I. De studiis in Sallustio Crispo a Pompeio Trogo et Iustino epitomatore collactis.* Sagani.

Sherwin-White, A. N. 1967. *Racial Prejudice in Imperial Rome.* Cambridge.

————. 1984. *Roman Foreign Policy in the East: 168 B.C. to A.D. 1.* Norman.

Shimron, B. 1979–1980. "Polybius on Rome: A Reexamination of the Evidence." *SCI* 5:94–117.

Shorey, P. 1921. "Τύχη in Polybius." *CP* 16:280–283.

Shrimpton, G. S. 1991. *Theompopus the Historian.* Montreal.

Sickel, G. 1876. *De fontibus a Cassio Dione in conscribendis rebus inde a Tiberio usque ad mortem Vitelii gestis adhibitis.* Göttingen.

Shumate, N. 2006. *Nation, Empire, Decline: Studies in Rhetorical Continuity from the Romans to the Modern Era.* London.

Smyshlyayev, A. L. 1991. "'The Maecenas Speech' (Dio Cass. LII): The Dating and Political Orientation." *GLP* 13:137–155.

Snowden, F. M., Jr. 1983. *Before Color Prejudice: The Ancient View of Blacks.* Cambridge, MA.

Soltau, W. 1891–1893. "Coelius und Polybios im 21. Buche des Livius." *Philologus* Supplementband 6:701–726.

————. 1894. *Livius' Quellen in der III. Dekade.* Berlin.

Steele, R. B. 1917. "Pompeius Trogus and Justinus." *AJP* 38:19–41.

Stelzer, I., ed. 2004. *The Neocon Reader.* New York.

Stevens, C. E. 1951. "The Will of Q. Veranius." *CR* 1:4–7.

Stier, H. E. 1969. "Der Mithridatesbrief aus Sallusts Historien als Geschichtsquelle." In *Beiträge zur alten Geschichte und deren Nachleben: Festschrift für Franz Altheim zum 6.10.1968*, ed. R. Stiehl and H. E. Stier, 441–451. Berlin.

Sumner, G. V. 1972. "Rome, Spain, and the Outbreak of the Second Punic War: Some Considerations." *Latomus* 31:469–480.

Swain, S. 1996. *Hellenism and Empire: Language, Classicism, and Power in the Greek World*. Oxford.

Swan, P. M. 1997. "How Cassius Dio Composed His Augustan Books." *ANRW* 2.34.3:2524–2557.

Syme, R. 1958. *Tacitus*. 2 vols. Oxford.

———. 1964. *Sallust*. Berkeley.

———. 1982. "Tacitus: Some Sources of His Information." *JRS* 72:68–82.

———. 1986. *The Augustan Aristocracy*. Oxford.

———. 1988. "The Date of Justin and the Discovery of Trogus." *Historia* 37:358–371.

———. 1992. "Trogus in the H.A., Some Consequences." In *Institutions, société et vie politique dans l'empire romain au IVe siècle ap. J.-C.*, ed. M. Christol, S. Demougin, Y. Duval, C. Lepelly, and L. Pietri, 11–20. Rome.

Taine, H. 1874. *Essai sur Tite Live*. Paris.

Talbert, R. J. A. 1999. "Tacitus and the *Senatus consultum de Cn. Pisone patre*." *AJP* 120:89–97.

Townend, G. B. 1960. "The Sources of the Greek in Suetonius." *Hermes* 88:98–120.

———. 1961. "Traces in Dio Cassius of Cluvius, Aufidius, and Pliny." *Hermes* 89:227–248.

———. 1964a. "Some Rhetorical Battle-Pictures in Dio." *Hermes* 92:467–481.

———. 1964b. "Cluvius Rufus and the *Histories* of Tacitus." *AJP* 85:337–377.

Tränkle, H. 1972. "Livius und Polybios." *Gymnasium* 79:13–31.

———. 1977. *Livius und Polybios*. Basel.

Treptow, R. 1964. *Die Kunst der Reden in der 1. und 3. Dekade des livianischen Geschichts-werkes*. Diss. University of Kiel.

Tresch, J. 1965. *Die Nerobücher in den Annalen des Tacitus: Tradition und Leistung*. Heidelberg.

Twyman, B. L. 1987. "Polybius and the Annalists on the Outbreak and Early Years of the Second Punic War." *Athenaeum* 65:67–80.

Ullmann, R. 1927. *La technique des discours dans Salluste, Tite Live et Tacite: La matière et la composition*. Oslo.

———. 1929. *Étude sur le style des discours de Tite Live*. Oslo.

———. 1932. "Quelques remarques sur Polybe, III, 64 et Tite-Live, XXI, 40–41." *SO* 10:57–60.

Urban, R. 1982. "'Gallisches Bewusstsein' und 'Romkritik' bei Pompeius Trogus." *ANRW* 2.30.2:1424–1443.

Van den Hout, M. P. J., ed. 1988. *M. Cornelius Fronto: Epistulae*. Leipzig.

Van Ooteghem, J. 1959. *Lucius Licinius Lucullus*. Brussels.

Van Stekelenburg, A. V. 1971. *De Redevoeringen bij Cassius Dio*. Diss. Leiden Rijksuniversiteit.

———. 1976. "Lucan and Cassius Dio as Heirs to Livy: The Speech of Julius Caesar at Placentia." *AC* 19:43–57.

Vasunia, P. 2003. "Hellenism and Empire: Reading Edward Said." *Parallax* 9.4:88–97.

Vázquez, J. C. D. 1989. "Sallustio, *Historiae*, IV, 69: Algunas notas para el estudio de la Carta de Mitrídates." *Baetica* 12:143–152.

Vlachos, N. P. 1905. "Demosthenes and Dio Cassius (D.C. 38, 36–46)." *CR* 19:102–106.

Volkmann, H. 1964. "Antike Romkritik, Topik und historische Wirklichkeit." *Gymnasium* Beihefte 4:9–20.

Von Carosfeld, H. S. 1888. *Über die Reden und Briefe bei Sallust*. Leipzig.

Von Gutschmid, A. [1872] 1894a. Review of F. Rühl's *Die Textquellen des Justinus* and *Die Verbeitung des Justinus in Mittelalter*. In *Kleine Schriften*, vol. 5. Leipzig. Pp. 348–356. = *Litterarisches Centralblatt* (1872): 657–661.

———. [1882] 1894b. "Trogus und Timagenes." In *Kleine Schriften*, vol. 5, pp. 218–227. Leipzig = *RhM* NF 37 (1882): 548–555.

Wachsmuth, C. 1891. "Timagenes und Trogus." *RhM* 46:465–479.

Walbank, F. W. 1957. *A Historical Commentary on Polybius*, vol. 1. Oxford.

———. 1963. "Polybius and Rome's Eastern Policy." *JRS* 53:1–13.

———. 1967. *A Historical Commentary on Polybius*, vol. 2. Oxford.

———. 1971. "The Fourth and Fifth Decades." In *Livy*, ed. T. A. Dorey, 47–72. London.

———. 1972. *Polybius*. Berkeley.

———. 1983. "Polybius and the Aitiai of the Second Punic War." *LCM* 8:62–63.

———. 1985. "Speeches in Greek Historians." In *Selected Papers: Studies in Greek and Roman History and Historiography*, 242–261. Cambridge.

Walker, B. 1968. *The Annals of Tacitus: A Study in the Writing of History*. Manchester.

Walser, G. 1951. *Rom, das Reich und die fremden Völker in der Geschichtsschreibung der frühen Kaiserzeit: Studien zur Glaubwürdigkeit des Tacitus*. Baden-Baden.

Walsh, P. G. 1954. "The Literary Techniques of Livy." *RhM* 97:97–114.

———. 1961. *Livy: His Historical Aims and Methods*. Cambridge.

———. 1982. "Livy and the Aims of 'Historia': An Analysis of the Third Decade." *ANRW* 2.30.2:1058–1074.

———, ed. 1986. *T. Livius: Ab urbe condita libri XXVIII–XXX*. Leipzig.

Walters, C. F., and R. S. Conway, eds. 1919. *Titi Livi Ab urbe condita*, vol. 2. Oxford.

Walton, C. S. 1929. "Oriental Senators in the Service of Rome: A Study of Imperial Policy Down to the Death of Marcus Aurelius." *JRS* 19:38–66.

Warmington, B. H. 1969. *Nero: Reality and Legend*. New York.

Warraq, I. 2007. *Defending the West: A Critique of Edward Said's* Orientalism. Amherst, NY.

Watson, A. 1993. *International Law in Archaic Rome: War and Religion*. Baltimore.

Webster, G. [1978] 1993. *Boudica: The British Revolt against Rome, A.D. 60*. London.

———. 1984. "The Site of Boudica's Last Battle: A Comment." *London Archaeologist* 4:411–412.

Webster, J. 1994. "The Just War: Graeco-Roman Texts as Colonial Discourse." In *TRAC 94: Proceedings of the Fourth Annual Theoretical Roman Archaeology Conference*, ed. S. Cottam, D. Dungworth, S. Scott, and J. Taylor, 1–10. Oxford.

———. 1996a. "Ethnographic Barbarity: Colonial Discourse and 'Celtic Warrior Societies.'" In Webster and Cooper 1996:111–123.

———. 1996b. "Roman Imperialism and the 'Post Imperial Age.'" In Webster and Cooper 1996:1–17.

Webster, J., and N. Cooper, eds. 1996. *Roman Imperialism: Post-Colonial Perspectives*. Leicester.

Weissenborn, W., and M. Mueller, eds. 1966. *T. Livi Ab urbe condita libri*, vol. 3. Stuttgart.

Welles, C. B. 1934. *Royal Correspondence in the Hellenistic Period: A Study in Greek Epigraphy*. New Haven.

Wellesley, K., ed. 1986. *Cornelii Taciti libri qui supersunt*, vol. 1.2. Leipzig.

———, ed. 1989. *Cornelii Taciti libri qui supersunt*, vol. 2.1. Leipzig.

Wells, P. S. 2003. *The Battle That Stopped Rome: Emperor Augustus, Arminius, and the Slaughter of the Legions in the Teutoburg Forest*. New York.

Whittaker, C. R. 1997. "Imperialism and Culture: The Roman Initiative." In Mattingly 1997a:143–163.

Wiedemann, T. 1986. "The *Fetiales*: A Reconsideration." *CQ* n.s. 36:478–490.

———. 1990. "Rhetoric in Polybius." In *Purposes of History: Studies in Greek Historiography from the 4th to the 2nd Centuries B.C.*, ed. H. Verdin, G. Schepens, E. de Keyser, 289–300. Louven.

Wilkes, J. 1972. "Julio-Claudian Historians." *CW* 65:177–192, 197–203.

Wilkins, A. S., ed. 1902. *M. Tulli Ciceronis rhetorica*, vol. 1. Oxford.

Winterbottom, M., ed. 1970. *M. Fabi Quintiliani Institutionis oratoriae libri duodecim*, 2 vols. Oxford.

Winterbottom, M., and R. M. Ogilvie, eds. 1975. *Cornelii Taciti opera minora*. Oxford.

Wirszubski, C. 1950. *Libertas as a Political Idea at Rome during the Late Republic and Early Principate*. Cambridge.

Wiseman, T. P. 1979. *Clio's Cosmetics: Three Studies in Greco-Roman Literature*. Totowa, NJ.

———. 1981. "Practice and Theory in Roman Historiography." *History* 66:375–393.

Wistrich, R. S. 2001. "Was Nietzsche a Fascist Thinker?" *Partisan Review* 68:201–217.

Woodman, A. J. 1988. *Rhetoric in Classical Historiography: Four Studies*. Portland, OR.

———. 2006. "Mutiny and Madness: Tacitus *Annals* 1.16–49." *Arethusa* 39:303–329.

Woodman, A. J., and R. H. Martin, eds. 1996. *The Annals of Tacitus: Book 3*. Cambridge.

Woolf, G. 1998. *Becoming Roman: The Origins of Provincial Civilization in Gaul*. Cambridge.

Wooten, C. 1974. "The Speeches in Polybius: An Insight into the Nature of Hellenistic Oratory." *AJP* 95:235–251.

Yakobson, A. 2009. "Public Opinion, Foreign Policy, and 'Just War' in the Late Republic." In *Diplomats and Diplomacy in the Roman World*, ed. C. Eilers, 45–72. Leiden.

Yardley, J. C. 1994. "The Literary Background to Justin/Trogus." *AHB* 8:60–70.

———. 2000. "Justin on Tribunates and Generalships, *Caesares*, and *Augusti*." *CQ* 50:632–634.

Yardley, J. C., trans., and R. Develin, intro. and notes. 1994. *Justin: Epitome of the Philipppic History of Pompeius Trogus*. Atlanta.

Yardley, J. C., trans., and W. Heckel, comm. 1997. *Justin: Epitome of the Philippic History of Pompeius Trogus, Books 11–12: Alexander the Great*. Oxford.

Young, R. 1990. *White Mythologies: Writing History and the West*. London.

Yunis, H. 2002. "Narrative, Rhetoric, and Ethical Instruction in Thucydides." In *Papers on Rhetoric 4*, ed. L. C. Montefusco, 275–286. Rome.

www.ingramcontent.com/pod-product-compliance
Ingram Content Group UK Ltd.
Pitfield, Milton Keynes, MK11 3LW, UK
UKHW031839110225
454967UK00001B/129